The Sapphire Staff

Walking the Western Mystical Way

The Ancient Path of Healing called the Tree of Life

*David
Blessings on the Journey
Megan Wagner*

By Megan Wagner, M.A.

Veriditas Publishing
Redwood City, California

Grateful acknowledgement is made to the following for permission to reprint previously published material:

Red Wheel/Weiser: Excerpt from *The Work of the Kabbalist*, by Z'ev ben Shimon Halevi. Copyright © 1984 by Z'ev ben Shimon Halevi. Reprinted by permission of Publisher, Red Wheel/Weiser, Boston, MA and York Beach, ME. To order call: 1-800-423-7087.

Chiron Publications: The story, "The Woman Who Honored the Bones", from *The Woman Who Was Wild and Other Tales*, by Karla Andersdatter and additional commentary by C.E. Brooks. Copyright © 1995 by Karla Andersdatter. Reprinted by permission of Publisher, Chiron Publications.

Harper and Row: The story, "The Demon in the Tree", from *Lilith's Cave: Jewish Tales of the Supernatural*, selected and retold by Howard Schwartz. Copyright © 1988 by Howard Schwartz. Reprinted by permission of Publisher, Harper and Row, San Francisco.

August House Publishers, Inc.: The story, "Sacred Snake", from *White Wolf Woman and Other Native American Transformation Myths*, collected and retold by Teresa Pijoan. Copyright © 1992 by Teresa Pijoan. Reprinted by permission of Publisher, August House Publishers, Inc.

Cover design and book layout by Liz Kalloch. www.lizkalloch.com

Library of Congress Control Number: 2004102868

The Sapphire Staff: Walking the Western Mystical Way
1. Spirituality. 2. Kabbalah. 3. Psychology. 4. Self Help

ISBN 0-9748665-7-1

Printed in the United States of America

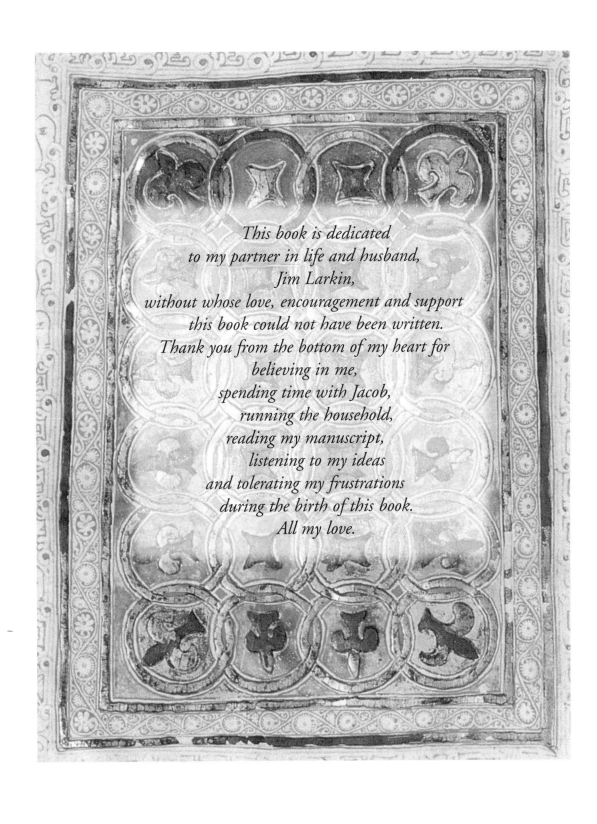

*This book is dedicated
to my partner in life and husband,
Jim Larkin,
without whose love, encouragement and support
this book could not have been written.
Thank you from the bottom of my heart for
believing in me,
spending time with Jacob,
running the household,
reading my manuscript,
listening to my ideas
and tolerating my frustrations
during the birth of this book.
All my love.*

Contents

Diagrams

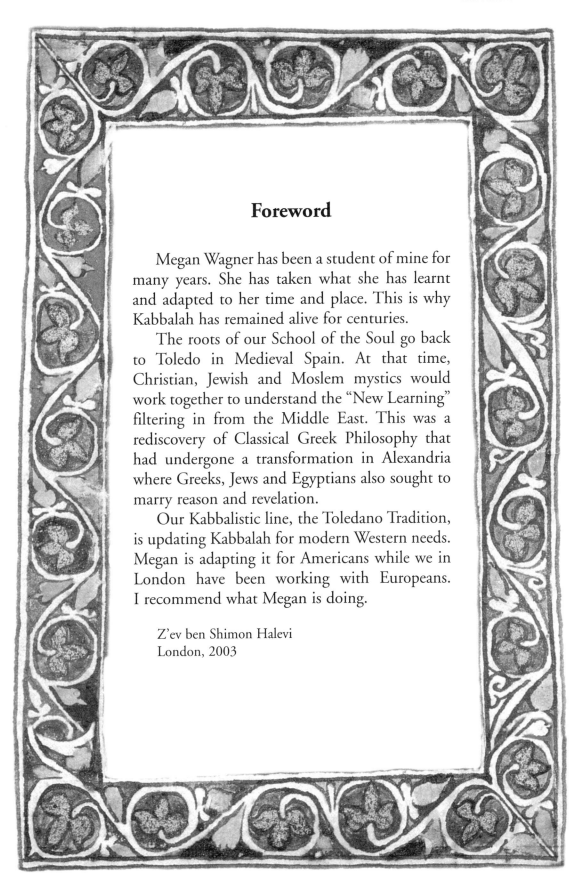

Foreword

Megan Wagner has been a student of mine for many years. She has taken what she has learnt and adapted to her time and place. This is why Kabbalah has remained alive for centuries.

The roots of our School of the Soul go back to Toledo in Medieval Spain. At that time, Christian, Jewish and Moslem mystics would work together to understand the "New Learning" filtering in from the Middle East. This was a rediscovery of Classical Greek Philosophy that had undergone a transformation in Alexandria where Greeks, Jews and Egyptians also sought to marry reason and revelation.

Our Kabbalistic line, the Toledano Tradition, is updating Kabbalah for modern Western needs. Megan is adapting it for Americans while we in London have been working with Europeans. I recommend what Megan is doing.

Z'ev ben Shimon Halevi
London, 2003

The Sapphire Staff:
Walking the Western Mystical Way

The Ancient Path of Healing called the Tree of Life

The Legend of the Sapphire Staff

Many intriguing legends surround the mysterious Sapphire Staff. According to the Kabbalah (the Jewish mystical tradition underlying Judaism and Christianity), the Sapphire Staff was given to Adam and Eve by the Archangel Raziel when they left the Garden of Eden. It was said to be adorned with ten descending sapphire jewels representing the ten divine emanations from the Tree of Life, which stands in the heart of Eden, sustaining all of existence with divine light and consciousness (see Diagram 1).

The sapphires on the staff - called "Sephirot" on the Tree of Life - are said to contain all of the mystical teaching, showing us how to awaken our true humanity, live consciously and connect with the Divine. So when Adam and Eve ventured forth from the garden, they carried with them a complete representation of the Tree of Life in the form of a staff, providing them with all they needed to grow, thrive and have a meaningful life.

The Sapphire Staff was then passed down through the generations as a staff of knowledge, from Abraham to Isaac to Jacob and then to Joseph, who had become one of top advisors to the Egyptian Pharaoh. When Joseph died in Egypt, legend says that the staff was taken into the Egyptian palace and, generations later, taken by Jethro, the priest of Midian.

It is said that Jethro was walking in his garden one day when he plunged the staff into the ground. Then, when he tried to pull it out, he discovered that the staff had transformed into a tree, sprouted roots and was blooming. From that time forward, no one could uproot the staff that had become a tree. It was said that the One who could easily take it would not only receive Jethro's daughter in marriage, but would also be the redeemer of Israel.

And so the story goes that Moses, who was in the line of Abraham, came to the land of Jethro after fleeing Egypt in search of a new life. As Moses spent time with Jethro and his family, he was eager to marry Jethro's daughter, Zipporah. Moses was therefore challenged to go into Jethro's garden and attempt to uproot the Staff/Tree. This was quite an ordeal as all other suitors had been devoured by the Tree. Moses went to the Tree and easily pulled it out of the ground, thus winning Zipporah's hand in marriage, reclaiming the great staff of knowledge and activating his destiny - to become redeemer of Israel.

Moses married Zipporah, settled in the land of Jethro and used his staff to tend flocks of sheep. For many years he shepherded and apprenticed with Jethro until one day, his life changed in a dramatic way, as did the function of his staff. On that fateful day, Moses was out tending his flock when he encountered the Divine in the form of a burning bush. During this numinous encounter, he received his calling to redeem Israel by returning to Egypt to liberate his people from slavery.

Moses wondered how in the world he would fulfill this task, so God told Moses to throw down his staff, and when he did, it became a serpent. God then told Moses to pick up the serpent by the tail, and when he did, it became a staff once again. Moses' staff had now become a staff of wonders, imbued with divine power. It was now a tool he could carry with him to remind him of his destiny, give him support on the journey and to grant skills to accomplish his mission.

After freeing his people from slavery in Egypt and fulfilling his role as liberator of Israel, Moses passed down the staff of knowledge - knowledge of mystical awakening and skills for conscious living - to the next generation and so on after him.

From this legend, we learn that the Tree and Staff are interchangeable symbols, transforming miraculously from one into the other throughout time. The story begins in the Garden of Eden with Raziel handing Adam and Eve the Sapphire Staff that embodies all of the teachings from the Tree of Life. The staff transforms back into a tree in Jethro's garden and again changes into a staff for Moses to carry with him on his journey of destiny.

Why is this interchangeable quality significant? Because it suggests that the Sapphire Staff is a portable form of the Tree of Life, the body of teaching that we can carry with us wherever we go. The Staff is available to us if we take it in hand and begin to walk the path of awakening. Each of us possesses a staff of knowledge - our own model of the Tree of Life - which is designed specially for us to guide us on our journey of discovery and destiny.

According to legend, the Sapphire Staff is no ordinary staff made of ordinary wood, but an extraordinary staff made of sapphires - translucent crystal, shining as if from a star. Sapphires are typically known as precious stones of blue. However, they exist in a variety of colors, including orange, yellow, red, green, blue, violet, white and even black. These rainbow colors are notably associated with the chakras or "centers of consciousness" as they are referred to in Kabbalah.

As we walk the mystical path, these centers of consciousness awaken, causing the sapphires to shine and illuminate our path more clearly. In turn, this helps us master each stage of development and facilitates psychological and spiritual maturity. Thus our Sapphire Staff becomes what royal staffs have always represented: a symbol of mastery, awakened consciousness, personal power, sovereignty and affirmation of our royal inheritance. Each of us has a right to hold our Sapphire Staff, for we are all children of God.

The Sapphire Staff

When the Tree of Life (image on left) is stretched out into a staff, we can imagine carrying this staff of knowledge as we walk the mystical path and grow in wisdom.

The Tree of Life

10 Divine Emanations or "Sephirot"

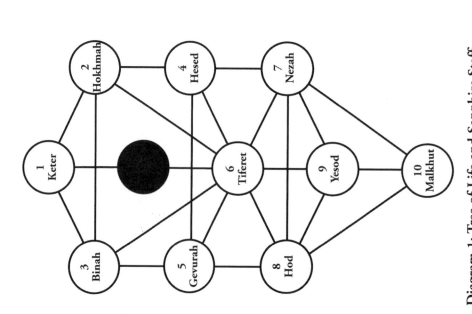

1 Keter	Crown
2 Hokhmah	Wisdom
3 Binah	Understanding
4 Hesed	Compassion
5 Gevurah	Justice
6 Tiferet	Truth
7 Nezah	Instinct
8 Hod	Communication
9 Yesod	Foundation
10 Malkhut	Kingdom

Diagram 1: Tree of Life and Sapphire Staff

The great Tree of Life sustains all of existence with divine light and consciousness.

Introduction

This book offers healing and inspiration for Western seekers who want to return to their spiritual roots. It also provides a universal path of psycho-spiritual development that can be used by any seeker from any tradition. It is designed as a workbook with practical instructions and creative exercises to guide us on the Tree of Life path of healing.

For thousands of years, the Jewish mystical teachings of Kabbalah have provided the Western spiritual tradition with a practical road map of self-discovery, a map called the Tree of Life. The Tree of Life leads us step by step towards psychological and spiritual health by guiding us through seven stages of initiation. As we follow the map and awaken our Tree, we can successfully work through and master each stage of development. The seven stages of initiation are:

1. **BODY**
2. **INSTINCTS**
3. **COMMUNITY**
4. **IDENTITY**
5. **TRUTH**
6. **TRANSFORMATION**
7. **WHOLENESS**

In Stage 1 we connect to the **body** and earth to become grounded.
In Stage 2 we learn to trust our **instincts** and flow with our own natural rhythms.
In Stage 3 we connect to the tribe to experience a deep sense of **community** belonging.
In Stage 4 we "leave home" to establish a separate **identity** and find our own path in life.
In Stage 5 we discover our personal power to creatively express our **truth**.
In Stage 6 we **transform** old patterns and open to Spirit to discover our higher purpose.
In Stage 7 we connect with the Divine to receive healing and experience **wholeness**.

The teachings in this book draw not only from Kabbalah, but also from a dynamic blend of Depth Psychology, Mythology, and Alchemy – offering stories to stir the imagination, visual images to activate healing, and archetypes to facilitate transformation. We will be guided through the seven stage initiation process so that we can let go of limiting patterns and beliefs and awaken to a life filled with heart, passion and purpose.

The Western Path of Initiation

An initiation path provides structured guidance from experienced elders through life transitions and stages of inner development. This guidance can take many forms, such as physical, emotional and spiritual exercises, meditations, rituals, instruction, tasks or dream interpretation. *The purpose of an initiation is to encourage inner development, expand consciousness and release emotional patterns that keep us blocked.* Initiations help us break through to new life and new possibilities.

Without a clear path of initiation guiding us through life transitions and inner development, we can experience loneliness, anxiety and disconnection from self and others.

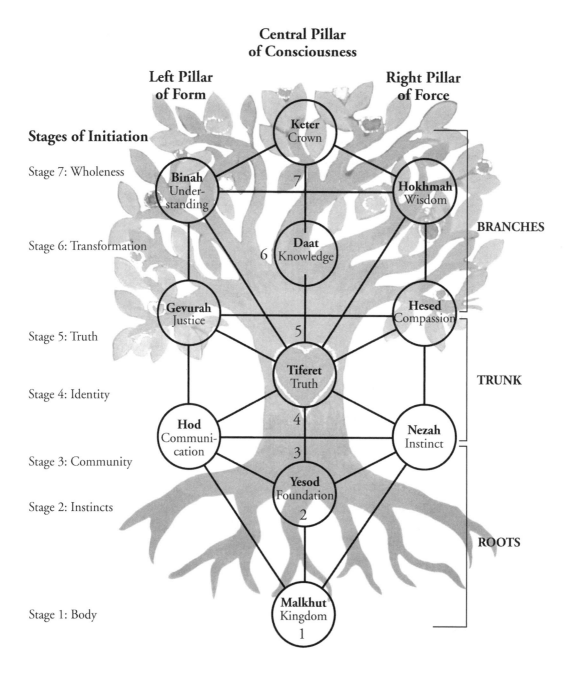

**Central Pillar
of Consciousness**

**Left Pillar
of Form**

**Right Pillar
of Force**

Stages of Initiation

Stage 7: Wholeness

Stage 6: Transformation

Stage 5: Truth

Stage 4: Identity

Stage 3: Community

Stage 2: Instincts

Stage 1: Body

Keter
Crown

Binah
Under-
standing

Hokhmah
Wisdom

7

Daat
Knowledge

6

Gevurah
Justice

Hesed
Compassion

5

Tiferet
Truth

Hod
Communi-
cation

4

Nezah
Instinct

3

Yesod
Foundation

2

Malkhut
Kingdom

1

BRANCHES

TRUNK

ROOTS

Diagram 2: The Initiation Model

The Tree of Life initiation model provides a beautiful analogy to human development as the roots, truck and branches of the tree depict body, soul and spirit and our journey of emotional, individual and spiritual development.

A path of initiation remedies this by equipping us with the skills we need to meet the demands of life and providing a sacred container to hold us while we develop and transform.

The path of initiation handed down to us from the Western tradition is called the Tree of Life. It is an ancient path of healing that has been tried and tested for thousands of years by dedicated men and women. The Sapphire Staff is another name for the path as the sapphires on the staff are said to be the same "Sephirot" decorating the Tree (see Diagram 1). The sapphires or Sephirot represent qualities such as truth, justice, compassion, understanding and wisdom, which are said to originate from the Divine Being.

As the Tree of Life is said to live within each person, we can develop these divine attributes within us if we know how to tend and nurture our Tree. However, exercising justice and compassion, understanding the meaning of life and developing true wisdom does not come quickly or easily, but requires determination and hard work. It requires the guidance, instruction, skills and support that only a path of initation can bring. (For deeper instruction on the Tree of Life and the Sephirot see Appendix A.)

The Tree of Life model

The Tree of Life initiation model provides a beautiful analogy to human development as the roots, trunk and branches of the tree depict body, soul and spirit and our journey of emotional, individual and spiritual development. I have divided the book into three parts corresponding to the roots, trunk and branches of the Tree (see Diagram 2).

Part I: Roots (Stages 1, 2 & 3)

Part One attends to the body and early emotional development. It addresses our need to be rooted in and connected to nature, instincts and community. This fosters healthy relationships and safeguards against feelings of isolation and abandonment. Without grounding in the body, stabilizing the ego and feeling part of a community, the bio-psychological body becomes traumatized, causing difficulties later as we develop and awaken to higher consciousness.

Part II: Trunk (Stages 4 & 5)

Part Two attends to the individuation journey and our need to eventually separate, establish and express our individuality. Without a model for healthy separation and individuation, we may never "leave home" psychologically and remain tied to the family or tribe, unable to live our own truth or feel a sense of personal power.

Part III: Branches (Stages 6 & 7)

Part Three attends to the spiritual aspect of our being by addressing our need to transform, renew and widen our vision of life. Without the guidance of a transpersonal vision, our personal power is used to serve the needs of the individual rather than serving the human community and breathing new life into the culture. (For further explanation and diagram of the Roots, Trunk and Branches, see Appendix B.)

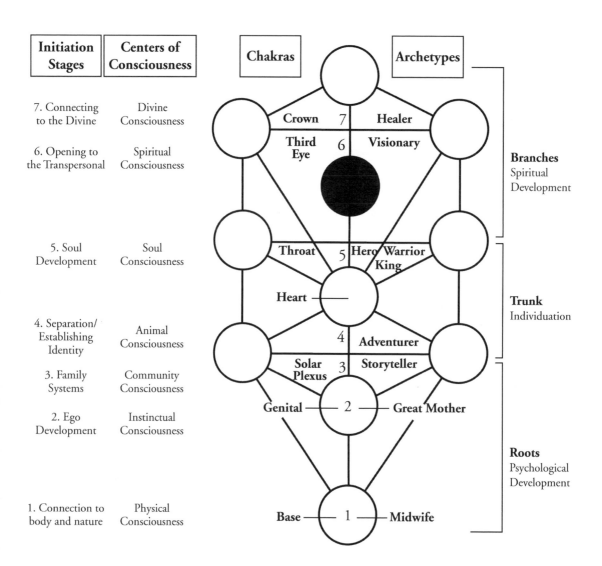

Diagram 3: Successful Initiation

For initiation to be successful, we learn the skills of each stage, awaken the various centers of consciousness and form a working relationship with the initiating archetypes. The aim of initiation is to complete the seven-stage journey and align the roots, truck and branches of the tree into an integrated whole so we can thrive with optimum health.

Aligning Roots, Trunk and Branches

The seven stages of initiation fit easily into this roots, trunk, branches model. Stages 1, 2 and 3 build the roots of the Tree, Stages 4 and 5 establish the trunk and Stages 6 and 7 develop the branches. *The aim of initiation is to complete the seven-stage journey and align all parts of the Tree into an integrated whole.*

This model of aligning the roots, trunk and branches offers a simple, powerful metaphor that we can quickly remember and easily apply to our life. For instance, some people want to heal their roots, resolving various family issues. Others want to strengthen their trunk, increasing their sense of personal power. Others work on the branches, deepening their commitment to a spiritual practice and exercising their creativity.

As you read, you will find a variety of creative exercises to help you complete each stage of initiation. At the beginning of each stage, you will find a listing of the strengths you can expect to gain if initiation has been successful and a parallel list of the problems that can arise when this stage has not been completed successfully. You can then quickly identify which stage you need to complete and which exercises will help you break through old patterns.

For example, if you are aware of a fear of confrontation, you will immediately see that the fourth initiation deals with this issue. You can then work through the exercises in Chapter 4 and find practical suggestions for managing confrontation, including meditations, writing exercises, rituals and a visual image of the archetype needed for successful initiation.

Successful Initiation and Archetypal Helpers

After each of the seven stages of initiation there is a threshold, a bridge that must be crossed to successfully complete initiation at that stage. Imagine this bridge stretching from one side of a river to the other. If we feel initiated in Stage 1, for example – grounded, contained and embodied – we will feel equipped to step onto the bridge and cross the river to the other side, ready to begin the second initiation.

Successful initiation requires that we gain **practical skills**, such as healthy boundary setting, in order to move on. If we have not internalized the necessary skills, then we limp across the bridge to the next stage rather than walking with pride, courage and confidence. Sometimes we get stuck and are unable to cross to the other side, which slows down or even halts development.

The other essential ingredient to successfully completing each stage is **personal will**. At the threshold of each initiation, the seeker must say "I will" in order to move through each transition point. When we experience emotional damage or trauma early in life, our will can feel crushed or crippled. A damaged will can be repaired, especially through the initiation process, but the journey can only be activated when the initiate finds the will to do so.

Although crossing each threshold involves risk and bravery, we are given help and guidance. Help at the crossing point usually comes in the form of what I call **initiating archetypes**. These archetypal helpers always show up at just the right time – both to activate further initiatory experiences in the stage we are in, and to help us cross the bridge to the next stage. Initiating archetypes arrive in the form of a teacher, a lover, or even an enemy. They may show up in a dream or in an everyday event or a crisis. (For more on initiating archetypes, see Appendix C.)

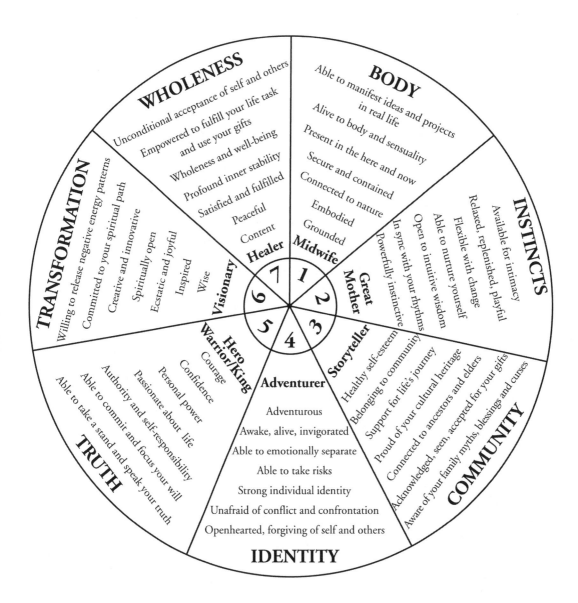

Diagram 4: Wheel of Initiation
The Wheel of Initiation shows the 7 stages, their archetypal helpers and a list of the strengths you can expect to gain if initiation is successful.

For initiation to be successful, we must embody the skills of each stage and form a working relationship with the initiating archetypes assisting us. For diagrams of successful initiation, see Diagrams 3 and 4, which show a completed Tree of Life and a circular diagram called the Wheel of Initiation. Some people find the wheel a helpful complement to the more linear Tree of Life symbol. On the wheel you will find a quick reference to the strengths that you can expect to embody at each stage when initiation is successful.

The Tree of Life as a sacred symbol

The Tree of Life is the central symbol of the Western mystical tradition and is also a universal symbol, found in many spiritual and mythological traditions around the world. In various cultures it is known as the Cosmic Tree, the World Tree and the Holy Tree.

The Tree of Life symbolizes many things, including Wisdom, Protection, Strength, Generosity, Bounty, Beauty, Longevity, Redemption and Solidity. This wise and holy Tree is like the Creator as it sustains creation with its abundant fruit. The Tree is also like human beings as we develop roots, strengthen our trunk and branch out to a wider vision of life.

Trees provide endless analogies to human development. They are amazing microcosms of exchange and flow of water, nutrients and gases. With sustenance from the earth, cooling water, refreshing air and the light of the sun, they grow in stature and strength and eventually blossom into full flower and fruit. They are earth-bound and yet reach up toward the heavens, trying to touch back to the Source. Their three main systems of roots, trunk and branches parallel human development of body, psyche and spirit.

These analogies and more will be unpacked throughout the book so that, in the end, we will have a full appreciation of why so many cultures use the Tree of Life to describe the Divine and our journey back to the Divine. The following are some examples of how the Great Tree is understood around the world.

Jewish Kabbalah - In the Kabbalistic tradition, two different Tree of Life symbols are used. The original Tree of Life emanates out of the Divine world of unity and is depicted as upside down, with its roots flowing from the divine place of unity and infinite light. The trunk and branches reach down towards us, penetrating the worlds of spirit, psyche, and physical existence. This is said to be the *Tree of Emanation* which flows downward from the Source.

The other Tree of Life symbol grows upward, back towards the Source, with roots in the ground and branches growing up to the sky. This is the Tree that the initiate climbs to return to the source and is the *Tree of Evolution* or the *Tree of Initiation*. It is the initiate's responsibility to evolve and awaken, climbing the Tree into the worlds of psyche, spirit and divine unity and reconnecting with the Divine source.

Christian - In Christian art, Jesus is often depicted as standing in the branches of the Tree of Life, presented as the living fruit of the Tree. In this capacity he is the bridge between the Divine and humanity, between heaven and earth. He is a vision of enlightened humanity and our potential to bloom and bring forth abundant fruit. The image of Christ on the cross is also a depiction of the World Savior on the Tree of Life, redeeming humanity through his death and subsequent rebirth.

Depth Psychology - From a Depth Psychology perspective, the tree is seen as a powerful symbol of growth, as the tree is the only living thing that continues to grow throughout its lifetime. The tree is also a symbol for the true self and serves as a positive, healthy model for the unfolding development of both psyche and spirit. As we grow and develop, a larger and more mature personality emerges and begins to flower and fruit, providing its gifts and bounties to the wider world.

Alchemy – From the Alchemical tradition, the Tree of Life is a symbol of the Opus Magnum, the goal of the alchemical journey, which is to find "the gold", "the philosopher's stone", "the elixir of life". A branch from the Tree of Life was said to protect the Alchemist on his or her journey through the alchemical stages of transformation. A quote from the *Teatrum Chemicum* says, *"Plant the Tree on the lapis that the birds of the sky can come and reproduce on its branches; it is from there that wisdom rises."* [1]

Nordic - In Nordic mythology, Odin is the god who rules all magic and guards the great well of wisdom and knowledge at the root of the World Tree Yggdrasill, whose strength supports the entire universe. Here, under the branches of Yggdrasill, Odin becomes an initiate magician and discovers a Shamanic vocation, obtaining inner sight and healing capacities.

Buddhist – It was beneath the great Bodhi tree, the great tree of Enlightenment, that Buddha was said to redeem the whole universe. Under this world tree, the Buddha transformed all negative temptations and energies and achieved enlightenment.

Minoan – From the ancient Minoan culture of Crete, the Tree of Life is connected to the Mysteries of the Labyrinth. The Tree of Life is said to occupy the very center of the maze. The goal of initiation is to claim yourself by winding into the center of the labyrinth, climbing the Tree of Life and connecting with your own divinity as well as the divine source.

Sacred Robes

Traveling the world and witnessing sacred initiations and rites of passage from various cultures, inspired me to find a new medium to teach the Western path of initiation. I wanted to supplement the oral and written teachings with a creative approach, to help my students and clients to experience the initiation process in a more embodied way. This led me to create a series of ceremonial robes that would tell a visual story of the archetypal initiation journey, robes that could be worn in ritual as well as contemplated as sacred art.

I knew from the Shamanic tradition that the Shaman's robe is designed to tell the visual story of the initiate's journey of awakening. The Shaman's robe is decorated with symbols received in dreams and visions during the vision quest. The Shaman is instructed to make and then don the robe as a sign that initiation is complete. The Shaman's robe is said to bring power, protection, healing, and illumination. In light of this, the sacred robe seemed the perfect medium to show the movement of the soul through different stages of initiation on its journey of awakening.

At the beginning of each chapter you will find an image of the sacred robe that corresponds to that particular stage of initiation. The figures, shapes and archetypal imagery are designed to activate the energy needed to facilitate and complete initiation at each stage.

How to use this book

I am often asked if one needs to know Kabbalah in order to "Walk the Western Mystical Way". It is not necessary to know Kabbalah to benefit from this book. Neither do you have to be Western in orientation. My goal in writing was to translate many of the mystical and psychological concepts into "lay language" that everyone could understand. The Tree of Life path of healing provides wisdom that is universal and can be applied by any seeker to any tradition. If you find the Kabbalah diagrams confusing in any way, please do not let them bog you down or interrupt your progress through the stages.

Although the book is designed as a step by step journey, inner development is rarely linear, but more often spiral in its unfolding. You can, therefore, work through the seven stages sequentially, or you can identify where your personal Tree of Life is out of alignment and turn to the relevent stage for help. As you work through each chapter, you will find writing exercises, rituals, meditations and art projects to facilitate successful initiation at each stage. You can also make use of **The Sapphire Staff companion CD's**, which include many of the stories and meditations to guide you along.

Because the initiation journey is so comprehensive in scope and may touch upon deep issues, it is very helpful to have a guide leading you through the various developmental stages. For in-depth guidance, I recommend my **Tree of Life Training**. This program combines individual and group work, personal consultations and communal rituals to support you through the journey. It also provides valuable connection with other companions on the path. For more on the **Tree of Life Training** and **The Sapphire Staff companion CD's**, see the last page of the book and my website, www.TreeofLifeTeachings.com

Preparing for the Journey

To get the most out of this Tree of Life journey, I suggest making a few preparations.

1. Journal - Find a special journal to answer the exercises in the book and to record your dreams so that you can chronicle your journey through the seven stages.

2. Art supplies - Have available some art supplies like large drawing paper, clay, colored pens, pencils or paint. As you go through the journey, sketch/draw/paint the symbols that emerge for you during each of the seven initiations. By the end of the journey you will have your own set of healing symbols to remind you of each stage.

3. Sacred Space and Altar – It is so important to have a quiet meditative space to work through some of the exercises. Set aside a sacred space where you live, and create an altar especially for this journey. Many exercises in the book require an altar on which to set candles, photographs, or symbols of healing.

How I Came to this Work

I wrote this book as a response to the growing need for Western seekers to have a comprehensive guide through the transformation process, including support for deep psychological healing and guidance for spiritual awakening. This is the book that I needed when my life was being turned upside down and I was searching to put the pieces back together again. I knew about initiations and rites of passage from my cross-cultural studies, and I had observed the kind of support and guidance that members of these communities received during times of change and transition. But as a member of modern Western culture, I had difficulty finding a road-map or wise elders to assist me emotionally, intellectually and spiritually, and I had to piece together a patchwork map as I went along.

My own experience of transformation began slowly with a series of awakenings that built in intensity over a number of years. The first important awakening occurred for me at the beginning of my adolescence. Although my mother and father came from Jewish and Christian backgrounds respectively, it was their intention to provide me with a broad, liberal and interfaith upbringing. They taught me religious tolerance, healthy intellectual skepticism, and the courage to trust my own intuition. To their surprise and mine, I followed my friends to the local Protestant church with its popular youth group, experienced a spiritual awakening and decided to get baptized when I was 13 years old.

The way I understood this with my 13-year-old mind and heart was that some fire had been ignited within me; a spark, a memory, a knowing, a core truth had penetrated into my heart. The small vision of life that I had held as a child suddenly opened and widened to a vision that included not just *my life* but *all life*. I began to understand things like forgiveness, compassion and honesty. I also began to ask questions like "What is the meaning of life?" and "How does prayer and healing really work?" This awakening at 13 propelled me forward on my spiritual search and the hunger grew within me to understand "why I was here".

During my undergraduate training at Stanford University, I had another awakening. It came in the form of a growing vision of starting a holistic academy to consider human experience from the physical, psychological and spiritual perspectives. I could see that our human design is multi-layered and that our physical health is intimately tied to emotional and spiritual well-being. I began to fill out this vision of the holistic academy by studying human biology, psychology and religion.

Also during my undergraduate years, I worked as a youth intern with a large group of teenagers at a local church. I counseled many of them on normal teenage issues of spirituality, sexuality, addiction, family problems, depression, eating disorders and more. The question that interested me was, **how do spiritual models address psychological problems, and how effective are they at healing?** The teachings of Jesus and the Christian spiritual model had much wisdom to offer my struggling teenagers, but also left some wide gaps in terms of addressing the deeper psychological issues of addiction, family systems and inner struggles. It became clear after three years of youth work that I needed more psychological training.

Staying true to my vision of a holistic academy, I began graduate school at a Theological Seminary with a department of Marriage and Family Therapy, where I grappled with both psychological and spiritual approaches to healing. Part of any good therapeutic training throws a student into her own healing process, uncovering family dysfunctions, individual challenges and existential crises so that she can experience firsthand what it is like to sit in the "client's chair". It was time for me to move beyond academic learning and experience holistic healing firsthand. Soon I found myself in the midst of psychological and spiritual upheaval as my ground was being tilled and stirred and all aspects of my life came up for review.

After my second year of therapy training, I spent the summer studying Jungian and Archetypal psychology. During this summer, on a nondescript afternoon, I had another profound awakening. It was late afternoon and I was resting on the bed when suddenly I became pinned to the bed with a force that prevented me from moving in any way. I could blink my eyes but that was all. An explosion of light filled the room, then a vision unfolded before me on the ceiling. In the vision, I saw a ladder reaching from the ground into the sky. There were people walking up and down the ladder. I noticed that at the top of the ladder there was a benevolent creature with wings perched in a cloud and looking at me intently, as if to get my attention. Our eyes met and we acknowledged each other's presence. The "angel" then made a gesture to the ladder and the moving people as if to say, "do you see this scene? Do you understand?" After a few minutes, the angel made another gesture and the entire ladder began to fold from the bottom up until it disappeared into the clouds. The angel looked at me again and then disappeared altogether, ending the vision. Immediately I could move once again, although I lay there for quite some time, stunned and bewildered.

After this vision, my life as I knew it began to change. My inner world broke open so rapidly that it was like being unpeeled at great speed, like an onion, layer by layer. The ladder vision opened a gateway to experiences that I could not explain and for which I was totally unprepared. I began having vivid dreams, visions, bursts of energy and creative ideas. I gained deep insight into my own family dynamics as well as insight into other people's psychology. At the same time, I was suffering from debilitating migraine headaches three or four times a week. Other symptoms included chaos, confusion, physical and emotional pain, overwhelming grief (not attached to any event or memory) and depression. Overall, I had a foreboding sense that I was somehow dying. Rationally, I knew I was not physically dying, but rather it felt as if my soul was dying and if I didn't remedy the situation, my soul was going to expire.

Fortunately, I was in graduate school and was being exposed to many different psychological and spiritual models that could help explain in various languages what I was experiencing. The mystics would say I was having mystical experiences, where my boundaries were dissolving and I was merging into realms of higher consciousness. From the Eastern perspective, I was having Kundalini experiences of rapidly awakening consciousness. The Shamans would say I was having Shamanic experiences. Scholars of mythology and world religions Joseph Campbell and Mircea Eliade documented many cases where a member of a community showed certain signs or symptoms similar to mine, suggesting that a "Shamanic call" was taking place. From the Jungian perspective, I was encountering the personal and collective unconscious. From a Developmental Psychology perspective, I was encountering primal, unprocessed material from my infancy and childhood.

I found it helpful to have interfaith and interdisciplinary explanations for my experiences, for each one brought new insight. Each tradition shed a little more light on what was happening. Having both psychological and spiritual perspectives gave me an appreciation for the complexity of the problem and the complexity of the solution. It became clear that depression, grief and emotional pain can be understood spiritually as well as psychologically and, considered jointly, can add tremendous insight during the healing process.

As I moved through my own healing and helped clients in my therapy practice, I was continually asking, **what do the great spiritual and psychological traditions say about emotional and spiritual health? What help does our Western culture offer in terms of support, guidance, initiations, rites of passage and mentoring for the developing soul? What models are available to provide us with healthy ego development as well as spiritual maturity?**

What I observed working with a spiritually active clientele was that the people who were open to spiritual realities were often lacking healthy self-esteem, a sense of personal power and developed will. Others who were not open to nor interested in spiritual realities, often had healthy ego development and a sense of personal power, but little connection to their passion and purpose. Clearly some bridges needed to be built between people's psychological and spiritual lives and between schools of psychology and spiritual traditions. More importantly, it was evident that our Western culture offers very little in the way of initiations or rites of passage to support developmental changes and spiritual awakenings which are designed to point people towards their passion and purpose.

To find some answers, I continued my intensive study of the Judeo-Christian tradition and went to many different kinds of "healing" services. I studied Jungian psychology, self-psychology, object-relations and psycho-dynamic models of healing. I studied the Christian mystics. I experienced individual therapy, group therapy, gestalt therapy, psychodrama and intensive Jungian Analysis.

My next awakening arrived as unexpectedly as the ladder vision. Three years after the vision, my husband and I had both graduated from Seminary and I had started a therapy practice at a local healing center. But I was continuing to have severe migraine headaches and mystical experiences which demanded that I make some serious changes in my life. Through a series of synchronous events, we applied for and accepted jobs at the American Church in London to set up a counseling service and work with youth.

Moving to England meant leaving our family, country and culture; a radical break from everything familiar, and one that I hoped would bring some clarity to my life. A few days before the plane flight to London, I was walking through my local bookstore to find a good book for the long flight. I passed a section marked "Jewish Mysticism" and was immediately struck with curiosity. I had been reading the Christian mystics for years and here was a chance to explore my Jewish roots and mysticism at the same time. As I looked at the titles, one particular book on the subject of Kabbalah leapt off the shelf and I found myself at the front register with money in hand.

The next morning, at the beginning of the ten-hour flight to London, I opened my new book called *The Work of the Kabbalist* by Z'ev ben Shimon Halevi. As I opened to the first page, I was stunned to find an exact depiction of my ladder vision. The subtitle read,

> *"Jacob's Dream. As the spiritually unawakened Adam lies asleep the angelic beings go up and down the great path that stretches between Heaven and Earth. This state of consciousness is the normal condition of most people until one day they wake up, if only for a moment, to say in awe like Jacob, "The Lord was in this place and I knew it not." This is the first rung for the Kabbalist on the Ladder of Realization."* [2]

My vision had, I discovered, come directly out of my own collective roots, from the pool of collective stories, dreams and visions of my ancestors. I had read the book of Genesis many times and known about Jacob's ladder dream for years, but had never connected it to my ladder vision. As I read through the book, I came upon my next discovery: a glyph of the Tree of Life, a strangely familiar diagram that resonated deep within my being (see Diagram 1). I learned that the Tree of Life was another version of my "Jacob's Ladder" vision and provided a detailed road map of how to walk the ladder of realization.

So there I was at 35,000 feet, somewhere over the Arctic Circle, when the puzzle started to come together. Through this synchronous event, I was introduced to the meaning behind my vision and to the Western path of initiation that considers body, psyche and spirit in the healing process. The ideas in the book resonated with my own philosophy of psycho-spiritual healing and brought long awaited meaning to my vision, and direction for my life path.

I understood from the book that the people walking up and down the ladder in my vision were those involved in the great work of unification, souls from every spiritual tradition interested in self-development and assisting other beings in waking up and working towards unifying self, others and the Divine. Even though I recognized Kabbalah as a Western spiritual path, I also felt from the author of this book that it was a path of inner development that any seeker from any tradition could practice. In addition, I discovered that many other traditions have some form of mystical teachings equivalent to this, guiding seekers in the great work of unification. The challenge for me in that moment was, would I commit to this path, enter a new gateway and follow my vision? Or would I simply see it as an interesting foray into my Jewish roots?

Because I had been asking and searching for so long, when this unfolded before me, I was open and ready. The word Kabbalah itself means "to receive" and I, apparently, was ready to receive this next step and move forward. Here was a mystical tradition from my own roots which also incorporated Depth Psychology. This seemed the perfect fit. I could stay connected to tradition and yet be true to my progressive soul.

After finishing the book on the airplane, I felt exhilarated and then disappointed, for surely the author must be some obscure Rabbi who was no longer alive. Where and how in the world could I take this further? Apparently life was answering this question for me: the Kabbalah master was very much alive and was living only a few miles from my new home in London.

After discovering where he was teaching, I attended his lecture series and asked on several occasions whether he had a weekly group where I could learn more, but he continually put me off saying, "When you go back to America, start your own group." Despite my protests that I was not returning to America, he continued to give me vague responses. I had discovered that he did run a group somewhere in London, so I waited patiently and deepened my studies of Kabbalah. I did not know then that he was giving me the traditional "three tests", to see whether I was really serious about entering a mystical school of the soul. According to tradition, the teacher is supposed to put off the student until he or she asks to join the group for a third time, proving the student's serious intentions.

One weekend I took the train from London to Glasgow, Scotland to attend Halevi's workshop on Kabbalah and Psychology. After the workshop was over, I ended up sitting across from Halevi on the long train ride home to London. I was a bit nervous so I quietly read my book, hoping not to disturb him as he read through several newspapers, unwinding from the long weekend. Three hours of silence later, he dropped his newspaper and asked me about my life.

I told him about my background, my Jewish roots, my training to be a minister and a therapist, my vision, how I bought his book and the synchronous events leading me to London. If I had any grandiosity about my great ladder vision, it was quickly deflated when I described it to him that day on the train.

He answered in the way only a Jewish teacher can (with that question mark inflection at the end of the sentence), "You were so thick they had to give you a vision?" We both laughed and after chatting for some time, he invited me to join his group. Soon afterwards, I excused myself, walked into the tiny British Rail toilet, shut the door, turned to look at myself in the scratched mirror and said out loud, "Your life will never be the same." I knew that I was crossing a vital threshold and making a deeper commitment to myself and to some larger picture that I was only beginning to understand.

I was right: my life was never the same. Entering a living mystical tradition like Kabbalah and attending an established school of the soul with mature and conscious companions brought deep contentment to my life and also accelerated my inner transformation.

Professionally during this time, I helped establish "Cornerstone", the London referral network of psychotherapists concerned with both psychological and spiritual perspectives of healing. We spent years together as professionals exploring how spiritual/mystical experiences affect the psyche and how early relationship dynamics affect our ability to relate to the Divine. Over the years, I became increasingly interested in what I call "spiritual dysfunction" - how spiritual models often hinder deep psychological change. I also became painfully aware of how people use spirituality as a defense against deep change and growth.

During my years in London, I also spent time studying and traveling. My main interest was in the Western wisdom traditions that address psycho-spiritual development and offer initiation for the genuine seeker. Friends and colleagues shared their Eastern knowledge of the chakra system, Kundalini Yoga, Sufi mysticism and more. It was exciting to discover the similarities of understanding and practice between East and West. I also discovered some ancient Kabbalists who traveled extensively and incorporated Eastern teachings, such as yoga breathing practices, into their teachings and writings. In fact, throughout history, Jews have traveled to and been exiled in so many countries, that they have assimilated knowledge from many cultures into their philosophy and spiritual practice. Kabbalah is by nature quite ecumenical in its outlook.

Although I was interested in the Eastern perspectives, I wanted to continue my search into the Western wisdom traditions because I was deeply interested in healing the Western psyche. Most Western seekers I was working with felt bereft of initiation practices to help them through transitions and transformations. So, to support my training in Kabbalah and Jungian Psychology, I studied Alchemy, Astrology, Mythology, Shamanism and the Western Mystery Traditions.

From Alchemy I learned the important metaphor of "turning lead into gold", a creative way to speak of the transformation process. By working with the evocative Alchemical images and stages of transformation, I learned a framework for transmuting one substance into another, the essential ingredient in making lasting psychological changes.

From Astrology I learned how each person relates to the planetary archetypes and how this affects their relationship dynamics, projections and their ideas about God. From studying Western Mythology, I learned about the great archetypal stories that spring from our collective psyche and identify common dilemmas that pose a threat or challenge to the soul's development.

While living in England, I discovered enthusiastic interest in Shamanism and was able to experience the ancient wisdom of the Wiccan, Druid and Celtic Shamans. I was struck with the wisdom of the many initiation practices, including vision quests and altered states of consciousness. I traveled to Stonehenge, Avebury and the sacred sites in Cornwall, Devon, Scotland and Ireland. I learned of the ancient people's reverence for the land, the trees and the animals and their use of drumming, chant and ritual to celebrate seasonal cycles and create communal initiations.

The Western Mystery Traditions I was most interested in were the Eleusinian Mysteries of ancient Greece, the Labyrinth Mysteries from Crete and the Ecstatic Mysteries of Dionysus and Ariadne. From these traditions I learned about the elaborate preparations, ritual sacrifices and the rites themselves that initiated members of the community into various stages of life.

An important question began to grow in my mind and heart. **Has modern psychotherapy replaced the ancient initiation traditions and become our new ritual space?** I am a firm believer in the healing nature of the intimate relationship that forms between client and therapist, but the ancient Mystery Traditions' emphasis on communal worship and communal ritual enactment intrigued me in terms of psycho-spiritual healing.

To complement my studies, I also traveled extensively to centers of history, art and culture, researching the role of sacred art in healing and facilitating higher states of consciousness. As I visited ancient sites and pored over sacred art and relics from Europe, South East Asia, Africa, Egypt, Sumaria, Greece and Crete, I wondered, **how did these cultures understand awakening consciousness and how did they initiate people into the mysteries of life?**

During frequent visits to the British Museum, I would meditate in front of particularly powerful statues that once stood in the ancient Temples. I imagined these sacred statues serving as evocative doorways, drawing the initiate into various states of mind and heart and providing access to the inner realms where awakening and healing can occur.

In the midst of this rich investigation, I had another awakening. One winter morning, I was sitting quietly at my kitchen table in my second-story flat in London, overlooking Hampstead Heath. I was preparing to lead a women's workshop on Crete that I had entitled, "Women and Initiation." I had been pondering a series of questions. **How were women initiated in ancient cultures? How are men and women initiated today in modern, Western culture? How do modern men and women spontaneously create rites of passages for themselves? Is there a comprehensive Western path of initiation that is suited for the Western psyche with our particular Western dilemmas?**

Spread in front of me on the table were various notes, books and a glyph of the Kabbalistic Tree of Life. I had been piecing together different initiation traditions, drawing from Joseph Campbell, Mircea Eliade, Jung, Shamanism, rites of ancient Greece, Minoan Crete and Judaism and Christianity. Suddenly, there at the kitchen table, I realized something that had been right under my nose all along. The Tree of Life, which I had been passionately studying and practicing all these years, clearly outlines the Western path of initiation and teaches initiates what they need to know about the journey towards psycho-spiritual health.

Suddenly I recognized the fulfillment of my ladder vision all those years ago: my life's work would be developing a comprehensive Western path of initiation, using my experience of psychological develoment and my expertise in the Tree of Life model.

I spent the next seven years researching each of the seven stages of initiation, distilling the main principles taught at each stage and the main qualities embodied as we complete initiation at each stage. I then explored what trials and ordeals are encountered at each stage and what symbols are used to facilitate healing. Next, I looked at which archetypes, myths and stories fit with each stage, and which archetypes activate initiation. I then matched the alchemical stages with each of the seven initiation stages on the Tree of Life (see Appendices E and F).

To pull it all together, I looked at how modern psychology informs our development of the roots, trunk and branches of the Tree. Developmental Psychology contributes to our understanding of ego development at the **roots** of the Tree. Jungian and Archetypal Psychology outline the individuation process and the development of the **trunk**. Transpersonal Psychology focuses on the **branches** and the impact of spiritual awakening on the psyche.

As I was developing my ideas on the Western path of initiation, I began working with various initiation and ritual experts who came to London to teach. Through large group rituals, I experienced first-hand the power of communal rites to shift people out of stuck patterns and initiate people into aspects of life where they had long felt wounded. Soon I was invited to drum for these rituals and then began leading and facilitating group rituals for others.

I had been working with people in the healing process for years in my consulting room, but it was not until I began using ancient initiation techniques such as drumming, chanting and ritual that I could see dramatic shifts in my clients and students. **I began to see the importance of providing both modern, structured therapy and the ancient creative arts in the healing process.**

When I introduce people now to the ancient healing arts of drumming, chanting and group ritual, it becomes obvious that we in modern culture have innate, archetypal wisdom that is accessed during these times of ritual space. Extraordinary wisdom, clarity, understanding, compassion and forgiveness come forth from the most ordinary people.

When people discover the initiation path and are given permission to access their wisdom, they can usually quickly identify where they have not been initiated and what kind of support they need to complete the initiation process. Most people "know" intuitively what initiations they have missed and discover creative rituals to heal past wounds and complete certain developmental stages. It is so crucial at this stage in the development of the Western psyche that we find ways to fill in the gaps where ancient cultures once provided explicit rites that initiated members of the community and blessed them on their path of development.

This book was written as a guide to help people identify exactly where they are on this developmental journey and what kinds of initiations they need to feel empowered, spiritually open and free. As we take our staff of knowledge, our Sapphire Staff, and begin the pilgrimage, we can shift from a life of bondage and wounding to a life of freedom and healing.

Part I – ROOTS

Stages 1, 2 & 3

According to Kabbalah, each individual human being is a Tree of Life in potential – with roots, trunk and branches ready and waiting to grow, flower and bear fruit. In order to encourage our Tree to grow, we must become like a loving gardener, nurturing and cultivating the roots, trunk, and branches – our body, psyche and spirit.

The fact is that often one or more systems of our Tree are out of balance, unawakened or wounded. In order to achieve optimum health, we must repair, rebalance and align all three systems of the Tree, consciously sinking down healthy roots, building a sturdy trunk and branching out to a spiritual perspective of life. This is what the journey of initiation is all about: *discovering and creating the optimum conditions for our Tree of Life to thrive.*

The initiation journey begins with rooting our Tree. The root system provides the emotional foundation for the entire Tree. Without a stable emotional platform, our Tree will eventually collapse. The only way to ensure a healthy and thriving Tree is to sink down roots into nutrient-rich soil. Here in Part I, we will forage into the underground landscape so that we can root our Tree in a healthy way.

Rooting our Tree of Life is a three-step process. **Initiation 1: BODY**, teaches us to feel at home in the body, honoring our sensual awareness and primary connection to the earth. **Initiation 2: INSTINCTS**, teaches us to root into our own instinctive rhythms. **Initiation 3: COMMUNITY**, teaches us to root into healthy community and experience a sense of belonging that anchors and stabilizes us in a profound way.

These first three initiations will help us discover which roots in our present root system are unable to soak up the water of life and unable to absorb the nutrients that feed the rest of the Tree. We will discover which roots are damaged or dysfunctional so that we can replant them into nutrient-rich soil. Sometimes our root system needs massive reconstruction in order to build a stable emotional platform. Other times, only minor repairs are necessary.

After completing the first three initiations, our root system will be healthy and thriving, and we can experience coming alive to sensual pleasures, trusting our deep intuitive wisdom, building a stable ego, balancing our emotional responses, and feeling part of a healthy community. At the end of Part I, we will possess the skills to plant our Tree of Life into soil that strengthens and nourishes us.

Chapter 1

Shekhinah
Robe 1

Initiation 1 - BODY

The initiation journey begins by rooting our Tree of Life, connecting with the earth and the body as the sacred ground of being. Through Biblical stories and creative visualizations, we will be guided to complete the first initiation so that we feel grounded, rooted and contained. When initiation is successful, we will feel profoundly connected to our body and nature, and will bring a dynamic presence to any situation. Others will experience us as solid, dependable and reliable, and we will be able to manifest projects and ideas.

In order to activate the first initiation, we call upon the archetypal **Midwife**, who helps us birth all aspects of our being into life. With the Midwife's help, we can stay present during the gestation period when parts of our personality are developing, and we can endure the labor and birthing process without giving up. The Midwife coaches us to persevere when new aspects of us are ready to be born. The Midwife's knowledge is crucial to learn at the beginning of the initiation journey because at each subsequent stage something new will be born within us and we must be able to nurture the new growth and remain steadfastly present with ourselves.

Qualities if initiated:

Grounded

Embodied

Alive to body and sensuality

Secure and contained

Connected to nature and the earth

Present in the here and now

Able to manifest ideas and projects in real life

Able to focus and follow through

Solid, dependable and reliable

Problems if initiation is not complete:

Ungrounded

Disconnected from body

Numb to sensual pleasures

Physically drained and stressed

Unrooted, lacking connection to nature/earth

Feeling unsafe in the world

Withdrawn from life, feeling invisible

Unable to follow through

Unstable or unreliable

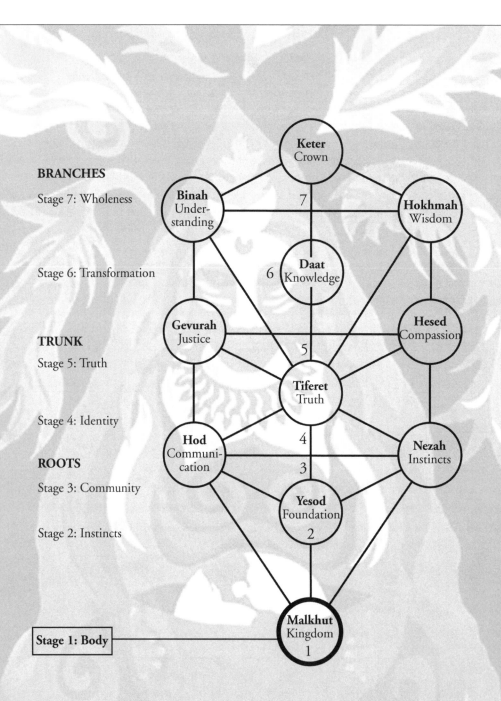

BRANCHES

Stage 7: Wholeness

Stage 6: Transformation

TRUNK

Stage 5: Truth

Stage 4: Identity

ROOTS

Stage 3: Community

Stage 2: Instincts

Stage 1: Body

Keter
Crown

7

Binah
Under-
standing

Hokhmah
Wisdom

Daat
Knowledge
6

Gevurah
Justice

Hesed
Compassion

5

Tiferet
Truth

Hod
Communi-
cation

4

Nezah
Instincts

3

Yesod
Foundation

2

Malkhut
Kingdom

1

Diagram 5: Stage 1
The first initiation invites us to cultivate a sacred relationship with the body and earth. This helps us to find our sacred ground in life so that we anchor our Tree of Life and give it the best chance of surviving and thriving.

Chapter 1 - Find your Sacred Ground

The root system provides the foundation for the Tree. When we root into our natural habitat of earth, and come to regard both creation and our physical body as sacred, our roots grow strong and sturdy, providing a platform for our trunk and eventually large branches and fruit. If we feel disconnected from nature, from our body and from our instincts, our roots will not be strong and our Tree will eventually collapse. This has dire consequences for the health and well-being of our Tree, and for this reason we begin the initiation path working diligently on the root system.

When I teach the Tree of Life model with its roots, trunk and branches, and ask people to identify where they need healing, most people quickly identify problems with the root system. They feel disconnected from their body, physically drained and stressed, and they feel disconnected from family and community. This is a natural response, especially for those of us raised in Western culture, because the roots are typically undervalued and underemphasized. Western psychology and spirituality tend to focus on the development of the trunk and branches, emphasizing the virtues of separation and independence. Developing the roots encourages connection, attachment and bonding within the family and clan and discourages separation and individual development. Because this model does not fit well into Western culture, the roots often get neglected.

In my experience with Western seekers, when little attention is paid or damage is done to the roots, individual Trees are often ungrounded. The result is that many people with good minds and hearts and wonderful ideas and talents fail to bring their many gifts to birth. When the roots are damaged, when there has been some trauma to the parental, family or communal environment early in life, then often our Tree of Life fails to thrive, fails to grow to full capacity, and fails to bring forth abundant fruit. Understandably, Western seekers who are aware of trauma to their roots are very keen to repair their root system so that they can enjoy the rewards of loving their body, feeling in tune with their instinctive rhythms, and having positive experiences in healthy family and community.

Exercise 1: Meditation - Rooting your Tree of Life into the good soil

The following is a meditation to help root your Tree of Life. You may want to try it in a standing position.

Focus your attention on the weight of your body, feel your energy sinking down and down towards the ground. Let the weight of gravity pull your consciousness down and down through your feet and into the ground below. Imagine that you are standing on the ground in bare feet, feeling the earth beneath you. Imagine that underneath your feet you begin to grow roots. Send your roots deep underground, spreading them wide and deep. Search for nutrient-rich soil. Search for a good water supply. Watch as your roots take hold and sink even further into the ground.

Do you feel secure in the earth? Is there anything stopping you from sinking down your roots? Is the soil around your roots rich with nutrients and moist, or is it dry and parched? If there is anything wrong with your ground, make it right. Add some water or nutrients. Ask for a stronger feeling of safety. Do what you must to make sure that your Tree has a healthy root system.

Take some time now to thank the earth for holding you and for receiving your roots. Breathe into the earth, and allow yourself to sink even further into the earth's holding embrace. If there is anything you wish to release, give it to the earth now. Any pain, any frustration, any anger – release it into the earth now. Feel the immense strength of the earth and its ability to hold anything that you bring to it. Feel how the earth surrounds your roots and holds you firmly in place. Feel yourself anchored and safe in the arms of the earth.

Bring your awareness now back up, up toward the surface of the ground. Follow your root system back towards the base of your feet. Become aware now of your body above the ground and breathe into your whole body. When you feel ready, come back fully into your body and open your eyes.

This is a meditation that you can return to whenever you feel unrooted or ungrounded. Make sure to note if there is anything getting in the way of sinking down healthy roots. Make sure to correct whatever is wrong with your root system and to ask the earth for what you need.

* Step 1: Root into nature*
Step 2: Ground in the body
Step 3: Feel contained
Step 4: Birth yourself into life

The first initiation invites us to cultivate a sacred relationship with the body and the earth. This helps us to find our sacred ground in life so that we anchor our Tree and give it the best chance of surviving and thriving. In Step 1, we begin the journey of initiation by rooting our Tree into nature and remembering our intimate connection with earth. In the subsequent steps, we will learn to feel more connected with the body, increase our feelings of containment, safety and security, and meet the archetypal Midwife, who teaches us to birth ourselves into life and to bring a strong and solid presence to any situation.

Sacred Earth, Sacred Origins

As I travel around the world and experience various indigenous cultures, it becomes clear to me that many spiritual traditions have basic training or initiation into the "Earth Mysteries", teaching members of the community about our sacred relationship with the earth. In these traditions, the earth is seen as the place of our sacred origins, a holy and holding container, our sacred ground. It is no surprise then that these cultures produce members who deeply appreciate the earth and its bounty and often have a relationship to the body that is easy, unashamed and beautifully embodied.

For most of us in the West, our relationship with the earth and the body does not come easily. This prompted me to ask of my own tradition: What do the Western mystical teachings offer in terms of initiation into the Earth Mysteries? What stories or teachings inform us of our sacred connection to the earth and to the body?

The answer was not hard to find. Let's start at the beginning.

From the Judeo-Christian tradition, our very first story – the creation of "Adam" and the Garden of Eden – has all the elements we need to activate this first initiation so that we can find our sacred ground of being. Almost all creation stories begin with the earth as the sacred origin of humanity, and the Western tradition is no exception. The following Creation story is from the Jewish tradition, both from Biblical and Midrash sources.

"And Yahweh planted a garden in Eden, and caused to spring up from the soil every kind of tree, enticing to look at and good to eat, with the Tree of Life in the middle of the garden. Its beauty of gold and crimson transcends all other things created; its crown covers the entire garden and four streams - of milk, honey, wine and oil - issue from its roots.

At the time when Yahweh God made earth and heaven, there was as yet no wild bush on the earth nor any wild plant yet sprung up, for Yahweh God had not sent rain on the earth, nor was there any human to till the soil. However, a flood was rising from the earth and watering all the surface of the soil. Out of the dust of the ground gathered from the four corners of the earth, Yahweh Elohim fashioned Adam. Then God breathed into Adam's nostrils the breath of life and thus Adam became a living being." [1]

The Garden of Eden is a place of sensual and visual delights. It is green, verdant and fecund – an inviting garden of rich soil, teeming with life. The earth within this garden is vibrating with a life force capable of birthing and sustaining the incredible diversity of all creation – including the great Tree of Life, whose roots seem to feed the whole world with its mighty rivers of milk, honey, wine and oil. The Tree of Life is anchored and strong, drawing its life blood and sustenance from the earth itself.

It is from this very same soil that our sacred ancestor "Adam" was birthed and formed. This is the crucial part of the story, for it means that we have a primal attachment to and intimate connection with the earth as our source of being. The earth is our mother, out of whose body we are birthed and sustained. Because we are made of the same vibrant matter and are birthed from the same mother's body, we are also intimately connected to creation, siblings from the same sacred source.

From this Genesis story we understand our sacred ancestor to be called "Adam" – which comes from the Hebrew word "Adamah", meaning "red earth". In the Western mystical teachings, Adamah represents both male and female, rather than a separate male entity. Therefore, Adamah is our sacred ancestor who emerges from the red earth as a divinely inspired male-female being.

When the traditional interpretation of Adamah evolved into "Adam", it came to mean "man" and lost the connection with the earth and with the feminine principle. With this loss in the language of the collective, we lose our memory of the rich red earth as our birthplace. We lose connection with the fructifying masculine-feminine pair who live inside us as archetypal animators, springing from the earth and becoming the sacred ground of our being.

Adamah is the first human name called by the Divine and reminds us of our sacred relationship with our primal ancestor. Adamah also connects us intimately to the sacred red earth, our "mother" who provides us with a physical body. Seeing the earth as the mother who births us into physicality returns to our consciousness the earth's maternal role in our sacred origins.

According to the Genesis story, we are then given the breath of life as God breathes into Adamah a living soul. Embracing the earth as "mother" by no means negates the Divine origins of humanity, but emphasizes the importance of the earth as our home and our need to respect this sacred relationship.

Exercise 2: Connecting to our sacred origins

The first initiation step to find our sacred ground is to learn our original name – Adamah – and to understand the true meaning of it. Our true name is our compass through life, orienting us to the sacred ground and setting us on the right path, the path of a true Adamah. The path of a true Adamah is to walk wholeheartedly on planet Earth, living in harmony with our body, respecting both male and female principles and respecting the beauty of creation.

Close your eyes and allow your imagination to conjure up images for each one of the Adamah sayings. Say each one aloud to yourself starting with "Adamah - red earth", and then wait to see what emerges. Move slowly through the list and focus on the image and feeling in your body.

Adamah - red earth
Adamah - our sacred ancestor formed from the earth
Adamah - dancing in the primal garden
Adamah - in harmony with the body
Adamah - respecting both male and female energies
Adamah - in harmony with creation

When you are finished, write down what happened in your imagination. What can Adamah teach you about connecting to nature and to the body as your sacred ground of being?

Anima Mundi

The next step in awakening consciousness in Stage 1 is to become aware of the dynamic spirit of the earth itself. This brings us into alignment with matter and corrects the dualism we inherit from Western theology and mythology.

Mystics from most traditions agree that matter is far from dead, but is alive as a vibrant field of energy, constantly infused with the divine life force. Not only is the earth our mother and birthplace, she is herself a vivacious entity, breathing her great seasonal breaths in and out. The living earth is constantly evolving.

Since we are the earth's creatures and made of this essential matter, we too are made of vibrant fields of energy – a microcosm of the macrocosm. *Anima Mundi* is the name that Archetypal Psychologists use to describe the earth as alive, and it means "soul of the world". The *Anima Mundi* speaks of the earth as a living reality – a dynamic, animated vision.

The *Anima Mundi* is the greatest advocate for finding our sacred ground, for she infuses all that is still unmanifested and waiting to be born with the desire for embodiment and incarnation. I like to imagine her inviting us and enticing us into matter, into life, into the sensual world, to be as present and embodied as possible.

The idea that incarnation, coming into the flesh and being matter-bound, is positive and desirable is a tremendous breakthrough for our dualistic minds. The lineage we inherit from our Western collective tells us that matter is somehow bad, evil, dead or something from which we must escape. Part of our initiation here in Stage 1 is to transform our vision of matter so that we can be truly present in the here and now, root into the earth and plant our feet firmly on solid ground.

The *Anima Mundi* is a unifying vision of matter that addresses the mystical law that matter is not separate from the Divine, but simply one manifestation of it. Living in this material world is therefore an experience to treasure.

The Alchemists also have profound teachings regarding the *Anima Mundi* that help transform our attitude toward matter. In alchemical writings, the seeker is encouraged to search everywhere for the *Prima Materia* - the primal material of oneself and of creation. It is said that within the *Prima Materia* is the divine fire or spark of consciousness that needs to be ignited. The Alchemist must set the primal spark alight and call out the inner fire, so that the Divine can be realized.

According to the Alchemists, the *Prima Materia* must be sought everywhere, even in the basest of matter. We are to search in the dung pile, in the filth and seemingly rejected parts of life, from the stones to the bones. If the Alchemist can "see" the divine spark within the *Prima Materia*, she is on her way to transforming the whole of her life and the whole of creation. The alchemical seeker must transform her vision to see the invisible divinity within the tangible. When the physical world is seen as alive and constantly infused with divine love and life, then the *Anima Mundi* becomes more consciously realized.

In traveling the world and observing cultures that are more oriented toward the earth, I am consistently made aware that they have a far more sophisticated understanding of the spirit of the earth. They recognize that the earth is radiating with divine energy, dancing and dynamically alive. Indigenous cultures tend to preserve a deep connection with their land, enabling them to root their consciousness into it. This gives them a tremendous advantage in terms of their emotional stability, for to be rooted in the land stabilizes the psyche.

When people do not feel rooted, they often do not want to be in their bodies. However, when the psyche feels embedded in the heart of nature, a cradle is created to hold and rock the psyche into wholeness. Next time you feel out of sorts, walk into a forest and let nature calm and hold you. Nature has a powerful healing effect because it is vibrating with natural divine energy. With this animated vision, how can we not see the earth as sacred, the sacred ground on which we stand?

Exercise 3: Meditation - Envisioning in the Anima Mundi

Think of one of your favorite spots in nature. Imagine everything you can about the natural surroundings of this place. What are the sights, colors, sounds and smells? Close your eyes and imagine being there and how you feel when you rest in your favorite natural place.

Imagine the life force of this place. Notice the radiance of each mineral, plant or animal. See the radiance of the dirt, water, air or fiery sunlight.

Now extend your vision to the greater landscape around your favorite spot. Extend your vision further out and out. Imagine yourself rising above this landscape, rising higher and higher until you are high above the earth.

You can now see the entire earth, teeming with life. See the earth as a great living being

– breathing, storming, raining, heating, cooling. See the vibrant field of energy encircling the earth – dancing, evolving and alive. What do you sense about the *Anima Mundi*, the world soul?

When you feel ready, come gently down towards earth, back gently down to your favorite natural spot. Sit quietly in your sacred space and bathe yourself in this vibrant field of energy. Let it be healing to your body and soul.

When you feel ready, return to real time and open your eyes.

When you are finished, write down your impressions of the *Anima Mundi*.

Moving from materialism to sacred ground

Western culture is fundamentally materialistic, which has its positive and, unfortunately, very negative consequences. Sometimes we can be blind and greedy consumers, often disregarding our sacred relationship with the *Anima Mundi* and our connection with Adamah. Sometimes we swing to the other extreme and reject matter as bad and impure. Either response severs our connection with matter, the earth and the body. As a result, we seem to be desperately trying to possess matter, devouring it in the form of materialism. Materialism seems to be a kind of manic attempt to repair the damage caused by this dualistic split in consciousness – we compensate for our denigration and rejection of matter by attempting to get matter inside of us and possess it. It is a culture-wide attempt to activate initiation into Stage 1, but it does not work. In fact, it fails miserably.

If it is true that in the West we tend to denigrate the Mother – body, matter, and the earth – how are we going to move from our ideology of materialism to matter as sacred ground? Without an earth tradition and earth initiations, we quickly become disconnected from the land. If we do not treat the land as the kingdom in which we dwell, and if we denigrate the land and fail to care for the land, then we fail to care for our bodies.

However, if we know our sacred origins and set down roots into rich soil, then we have the awareness and capacity to treat the land as the kingdom, the royal home in which we dwell. We must begin by acting as a king or queen of the land. A good king or queen protects the land and the natural resources, and perceives the land as a sacred dwelling place.

Find your nutrient-rich soil

As we become conscious of our true name "Adamah" and experience the earth as source and sacred ground of being, we can truly make the earth our home and sink our roots into the land. This transforms our vision of the land as a home – not to be exploited or destroyed, but to be a place that sustains and supports us. To feel supported by the land, we must consciously choose to sink the roots of our Tree of Life into the land and find nutrient-rich soil that will provide our Tree with the nourishment that it needs to grow and develop.

The teachings from the Kabbalah provide helpful insight into finding nutrient-rich soil and rooting our Tree. According to Kabbalah, the first stage of initiation begins at the base of the Tree in Malkhut (pronounced "mal-koot"). We can see on the diagram that Malkhut is the anchor point where life takes root (see Diagram 5).

Malkhut represents the earth and the human body. It is the place of physical manifestation, where we birth ourselves into life and root into nature and the body. It is the place of incarnation, which literally means coming into the "carne", the flesh. At the base of the Tree, Malkhut exerts a force of gravity that pulls whatever is unmanifested further and further into physical manifestation. Initiation in Stage 1 pulls us into life and encourages us to root.

How do we find the right kind of soil to sink our roots into, soil that will eventually yield a healthy and fruitful Tree? The great teacher Jesus addresses this issue in a story called the parable of the sower. In the Gospel of Mark 4:3-9, Jesus says:

"Listen! A sower went out to sow. And as he sowed, some seed fell on the path, and the birds came out and ate it up. Other seed fell on rocky ground, where it did not have much soil, and it sprang up quickly, since it had no depth of soil. And when the sun rose, it was scorched; and since it had no root, it withered away. Other seed fell among the thorns, and the thorns grew up and choked it, and it yielded no grain. Other seed fell into good soil and brought forth grain, growing up and increasing and yielding 30 and 60 and 100-fold." And he said "Let anyone with ears to hear listen!" [2]

Every parable has many layers of interpretation. For our purposes here, let's look at what it has to say about the sacred ground.

In the story, there are four kinds of ground onto which the seed falls. The first ground is hard, the second ground is rocky, the third ground is thorny and the fourth ground is fertile soil.

When the seed falls on the hard path, it finds no supple soil that is conducive to rooting. Nothing penetrates this hardened ground and the birds gobble up the seed.

The seed can be seen as our soul in potential. Is our soul going to find the right atmosphere in life to flourish and grow? The hardened path represents the attitude of someone who cannot let the seeds of the soul come into life. With the hardened ground there is resistance to softening and receiving the seeds, and therefore the potential unfolding and flowering of the Self gets cut short. This speaks of the person who actively resists their own development and whose soil is hard to penetrate.

In the second scenario, when the seeds of the soul fall on rocky ground, there is enthusiastic reception and rapid growth. However, this is not the stable, sacred ground that we want for our initiation path because when the light and heat of the sun arrive, the new growth of our Tree will burn. In the language of Depth Psychology, when the archetype of the Self – represented by the sun – comes into conscious realization, the consciousness and radiance generated will scorch our Tree. In this scenario, the roots have not taken hold and the psyche does not have sufficient grounding to hold the dynamic energies of the Self when they shine.

The seed among thorns is another problematic situation. When the seeds fall among the thorns, they take root, but the greedy thorns take all the nutrients so there is little to spare for the seedlings. Just as growth is taking hold, some kind of "weeds and thorns" threaten to extinguish our seedlings. The thorns may represent an atmosphere of criticism and judgement or an environment depleted of nutrients. With this kind of soil, our new growth will be choked and cut off from its lifeline of encouragement.

In the fourth scenario, everything works. The good soil receives the seeds and yields a terrific crop. The good soil represents a basic attitude of openness to life and to the seeds of the soul that can only take root if we are willing to awaken along the path. Without this supple, moist, receptive attitude towards the soul, our ground will not encourage growth. If we can consciously hold the vision of our whole Tree, which is contained within the seed, then we provide the fructifying ground that encourages our seed to yield its full potential.

Remember, the good soil is called "Malkhut" or "Kingdom". This implies that the good soil into which we root our Tree of Life is a royal container. We need to spend some time preparing the soil around us so that our roots have a royal container. We can develop an attitude of openness to life and a commitment to our unfolding. We can visualize the seed as our potential Tree of Life and encourage it to grow into fullness and become whole.

It is also vitally important to be concrete about the soil. We must search for and find the actual physical land that allows us to feel at home. We can frequent natural atmospheres that are nutrient-rich and make us feel replenished and alive. This could mean living in the landscape that nourishes our body and soul, spending quality time in beautiful places, or surrounding our office cubicle with plants and flowers. We need to find the good soil that will increase our yield a hundredfold.

Into the heart of nature

So far in Step 1, we have connected to Adamah and the *Anima Mundi* and committed to rooting our Tree in nutrient-rich soil. To deepen our initiation, let's explore the healing aspects of nature and how connecting with the earth and nature brings us into deeper connection with the body.

When people feel out of sorts, they often go into nature – to a river, a lake, the ocean or a forest – because it feels healing. Nature does what it naturally should do: it vibrates and sings to its natural rhythm.

Human beings can be very out of balance in terms of following their own rhythms, and being in nature helps to anchor the personality in the body and anchor the body to the earth. So when we come into the heart of nature, we rebalance the Malkhut aspect of our being. Feeling held by Mother Nature is a powerful experience. Lying on the earth and allowing the earth to soak up our pain or our fragmented state of mind is truly healing to the body. If we feel disengaged, stressed or disembodied, we can go to an apple orchard and pick apples, go to a vineyard and pick grapes, work the land, dig in the garden and engage the senses.

In order to move more fully into the heart of nature and to activate initiation, I recommend going into nature to do ritual work by yourself or with a group. You can build natural shrines to the elements of earth, water, air or fire and allow their wisdom to guide you in the ritual and heal you in various ways.

Several years ago, I had the privilege of working with some experienced women ritual leaders who led a group of women in a powerful "earth" ritual. More than any other ritual I have participated in, this particular one put me literally into the heart of nature. During the retreat, we were asked to build an earth shrine together in the forest and create a way for the group members to have an experience of the healing powers of earth. We learned some basic principles about the element earth and its role in the healing process. For example, earth is a grounding element and is also very receptive to human suffering and pain. It easily and willingly absorbs chaotic emotions and fragmented states of mind. Earth helps us "come back to our senses" and be present in the here and now.

During the ritual, I was assigned to the group in charge of building the actual earth shrine. We decided to get some shovels and dig a human size grave-like pit which would act as our grounding rod for the ritual. It was not meant to be morbid but was meant to offer the women a holding container for them to experience rooting into the ground and, hopefully, healing in some form. The ritual evening began with drumming around a central fire while others went off into the forest to the earth shrine.

Each woman waited at the edge of the threshold and when the time came, two escorts led her along a candlelit path through the dark forest to the earth shrine. Each woman could choose to do whatever she wanted at the earth shrine, which was attended by two women. When it was my turn, I chose to lie down in the grave and surrender to a burying of warm mud packed over my whole body.

Many thoughts and feelings were awakened while I was buried. When I first experienced the weight of the earth packed on my body, I initially felt anxious and claustrophobic. There was no way to get out of the grave unless I was helped by the attendees. I had to mentally relax my muscles and try to feel with my body and "hear" with my inner ear what it was that the earth wanted to teach me. Eventually I relaxed into the experience and allowed myself to really feel the nakedness of my body next to the warm earth. I imagined letting go of my anxiety and fear and felt it drain out of me into the ground. After some time I began to feel truly held and anchored by the earth itself, and it was healing to both body and mind. The ritual ended with a celebration around the fire, dancing into the heart of the night with my sisters covered head to toe in the dark, wet earth.

Step 1: Root into nature
Step 2: Ground in the body
Step 3: Feel contained
Step 4: Birth yourself into life

The body and its connection to the four elements

After rooting into nature, the next step in the initiation process is to feel grounded in the body. This involves embodying life, being fully present in the here and now, and placing our feet firmly on the ground. It means being solid, reliable and stable.

In order to accomplish this, *we must desire embodiment*. We must want to be here in life. According to the Western mystical teachings, the process of incarnating into the physical body is a miraculous event. Incarnation has often been misunderstood and referred to in the West as "The Fall". In Kabbalah, we describe the process of incarnation as "the descent", which offers a more positive image of the soul arriving into the physical world. The "descent" describes how the arriving soul experiences a gravitational pull from the upper worlds towards the physical world, where the soul has agreed to come and fulfill its destiny.

According to Kabbalah, the physical body is the most visible and tangible of four different bodies that we inhabit. It is said that we have divine origins and therefore have a divine body that corresponds to the element fire. During the creation process, we then descend into the world of Spirit and are clothed in a spiritual body which corresponds to the element air. Next we descend into the world of the psyche and are clothed in a psychological body, corresponding to the element of water. Finally we are given what Genesis calls "coats of skin": a physical body that corresponds to the element earth. Our physical body, therefore, holds and contains all four bodies.

The four-world/four-body schema increases our appreciation for the physical body as the miraculous container of our totality. It is truly mysterious that this flesh-and-blood body of ours is the container for our psychological, spiritual and divine natures. As we are grateful for our physical vehicle, we are also reminded of our intimate and vital connection to the earth that provides the physical material of the body. The physical body itself is borrowed from Mother earth, as it is made of the natural substances of earth, water, air and fire. If we do not have sufficient respect for the earth as mother in this way, we are negating the creator of our physical body.

Exercise 4: Meditation - The body and the four elements

An important aspect of initiation into Stage 1 involves expanding our awareness of the physical vehicle itself. The following is a meditation that helps connect you with the elements and helps you to ground in the body:

Relax and breathe deeply. Become aware of your body as it sits on the chair or floor. Focus now on the earth element of your body, the density of its matter, the flesh and bones which make up the skeleton. See how this resonates with the earth itself. Imagine how the solidity of your body is like the solid earth. Imagine the stones, the dirt, the rock and mountains, the bones of the earth itself.

Now shift your awareness to the element of water inside your body. In your mind's eye, follow the flow of blood throughout your arteries and veins. Imagine all the fluids between the cells, lubricating the joints and generally filling the spaces of your body. The water element in your body is shared with the great waters of the earth, and is subject to tidal pulls, like the sea swaying in and out by the pull of the moon. Imagine that the water inside you is like the rivers, the lakes, the seas and the great oceans of the planet.

Now shift your awareness to the element of air in your body. Breathe in the air and let it fill your lungs to capacity. Imagine the oxygen penetrating into your bloodstream and being carried to all your cells. Allow the oxygen to breathe into each cell the breath of life. Your own breath is like the great breathing of the planet, as oxygen and carbon dioxide are exchanged by the trees and plants in the atmosphere surrounding Earth. Imagine the Earth breathing a great breath of wind in and out. See the mighty winds encircling the planet.

Now shift your awareness to the fire element in your body, the fire of consciousness surging through your whole system. Experience the heat of your body and how your body maintains a warmth of around 98.6 degrees. Become aware now of the fiery aspect of the Earth, the molten core bubbling at the center. Experience your own heat that arises from some core central point inside you.

Become aware of your connection with every living thing on Earth. We are made of the same elements as every other living creature: earth, water, air and fire. Give thanks and gratitude to the Earth, the elements, and the miraculous physical design of your body.

Come back now into the present, into the room where you sit and back into this reality and open your eyes.

When you have finished, reflect on which element you relate to most easily in your body and which element was most difficult for you to relate to. Which element would you like to strengthen your awareness of?

Anchoring in the body

Most spiritual disciplines begin with attending to the body because wise spiritual teachers know the value of anchoring in the body. We need to train the physical vehicle, awaken the senses and embody ourselves as much as possible, so that we are anchored in our sacred ground. Breathing exercises, chanting, toning, focused meditation, yoga, Zen sitting and martial arts are all ways to ground the body and prepare the body for the awakening of consciousness.

It is an unfortunate fact that often those who search for a spiritual tradition *seek spirituality as a defense against the body*, to get away from the body. Why do we want to escape from our body?

From developmental psychology we learn that powerful feelings are aroused in the body when we are infants. In this vulnerable state we can experience terror, rage, helplessness, isolation and abandonment. These feelings are sometimes unavoidable in our early life. If the infant is left long enough or frequently enough in these states with no help, the primitive fear or anxiety becomes overwhelming. As a result, these intense feelings often get projected into the body and the body itself is rejected or felt to be a place that is unsafe. This makes it hard to feel anchored in the body, and often forces us to take flight into the mind or spirit.

An important aspect of the first initiation is to find a creative way to feel anchored in our body, so that primitive feelings are held and contained and negative body projections withdrawn and healed.

Human beings are built with a natural desire to attach to others. In early childhood, we trust our elders to facilitate healthy attachment and therefore help us feel comfortable in the body. We count on them to be grounded and connected to their body so that they can help us to enjoy living in our own flesh and bones. We trust them to hold us physically and emotionally and to deeply value touching and holding. We depend on our elders to be able to contain the infantile torrential emotions and the infant's sense of helplessness. If our elders are initiated, they can anchor us by physically holding us until we feel secure and anchored in our own body. But if they are not initiated or anchored themselves – and many are not – then they do not know how to hold us in a healthy physical and psychological way, resulting in our lack of deep connection with the body.

Some years ago, when I was exploring my own difficulties connecting to my body, I had a dream about the importance of anchoring in the body. It speaks generally to all of us needing to be held and anchored by a benevolent source so that we can move towards our body and not defensively away from it. I call the dream "In the Body of the Forestmother."

I am in the depths of a large forest. A friend of mine is sitting next to me. I am lying on my back looking up at the sky. Except for my head, my entire body is buried under several feet of earth. I am lying comfortably with my head resting on some dirt which is acting like a pillow. I can feel the earth creatures all around my body but am not directly touching the dirt because I am wrapped in a lining or some sort of cloth protecting me from the underground creatures on the forest floor. The friend who sits beside me is from England and is a self-declared pagan who loves the forest. He is initiating me into the ways of the forest. Sometimes I listen quietly and sometimes we talk about the mysteries to be found there. I feel safely held in the body of the Forestmother.

In the dream, my pagan friend teaches me the secrets of the forest and holds the space for my initiation. I cannot move and therefore must remain still and attentive to my physical surroundings and my body. I can no longer run away from the ground of my being. Because I am immobilized and buried, I cannot leave the body of the Forestmother and must allow her to hold me as I experience a new kind of embodiment. As I lie there, I begin to feel relief at having found a holding mother who can help me stay in my body so that I do not take flight. I am still reluctant, however, to really touch ground as I am wrapped in a cloth and do not yet have direct contact with the ground. The question arises whether I will trust the earth mother to be big enough and benevolent enough to really contain and support me.

Many people associate anchoring and rooting with feeling trapped or being in bondage. This is how our negative body projection or body hatred gets translated into feelings. We often carry a great deal of anxiety about being held, even though it is what we want and need. In my own case, my defensive solution was to feel trapped, and I would move away whenever genuine physical or psychological holding was offered. In the dream, the fact that I could allow myself to be held by the safe Forestmother indicated that a transformation was happening in the depths of my psyche. The dream heralds my readiness to surrender more fully to the anchoring process and demonstrates that my anxiety about being embodied is waning. The dream also indicates that my ideas about bondage and rooting are changing, which opens the possibility of seeing my body as a comfortable place to be. It means I can be still and stay where I am, rather than defending against anchoring by running away from commitment to my body and to the land.

Exercise 5: Anchoring in the body

1. Do you feel adequately anchored in your body? Do you ever feel anxiety about being held? Do you ever feel body hatred, shame or disgust?

2. Were the elders in your family comfortable in their own bodies? Were they able to lovingly hold you physically and psychologically?

3. What would it be like to be held by a loving elder, whether it was the warm earth herself or a trustworthy person? In what ways do you want to become more anchored in your body? How might you initiate some body healing experiences?

Trusting the body's innate knowledge

In order to feel truly grounded in the body, we must learn to trust the body's innate knowing. One of the things that we can trust about the body is its miraculous design, which has been perfecting itself over millions of years. Imagine the span of evolution that has occurred and the vast experience that has preceded a single human life. The body is an amazing system of organs, tissues, muscles, nerves, arteries and veins, a system that must coordinate thousands of interactions at any given time. Our job is to acknowledge the body's innate knowing and to learn to trust the body's vast experience. Our awareness of Nature's wisdom and our gratitude for our physical vehicle determines the amount of joy we experience in the body and whether we feel at home here.

Over the millennia, the human physical design has been perfecting and gaining experience. This experience from prehistoric days up to the present is stored in our DNA. Our body knows instinctively how to fight infection, how to regulate temperature, how to eliminate toxins, how to circulate the fluids, how to breathe, how to store energy, how to release energy, how to move, how to send messages to all parts of the body and so on. Anyone who has ever seen the interior of the body and observed the complexity of its design knows how brilliant it really is.

During my own experience of pregnancy, I had a profound experience of deepening trust in the body's innate knowing. I became keenly aware of the wisdom of my body and the miraculous development of the fetus, as every cell, every organ and every neuron of my baby's body was building and forming. I surrendered to the wisdom of the body and realized that my main job was to create the conscious sacred space, the environment where the baby could grow and flourish.

Take care of your body

So far in the second step, we have connnected with the four elements, anchored into the body and learned to trust the body's innate knowing.

Another important way to anchor further into the body is to make great efforts to take care of our bodies. After all, it has been said that the body is the "Temple of the Spirit". Treating the body with tenderness and care may sound simple, but consider how many people you know who do not take care of their bodies. If the body is the Temple of the Spirit, we have a long way to go in terms of sanctifying our bodies.

In Kabbalah, the body is seen as the sacred Temple of the Spirit because the body itself is an individual Tree of Life. To see how the Tree of Life fits on the human body see Diagram 6. An important aspect of Kabbalistic practice is to activate the Tree in the body. This can be done by imagining light coming in through the bottom of the feet and imagining the Sephirot/sapphires coming alive as you invite light to swirl and move up into the body. When the entire Tree is awakened within the body, the body can feel refreshed and invigorated.

Another way to treat the body as sacred is to listen carefully to what our body wants, needs and enjoys. Body pleasure is crucial if we want to develop a sacred house for the Divine to inhabit. Find creative ways to care for your body. One of my favorite rituals to activate grounding in the body and stimulate Malkhut (and the base chakra) is drumming. When I spend time playing my *djembe*, a West African drum, in no time at all I feel pulled into the present and grounded in a profound way.

Create some engaging practice in your daily life to open the senses and pleasure your body. Drum, dance, take a hot bath, explore sensual and sexual experiences that are pleasurable for you. Treat yourself to massage and body work. Go to a day spa, hike in the mountains, get on your dirt bike. Find a way of eating which is satisfying to you and healthy for your body. Spend time finding out what your body wants and needs, and then spend time giving your body what it wants and needs.

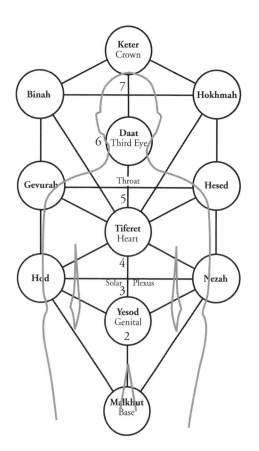

Diagram 6: The Tree of Life and the Human Body

In Kabbalah, the body is seen as the sacred Temple of the Spirit because the body itself is an individual Tree of Life. An important aspect of Kabbalistic practice is to activate the Tree in the body. This can be done by imagining light coming in through the bottom of the feet and imagining the Sephirot/sapphires coming alive as you invite light to swirl and move up into the body. When the entire Tree is awakened within the body, the body can feel refreshed and invigorated.

Step 1: Root into nature
Step 2: Ground in the body
* Step 3: Feel contained *
Step 4: Birth yourself into life

Build internal containers for holding and gestating

Once we feel rooted into nature and grounded in the body, the third step towards finding our sacred ground is to develop a sense of profound **safety**, **security** and **containment** within ourselves. This means building a container inside that acts like a womb or holding place so that we develop a deep sense of security in life. This enables us to contain whatever stormy experiences or emotions broadside us from time to time.

Feeling safe and contained gives tremendous stability to the psyche. From the stories I hear in my consulting room, it is clear that many people feel uncontained, unsafe and insecure within themselves. Let's see what we need to do in order to strengthen our sense of internal containment so that we feel good being in our own skin.

Our first language during infancy is touch. In order for the body and psyche to integrate and feel at home together, we need to be held, touched and contained. Physical loving and holding translate to the growing psyche as containment for all the emotions of life – especially anxiety, fear, confusion and chaos. Holding and containing also provide the psyche with a template for future intimacy. To attain true intimacy, we must be able to contain love within our system and hold the beloved – the other person – in our mind and heart. If we have a stable parental figure who can hold us both physically and psychologically, then we are on our way towards intimacy and successful initiation at Stage 1.

Unfortunately, many people do not experience enough loving containment and so need to develop this capacity inside so that they can feel safe, contained and emotionally stable. Developing a container inside also creates a loving atmosphere that encourages all parts of the personality to show up and be present. We need a container inside that can be filled with unconditional love and can grow big enough to hold and gestate whatever we need to bring to birth: a new idea, a new attitude, a new talent.

Looking back at the Shekhinah on the first Sacred Robe, notice that she holds a cauldron which is birthing the earth. The cauldron reminds us of our need to construct a womb-like container within us that prepares a sacred internal space.

Why is the womb such a good symbol for a healthy container? The womb has defined boundaries and it is warm, safe and protected. The womb is alive and nourishing and provides sustenance, as well as providing an outlet for toxins and waste. The womb is a holding environment that allows growth in its own time. It is a flexible container and expands with the growth of the baby. It waits patiently for the full term of gestation. It offers consistency, continuity of care, and presence. A womb provides active and loving holding.

A negative container, on the other hand, is one that is either smothering in its containing or diffuse, lacking boundaries and holding capacity. A negative container has holes in it like a sieve. A negative container is unstable, inconsistent, scattered, unfriendly, indifferent, hostile or even violent.

As we can see, there are many different kinds of containers. During this first initiation, it is important to assess *what kind of container was provided for us as a child, what kind of container we now have inside, and what kind of containment we can offer others.*

Building a container inside creates a holding space where we can process emotions such as anxiety, rage, confusion and frustration and where we can consciously hold our gifts and talents. With healthy containment, the body then feels like a home, the place we want to be. A safe inner container makes us feel contained, embodied, rooted and grounded.

An inner container also helps us to remember things. For example, during a conversation, if a friend tells us very intimate and important things about what they are struggling with, our good container can retain the information and profoundly hold what they say. We can then reflect on it, maybe we dream about it, chew it over and then call back our friend and ask, "How are you doing?" This is how we can hold another person in our cauldron. Imagine if we could do this for our own needs, worries and feelings. Our inner container would be holding us in a transformative way.

When our internal container or symbolic womb is not fully developed, it becomes difficult to hold all of our emotions within our body space and process them in a satisfying way. When this is the case, the body does not feel like a safe and secure container. We may want to escape our body or find ourselves moving into the mind to try to make sense of what is going on.

In my psychological and spiritual work with others, I encounter many people who feel uncontained, unsafe and uncomfortable in their own skin. They find other people whose containers seem safer and more secure and develop a fantasy of wanting to be inside the other person's skin, wanting the other person's womb space. This dilemma resolves when they experience enough direct and tangible holding to make their own container feel safe. With enough physical and emotional holding, we can feel comfortable inside our own skin.

Exercise 6: *What kind of container do you have?*

Attributes of positive containers:	Attributes of negative containers:
safe environment	unstable
predictable, emotionally/physically consistent	unpredictable
consciously holding	inattentive
holding without controlling	preoccupied
attentive	scattered
stable, solid	manic or depressed
healthy structure, clear boundaries,	unhealthy and unclear boundaries
healthy separation, pliable with boundaries	unfriendly
present, actively listening	hostile
compassionate, warm, empathetic	indifferent
quiet, allowing	smothering
defined space	discouraging separation
providing enough sustenance	encouraging separation too quickly
good food comes in and toxic waste goes out	lacking a toxic waste system

1. Looking at the above list of positive and negative containers, **what kind of containment did you have as a child?** Did it resemble a positive container or "good womb" that was alive and nourishing, providing sustenance as well as an outlet for toxins and waste? Or did your holding environment more resemble a "negative womb", one that was either smothering in its containing or diffuse, lacking boundaries and holding capacity? Did it have holes in it like a sieve? Write down a list.

2. Looking at the same list of positive and negative containers, **what kind of container or containment do you have inside you now?** Write a list. Are you able to contain your emotions? Which feelings are hard to contain – anger, anxiety, chaos, fear? Is it difficult to hold your gifts and talents? Are you able to hold on to conversations, remembering details and following through with people?

3. **What kind of container do you offer others**, especially to your intimates?

Imagining and making sacred vessels

For initiation to be successful in Stage 1, we must learn to create a sacred internal vessel that is safe and secure, one that does not leak. Growing an internal container is fundamental to psychological and spiritual work, for if our container/womb is unfriendly, hostile, indifferent or insufficient, parts of the personality cannot be born and will be hidden in the unconscious and inaccessible.

There are several ways to develop an internal container. One way is to use active imagination to begin thinking about what a sacred vessel is and how it functions. I have spent many years looking at photographs, drawings and actual artifacts of ancient sacred vessels. I have been to many museums in the United States, Crete, Israel, Turkey, Europe and South East Asia, looking at sacred objects – and I am always drawn to the containers, offering bowls, chalices, ablution cups and baptismal fonts.

Observing sacred vessels is a helpful way to begin creating an internal container, for these vessels are exquisitely crafted and are anything but unfriendly, hostile or indifferent. Go to a museum, get some books, go to a spiritual temple or church and you are sure to find some beautiful vessels. Begin imagining your favorite container as a beautiful holding place inside of you.

When I think of containers that could house and birth the whole of me, my imagination is drawn to sanctuaries, caves and iron cauldrons. One of my favorite images is a *kiva*, a Native American holy space, which is a meeting place dug into the ground. The *kiva* is architecturally designed to give one the sense of being held by the earth but also connected to the sky by way of a ladder.

There are also wonderful images from Alchemy of womb spaces for birth. Alchemical vessels of all kinds were used to house the raw materials which would be cooked and baked, boiled and steamed. We too need a vessel that will hold our raw material – the thoughts, feelings, instincts and urges which may seem frightening, but which certainly need containing and loving while we cook, bake, boil and steam through life. Pots, bowls, chalices and earthenware are succulent images for the first initiation. These objects conjure up images associated with mother, such as roundness, circle and breast, and they conjure up feelings of warmth, softness, cuddling and resting. The universal energy that they represent is unconditional love.

Exercise 7: Creating your own clay container

For this exercise you will need about one pound of self drying clay, a plastic tarp to cover your work surface and a small bowl of water to moisten your clay. Hold your slab of clay in your hands and close your eyes. Imagine what it would be like to have a safe, strong and secure container within you. Allow the container that wants to be born from your slab of clay to form in your hands. Give yourself plenty of time to create your container. When the clay dries you can place your hand-made container on your personal altar to remind yourself that you are seeking initiation at Stage 1, seeking to grow a safe and sacred container inside.

The cave as container

Another way to develop a secure internal container is to have tangible experiences in physical places that feel like safe containers. I have had many powerful experiences that led to the growth of my internal container by venturing into the caves found on the island of Crete.

Caves seem to powerfully reenact the womb experience and test our ability to trust the earth as a container to hold us. If we can trust the cave to be a holding container, it helps us to internalize a positive and holding container.

During a women's retreat I was co-leading in Crete, my colleague and I took a group of women down into a cave to do a powerful ritual where we would test our ability to allow Mother earth to hold us safely in her cave/womb. The cave is tucked up in the mountains, accessed by a narrow 40-foot vertical slit into the rock. The cave has two main chambers. The first is accessed by climbing down a series of extremely steep ladders to a large, round underground room that is illuminated by sunlight pouring down from the cracks in the opening of the cave above. In this first chamber, an altar is set up with many candles, creating a sense of reverence and awe. For some women, entering the first chamber of the cave proved challenging. As we ventured into the second chamber, deep into the darkness of the mountain, more women joined the ranks of the frightened and wanted to turn back.

It was a 15-minute walk, through the pitch black, from the first chamber to the second chamber deep into the bowels of the mountain. We had prepared the women ahead of time, speaking of the fear that could arise. We had flashlights and headlamps and at times found ourselves scrambling up and down huge rocks and walking through narrow slits between the rock walls. For the women whose internal containers were solid and secure and who therefore had a positive relationship with the archetypal Mother, it seemed easier to walk into the darkness and depths of the cave without feeling claustrophobic and panic stricken. For those who felt their internal containers were shaky and insecure, the cave adventure proved extremely challenging. Some women had fantasies that the cave walls would collapse and found it difficult to trust the holding womb space of the Mother.

The second inner chamber was literally shaped like a womb, a round space, approximately 15 feet in diameter. The only activity inside this part of the cave was the slow dripping of water from the rock ceiling. When we all arrived safely, albeit with some anxiety, we sat in a circle, lit some candles, and did some meditation and chanting. At some point, we blew out all the candles. In the complete and utter darkness of the cave we sat in silence together for a long time. This experience of being in the bowels of the cave helped us understand both the earth's benevolent aspects and her malevolent side as well. Some women felt crushed and overwhelmed by the cave, others felt sweetly held. Some women had rebirth experiences and some allowed themselves to be rocked by the silent, cool, solid cavemother.

This was a fantastic experience of trusting. We allowed the darkness and the sounds of the dripping water to permeate our bodies and minds. When some women encountered the dark mother who felt crushing and deathlike, it was frightening. They were grateful for the warm hands of the women beside them. Others enjoyed the silence and solitude of the cave and experienced profound inner peace. This experience gave all of us insight into the state of our inner containers. We learned first hand whether we could emotionally afford to surrender to the dark womb space or whether we felt overwhelmed by the experience. This ritual forced us to develop trust at a very basic and primitive level that was important to each person.

In the end, each woman, with the help of the whole team, made it all the way into and out of the cave. This ritual proved to be supportive for those who had apprehension and provided a place to face the fear. It also strengthened our internal containers and helped us to feel more grounded and connected to earth.

The hermetically sealed vessel

The Alchemists had a name for the safe container that was air tight and did not leak. They called it the "hermetically sealed vessel".

The Alchemical laboratory was filled with vessels of all sizes that were closed tightly and protected. With this design they were able to survive heat, burning, cooling, distillation and vast changes of the substance within the vessel. The Alchemists knew that if the hermetically sealed vessel was broken, the operation was aborted. So how do we ensure that our internal vessel is hermetically sealed? We must first and foremost create *appropriate emotional boundaries around whatever process we are in so that we are safeguarded from external energies that may damage the process of our development.*

For example, there are times when it is important to protect ourselves from doubt, criticism or opposition to our personal development. If we have an idea about a creative project, it may need to be kept secret. If we are trying to develop some new aspect of ourselves and speak about it repeatedly, this may dissipate the energy. Rushing into a relationship or project too soon, without the proper foundation, may bring about a premature birth. We must learn to wait patiently until all stages of gestation are complete. We must stop talking, live with silence and draw around us appropriate boundaries. We must protect our process, our initiation experiences, reserve our energy and try to seal our vessel.

The inner container must be hermetically sealed during the entire gestation process, however long that may be. Think about the gestation of a real baby. A baby needs a safe place to grow. The whole gestation period is a wonderful metaphor for the amount of containment that we need to process feelings and experiences. We have to hold and be patient for the symbolic nine-month period in order for something to grow. If our energy is leaking out of our womb space, the process of development will not go through to birth.

Some years ago, I had a dream about my ancestral alchemical vessel whose seal was broken. The dream informed me which particular vessel was broken and clearly showed the devastation that results when a container is damaged and leaks over many generations. The dream also offered suggestions for healing and spoke to the importance of building a hermetically sealed vessel to contain all of me. I named the dream "Ancestral house in ruins - an anointing in the wilderness."

> *I am a young adult in my family home amidst a crowd of people participating in a large party. During the course of the party, I am betrayed in a deeply painful way by a maternal figure. She is giving away private and sensitive information about me to a stranger. I feel exposed and unprotected. In a moment of boldness, I go to her and face her squarely to declare my protest but I am totally unable to speak. I have literally lost my voice. In desperation I run out of the house and run for miles and miles, eventually finding myself in the midst of a desert wilderness.*
>
> *The maternal figure follows me into the desert. It is here in the desert that I finally find my voice and the words to address my pain. I weep for her to understand me and I cry, "I want you to listen to the child inside of me." But the dream mother ignores my feelings and begins intellectualizing, unable to hold my pain and concerns.*
>
> *In despair I turn away, hopeless at ever finding a solution to this problem or healing my*

pain. As I turn around to walk away, I see the site of an old ruin. I walk towards it with curiosity, and as I approach, I realize that it is the remains of an ancient Jewish home. Standing within the rubble is a female anthropologist who confirms that this is indeed an ancient Jewish home "in ruins". We greet each other and she begins to show me around. The anthropologist shows me the old customary salutation which would accompany a visit into a Jewish home and demonstrates the kind of ritual that would be performed. She says to me, "When a Jew invited you into their home, you would enter through the arched doorway into the brick structure and the host or hostess would say, 'This is the hearth of many colors, come in and be welcome.' As the guest, you would then walk down a few steps to a communal room and sit on the floor."

I do as she suggests and sit on the floor of this old house where I come face to face with an ancient stone tablet about three feet high and two feet wide. As I observe it closely, I see the face of a wise old sage carved into the white stone. Underneath the head of the sage are carved four hands, positioned in such a way as to convey a particular message. Apparently, the hand signals tell a story in ancient Hebrew. As the guest in the home, my job is to figure out what the hand signals mean and then interpret the Hebrew story. After successfully interpreting the tablet, I am able to get the "anointing." On top of the stone carving I find a slight dip in the marble, creating a small well where scented oil is resting in a pool. I dip my finger in the oil and anoint my forehead. After this I awaken.

The dream quite clearly informs me that one of my main alchemical vessels has broken a seal. The dream tells me it is my ancestral maternal vessel that has been damaged. When the maternal vessel is broken or damaged in some way, the internal devastation can be tremendous. I am left with feelings of abandonment, betrayal, rage and hopelessness. I feel exposed and unprotected. I lose my voice to protest about the things that hurt me and lose the ability to ask for something different. I feel helpless to find any solution or to communicate what I am feeling. I feel alienated from my own home and must take flight into the desert which is hot, dry and without the moisture of a warm, emotional life.

When I come upon the Jewish home in ruins, it confirms to me that this maternal vessel has been leaking for generations. Remember, a hermetically sealed vessel should be strong enough to survive the vast changes of temperature and transformations within the vessel. I know from my family history that my maternal ancestors of Jewish lineage endured many hardships resulting from the pogroms in Eastern Europe. They were forced to flee their home and seek refuge in a new land.

Many other circumstances contributed to the chipping away of the maternal container. Abandonments and hardships along with personal and collective persecution can break open the vessel. After some generations, I inherited a maternal container that leaks. The dream clearly identifies the consequences: my boundaries are not properly protected, I have lost the ability to ask for what I need, I do not feel safe in my own home or body, and find myself in defensive flight away from home into the desert. Even when I find my voice again to speak my pain, my internal dream mother is unable to hold and contain my feelings.

I need to patch up the leaks and restore my internal vessel. I need one that has a strong seal to withstand the twists, turns and storms that life brings. The dream offers some suggestions for healing and rebuilding my alchemical maternal vessel.

The first step is to access my "anthropologist", that part of my personality that can reconstruct the past in a more objective way, more detached from the emotional complex, and then put my house back together piece by piece. The woman anthropologist can do something constructive with the rubble. She is the beginning of a new maternal vessel because she has knowledge of history, she knows what this Jewish house or inner container was like when it was whole. She also knows how to make this house into a hearth and home. She knows the proper greeting to welcome everyone into this inner home. If I pay attention and follow her lead, my inner container can become the "hearth of many colors", a safe place where all the diverse parts of me are welcome to show up. She will help me create the hermetically sealed maternal vessel that I need.

The anthropologist also reminds me that the foundation of my container is intact. There is rebuilding to do amidst the rubble, but the thread of continuity from generation to generation is there. However, there is a mysterious riddle to be solved in order to get to the blessing and anointing which would take the healing to a new level. In the dream I must "step down" into another room in the house, into a deeper aspect of the unconscious and do some digging and deciphering. The old Hebrew sage on the stone tablet has something to say to me. The hand signals remind me of the holding and loving touch I need to rebuild the ground of my being. The hands also seem to hold a Jewish story – perhaps the story of my ancestors – that reveals how the maternal vessel became broken and sprang some leaks.

I had this dream during a deep search into the unconscious to reconstruct my roots. I was mothering myself in more tangible ways, making solid boundaries and protecting my emotional process. The dream indicates that I have done enough deciphering to warrant the anointing at the end of the dream. The anointing with oil on my forehead signals that initiation is taking place and healing is in progress. Brick by brick, I am rebuilding this inner container so that my house can become a hearth and home.

The Tabernacle in the Wilderness

In the "Anointing in the Wilderness" dream, the anthropologist represents an archetypal helper who can assist us in reconstructing our inner home, our internal container. The purpose in building a sealed container is to restore to our physical and psychological life feelings of security, safety and inner solidity, so that no matter what trials we encounter in life, we will have a sturdy platform to stand on and a deep root system that will keep our Tree firmly planted in the ground.

Another archetypal helper that we can call upon in Stage 1 to take this initiation even further is the *Master Craftsman* who not only knows how to construct a solid container, but knows how to create a sacred internal space that has style, flair and originality. There is a wonderful Jewish story from the book of Exodus of a Master Craftsman named Bezalel, who is chosen to build the Tabernacle for the Israelites while they are living in the desert after leaving Egypt. The Tabernacle is the mobile Temple that houses the sacred paraphernalia and becomes the tent of meeting where Israel gathers to celebrate the presence of God. In the Western mystical teachings, the Tabernacle is seen as a symbol of the inner temple, a sacred container that is built in such a way as to attract the Divine. As an initiate on the path of awakening, each one of us is a Master Craftsman building our life into a beautiful temple where the Divine can set up home.

In the Anointing dream, reconstruction of the container begins in the desert. In the Exodus story, the building of the Tabernacle also takes place in the desert environment. This says to me that even in the most dire, parched and extreme environmental and emotional circumstances, we can still build an inner temple to house the soul and attract the Divine.

In the book of Exodus, the Israelites have been in the desert for some time after leaving Egypt, where they had been slaves to the Pharaoh for hundreds of years. Moses has been leading them through the desert and now the people have arrived near Mount Sinai. It is here that Moses climbs the mountain to receive the Ten Commandments and the instructions for the building of a sanctuary according to principles of sacred architecture. The shape and design of the Tabernacle will facilitate the raising of consciousness up to the Divine, and the beauty of the gold and silver sacred objects placed inside the Tabernacle will help focus divine attention down to earth.

After Moses receives the instructions for building the Tabernacle, a master builder and craftsman is chosen to construct and build it. The man who is selected, Bezalel, is chosen because of his righteousness, skill and ability to create with originality. Bezalel represents the archetypal force within us who has "righteousness" and knows the right way to live. He knows his sacred ground of being. *Bezalel is the part of us that has the focus of mind and heart to build our container in the most original way so that our unique expression can attract the Divine.*

Follow along now with the story of the Master Craftsman and pay attention to what happens when the Tabernacle is finally built. Imagine yourself as Bezalel and imagine what gifts you possess that will help to build your inner temple in an exquisite way.

"God has singled out Bezalel of the tribe of Judah to be the craftsman for the sanctuary. God has filled him with the spirit and endowed him with skills and knowledge for every kind of craft: for the art in designing and working in gold, silver and bronze: for cutting stones to be set, for carving wood, for every kind of craft. God has filled him with the skill to carry out all the crafts of engraver, damask weaver, embroiderer in purple stuffs, of violet shade and red, in crimson stuffs and fine linens. He is able to do work of all kinds and do it with originality.

When the Tent of Meeting was erected and consecrated, a cloud (the Shekhinah) covered the Tent of Meeting, and the Glory of Yahweh filled the Tabernacle. At every stage of their journey, whenever the cloud rose from the Tabernacle, the Israelites would resume their march. If the cloud did not rise, the people waited and would not march until it did. For the cloud of Yahweh rested on the Tabernacle by day and a fire shone within the cloud by night for all the house of Israel to see. And so it was for every stage of their journey." [3]

This sacred space was built to attract the divine presence and call in the mystery of the divine force, the Shekhinah. In order to be initiated at Stage 1, we must do what the Hebrew people did in the wilderness those many generations ago: we must build our lives like a Temple, to attract the Divine and create a sacred space for the Divine to come and live. Like the Shekhinah, we then become the dwelling place for the mystery of life. Not only are we building a safe container that is like a home, we are building an inner Temple, filled to the brim with the beautiful aspects of the soul. The gold and silver, the purple damask and the white linen can be seen as qualities of inner radiance such as love, gratitude, kindness and abundance.

It is up to each one of us to build a living Temple, placing brick upon brick, stone upon stone. A firmly grounded Tabernacle will eventually be strong enough to hold all of ourselves. When we awaken further down the initiation path, our inner Temple will need to be strong enough to hold the great inspirations coming to us from Spirit.

External containers - creating sacred space

So far in Step 3, we have learned ways to build an internal container for holding and gestating, and learned the value of sealing our vessel and building our inner Tabernacle with style and flair. The story of the Tabernacle in the wilderness is also a beautiful story about how to set up sacred space in the *external environment*. When our outer, as well as our inner environment becomes a safe and holding container, we feel profoundly grounded and stabilized.

Imagine being in the middle of the parched desert and setting up an enormous white linen tent, a mobile sanctuary, a sacred meeting place. Imagine the sides of this Tabernacle covered in archetypal figures and inside decorated with beautiful sacred objects. The Tabernacle was designed architecturally and aesthetically to call down the spirit of the Divine. In our own homes we can do the same by creating conscious, sacred space to attract the Divine. Shrines and altars are not just reserved for the church, mosque, synagogue or temple. *We need to bring sacred intention into the home so that we anchor the Divine in real time and space*, anchoring memory, anchoring intent and honoring spirit.

There are a variety of ways to create sacred space in the external environment. Much can be learned from visiting sacred temples, churches, synagogues, mosques and other natural sacred sites. As I travel the world, I am amazed at the beauty, variety and creativity of sacred places. I love to see the foods, colored banners and stone carvings at the temples in Bali, the totem guardians encircled against the backdrop of towering palm trees at the Place of Refuge in Hawaii, the pure gold Buddhas scattered throughout the temples in Thailand. I am awed by the exquisite European cathedrals in Chartre and Siena and the simple beauty of the stone circles in Britain.

Sacred sites are often decorated with some form of nature – flowers, food or plants. Often they have candles, music, incense, fresh water and sacred works of art. These sacred objects facilitate inner silence, contemplation, prayer, worship, focus on the Divine, inner peace and healing. Think of the atmosphere we can create if we spend time beautifying our home in this way.

The Hestia archetype is helpful here. Hestia is the Greek goddess of the home fires, the hearth. She oversees the creation of sacred space within the home. If we do not replenish ourselves within the home and cannot rest within the home, what kind of sacred container are we building? However large or small, Hestia can make a house a real home, a sacred container where the Divine can be honored. She shows the importance of creating sacred space where we can truly rest. Like the temple priestesses of old, we too can learn how to keep an external space clean and clear of emotional negativity. Cleansing with incense or sage is effective. Drumming or singing can help build up a positive atmosphere.

Another way to create sacred space in our home is to set up an altar or shrine. Shrine making is "honoring with intention". We can set up an ancestral shrine with photographs of our ancestors, setting aside a small sacred place to remember our origins and roots. Or we can have a shrine to our spiritual teachers, honoring their wisdom and knowledge. Creating a special altar with our sacred objects and favorite art pieces produces an ambience of reverence and awe. There is an amazing difference in atmosphere as we raise the level of consciousness within our home.

Most cultures have a great respect for shrine building and creating sacred space. When I stayed in Bali, for example, I noticed how the people created beautiful shrines to their ancestors in their homes and in the local temples where the gods and goddesses of the Hindu pantheon are honored. Each morning as I awoke in my small homestay, I would find a fresh offering plate outside my door, an offering to the local deities to protect me and bless my stay. Having a shrine made for me of rice, banana leaf, incense, and a candle grounded me, connected me to nature and reminded me to be grateful each day.

Step 1: Root into nature
Step 2: Ground in the body
Step 3: Feel contained
* Step 4: Birth yourself into life *

So far in the first initiation, we have rooted ourselves into nature, grounded in the body, and learned to feel contained, safe and secure. Step 3 helped us to create the symbolic womb that will now provide the space we need for gestation and birth. Without this strong container, it is not possible to birth ourselves into life.

In Step 4, we will call forth the Midwife, the central archetype to activate the first initiation. *The Midwife will guide us step by step through the birthing process so that we can birth our dreams and manifest our gifts into the world.* With the Midwife's help, we can bring anything to birth, whether it is an organization, a book, a product, a piece of art or a professional qualification. Step 4 will take us through the birth process – from gestation through the labor pains and active birth – so that we can incarnate and embody our life goals and dreams. With the Midwife's help we will become radically embodied and radically present with ourselves and others.

Incarnation

What is incarnation? According to the Kabbalistic tradition, the Divine, whose essence is in all things, is seeking continually to come into matter, into physical form. All things in Spirit desire manifestation, unfolding and embodiment. As Spirit incarnates, God makes God's self known in tangible form so we can touch, feel and experience the Divine in our everyday lives. This sensual experience of the Divine is referred to as the Shekhinah, who enlivens the senses and invites us into the pleasures of incarnation. She encourages us to show up fully in the present moment and to enjoy the physical world in all its diverse glory.

The Shekhinah also represents the active, divine presence which is desiring to come into incarnation, and as we are created in the divine image, we too must be infused with this same desire to come into full form. I take this to mean that we desire to fulfill our Tree of Life and blossom fully, expressing what we are created to do.

The Alchemists understood and deeply appreciated the process of incarnation and were open to the mystery of what was incarnating before them in the alchemical vessel. They were also open to the potential of what was incarnating within themselves. The incarnation story told by the Alchemists was that life begins with the *Prima Materia*, the primal matter that must be searched for, found and brought through a series of operations, ending with the beautiful "gold", which represents the fully incarnated object or person.

The Alchemists began the incarnation process digging into the earth, mining for the raw ore, the *Prima Materia* that had all potential encoded within it. The *Prima Materia* contained the divine spark, and the Alchemists' job was to locate this spark wherever it was and become more aware of the divinity within nature and within themselves. Like the Alchemists, we too must dig into the earth of ourselves, finding the spark of gold. We must hold and respect that precious metal inside of us, letting go of control in order to see who will emerge. Our job is to mine the gold from the deepest part of ourselves and acknowledge the beauty of each part of ourselves as it is being born.

Another incarnation story in the Christian scriptures, the birth of Christ, is a beautiful example of how we can become sacred vessels for birth. The incarnation story begins with Mary who was specifically chosen to birth the Christ because she had developed her inner vessel to the point where she was capable of birthing this level of consciousness. Mary represents the feminine container that is conscious enough and solid enough to gestate and grow Christ consciousness. From a Depth Psychology perspective, it is a beautiful story demonstrating that in order to birth the Christ, we must have a conscious vehicle, a womb space that is open to be fertilized by the archetype of the Self. Then we must have a willing inner vessel that can hold, gestate and be present with the authentic Self that wants to be born.

These examples of incarnation stories bring us positive images of incarnating and help us look forward to embodying ourselves fully. The rewards of birthing the gold and birthing the Christ seem a worthy prize at the end of the initiation process. Why then do many people resist incarnating?

Many fears contribute to our refusal to bring the whole of ourselves to life, including fear of success, fear of failure, fear of our greatness and fear of our power. According to the Western mystical tradition, when we come into the physical world, we face our greatest challenges and changes. When we incarnate, we come into present time and therefore must face reality. Many people do not want to face reality and would rather live in their illusions, live in the past or live in the future. The most difficult place to stay is in the present. In the present we come face to face with ourselves and face to face with what we can and cannot do. One of our tasks in the incarnation process is to face our fears and develop ourselves through embodied experience in the world, climbing up every rung of the ladder, polishing every sapphire and doing the work that initiation demands.

Calling the Midwife

The Midwife is the primary archetype that helps us successfully complete the first initiation. The job of the Midwife is *to bring unborn babies into life, to oversee and manifest projects and to help birth our ideas and new levels of consciousness.* If we have not called the Midwife energy to assist us in whatever we are bringing to birth and have no one overseeing or holding the sacred space, there could be great difficulty in the birth. Projects and ideas can be abandoned or aborted.

The Midwife teaches us how to be profoundly present as we actively open to our own creative process. She teaches us that birth is always accompanied by birth pains, including the contractions and expansions of our imagination as we create, and the contractions and expansions of our emotions as we grow. The birth pains also manifest in the pushing and pulling as we begin a new phase of life, such as parenthood, marriage or a new job.

The Midwife within us is specifically interested in what is coming to birth, preparing the space in every way she can. This corresponds to the part of us preparing the soil into which the new birth will come. The Midwife is the coach, encouraging us to move through the process and not give up. There are so many ways that we sabotage what we are trying to manifest, but the Midwife keeps us on track through the gestation and incubation stage, through the labor pains and through to the final birth.

Another aspect of the Midwife is that she operates in that borderland between the inner and outer worlds, between the fetus and the newborn. She holds the boundary between what is not yet formed and what is being birthed. She has knowledge of both worlds and witnesses the mystery of birth when we cross from one land to the next. She teaches us the art of holding open the space in an excited and inviting way without knowing exactly what or who is coming as we birth new parts of ourselves.

The Midwife guides us through the three main phases of birth: **gestation**, **labor** and **active birth**. During the gestation time, the Midwife teaches us to set our intention, invite our project to manifest and let go of control. During labor, the Midwife teaches pain management, focus and presence. During active birth, she teaches us the art of coaching, manifesting and following through until the very end. When we have fully internalized the Midwife, we will feel embodied, able to show up, able to keep our promises, be on time, stick it out, stay present and bring a solid presence to any situation. We will be known to others as solid, dependable, reliable and powerfully embodied.

Exercise 8: Calling the Midwife

1. From the following list, write down the qualities of the Midwife you already possess and then list the qualities you would like to internalize by the end of the first initiation: feel embodied, be able to show up, be able to keep my promises, be on time, stick it out, stay present, bring a solid presence to any situation, be known to others as solid, dependable, reliable and powerfully embodied.

2. As we move through the three phases of manifesting and birthing, begin focusing on what you are trying to birth now in your life. Some examples are: starting a new career, applying for a new job, implementing a better discipline structure for your children, starting a new organization, beginning a new exercise routine, producing a piece of art, revitalizing your relationship, or adding a new management style to your work. What are you bringing to birth at the moment?

Gestation

Gestation is the phase of birthing that includes planning, incubating, toying with options, holding the space and waiting patiently. During gestation there is incredible growth of the fetus or whatever we are trying to bring to birth. For gestation to be successful, we need to learn the art of active holding and living with patience in the darkness of the womb, while our "baby" is incubating, growing and gaining strength before anything is manifested. The gestation phase allows us plenty of time to incubate an idea, expand on it, change it, improve it, see its relevance and understand its importance. To keep us on track during gestation, the Midwife teaches us about **intention**, **invitation** and **letting go of control**.

To make this process practical, let's follow the case of a man we will call Thomas through his process of "birth". Thomas is a therapist who wants to start a men's center, helping men with issues of anger management, sexuality, self-esteem around money and success, and other relevant topics. His intention is to get the money together and find qualified, trustworthy men to lead groups, make appropriate referrals, and care for the men who will use the center.

The beginning of the birthing process requires us to set our intention for exactly what we want to manifest. The intent is the original idea, the original spark. This may change in the course of the process, but it is important to be true to our original impulse and be specific about what we want. When Thomas set his intention, it was to create a healing center for men. He saw the need in his community for a center that dealt specifically with men's issues and was a sacred space for men only. He knew it was a practical idea, since there was nothing like it around and he had the financial resources and connections that could bring this dream into reality. He had spoken to many of his colleagues who agreed that their male clients would benefit from such a service and were willing to refer them to the center once it was in operation.

After setting the intention, it was time to invite the center into being. Making the invitation can be a simple internal process that we do in the privacy of our own home. The invitation to bring this baby to birth requires an internal attitude of love and desire and a commitment to paving the way for the baby to successfully come into the world.

I remember during the gestation time before the birth of my son, my husband and I intentionally held a focus of invitation for the baby, inviting him to come and be with us. We spoke to him in utero and told him of our anticipation. The loving invitation for the "baby" to birth into the world gives a forward-looking and forward-moving energy to the project.

Thomas was able to make the invitation both privately and publicly, by personally choosing male therapy colleagues to support the project as it was forming and manifesting. Together they had a small dedication ceremony, inviting this center into being.

During this gestation phase, Thomas's colleagues began to feel impatient to get things started. Because Thomas had experience with this kind of organization, he knew the importance of incubating the ideas and waiting until they had processed and formulated the true foundation of the center before rushing into the birth too quickly.

Many people try to control what is coming to birth, and this actually kills the spirit of what is emerging. When we are birthing something, we are inviting a tremendous life force into being. Therefore, we must provide structure and form to contain the dynamic force of what we are being asked to hold. There is an art to holding a space for birth without controlling. This can be done if we learn to tolerate the darkness of the gestation period with patience and anticipation. The symbolic "nine months" is a long time to tolerate the darkness when we do not know exactly what the end product will be. It is imperative to surrender to the gestation time and allow the natural incarnation process to unfold without interfering.

During my own pregnancy, I experienced a growing curiosity about what soul was manifesting. Who was this emerging person? What kind of creation was coming to fruition? I could feel my son growing and developing and I could experience his soul's unique energy while he was in utero. But this new creation was mysterious to me and filled me with awe and wonder. I had to completely surrender, not only to the timing of my son's birth, but to the kind of person he would be, separate from my desires and expectations.

When I am creating one of my Sacred Robes, I also must surrender to its incubation and birth time and the character that will emerge separate from my hopes and wishes. I can try to be prepared for the spirit that will emerge on the robe and the time when it will come to fruition, but most of the time I am deeply surprised. The Robe never births when I expect. When we can allow organic growth without interference, we are preserving the natural state of what is incarnating and can then thoroughly enjoy what is unfolding in our presence.

In the case of Thomas' men's center, letting go of control did not mean lack of involvement, but it meant not being overly attached to the final product. Thomas wanted to preserve the essence of the original idea - a healing center for men - but during gestation, new ideas emerged regarding how men needed healing. His colleagues gave invaluable input about the various issues facing men today, and they decided to add drumming and martial arts classes to their repertoire, to include more body-centered approaches to healing.

Exercise 9: Attending to the gestation period

1. Intention - Set your intention about what you desire to bring to birth. Be practical and realistic in your goal. How much energy are you willing to put into this project to bring it to birth? Are you giving it enough nourishment and sustenance? Are you spending enough time formulating each aspect of the project? Are you inviting others to join you? Are you being realistic in your goal?

2. Invitation - How are you going to invite your "baby" to manifest? You can do it either privately or publicly, with a small ritual. How can you show an attitude of love and desire?

3. Let go of control - Hold to your original impulse and then surrender to the unknown. How does it feel to let go of control? What are you overly attached to? What can you let go of? Is the birth taking longer than you expected? Are you trying to control the timing of the birth?

Labor

Labor is the aspect of birthing that hurts the most. Labor pains come when the birth is imminent and is a time fraught with chaos, instability, ups and downs, expansions and contractions, frustration, pain and sometimes even screaming. It is a precarious time in the life of any new project, and therefore must be attended to with close scrutiny. We must also keep our wits about us because when the labor pains hit, rationality goes out the window. If we are unprepared for the pain, we will be disappointed, disillusioned and may give up. To keep us on track during labor, the Midwife teaches us the important skills of **pain management**, **focus** and **presence.** With these three skills we can steer our way through the inevitable difficulties with a steady heart and mind.

Thomas was close to manifesting his dream. He had found a space for his men's center, hired the colleagues he most trusted, and had even begun offering a few groups to interested men who were willing to try it out. Some of the classes went well, especially the groups dealing with issues of self-esteem, money and career. But the classes on sexuality and anger management did not go well and it took some investigating and soul-searching to understand why they were failing.

The class on men's sexuality was a good idea, but it turned out that the facilitator was introducing subjects that the men were not ready for. The men in the group reported needing a lot more time to get to know each other before discussing issues of sexual dysfunction or histories of sexual abuse. The facilitator had been too confrontive too quickly, and the men were threatening to quit.

The anger management group was also in some chaos. It turned out that Thomas and his colleagues had not thought through the anger management course thoroughly and there was not enough containment built into the course. Some of the men felt that their anger was escalating and they were not being taught the right skills to neutralize it. The course needed to be redesigned.

The center was getting mixed reviews. Some of the participants raved about the center, others were unimpressed, and still others were critical and vocal with their negativity. Thomas and his staff were in the throes of the labor pains. They felt at times disappointed and dejected and it was painful to see their "baby" criticized by others. They felt unstable, unprotected and vulnerable. They really began to wrestle with the chaos coming from both the clients and staff. With the feedback they were getting, they went back to the drawing board and redesigned some of the courses and groups. Thomas and his staff had a crash course in pain management and learned how to survive the ups and downs of labor.

During labor, it is imperative to focus our energy and be expedient in our decisions. All energy must be concentrated on the end goal. We cannot get sidetracked or take things personally. We must exercise discernment and discrimination. During actual physical labor, when we are birthing a child, focused concentration is the only way to manage the pain and keep moving forward towards the goal of birth. During the labor of any project we must also be in shape to sustain this focus over the entire period, which may be days, months or even years.

During the time that I was pregnant with my son and getting close to delivery, I had a significant dream about the nature of the creative process and the importance of focusing through the expansions and contractions of labor. The following dream is entitled "Birth Mysteries".

I am encircled by a group of wise women who are initiating me into the secrets of childbirth according to the Kabbalistic Tree of Life. As they gather in a circle around me, they tell me they are the Inner Midwives, ancient wisdom keepers who share secrets of birth with pregnant women. They tell me how a woman's body is designed to imitate the cosmic birth process. They point to the Tree of Life diagram and show me how the contractions of labor correspond to the left hand pillar, which I know as the pillar of Form, Structure and

Contraction. The contractions of labor, they say, set off an opposite response on the right-hand pillar of Force, countering the contraction with an expansion and opening of the cervix which must fully dilate in order to give birth.

In a flash I understand what they are trying to say, that the action of the left and right pillars are in a dynamic dance of birth – a dynamic which is constantly surging throughout the universe. They tell me that my female body is designed to move through this incarnation dance because it is encoded in my DNA. The dream Midwives show me that during labor, the contractions and expansions are imitating the spiraling kundalini force, weaving back and forth between the left and right pillars, activating the body's contraction and release, contraction and release. I then understand that my job as the birthing mother is to surrender physically to this spiral dance, to the incarnational forces channeling through my body, and to hold a sacred space for this tremendous birth dance to unfold. This means holding a solid focus on the central pillar of consciousness to facilitate and recreate the cosmic creation process as fully as possible.

The next lesson from the dream Midwives again involves the Tree of Life. They tell me that the ten Sephirot on the Tree (the ten archetypal spheres or sapphires, Daat not included) correspond to the ten centimeters that a woman must be dilated before the active birthing phase can occur. When they point this out to me, I realize that the birthing itself occurs in the sphere of Daat, which represents the birth canal, the transition space, the transformational tunnel. I understand that my body and psyche must open to such an extent that I travel through all the Sephirot, all states of consciousness – from Malkhut to Keter – as I am giving birth.

After waking from this dream, I am profoundly moved and awestruck at the beauty of the incarnation process. It confirms to me that our job during gestation and labor is to hold an intense focus and conscious space for birth to occur. During any creative project, we must be able to hold the fluctuations between times of expansion and action and times of receptivity and reflection. This kind of holding is so much more dynamic than I had ever realized. It involves more than holding with consciousness – it is a holding with a fierce focus of concentration and a steady heart and mind.

This fierce concentration was required of me during the birth of my son. Thirty hours after my labor began, I was finally allowed to come into the hospital. I was exhausted and disappointed that labor with my first child had already been extremely painful and difficult. Things were not proceeding normally, and hour by hour I was hooked up to more monitors and intravenous drips. I had wanted a natural childbirth but the baby was dangerously positioned, and my husband and I had to make a series of choices regarding how to best birth this child.

There was no turning back. I remember thinking this somewhere at the zenith of labor. This was the one time in my life when clearly I had to follow the process through to the end. I could not quit, I could not be somewhere else and I could not think about the past or future. I had to be fully present in the moment, and each moment consisted of managing the pain and concentrating through each contraction with as much consciousness as possible.

The initiation lesson here is about *staying in the present and being fully embodied even though it may involve pain*. During the labor phase we cannot run away from the pain or the situation at hand when things heat up or increase in intensity. Holding an intense focus for incarnation requires concentrating all our energy in the moment. Every person in the labor and delivery room during my birth experience was totally focused on getting this baby out without any harm to baby or mother. The Midwife cannot turn her mind to anything else. There is a concentration of energy in and on the present, being in the here and now. If we turn our attention for one moment, the birth could go wrong. So we have to hold that focus to the very last point, until the baby's first breath is taken or the project comes to full term.

I will never forget the feeling I had when my Midwife entered the birthing room. I was in an altered state from the pain and exhaustion. But when the Midwife came to my bedside, she brought with her a confident presence that totally changed the atmosphere of the room. This presence was powerfully palpable and I could almost smell and taste it. I perceived her holding presence all around, and suddenly all was well. I remember feeling a resurgence of hope that I could keep going, no matter how difficult it was.

This kind of strong and confident presence is crucial during the labor pains. When we invite our Midwife into the expansions, contractions and chaos of labor, she can quickly assess what is working and what is not working, how much to push and how much to wait, what procedures should be followed and what should be scrapped. The Midwife brings her solid, reassuring and hopeful presence.

Exercise 10: Attending to labor

1. Pain management - What are you wrestling with as you bring your "baby" to birth? What ambivalence do you have? What chaos are you experiencing? What aspects of your project feel unstable? Where do you feel vulnerable, exposed or unprotected? Are you successfully managing the pain? What do you need from the Midwife to be more successful at pain management?

2. Focusing - During the throes of labor, are you focused or scattered in your energy? How is your stamina? Do you need to pace yourself for the long haul? Describe in detail for yourself the expansions and contractions of your particular birth. What aspects of the project are opening and expansive, and what aspects bring contraction and constriction? Are you able to hold your focus during the expansions and contractions? As you keep your end goal in mind, how can you be more expedient and discerning?

3. Presence - What quality of presence are you bringing to your project? Are you bringing a confident and solid presence? If not, why not? How can you make your presence more palpable? Are you staying in the present or dwelling in the past or the future?

Active birth

To keep us on track during active birth, the Midwife teaches us skills of **coaching**, **manifesting** and **follow-through**. Active birth is the last stage of the process, when we are actively pushing to manifest our "baby" in real life. For Thomas and the men's healing center, this came after he and his colleagues had ironed out many of the wrinkles and put out many of the fires. They had listened to the negative feedback and redesigned some programs to better suit the needs of the men who wanted to use the center. Now they were ready for their grand opening and their big marketing push, which included press releases, radio advertising and a spot on a local television station.

The active phase is the last push before we can celebrate the birth. During this last phase, we need the coaching and encouragement of the Midwife to steer us confidently through because there are dangers at this late stage. Just when we think we have everything in place, often something unexpected arises. Sometimes the unexpected comes from the outside and sometimes it comes from within. How many times do we hear of people who get nine-tenths of the way through a degree program and then quit?

The Midwife coaches us through by encouraging us: "You birth this degree, don't give up, look how far you've come, you're doing well, keep going." Often we hit the voice of sabotage during the active birth stage and come close to throwing it all away. With the Midwife's help, we can stay positive and forward-looking even though we may have doubts. The Midwife remains steadfastly at our side, coaching us to reach the goal, do our best, go the extra mile and make one last push.

As the men's center was manifesting in real life and becoming known in the community, Thomas and his staff needed to stay focused on their goal of offering groups and courses to men that were healing to body and soul. With their growing popularity, it became clear that they needed to stick with what was practical, realistic and feasible for the center to accomplish, rather than becoming inflated and grandiose, offering too much too quickly. The staff was tempted to expand and inflate because of their growing status within the community, but they decided to celebrate what they had originally birthed and nurture this baby for a while until it could crawl and then walk confidently in the world.

During the manifestation time, our energy must be focused on what is practical and realistic, what is solving the problem and meeting the need. We must concentrate on what is working rather than on what is not working, what we can do rather than what we cannot do.

The very last phase of the birth is when the beautiful newborn appears in the world and takes its first breath. We have survived the birth pangs, weathered the storms, and stayed positively focused and true to our original impulse. This is a miraculous moment and should be celebrated. Following through to the end provides the necessary energy for birth and subsequent growth. When we can overcome the sabotaging voice and complete our degree or finish our project, successfully engaging until the birth, we have a much better chance of manifesting our dreams in real life. We have internalized the capacity to manifest our gifts and bring this presence into the world.

Exercise 11: Celebrating the birth

1. Coaching - What are the last pushes needed for your project to come into life? If you could hire a real life coach for your project, what would he or she say to you?

2. Manifesting - As you manifest your project and bring it out into the world, are you following your original goal or departing from it, getting sidetracked? Are you being practical and realistic in what you can actually manifest? Are you tempted to birth too much too quickly?

3. Follow through - Can you follow through until the end, until every aspect of your project has been birthed? How are you going to celebrate the miraculous birth of your project?

Conclusion – Initiation 1: Find Your Sacred Ground

Rooting our Tree of Life and finding our sacred ground is the crucial beginning for the soul on its journey of initiation. Although the soul has within it the spark of divinity that will eventually ignite and burst into flame, we must be firmly anchored and rooted in order to hold the intensity of our inner fire once it has awakened. For this reason, we begin the initiation journey by connecting with the earth and with the body as the sacred ground of being.

When we complete the first initiation, we can enjoy feeling some or all of the following: groundedness, embodiment, connection to nature and the earth, aliveness to the body and sensuality, security and containment, the ability to bring a solid presence to any situation, and the ability to manifest ideas and projects in real life. We are now ready to cross the threshold to Stage 2 and begin the second initiation of trusting our instincts, where we will root our Tree of Life into the instinctive soil and bring our instinctive power into life.

Chapter 2

The Great Round
Robe 2

Initiation Two - INSTINCTS

In Chapter 2, we will root our Tree of Life into instinctive soil. Through the ancient Greek myth of Persephone, we will be led on a journey to retrieve our instinctive power. When we complete the second initiation, we will trust our instinctive responses to life, know our own rhythms and be able to flow with the ever-changing cycles and seasons of life. We will be able to comfort and nurture ourselves so that we feel deeply rested and replenished. We will be imaginative and playful and available for intimacy.

In order to activate initiation at Stage 2, we call upon the **Great Mother** archetype who works endlessly to help us retrieve our instinctive knowing. The Great Mother steers us back to our own natural rhythms of rest and play, attractions and repulsions, wants and needs. We can rest in her arms and be in our child energy, enjoying play and imagination without anxiety or fear. Trusting the Great Mother is the bedrock for emotional attachment and bonding with others, creating lifelong satisfying relationships.

Qualities if initiated:	**Problems if initiation is not complete:**
Powerfully instinctive	Unaware of our instinctive power
Flexible with change	Unable to tolerate change
In sync with body/emotional rhythms	Out of sync with body/emotional rhythms
Self-nurturing and self-comforting	Unable to self-nurture
Able to ask for what we want and need	Unaware of our needs
Available for intimacy	Difficulty forming attachments/intimacy
Imaginative, creative and playful	Blocked imagination, unable to play
Relaxed and replenished	Emotionally stressed
Possessing an internal Good Mother	Possessing an internal Negative Mother
Valuing wisdom from the unconscious	Blocked from unconscious wisdom
Connected to the cycles and seasons of life	Disconnected from the cycles and seasons of life

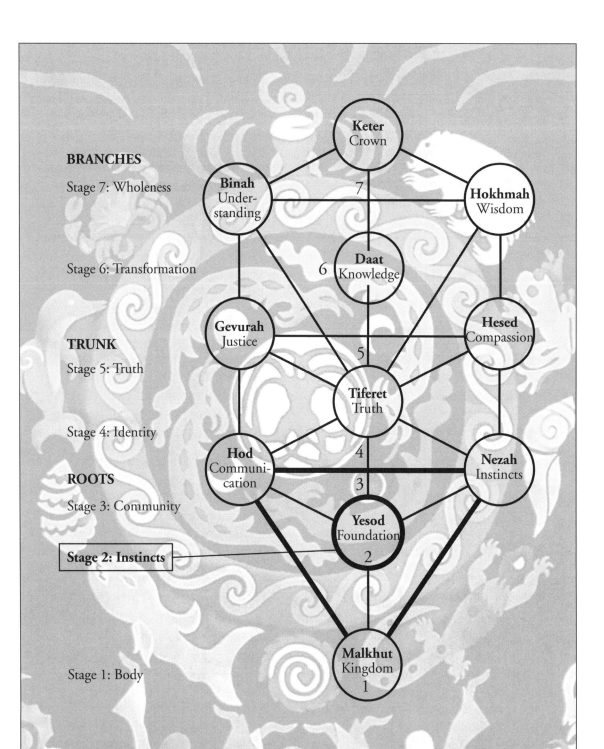

BRANCHES

Stage 7: Wholeness

Stage 6: Transformation

TRUNK

Stage 5: Truth

Stage 4: Identity

ROOTS

Stage 3: Community

Stage 2: Instincts

Stage 1: Body

Keter Crown

Binah Under-standing

Hokhmah Wisdom

7

Daat Knowledge

6

Gevurah Justice

Hesed Compassion

5

Tiferet Truth

Hod Communi-cation

Nezah Instincts

4

3

Yesod Foundation

2

Malkhut Kingdom

1

Diagram 7: Stage 2
In the second initiation we stabilize the root system by rooting our Tree into instinctive soil. Instinctive soil connects us to a deep underground well of intuitive wisdom and the raw vitality and power of instinctive drives. If our roots anchor into the instinctive ground and get the nutrients they need, we will build a stable psychological foundation that will allow our Tree to thrive.

Chapter 2 - Trust your Instincts

In the first initiation, we began to root our Tree of Life by anchoring ourselves into the earth and into our bodies. In the second initiation, we stabilize the root system even more by rooting our Tree into instinctive soil.

Instinctive soil connects us to a deep underground well of intuitive wisdom and the raw vitality and power of instinctive drives. Instincts are natural impulses and inherent tendencies that do not involve reason or the higher mind. Our instincts can be described as our natural attractions and repulsions, our inherent draw towards people and things that satisfy our basic physical, sensual and emotional needs. When the roots of our Tree are nourished by instinctive soil, we feel replenished, we can enjoy play, explore our creativity and nurture ourselves like a good mother. If our roots sink deeply into the instinctive ground and get the nutrients they need, we will build a stable psychological foundation that will allow our Tree to thrive. The emotional stability that results from awakening and trusting the instincts is as strong as the steel and concrete foundation of a house.

The roots of human instincts reach far back into our ancient, evolutionary past, connecting us to our ancestors who, out of necessity, were far more in touch with the rhythms of nature, survival instincts and psycho-biological life in general. As the human race has become more civilized, our instinctual responses to life have become dulled. This is especially so in the West as we have moved into the cities, become more refined, intellectually educated and religiously schooled. We have distanced ourselves from instinctual life and tend to devalue the sexual, aggressive and survival drives as uncivilized and base. Often we are taught to "rise above" the instincts. This is dangerous for our psychological stability, because rising above the instincts can push them into the unconscious, forcing them to arrive in our conscious life in the form of nightmares, crises or psychological breakdowns.

Aligning with our true, natural, instinctive rhythm is crucial to our emotional health. As I watch my young son, I am amazed at how instinctively aware he is of his rhythms and how clear he is in communicating his needs. He knows exactly when he is hungry, tired, excited, needing stimulation, rest, play, intimate contact and time alone. He is very much in sync with his needs and the rhythm of his instinctive world. As the mother, my job is to hold a space for his natural rhythms to establish themselves and for his own personality to develop within that safe space.

For most of us, somewhere along the line we lost this connection to our instinctive responsiveness to life and lost the voice to communicate our needs. Perhaps we did not have the safe holding place where our natural rhythms had a chance to establish themselves. If we do not know how to flow with the natural currents of life, we are unable to rest in our own rhythms and this causes suffering to both body and soul. We must be able to contact our natural instinctive rhythms of sexuality, pleasure, play, sensual awareness and creativity.

Many people in the West feel disconnected from instinctual life, out of sync with their body cycles, and have little knowledge of how to care for themselves in basic physical ways. Some are out of sync with their emotional cycles, with no road map to survive grief, rage or loneliness. Not only have we lost connection to our most basic needs and rhythms, but we are also disconnected from the animal and plant life of the land, which preserves the instinctual mysteries of life. Our senses have numbed and our instincts have gone to sleep. It is imperative that we reawaken the ancient instinctual memories buried deep within us.

Initiation into Stage 2 awakens our instincts so that we can root and stabilize our Tree. By exploring our impulses, attractions, repulsions and instinctive urges for survival, attachment and sexuality, we can call back our instinctive power. We no longer have to spend enormous energy repressing our instinctual life. When instinctive energy is retrieved from the unconscious, we can feel a tremendous amount of vitality return to our waking life; the juice will begin to flow and our blood will feel hot coursing through our veins once again.

Exercise 1: Meditation - Rooting our Tree in instinctive soil

The following is a meditation to help you root your Tree into instinctive soil.

Imagine once again your great Tree of Life. Imagine yourself down in the great root system of the Tree, resting in the earth. You notice that there are three main taproots to your Tree: one that feeds and nourishes the body, one that feeds your instincts, and one that connects you to your ancestors and family inheritance.

Focus your attention on the root that nourishes your instinctive life. This root connects you with primal instincts of survival, instincts that have kept animals and humans alive since the beginning of time. Feel the vitality of the primal instincts surging up this root and into the whole of your Tree.

Imagine going back in time, back to when we lived in caves and built fires to stay alive and keep safe from animal predators. In this environment, you must survive in the wilderness, your senses come alive and you keep vigilant watch as you move through the primal forest. You live close to the land and celebrate the seasonal changes as the great wheel of nature cycles and circles through the seasons. The sun and the moon are worshiped as great and powerful deities. Your life moves in rhythm with these great cycles of life and death. Allow the great instinctive cycles of nature to rock you as you surrender to their rhythm.

Now turn your attention inward to the rhythms of your own instinctive life. Your instincts lead you naturally towards what you desire and what is pleasing, and quickly away from what you do not like. Allow yourself now to flow from one instinctive state to the next. Now you are hungry, now you feel tired, now excited, now you want to rest, now you need stimulation, now you want to play, now you want intimate contact, now you wish to be alone, now you feel competitive and want to work out some aggression, now you want to daydream. Allow yourself to flow from one state to the next, flowing with your own rhythm.

Imagine once again the roots of your Tree and see the instinctive taproot firmly grounded in rich, instinctive soil. This is your connection to the instinctive power of all beings. During this initiation, you will open this channel more and more and learn to harness your instinctive power, flowing with your own rhythm. Bring yourself back to the present and, when you feel ready, open your eyes.

Write down in your journal what you experienced. What is your relationship to instinctual life? How in touch are you with your attractions and repulsions? How easy was it to allow yourself to flow from one instinctive state to the next?

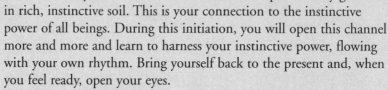

* Step 1: Flow with cycles of change *
Step 2: Honor your instinctive rhythms
Step 3: Explore the unconscious
Step 4: Trust the Great Mother

Identify the life-death-rebirth cycles of regeneration

Instinctive life is fundamentally connected to the great cycles of nature – both follow the archetypal pattern of life, death and rebirth. In Step 1, we will learn how to *flow with the cycles of change by experiencing the full turning of the great life-death-rebirth wheel.* We will learn to handle all the stages, including separation, loss, descent, death, reintegration and rebirth.

All cycles of regeneration are modeled on the great **life-death-rebirth** template, beginning with a state of **oneness** and moving through stages of **separation, tension, resolution** and **reintegration**. Without initiation into the great cycles of regeneration, we can easily get stuck around the wheel and not experience the great release and development that occur at the end of each cycle. Regeneration can only occur if there is death of some kind. In the natural world, for example, the death of a tree means food for the insects and fertilization for future generations of trees and plants. In the human world, periodic psychological death to outmoded ideas or emotional patterns ensures regeneration for the psyche as a whole.

The following are some other examples of cycles and their progression around the wheel:

The cycle of regeneration in *nature* begins with the birth of a tree and moves through stages of growth, flowering, decaying, death and inevitable rebirth.

The cycle of *relationships* begins with symbiosis (psychological fusion between two people), and moves through stages of separation, loss, reparation and eventual reunion.

Groups also move through cycles of regeneration, beginning with homeostasis (when the system is balanced) and moving through stages of change, transformation, return and restoration on a new level.

Sometimes a family group can get stuck in the homeostasis phase and not allow any outside influence, any new ideas or people, into the group. When the group cannot move around the natural regeneration cycle, a crisis usually occurs during developmental stages, particularly adolescence. The family system must be able to adapt the family rules as the children are developing and accommodate to changes so that a restoration of the family unit can occur, but on a more expanded level with age-appropriate family rules.

If we can survive the death phase of the cycle, we will experience a surge of renewing life force. This means that we can look forward to relief, restoration, reunion, reparation and regeneration. Hopefully with each turn of the cycle, we gain more and more consciousness, so that the cycles become like spirals, facilitating renewal and helping us to expand consciousness and develop internally.

In addition to experiencing renewal, there are several other reasons to be initiated into the great wheel and flow with the cycles of change. Probably the most important reason is that experiencing continual life-death-rebirth cycles instills in us the principle that *nothing in life is permanent.* This instinctive knowledge is crucial to help us cope with the constant changes of life.

Life is in a continual tidal dance of ebb and flow. Sometimes life is lean and other times abundant. Sometimes we experience joy, but it will inevitably be followed by some kind of change. Flowing with these circular changes gives our Tree the flexibility to bend with the various storms that hit us from time to time. Cycles teach us that nothing stays the same. All of life is in a dynamic movement of change.

Flowing with cycles of regeneration also *helps us cope with loss and death*. Knowledge of the whole cycle offers a container for the intense grief of loss during the death phase and offers a holding space for recovery. Knowledge of the entire cycle also brings a sense of continuity to life, helping us see that death is not final, but rather the precursor to new life. Both individuals and communities need the hope of revitalization and inspiration. We need to know that life somehow continues and that "Spring" always follows "Winter."

Knowing how to flow around the entire cycle ensures that new life and growth are infused after each turn of the cycle so that life continues to move and does not get stuck. Humans have a tendency to get stuck because of fear, resistance or sentimentality. We want to hold on to things because of our desire for permanence. We must tune into our instinctual body and learn to flow with the great river of life and not against it. If, as individuals or a collective, we fail to grasp that life always flows in cycles, we inevitably get stuck at some point around the wheel. Western culture is notorious for getting stuck at the flowering stage and we can barely tolerate the decay and death phases. We worship the flowering of youth, try to look younger with plastic surgery, shun our elders, and whisk away our dead to funeral homes. One of our deepest challenges is to learn to accept the decay and death phases so that we can keep the instinctive wheel turning.

Exercise 2: Flowing with cycles of change

1. What cycle of change are you in at this point in your life? In terms of the life-death-rebirth cycle, identify which phase you are in at this moment: **birth, growth, flowering, decay, death, or the pause before rebirth?**

2. Does your Tree feel flexible and able to flow with cycles of change? How well do you cope with change?

3. Which phase of the life-death-regeneration cycle is easiest for you? Which phase is most difficult?

The great cycles in mythology and religion

We need to raise consciousness collectively about the nature of instinctive cycles and consider developing some cultural or communal rituals to enact the entire life-death-rebirth cycle. Symbolically enacting the cycle through ritual would provide a cultural safeguard against tragic violence and acting out the death phase concretely.

There is historical precedent for communal life-death-rebirth rituals. The most famous rites in the Western world were known as the Eleusinian Mysteries. These Greek initiation rites enacting the Demeter-Persephone myth were celebrated for 2,000 years until the birth of Christianity.

The rite began in Athens where the initiates would gather to prepare, cleanse, fast and sacrifice. After several days, the initiates would gather once again and would walk in procession from Athens to Eleusis. Once in Eleusis, there would be more sacrificing and preparing. Then the initiates would enter the large amphitheater where the myth of Persephone would be reenacted, from her descent into the Underworld to her eventual rebirth. At the end of the drama, Queen Persephone would rise from the Underworld with her new child. It is said that the initiates were given a potion, some say a hallucinogenic substance, that facilitated an experience of death and rebirth as Persephone emerged from the Underworld. Through annual reenactment of this ritual, initiates came to understand what it meant to descend into the Underworld, to be buried like a seed in winter, to incubate and gestate, and then to be reborn in the spring. The Eleusinian Mysteries initiated the people into the life-death-rebirth cycle, ensuring for the individuals and the community the continuity of life after death.

The Christian story of the life, death and resurrection of Jesus portrays another powerful cycle of regeneration. This story begins with the archetypal oneness between Jesus and God. This primal bond undergoes separation when Jesus is born on earth as a human being. During his time on the cross, Jesus shows despair at the separation and eventually moves through death and descent into the Underworld. After three days in the Underworld, Christ resurrects and with this act there is reparation and reunion with God in heaven. There is also reconciliation among humanity on earth by the active, binding force of the Holy Spirit. This brings physical, psychological and spiritual regeneration for those who are willing to follow Christ by moving through their own initiation around the cycle.

From the Kabbalah we learn the nature of instinctive cycles by contemplating the great vegetable triad of Malkhut, Hod and Nezah (see Diagram 8). The vegetable triad is centered on Yesod and – along with the animal triad – forms the instinctive body or *Nefesh*. Our instinctive body is subjected to the vegetable processes of life: birth, growth, flowering, decay, death and regeneration. Far from being negative, this cycle keeps human beings and the universe circling, moving and evolving. It is possible that our instinctual body, with its inherited patterns, can get stuck in ever-repeating compulsive cycles. However, *if we accept and flow with the inevitable flowerings and decays of life, we can move around the circle, rebuilding and renewing our foundation at Yesod and eventually constructing a healthy platform that is flexible and ever evolving.*

Natural cycles of regeneration

Initiation into Stage 2, trusting our instincts, involves a deep exploration of the cycles of life. Let's begin with the cycles of nature.

All of life follows this universal life-death-rebirth pattern of change and transformation. The earth follows this rhythm, as does the moon, sun and stars. As human beings, we participate in this cycle physically in that our bodies grow, bloom, decay and eventually die. The psyche also participates in the life-death-rebirth cycle, moving through times of emotional loss, withdrawal, mourning, and revitalization and joy.

Let's explore more deeply the natural cycles of regeneration and discover how connecting with these cycles helps us to flow in sync with our own instinctive depths. The following is a review of three regeneration cycles in nature: the vegetable, lunar and seasonal cycles.

Vegetable cycles

Let's begin by looking at the vegetable cycles of life that we have previously identified as birth, growth, flowering, decay, death and rebirth. These cycles can be obviously identified when

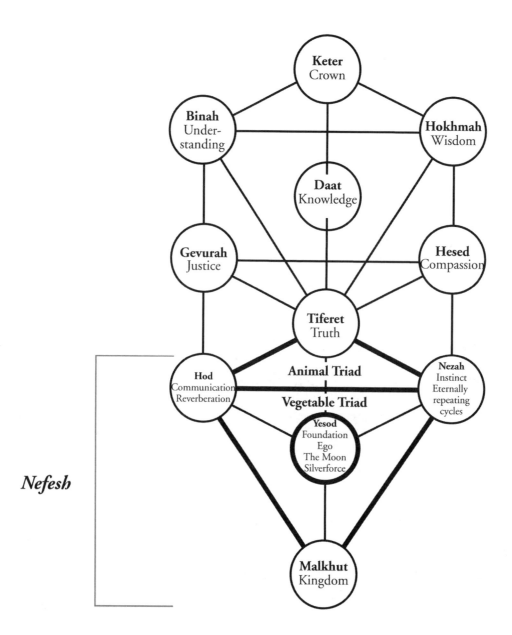

Diagram 8: The *Nefesh* and the Vegetable and Animal Triads
Our *Nefesh* or instinctive body participates in the vegetable and animal processes of life. The "vegetable" cycles of birth, growth, decay, death, and regeneration keep human beings circling, moving and evolving. The "animal" drives help us break free of the purely vegetable state and keep us vital, strong and adventurous.

we walk into a forest and observe the different aspects of the cycle at work. From the base of a redwood tree, a new green shoot is sprouting into *birth*. Steady *growth* can be seen in the bright, lime-green tips of the branches of the older trees. Wildflowers are popping up and opening their full *flower*. Old *decaying* logs are decomposing and providing *new life* for insects and animals.

There is a wonderful term from Alchemy that describes this regenerative force of nature, called *silverforce*. Silver is the alchemical metal associated with the second initiation, for silver is the metal of the moon, which is placed at Yesod on the Tree of Life. Silver, therefore, is the metal associated with the great regenerative cycles of nature. *Silverforce* describes the rhythmic pattern of nature that generates and regenerates time after time, season after season. (For more about the placement of the Alchemical metals on the Tree of Life, see Appendix F.)

When we observe a cut-away section of a tree trunk and notice the rings, we can see an original circle and then ring upon ring of yearly growth flowing outwards from the original sapling of the tree. This same *silverforce* can be observed by throwing a pebble into a still pool. The pebble sets in motion an original impulse, followed quickly by the waves and ripples reverberating the original pattern in an ever-widening circle. When we observe the growth of plants in a rain forest through time-lapse photography, we can really get a sense of the power in the *silverforce* as it generates and regenerates new life. Jungle vines creep up the trees towards the light, fiercely stomping out weaker foliage, beating out their competition for the sun. There is a kind of ferocity in the life-death-rebirth cycle of the jungle. This demonstrates the natural cycles of regeneration in the vegetable world.

Lunar cycles

Over the years of doing cross-cultural research, I found that many cultures initiate their community into the life-death-rebirth cycle by reenacting some form of the Lunar Mysteries. The Lunar Mysteries teach the principles of regeneration by focusing on the various phases of the moon and the associated changes that come during the waxing, full, waning and new moon. On the Tree of Life diagram, the moon is associated with Yesod, the foundation. Participating in the lunar rites helps to establish a healthy emotional foundation because it helps people cope with the inevitable changes and transformations of life. For example, if we become accustomed to the waxing and waning cycles of the moon, then we can flow with the tides of abundance and scarcity, light and dark, health and sickness, sorrow and joy in our life without too much anxiety and fear.

Learning the lunar cycles in depth is particularly important because it teaches us to flow with the different phases of life: when there is potential, when life is full-bodied and fruitful, when some phase in our life is in decline, and when there is pause before a new impulse. The waxing moon is the stage of life that is budding into new growth, full of potential. The full moon represents the stage of life when things come to fruition. The waning moon symbolizes the movement towards decay and ending, but also towards introversion and harvesting. The new moon phase brings us to death, completion, and the silence before rebirth.

Seasonal cycles

The seasonal cycles are the Spring, Summer, Fall and Winter. Each season has particular qualities influenced by the sunlight, moon and stars, and each season reflects one phase of the life-death-rebirth cycle.

In Spring we begin with new life in both the plant and animal kingdoms. There is increasing sunlight and a feeling of joy and anticipation during this time in the northern hemisphere. It is the Christian season of Easter, focused on rebirth through the resurrection of Christ, bringing hope and promise of renewed life. It is also the Jewish season of Passover, the story of freedom from slavery and promise of delivery and new life.

Summer is the season of light and solar consciousness, when the daylight is longer than the night. It is a time of outward focusing and "doing" rather than "being." This makes it the most active or extroverted of seasons.

Fall is the season of harvesting and slowing down. It is a time of communal focusing and celebrating the bounty and abundance of life. It is a time of gathering the harvest in preparation for Winter.

Winter is the season of night, dreaming, darkness and reflection. The nights are longer than the days in the northern hemisphere, and it is a time of being rather than doing. This makes it the most reflective and introverted of the seasons. During Winter, the solstice marks the time when the light is birthed in the darkness. During this time, Hanukkah, the Jewish festival of lights, is celebrated; and Christians celebrate the birth of Christ. Amidst the darkest season of the year, the birth of the divine child brings light, hope and the promise of regeneration. Winter soon turns into Spring.

Exercise 3: Vegetable, lunar and seasonal cycles

1. Vegetable cycles - Take a walk in nature and observe the various cycles at work. Pick a particular cycle, such as the life-death-rebirth cycle you observe by a small pond, and try to follow the cycle all the way around the wheel – birth, growth, flower, decay, death and rebirth.

2. Lunar cycles - What is your favorite lunar cycle and why? For a creative project, get a piece of black construction paper and some white pastels, oil pastels or a silver pen and draw the different phases of the moon. Then write some poetry to go along with each phase and the feelings that each phase evokes for you.

3. Seasonal cycles - What is your favorite season and why? What is your least favorite season and why? What can you do to take care of yourself during your difficult season?

Human cycles of regeneration

Now let's turn to the human realm and see how we are intimately connected to these great regenerative cycles of life. Human cycles of regeneration are remarkably similar to the cycles found in nature. Initiation in Stage 2 requires us to learn about our physical, emotional and collective cycles so that we can move through them with ease, flowing around the entire cycle without getting stuck.

Physical cycles

From the vegetable cycles of life we learned about *silverforce*, the power of regeneration in nature. There is also a *silverforce* of human regeneration that manifests itself in the propagation of the species. Any woman who has given birth can describe this *silverforce* as the life force surging through her body during pregnancy and birth. This is a powerful archetypal force at work, ensuring our instinctive survival as a species.

In order to activate our physical *silverforce*, we can expand consciousness to the second chakra (or center of consciousness, as it is called in Kabbalah), which is the energy center around the genitals of both men and women. When we activate the second chakra, we become aware of the powerful *silverforce* of regeneration that naturally surges through our body. It makes no difference whether you have had surgery or problems connected to your reproductive system, because the second chakra is an energy field located around the genital area. Even if you have not engaged in propagating the species, you can still experience the instinctive power that brings a sense of regeneration to your body.

In a more tangible way, our physical body is moving through cycles of regeneration on a daily basis. Although the physical life span of the body is limited as it goes from birth through its flowering at adolescence and eventual decay and death, the body itself is in a continual process of regenerating itself day by day, cell by cell, through anabolic and catabolic activity. Through anabolic processes, new cells and tissue are forming; and through catabolic processes, old cells and tissues are breaking down and dying in a cyclical dance. This life-death-rebirth cycle in the body is the way that the body stores and uses energy. Energy is stored through anabolic activity and is released through the catabolic death phase, breaking down the stored sugars and carbohydrates. This is tangible evidence from the body that death precedes rebirth and provides new energy.

Women, in particular, move through monthly life-death-rebirth cycles during ovulation and menstruation, potential life and symbolic death when life has not been fertilized. If the ovum is fertilized, then a woman experiences conception, gestation and birth. She then holds the space for the flowering and growth phases; and when the baby is born she endures labor, which is a kind of death-rebirth experience.

Emotional cycles

Human emotions also cycle through their seasons. Our moods and feelings, joys and sorrows follow particular archetypal patterns that move around the life-death-rebirth cycle. It is crucial to be able to identify which emotional season we are in so that we can guide ourselves gently around the whole cycle without getting stuck. Having knowledge of the full cycle, of the Spring, Summer, Fall and Winter emotional states, gives us a container as we move through states of excitement, joy and satisfaction, as well as loss, anger and chaos.

All of the emotions have organic seasonal cycles. Love, for example, begins with a *honeymoon* period filled with blissful feelings and idealized projections. There is eventually a *disillusionment* phase when the idealizations and illusions are withdrawn and we see the other person more realistically. Hopefully, if the partners can move through the *death* phase, there can be *regeneration* in the relationship and deepened respect. Love moves through many life-death-rebirth cycles and we need to learn to dance gracefully around the cycles, accepting the seasons of love.

Emotional cycles have a natural, unfolding process that needs to run its course. Grief, for instance, will move towards resolution if allowed to flow all the way around the wheel. If we try to control the organic grief cycle, then we will inevitably get stuck in one of the phases. Fear usually stops us from fully surrendering to the grief cycle. Some people control grief by over-spiritualizing, saying that God is in control. Although that may be technically true, this usually prevents them from plunging headlong into the chaos of grief. Other people control the cycle by over-intellectualizing, wanting to understand and find meaning while avoiding the feelings. Meaning will come, but only if the grief is felt deeply and sincerely. The alternative to controlling the feelings is to surrender to the cycle of grief and move into the depths of feelings. This means embodying feelings by crying, wailing, despairing or raging until the chaos eventually and naturally resolves.

The grief cycle or any cycle of emotions, if allowed to unfold organically, leads to a resolution where the psyche feels more integrated and embodied. Over-spiritualizing and over-intellectualizing can block the unfolding of the entire emotional cycle and the psyche stiffens up, deprived of the release and relief at the end of the cycle. If we can trust the instinctive cycles and feel all the feelings around the wheel, the resolution will bring understanding, forgiveness and renewed strength.

Collective cycles

History is filled with the birth and flowering of civilizations, a renaissance of one kind or another. Florence, Italy had a flowering renaissance in the late 15th Century that brought tremendous renewal into art, music, literature, architecture and spirituality. This renaissance spread to all of Europe and influenced Western culture for hundreds of years.

Eventually, however, after a flowering stage, there is an inevitable decadence and decay – morally, politically and often spiritually – which may decline even further into war or some kind of destruction of the culture altogether. The Roman Empire had its time of triumph and glory and then its time of destruction. The rise and fall of the Third Reich is another example of the life-death cycle in history.

Collective cycles are influenced by the guidance of religious and political leaders – by those who are visible and by those behind the scenes like mystics, scientists, artists and writers. Spiritual leaders such as Moses, Buddha, Christ and Muhammad bring collective reform by injecting a new spiritual impulse into the culture. Others, like Martin Luther, bring spiritual reformation, putting to death religious forms that were constricting and limiting to the people of that time. The Protestant Reformation in the early 16th Century caused death to some of the Catholic practices and opened the way for new life and growth within the Christian community of Europe. It also caused the death of thousands of people in subsequent religious wars.

All cycles move through the birth, growth, flower, decay, death and rebirth phases. Cycles, both in nature and in human life, keep the world moving and evolving. Cycles give us chances, time and again, to regenerate ourselves. The more conscious we become of the various phases of change and transformation, the more benefits we can draw from each phase and the more flexible we can be with change. This will enable us to let go during the death phase, knowing that regeneration is on its way. We will be able to glimpse the impermanence of life and learn to move gracefully with the ups and downs and the inevitable flowerings and decays of life.

Exercise 4: How are you evolving through your cycles?

    1. Take stock of the various cycles you are in: (a) Physical (b) Emotional (c) Collective

    2. Are you stuck circling round and round, or are you evolving through these cycles of change?

    3. Write down several ways that you have evolved emotionally in the past year, so that you can see your progress.

    4. How are you participating in the cycle that your collective is moving through now?

Step 1: Flow with cycles of change
* Step 2: Honor your instinctive rhythms *
Step 3: Explore the unconscious
Step 4: Trust the Great Mother

Into the instinctive ground of being

In Step 1, we learned about the great cycles of life and how to flow flexibly around the life-death-rebirth wheel and not get stuck. Here in Step 2, we will be guided to honor our own instinctive rhythms and call back our instinctive power. To help us, let's turn to a powerful Western myth that will help us root our Tree of Life further into the instinctive soil. This is the popular myth of Demeter and Persephone. Although this story has been often told and discussed, I want to present it again using a modern form with a liberal interpretation.

The myth of Demeter and Persephone is a traditional life-death-rebirth story, an agricultural myth connected to planting seeds in the winter and awakening to new growth in the spring. For thousands of years, it was the myth at the heart of the Eleusinian Mysteries of ancient Greece. This initiation rite belonged to the Lunar Mystery tradition and was designed to initiate the community into the instinctive cycles of life. By listening to the deeper levels of the story, we will gain instinctive wisdom and find practical help to complete initiation at Stage 2.

Open your imagination now and follow me on the journey into the instinctive ground of being.

The myth of Demeter and Persephone

Our story begins with a young maiden named Persephone. Persephone is the daughter of the Great Mother Demeter, the powerful goddess of growth, fruitfulness and all sprouting life on earth. Every day Persephone plays in the wondrous expanse of her mother's garden, the endless fruitful foliage of forests, flowers, brooks and streams. Persephone often wanders with her maiden friends to a favorite meadow to pick flowers. She runs and laughs without care, worry or responsibility, playing endlessly in her mother's beautiful garden.

One day she walks to her favorite meadow and notices great beauty in the batches of white flowers that dot the meadow and give off a sweet and enticing smell. She begins to pick the white narcissus flowers and place them in a basket that she brought with her this morning. One by one she plucks the narcissus, and one by one she finds herself mesmerized by the rhythm of her movement. As she bends down to pick the next flower she touches the earth with her fingers, feeling the wet ground as she pulls up the bulbous root, stem and flower in one swooping movement of her hand. She stands up and places the beautiful white flower in the basket and moves back toward the ground again. Down and up, down to the ground and up again she moves, touching the earth in a dancing rhythmic pattern. Each time she puts her hand into the earth something inside her trembles, and an ancient memory deep within the recesses of her being swings open. All her senses come alive and open to the sweet smell of the flowers, the pungent odor of the damp soil, the touch of the velvety flower petals, and the warmth of the sun on her back.

As she dances around the meadow this day, finding her own natural rhythm, she sends a vibration surging into the ground, penetrating layers of dense earth. The vibration of Persephone's movement penetrates all the way down to the center of the earth, into the Underworld where it catches the attention of the great Lord who presides over that realm, Lord Pluto. When Persephone's vibration catches Pluto's attention he is seized with an unquenchable thirst, a forcible desire. As great Pluto gazes upward toward the surface of the earth, there he spies the lovely Persephone moving rhythmically toward the ground.

Pluto cannot contain his passion and immediately calls for his two dark horses and mounts his chariot, steering them straight up from the Underworld toward the innocent and unsuspecting maiden dancing in the meadow. As Pluto's desire is rising, he gallops faster and faster, closer and closer to the surface of the earth. Persephone stops her dance for a moment as she feels a faint rumbling beneath her feet. The vibration gets stronger and stronger, and a terrible sound bellows forth from the ground. Suddenly Persephone sees a crack open out and then the whole ground beneath her feet splits open. Up from the ground lunge two gigantic dark horses, and suddenly a pair of unknown arms grabs her. The Lord Pluto snatches her up into his chariot, turns abruptly around and rides straight down toward the Underworld, swallowed back up into the ground – and all is darkness.

One moment Persephone sees the ground beneath her opening up, and the next thing she knows she is flying down through the darkness, held against her will, terrified and disoriented. Persephone is frightened and deeply confused. Her world as she knows it is lost in one instant of time, shattered and scattered into a million pieces. All she knows is descent, going down and down and down. With each gallop of the horses a myriad feelings flood her mind and heart. At once she is surrounded by fear, loss, devastation, chaos, and rage.

At last when the horses come to a stop, Persephone finds herself in the heart of the Underworld, far from the surface of the earth and from the warmth and heat of the sun. She is far, far from her maiden friends, far from the dance and play of the garden, far from the comfort of her mother Demeter. Here in the Underworld she is left by herself and to herself. She has only the company of the Lord Pluto and the creatures inhabiting this realm who know only darkness and the happenings of the Underworld.

So here she is in the darkest and the densest of places, in the belly of the earth, totally alone. As time goes on, her mother Demeter learns of her disappearance and tries to find where her daughter is, but to no avail. Demeter goes into deep mourning and allows all the vegetation on the surface of the earth to die.

In the meantime Persephone, too, descends into a deep and mournful season, forced to face her fate in this underground place. Until her mother finds her and eventually secures a passage for her return, Persephone has no choice but to stay in the belly of the earth and face the darkness.

Days go by, and Persephone sits. Weeks go by, and still Persephone stays in her dark cave.

She cannot run and she cannot hide from herself. Months go by, and still she sits. Years go by, and she forgets time and her old distant life on the surface of the earth. The more time Persephone spends in the Underworld, the more she understands about the laws of darkness and the great cycle of death and transformation. Eventually, after much time has passed, she weds the Lord Pluto and becomes the Queen of the Underworld realm, for she has survived her dark ordeal and grown wise in the ways of the Underworld.

Meanwhile, the goddess Hekate has pointed Demeter in the right direction to find and recover her lost daughter. Demeter perseveres and finally secures Persephone a safe passage of return to the Aboveworld so that they can be reunited as mother and daughter. The messenger god Hermes is sent into the Underworld to retrieve and escort Persephone back home. But Pluto gets wind of the deal and slips Persephone a pomegranate, which, if eaten, will keep her tied to Pluto forever. Persephone takes the pomegranate and breaks it open, revealing the fruitful and ripe seeds that look glorious to eat. She does not hesitate, and bites heartily into the pomegranate, tasting its sweet and sour fruit, ingesting the seeds and binding herself to Pluto forever.

Soon after, Queen Persephone becomes ripe with child and births a baby with her husband Lord Pluto. In the end, she does follow Hermes out of the Underworld, but must return for part of each yearly cycle to the Underworld to reign as Queen. She returns to her mother Demeter with her new son in her arms, reunited at last with the Great Mother, no longer a maiden but a triumphant Queen, ripened with the seeds of fertility and wise in the ways of the Underworld.

The Maiden's Dilemma

The story of Persephone takes us deep into the instinctive ground of being. As we follow her heroic journey, we are reminded of both the horror of being abducted and knocked off our instinctive rhythm and the beauty of recovering our instinctive power. Persephone's journey is long and painful, but as she moves through the entire life-death-rebirth wheel she gains valuable experience of each phase of the cycle. In the end, she becomes Queen of the Underworld – embodied, fruitful, powerfully instinctive and able to hold her own ground of being.

At the beginning of the story however, Persephone is in a very different state of mind and being. She is the innocent maiden frolicking in her mother's garden. She has no cares, worries or responsibilities. She is surrounded by beauty and friends and has the freedom to wander aimlessly in nature. The Great Mother Demeter protects her, gives her sustenance and holds the ground; she is the container.

In many ways, Persephone's maiden life describes an idyllic childhood, the archetypal dream of freedom and safety, exploration and beauty. This may seem like paradise and a state of being that we long for (especially if we did not get enough of it), but Persephone's maidenhood also leaves her in a predicament. *She is in the classic maiden's dilemma – she lives in "paradise" yet lacks the skills to deal with real life.* She knows the "life" in the life-death-rebirth cycle but has not yet experienced the death and rebirth phases and therefore remains innocent and immature. In this state, Persephone is particularly vulnerable to "Pluto abduction", the archetypal fate for the maiden in all of us.

Let's look more closely at the maiden's dilemma to understand the function of Pluto's abduction and the necessity of descending into the Underworld to gain experience.

The maiden's dilemma begins with her closeness to the mother; she has not yet separated. This means that the mother is still actively containing, holding and providing, which means that Persephone cannot yet contain, hold or provide for herself. The maiden is inexperienced and has not yet explored the full range of her instinctive responses to life, including her sexuality. She also lacks experience of her instinctive power. She has desires and longings but does not know the consequences of her longing. The maiden is unaware of the instinctive patterns and complexes she carries. She has not yet confronted difficult emotional situations such as separation, conflict, pain, suffering and loss. She has no experience of the Underworld, of her unconscious, and the latent potential residing there. Her personality lacks depth; she is one-dimensional rather than multi-layered.

As you can see, Persephone needs experience of the full life-death-rebirth cycle in order to solve her maiden's dilemma and gain the skills necessary to deal with real life.

Picking Narcissus – Exploring our Instinctive Rhythms

According to the Kabbalah, each person's instinctive body or *Nefesh* has its own particular rhythm, which is generated by the Hod and Nezah of each person's Tree of Life (see Diagram 8). Hod reverberates our natural curiosities, interests and intuition; and Nezah generates our instinctive attractions and repulsions to things like people, situations, colors, sounds and foods. Together Hod and Nezah set up a particular instinctive rhythm that is unique to each person, sounding out a particular rhythmic pattern like a drumbeat that has a certain style and flair.

At the beginning of the story, Persephone has only a vague recognition of her own deep rhythm, for she is still in the maiden stage of exploring her instincts. In order to discover and get in sync with our own rhythms, our instinctive body needs time and space to explore our sensuality in all its forms. Persephone begins this investigation by following her natural attraction to the beautiful narcissus flowers that dot her favorite meadow. The flowers have a sweet and enticing smell that draws Persephone into a mode of exploration. She notices the sensual beauty of the flowers, their fragrance and the rhythmic movement of her body as she picks the flowers and places them in her basket. She presses her fingers and hands into the wet earth, and each time she bends down toward the ground, she awakens another aspect of her instinctive rhythm.

The white narcissus flowers are a crucial symbol in the story. The name "Narcissus" refers to another myth about a boy who falls in love with his own image when he sees it mirrored and reflected in the surface of a pool of water. In modern psychology, "narcissism" describes the state of mind of a person who is caught up in their own reflection to such a degree that little else can be seen and experienced. They are trapped in a state of self-mirroring and self-reference. Yet the narcissistic person longs to be mirrored and seen by others because they have been abandoned over their own reflecting pool with no one to give them outside feedback.

As Persephone picks narcissus, it is as if she is longing, like Narcissus, to be mirrored and seen. Our instinctive self, our *Nefesh*, needs enthusiastic mirroring, wholehearted response and feedback from others who are instinctively aware. I like to imagine that each time Persephone picks a narcissus she identifies another part of herself that longs to be awakened. When another person sees, mirrors, encourages and invites our new instinctive response into life, we then feel safe to express it.

Every person has different aspects of the *Nefesh* that need to be mirrored and seen. Some people want to feel more comfortable with their body and sexuality; they long to be touched and to be more sexually free and expressive. Others are sexually confident and yet need intellectual encouragement; they long to express their ideas and feel more intellectually secure. Others wish to explore their unexpressed desire to dance, sing or sustain a loving partnership. Parts of us that have never been mirrored remain immature, dormant or unconscious. They have not yet been assimilated into the conscious personality and are like Persephone in her innocent and inexperienced state.

In order to honor our own instinctive rhythms, we must identify the parts of us that long to be seen and then move toward the beautiful narcissus, exploring our sensual experiences and our natural rhythms that flow forth from our instinctive body.

Pluto's Abduction - instinctive wounding

As Persephone dances around the meadow that fateful day, she opens the door to her instinctive world. She sends a vibration surging into the ground, penetrating through layers of dense earth, where it catches the attention of Pluto. Far below in the Underworld, Pluto senses her, feels her vibration, and is seized with an unquenchable desire for her. It is the Pluto within our underground life who can quickly recognize what our natural instincts are. Pluto represents intuitive wisdom that lives in our underground world, instinctive life that is repressed, unrealized and still in potential. When we pick our narcissus and attract Pluto, he rises up from the Underworld and responds to our need to be seen. Pluto sees, hears and feels our rhythmic movement towards the instinctive soil and responds.

To the inexperienced Persephone parts of the personality, it is terrifying when the ground opens and Pluto arrives on the scene. To the unsuspecting maiden, Pluto seems awesome, powerful and dangerous. Pluto is called "Lord of Death" because he is known to stir up disastrous crises that can feel like death to the old way of life. He is known to crack open our ground in a harsh or violent way, rather than arriving with a friendly knock. This can feel to the maiden parts of us like a rape or abduction.

However, Pluto's real name means "bringer of riches" implying that he has another agenda behind these ground openings and abductions. As "bringer of riches," Pluto is dedicated to death in service of new life. He exposes us to separation, conflict and loss to help us gain experience of the complete instinctive life-death-rebirth cycle. So behind the terror of the open ground is the larger vision of wholeness and the riches that come after rebirth - *sensual awareness and instinctive power.*

In order to accomplish this, Pluto opens the ground and brings Persephone down into the Underworld so that she learns to face the darkness and process her pain, loss, and suffering. The maiden within us does not consciously volunteer to go into the Underworld however, and thus the ground-opening events are often felt to be abductions against our conscious will. When the ground opens, it usually feels like a crack in the ego foundation and although this cracking in the membrane around the ego helps expand it, making it more adaptable to real life, it is also painful and frightening. To survive the ordeal, we must remember that Pluto is always concerned with integrating the total personality, and so bypasses our resistances to become whole.

One of the most difficult things about the "abduction into the Underworld" experience is that our innocent, childlike parts are so unaware of the coming trauma. This surprise delivers a tremendous blow to our instinctive body and our tender, budding feelings get crushed. For example, when we hit puberty, we naturally desire to have our sexuality acknowledged and seen. Sexual exploration then becomes one of the narcissus we pick in the garden. As soon as we start the instinctive picking, our wondrous sexual urges to be desired and to be creative can precipitate a crisis, attracting a Pluto character or a "plutonic" experience. When an unsolicited sexual advance or an experience we are not ready for occurs, our sexual innocence gets crushed and the little green shoot of new life that could grow into a healthy sexual response gets squashed. The natural rhythm which would have established itself if the desire was satisfied in a safe way gets cut off, and we feel unable to contact our own instinctive rhythms.

As a therapist, I work with many people who feel out of sync with their natural rhythms. When asked to try and pinpoint when they lost touch with their own rhythm, they often identify an event, relationship or crisis that traumatized them and knocked them off their rhythm. Whenever I hear their stories, it reminds me of Pluto's abduction of Persephone. Most people can identify when the ground opened, when the abduction and loss of innocence occurred, what it felt like, and how they lost touch with their instinctive responses to life.

The following are some examples of **ground opening events** that knock people off their natural rhythm and deliver an instinctive wound:

Early loss of parent, home, country or loved one
Negative early sexual experience
Rejection from parent or significant other
Violation of personal boundaries
Overt criticism around instinctive urges
Excessive parental rigidity regarding instincts, sensuality, sexuality, play
Excessive parental control of instinctive responses
Hospitalization early in life
Experiencing a violent or abusive relationship
Drug or alcohol addiction
Drug or alcohol addiction of a parent or family member

The following are examples of **instinctive powers that are lost through trauma**:

A man recalls the time that a teacher criticized and shamed him in front of the class and his natural *desire to learn* was cut off.

A woman remembers the day in her adolescence when her father, in a rage, called her a whore. This incident sent her *sexuality* underground.

A man recalls from his childhood a critical mother who continually accused him of being lazy when he was really in a contemplative or artistic mode, creating with his imagination. This trauma pushed his natural *creativity* into the background.

A woman remembers the traumatic adolescent sexual experience that made her body go numb with grief and humiliation. She now has trouble making boundaries and trusting her *instincts to say no*.

A man recalls in his childhood an abrupt family move from a rural to urban setting, which sent his *fun-loving, spontaneous, wild boy* underground for many years.

Exercise 5: Identify your Ground Opening Event

1. Identify a past event that was like a Pluto abduction for you. Did it involve an external event, relationship or internal crisis? Who was your Pluto character? What were the circumstances? How old were you?

2. What wounding did you suffer? What loss of innocence occurred?

3. What instinctive powers were lost?

4. How did that push you out of sync with your natural rhythms?

Responding to instinctive trauma

After identifying your ground opening event and the subsequent trauma, the next step is to identify how you *responded to* the trauma when it occurred. When Persephone is snatched up by Pluto, swallowed up by the ground, forced into the Underworld, thrown into darkness and held against her will, she is terrified and disoriented. She is frightened and deeply confused. Her world as she has known it is lost in one instant, shattered and scattered into a thousand pieces. From the story, we hear that with each descending gallop of the horse, a myriad of feelings flood Persephone's mind and heart. At once she is surrounded by fear, loss, devastation, chaos and rage. The following is a list of **responses to instinctive trauma**:

Body shame   Sexual shame, sexual dysfunction
Confusion and chaos   Grief
Anxiety/fear/panic attacks   Substance abuse or other addictive behavior
Obsessive or compulsive behavior   Acting out irresponsibly or uncontrollably
Fragmenting   Inability to feel certain emotions
Denial   Repressing or forgetting
Exploding into rage   Imploding into depression
Going mad or feeling you might go mad   Manic behavior
Insomnia   Physical illness

All of these responses are appropriate at the time of the trauma, as we try to make some kind of sense of the horror, violence, betrayal, loss, abuse or neglect. When we sustain an instinctual wound, our physical, psychological and spiritual systems go into a state of shock and we react in any number of ways. Our reaction, however, can set into motion patterns of behavior that can continue for years until we learn healthier ways of coping. In light of this, it is important to notice how your past wound is affecting you now, in the present. It is helpful to notice what present-day behaviors are results of this past trauma.

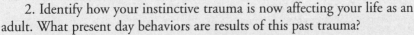

Exercise 6: Your responses to instinctive trauma

1. Prompted by the above list, write down the ways in which you responded to your instinctive wound.

2. Identify how your instinctive trauma is now affecting your life as an adult. What present day behaviors are results of this past trauma?

For example, remember the woman who sustained a traumatic adolescent sexual experience. She responded to her instinctive trauma by going numb both physically and

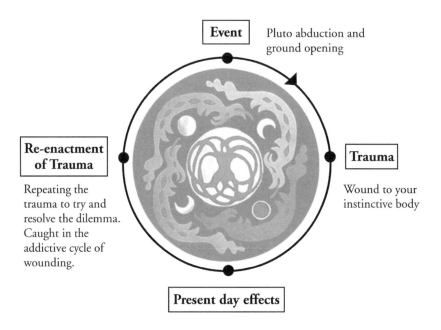

Event — Pluto abduction and ground opening

Trauma — Wound to your instinctive body

Re-enactment of Trauma — Repeating the trauma to try and resolve the dilemma. Caught in the addictive cycle of wounding.

Present day effects

Diagram 9a: The Addictive Cycle of Instinctive Wounding

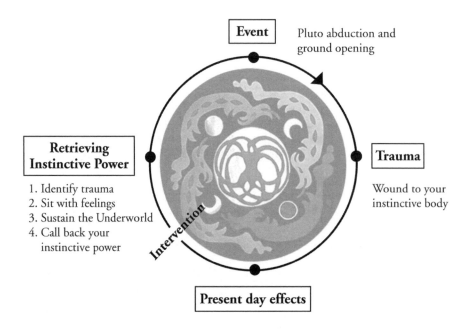

Event — Pluto abduction and ground opening

Trauma — Wound to your instinctive body

Retrieving Instinctive Power
1. Identify trauma
2. Sit with feelings
3. Sustain the Underworld
4. Call back your instinctive power

Intervention

Present day effects

Diagram 9b: Breaking the Addictive Cycle of Instinctive Wounding

emotionally. Her body shut down and she pushed away sexual experiences. In her present life, she now has trouble setting appropriate boundaries in her relationships and trusting her instincts to say no when she needs to protect herself.

Reenacting the trauma – the addictive cycle of instinctive wounding

If we remain stuck in our unhealthy pattern of response, we get caught in the addictive cycle of instinctive wounding and unconsciously reenact the trauma (see Diagram 9a). We do not *wish* to be re-traumatized, but we do not yet have the language to ask for what we want. Instinctive wounding causes us to "forget" what we want, forget how to ask for what we need, and therefore our instinctive desires remain hidden and we are left in a state of longing. Because the longing to fulfill our instinctive needs is so great, we pick people and situations to reenact the trauma to try to *resolve the dilemma*. Unfortunately, unless we are conscious, this tactic does not work but only makes it worse; we get stuck in the addictive cycle of instinctive wounding.

For example, the man whose wild boy went underground, continually picked situations where he took on the role of "policeman" rather than wild boy. In groups he would stand on the outside and police the behavior of others, making sure everyone followed the rules. His peers would then avoid him and he got pushed further and further away from friends with whom he could play and have fun. His isolation and role of policeman would then reenact his trauma and reinforce his feeling that he was not allowed to be wild.

Another example is the woman who was sexually traumatized in her adolescence. When she grew into adulthood, she continually picked men to be in relationship with who violated her boundaries. It was very difficult for her to know what her sexual boundaries were, let alone enforce them, which set up situations where her trauma was reenacted time and again.

Another example is the man who was criticized and shamed in front of the class and his natural desire to learn was cut off. When he had his own children, he criticized and shamed them instead of supporting their natural desire to learn. This behavior kept him and his children in the addictive cycle because instead of soothing and repairing his instinctive wound, his own parenting techniques reopened the trauma and there was no resolution. The shame and humiliation he carried with his own wound was then recreated in his children.

Retrieving our instinctive power

Even though most of us get knocked off our rhythm and stuck in the addictive cycle of instinctive wounding, the story of Persephone provides hope. The story shows that if we can remain in the Underworld and face our fate squarely, as Persephone does, we will eventually solve our maiden's dilemma and retrieve our instinctive power in a full and embodied form. Let's look at how Persephone accomplishes this feat.

The hope really begins with Pluto, for he is determined to hold on to Persephone no matter how hard she struggles to be free. Pluto's arms are strong and his passionate determination to bring wholeness even stronger. We can trust that the Plutonic forces in life and within us will hold the larger vision and will hold us in the Underworld until we discover our feelings and actively participate in our instinctive life. Soon we will discover that resistance only makes it worse and extends the length of time in the Underworld.

When at last the horses have completed their descent and stop in the Underworld, Persephone finds herself truly alone. She is far from her old life and far from her mother and friends. As Persephone is held in Pluto's world, held in the arms of her instinctive soil, she cannot run away from herself and is forced to be with herself in the dark place. Here Persephone finds her instinctive ground and is pulled to the center of her being. Day after day, month after month, she must face her particular fate and wrestle with the feelings of resentment at having her innocence taken from her. We too must wrestle with our abduction and subsequent loss of instinctual life and the bitterness, grief, loss, rage and fear that accompany our abduction. If we can surrender, as Persephone does, to the darkness and grief of the Underworld experience, there is hope.

As Persephone is held in the dark place day after day, the instinctive soil creates the safety she needs to contain her feelings. Some people experience this kind of descent as a tomb, some as a womb. Plutonic descent is almost always accompanied by depression, silence, confusion and chaos, and is therefore a difficult experience. On the other hand, if we can see the Underworld as a place of incubation that will help us retrieve our instinctive power, we can survive this experience in the darkest of times.

Persephone's fate sets her on a course of descent to gain knowledge of the life-death-rebirth cycle, and to become Queen of the Underworld. Her fate, like ours, is to learn how to acknowledge the trauma that has occurred to our instincts, face our true feelings, and recover our instinctive power.

After her abduction experience, Persephone could have responded to her fate in several ways. She could have gone into states of denial, fragmentation, body numbing, cynicism, sexual dysfunction or bitterness. These responses are, of course, appropriate protections at the time of the trauma, but they are no longer useful when they take us away from our instinctive power. Persephone's response is that she does nothing but sit with herself in the Underworld. She does not crack open. She does not go mad. She simply sits with herself.

In our expanded version of the story, Persephone feels the loss, feels the separation from what is familiar, and feels the grief and anger caused by the trauma itself. *She models the key to surviving and righting the trauma to our instincts: staying long enough with our feelings so that we truly experience their impact, feeling them in our flesh, our bones and our cells* (see Diagram 9b).

We can recognize people who have not recovered their instinctive power because they do not have enough gravitas or "weight" to them. They have not embodied their feelings or felt their true impact on their body and soul. We can also recognize those who have endured the Underworld, felt their grief and survived. They are like elders who have gray hairs to prove their embodied experience. They have survived the death and are thriving with new life. They are rooted in their instinctive ground of being, embodied with radiance and presence.

Persephone shows us how to stay inside our own skin during the descent and bondage in the Underworld. She shows us how to be surrounded by a dark, earth place and not run away from ourselves. She shows us how to become embodied in our instincts and feel weighty and knowledgeable. She shows us how to be the Queen of our own Underworld, with a truly embodied presence.

Exercise 7: Retrieving your instinctive power

1. Identify the feelings that you need to sit with in your Underworld in order to heal your instinctive wound - shame, humiliation, fear, rage, hatred, betrayal, grief. Is your container strong enough to do this? Do you need some companionship?

Make a commitment for at least one month to set aside sacred time each day, preferably 20 - 30 minutes, with your journal, and allow your feelings to emerge - the feelings you have had difficulty allowing yourself to feel that are a result of your instinctive wounding. Don't worry if it feels like "nothing" is happening during your sacred time. Your psyche knows that you are honoring the instinctive wound and that something is happening. Try to imagine yourself as Persephone held in the Underworld. If you can stay with your authentic feelings and be held by Pluto for long enough, you will experience instinctive energy returning.

2. Identify the instinctive power that you are calling back. Identify exactly what energy you want to retrieve. What instinctive power are you reclaiming? It could be passion, sexual desire or the ability to discern your own attractions and repulsions.

3. Invite the lifeblood to return. Actively call back your instinctive power. Notice what parts of your body have been affected by your instinctive trauma. Where does your body feel numb? Where does your psyche feel numb? Where do you carry your rage or grief? Identify what you need to heal this wound and to call back the flow of blood to this area of your body and your life.

You can actively call back your instinctive power by getting a drum, rattle or percussion instrument and find a space where you can make as much noise as you want. Open your throat and yell, speak, shout, sing or sound whatever needs to be vocalized. Call back your power. Imagine these parts coming alive and feeling the full range of sensations. When you do this with love and intention, the numb places begin to awaken, lifeblood begins to flow and feelings return.

4. Celebrate the return of your instinctive power. When you feel the lifeblood returning, make sure to honor your instinctive power in some tangible and sacred way. Do something sensual to mark this initiation. Buy a sacred object to commemorate this transition. You deserve it!

Honoring Pluto

I want to end this section with a fresh look at Pluto. It has already been suggested that hope for instinctive recovery lies with Pluto, for he is the archetypal energy within us that holds the larger vision for healing, and understands the necessity of the death–rebirth phases of the cycle. In his yearning for union with Persephone, Pluto becomes the initiator and agent of greater consciousness and of our ability to become ruler of our own Underworld. In order to honor Pluto, we can try to imagine a positive relationship between Pluto and Persephone, a sacred pair within us that can honor our instinctive responses to life. Using active imagination, we can set up a dialogue with the Pluto character inside us that responds to our instincts with enthusiasm and desire.

Honoring Pluto involves spending time exploring our natural responses to life and imagining how we would have responded before we got out of sync with our natural rhythms. It involves discovering what we are naturally attracted to or repulsed by. Honoring Pluto means discovering the ways our energy naturally flows – towards certain kinds of people, certain foods, certain kinds of atmospheres and living situations.

As we call back our instinctive power and honor our own instinctive rhythms, we will honor Pluto who desires to make us whole.

Step 1: Flow with cycles of change
Step: Honor your instinctive rhythms
* Step 3: Explore the wisdom of the unconscious *
Step 4: Trust the Great Mother

Be curious and receptive

In Step 1, we learned to flow with cycles of change as we moved around the great wheel of life-death-rebirth. In Step 2, we learned the importance of honoring our own instinctive rhythms and the necessity of spending time in the Underworld to become one with Lord Pluto, bringer of riches. Now, in Step 3, we will explore the riches of this underground realm and learn to *forge a working relationship with the unconscious* so that we can flow freely, as Persephone does at the end of the story, between the world above and the Underworld, between our conscious and unconscious life.

In order to trust our own instinctive depths and honor our own true rhythm, we must adopt an attitude of openness and receptivity to the unconscious. Like a curious explorer, we can wander and meander in our underground world, playing and dreaming. Like Persephone, we can dance with the bringer of riches and explore the rich treasure house of the unconscious. The Persephone/Pluto dance will go on as long as we are alive, as we dip down into the unconscious to get some riches and return again to the world above to gain clarity. We must learn to descend into the unknown parts of ourselves with open curiosity. In this way we are listening for Pluto's call, listening for opportunities to descend into the unconscious and retrieve the riches there.

Exploring lunar wisdom

One of the most important cycles for humans is the mysterious cycle flowing between conscious and unconscious life. The psyche is dynamically alive, able to move and develop because it flows in a cycle between waking consciousness, with its clarity and enlightenment, and another kind of consciousness that dips into other realms like sleep, dream, fantasy and myth. There are many names for this "other" kind of consciousness - the Underworld, the Netherworld, the unconscious, Hades or Middle Earth. Whatever the name, it is one of the psyche's inevitable destinations, and is the place around the cycle that brings replenishment to our whole being.

Returning to the Sacred Robe for Stage 2 – "The Great Round" – take a look at the central image in the middle of the great mandala. In the center of the robe, we find a Celtic

Tree of Life with its branches and roots connected and intertwined. It teaches us the important relationship between the richness above the ground as well as the richness below. Here is an image of the intertwining of solar and lunar consciousness.

The solar realm is one of light, day, clarity and reason. The lunar realm is one of darkness, night, shadow and dream. By nature, lunar consciousness is opposed to solar consciousness, and yet both must function together for the psyche to feel whole. We must be able to move from rational solar awareness to the more fluid, intuitive lunar awareness on a day-to-day basis.

Each day in the 24-hour cycle, we enact the dance as we move into lunar consciousness, sleeping and dreaming, and in the morning wake into solar consciousness, trying to make rational sense of things. The trick is being able to move between the worlds in a way that feeds and nourishes our inner life. When we build a healthy channel between the two worlds, we gain access to our imagination, to dream images, and to the unconscious.

The Celtic Tree on the robe is set against a large silver disc. This represents lunar wisdom in its fullest form – the full moon. Silver, as we know from the Alchemists, is the metal associated with the moon. Silver is the color of moonlight, a diffuse and reflected glow from the sun. One of the great advantages of silver light is that it illuminates things only dimly, not exactly, and this makes the journey much more interesting. If you have ever walked through a forest at night when the moon is up, you have only a vague sense of where you are going. In the moonlight, we must begin using other senses to find our way through the forest. When the blazing golden light of the sun is dimmed and silver light rises in the sky, we must begin to use our imagination. This allows us to explore unseen territory, to tap into dormant senses and instinctive feelings just below the surface. Silver light opens the door to our imagination and allows our intuition to rule. This is the lunar way.

Surrounding the Celtic Tree is a circle of lunar dragons that carry the various phases of the moon on their backs. They move in the cyclical dance around the lunar wheel, offering us the waxing, full, waning and new moon. The dragons remind us of the cyclical seasons of the unconscious, when instinctive feelings are rising and coming into full expression and when they are waning and silence descends upon the inner life. The dragons facilitate the life-death-rebirth cycle of lunar wisdom that Persephone learns in the Underworld.

As Persephone spends more and more time away from her mother and the world above, the world of sunlight and solar consciousness, she learns to adjust to the darkness. She becomes acquainted with moonlight and the lunar ways of the night. As she moves away from the light of day, she must tolerate a new way of being in life, living with the night, where darkness reigns and other senses are operative. Like moving through a forest at night, being in the lunar realm enhances our senses of intuition, inner sight, touch, body sensations, listening and smell. We have to feel our way in the dark, sniff things out and use a gut sense.

We need to watch what happens in our moonlight times when we cross over into the lunar realm, and follow our hunches and the dim shadows of awareness. We must stay open to our dream life and be curious about the rich images that emerge, remain open to fleeting fantasies and daydreams, and follow their thread in our imagination as far as we can. We must be receptive to our wild feelings and crazy ideas and – rather than pushing them aside – take them seriously, give them room to breathe.

Riding on the backs of the lunar dragons will lead us into the unknown territory of the unconscious, and if we are not afraid, we can wander on the far outskirts of this realm.

Exploring our invisible inner world may seem toxic, dangerous and frightening to our ego and to our conscious solar standpoint. However, risking the adventure means that we can recover the lost instinctive drives, urges, wishes, fantasies and dreams that carry tremendous vitality back to the conscious personality. The "bringer of riches" will help us recover feeling, vitality, lifeblood, energy, and joy.

Image-based wisdom

Unconscious wisdom is different from conscious wisdom because it is image-based. It comes to us in the form of images and symbols, clearly evident from our dream life. Rather than having one clearly defined meaning, images and symbols have multi-layered meanings. Images bring non-linear and non-rational wisdom that cannot be easily "figured out" with the mind. Unconscious wisdom is therefore sense-based and primal, and the images usually come to us in a loose, unstructured and chaotic form.

For example, Alchemical images are filled with non-rational symbols: a green lion eating the sun, a wolf devouring the king, a woman suckling a frog, black ravens flying out of open graves, a salamander in the middle of a fire but not consumed, a man flying in the air trying to eat a large stone, an eagle chained to the ground, a hermaphroditic figure in a bath. Although these images are tied to various Alchemical operations and can be explained, they are fantastic lightning rods for active imagination. These interesting, dreamlike images can be pondered indefinitely, and our various subjective associations can lead us into deep personal reflection.

Personal dream images can be even more powerful and stirring. I remember once waking from a startling and disturbing dream where two wolves had crashed into my bedroom and were locked in mortal combat. They were fighting to the death – snarling, biting and thrashing. I tried to get away, but I was caught in the middle of the wolf fight. One of the wolves pinned me down with its paw while it delivered the fatal blow to the neck of the other wolf. I was forced to lie on the floor while the dying wolf bled to death and filled the bedroom with wolf blood.

This dream can be interpreted in different ways, including the way many of us are familiar with, where we go into the "meaning" of the dream images in a very solar way. The lunar way to approach this dream is to stay with the energy elicited by the image. For example, what is my visceral response to the snarling wolves? How does it feel to be pinned down by a killer wolf? What would it be like to be the less capable wolf? If I were the killer wolf, what would that feel like? What happens to me as I lie in a pool of wild animal blood?

Exercise 8: Dream Amplification - *the healing power of images*

The following are some ways to be creative with dream images.
Write out an entire dream sequence and play with the following:
   1. Identify the general **mood** of the dream.
   2. Free associate with the **main characters**.
   3. Notice the **themes**: conflict, chaos, separation, betrayal, dismemberment, dissolution, unbearable choice – or – healing, redemption, reconciliation, salvation, preparation, death and rebirth, union/marriage. There are many more.

4. Write down **verbs** you see in the dream. Where is the **action** taking you?

5. Play with the various **levels of meaning**: personal meaning, cultural meaning, mythological meaning, religious/spiritual meaning. For example, an image from one of my dreams that was evocative for me involved a man down in my basement, building a library of bronze, silver and gold books. The **personal** meaning has to do with my love of books, libraries, ancient texts and my desire to write books. Another personal level to the dream is my association of the man with my brother, who is well-read and intelligent. The **cultural** meaning may have to do with Western values of intellectual "book" learning. The **mythological** reference is clearly Alchemical, with bronze, silver and gold books representing stages of the Alchemical transmutation process. One **spiritual** association I have is with sacred books and sacred texts, which have always captured my interest. This was a powerful image for me, seeing this great library being built in my own basement. I could go on associating...

6. Do **active imagination**: go back into the dream in a meditative space and see where the dream characters and the dream take you further.

7. Give the dream a **title**.

8. Now read through your amplification of each dream and **identify how these images are healing for you**.

The instinctive power of images

Unconscious images pull up instinctive energy right from the ground of our being. We have to stay with our senses and our primal responses when working with images.

When I was making the Sacred Robe for this second initiation, I had a full sketch of what I wanted the robe to look like. As I was working with the images around the mandala, an interesting thing occurred. One by one, each animal that had originally been placed around the mandala began to change. I found myself drawing dolphin, then crab, lizard, snake, fish and sea snail. I dropped into a dreamlike state and allowed each image to pull me into an active dialogue. Each image had a story to tell about instinctual life and about thriving in the lunar realm. The following is the wisdom that emerged from my encounters with the animal images.

At the base of the mandala, a snake lies coiled, like the coiled Kundalini, like the coils of the Labyrinth, like the coils of our guts. The snake sheds its skin and guides us in the death and transformation phases, letting go and regenerating. The next image to the left of the snake is a primitive sea creature from the unconscious, reminding us to respect the depths. This deep-sea fish can breathe underwater, giving us stamina for the journey into the primal depths. Next is the scallop-shelled creature whose chambers echo the sounds of lost voices, buried deep under conscious recognition.

The dolphin teaches us how to stay conscious underwater. Dolphins can play in the depths and retain freedom to move to the surface to get the air that they need to stay alive. They help us to forge a pathway between the outer world and the inner world of unconscious thoughts and fantasies. The crab represents the sign of cancer and signifies the privacy of our own watery, emotional world. When we go into our private, emotional space, we need to have protective boundaries. The crab also holds on to things that are nurturing, comforting and safe. This is so important when we need replenishing at the instinctive level.

There is a drummer at the top of the mandala who helps us find our own rhythms, the beat that brings us harmony and puts us back in sync with ourselves. The bear teaches us how to move into the cave for hibernation during the winter phase. At times, we must reflect and become introspective, dreaming ourselves anew, preparing for the next season. The frog initiates us into the mysterious properties of water and its miraculous cleansing and healing capacity. Water is used for baptism and symbolizes a return to the womb for rebirth. Dipping into the pool replenishes and refreshes us.

The next image shows the spiral shell of a sea snail that can curl deep inside and hide secretly, coming out only when it is safe. This is unconscious timing we can trust. The last image is the lizard that holds the knowledge of shadow. He hides under the cracks and crevices of rocks, sleeping and holding knowledge of the shadow lands and what lies beneath the surface.

This is a brief version of the wisdom that arrived with these powerful symbols. Image-based wisdom stirs the imagination and sets us on a journey of meandering through our unconscious depths like the winding path of a Labyrinth.

Meander through the Labyrinth

Since ancient times, the Mysteries of the Labyrinth have taught men and women how to walk the lunar path and how to integrate lunar and solar consciousness. The Labyrinth is always constructed with the same principle in mind – lunar meandering. Every Labyrinth, no matter where it originates, takes us on a winding journey, wandering around a central point, sometimes nearer, sometimes farther away from the center. The central point is the Self, our true center. According to lunar principles, we do not make it to the center in a straight line, but spend time exploring our inner world – meandering, wandering, wondering, marveling and questioning.

On the robe, the circle of spiraling waves that surrounds the lunar dragons depicts the spiraling path of the inner Labyrinth where we meander closer to and then farther from our center. What we are being initiated into here is not goal orientation, but instinctive wandering. The Labyrinth is a maze, but with no dead-ends or blind alleys, a non-linear model of life, and a spiral way of being. When we have no solar goal, no beaming light trying to extract the truth, we can begin to make associations and connections between parts of the psyche that have never related to one another before.

Meandering requires patience and requires slowing down our pace. As we adopt a wandering attitude, we must surrender to unconscious timing, not the hurried pace of solar time with its deadlines and precision clocks. We must learn to let go of the linear way and trust our instincts. Solar time always demands a faster pace and an attitude of mastery and reaching the goal. For those of us steeped in Western, solar culture, walking the Labyrinth is no easy task, for we feel impatient and have no time to learn the foreign language of the unconscious. Instead of surrendering to the wisdom of unconscious timing, we set unrealistic, solar-oriented goals, believing that we can make it into the center of the Labyrinth within a certain prescribed time frame. This is a dangerous method according to lunar principles, for it sets up an inevitable Pluto abduction.

In order to surrender to the labyrinthine lunar way, we need some reliable guides. These guides are depicted at the base of the Sacred Robe – the three feminine figures rising out of the lunar sea with its frothing, spiral waves. The three figures uphold the large wheel of life that represents a Labyrinth as well as a mandala of the instincts. The three figures represent the triple goddess of maiden, mother and crone. Sometimes they are called the Three Fates, the daughters of Mother Night. On the left, we see the maiden Clotho, who spins the thread of fate. In the middle, we see the mother Lachesis, who measures the length of the thread of fate. On the right, we see the crone Atropos, who cuts the thread of fate. Her name means "she who cannot be avoided," for it is Atropos who knows the number of our days and knows that we can never escape her final thread cutting. These three goddesses are the archetypal characters overseeing our fate, the particular life-death-rebirth cycle that is unique to each one of us.

The Three Fates challenge us to find the thread of our own fate and to walk the Labyrinth of life with dignity and finesse. The key to this challenge is to trust the wisdom of Clotho, Lachesis and Atropos, who hold the thread that can lead us into and out of our Labyrinth safely. As the maiden, mother and crone, they provide three different archetypal energies that we can call upon as we are going through initiation at Stage 2. Sometimes we need to access the maiden, when life is still incubating and coming to fruition. Other times we need to access the mother energy, when we are giving birth to something and nurturing new life. Sometimes we need to access the crone energy, when we are at a crossroad, when we need to be silent or when we need to stretch into the world of dreams to retrieve dream wisdom.

Allow yourself to play

When confronted with images, symbols and nonlinear reality, can we allow ourselves to play? Can we allow ourselves to fall into non-rational space where things do not have to "make sense"? In order to play, it is important to not categorize images according to this theory or that, but play with them by free-associating. It is important to make connections to whatever comes to mind. We can taste and smell the image, touch it and turn it over, look at the symbol or the dream material or the fantasy from different angles. I am learning about play by watching my son. He has no goal in mind when he picks up a rock or a toy. He turns it over, observes it, knocks it on the ground, tests its strength and its integrity, experiments by dropping it in water and so on. He has no idea what is going to happen next. The spirit of play is filled with limitless possibilities and associations.

This loose and unstructured way of being with ourselves gains us entrance to the great sandbox of life, where we can play to our heart's content. As we enter the sandbox, we will find new ways of being when we loosen up and explore life like a child. We will find new and creative solutions to problems. We can start with a powerful dream image that strikes us in some way, or an image from a painting or a poem or a film, and begin playing with it. We can take hold of the Labyrinth thread and follow its winding path from one free association to the next.

For example, the following is a powerful image taken from a larger and more complex dream. Follow along as I play with the dream images:

> *I am trying to get into my Labyrinth but I have to cross a large swamp, out of which are emerging hundreds of frogs the size of cats, dogs and lions.*

As I let myself play with the images, I am drawn to the swamp, which feels very primitive and both frightening and exciting. The frogs are juicy, wet and amphibious, living in both water and on land. They live in the primal soup. There is generativity in this swamp. The force of nature is coming toward me. I remember the fairy tale of the frog who is really a prince, who has been put under a spell. I wonder what instinctive parts of me are under a spell, which instinctive bits of me need to be kissed and transformed, honored and loved. They are trying to get my attention. They are huge and have taken on the proportion of the king of beasts, the lion.

I could go on playing with the images, but you get the flavor. With dream images, we can allow our imagination to soar and do not have to figure things out. We can wonder, question, be curious and enjoy the chaos.

Playing with others is also important when we are exploring the wisdom of the unconscious. It is helpful to find a friend we can spark with and have a lunar dialogue. One subject will spark off an association that will trigger an image or memory that we can follow as far to the outer reaches as we like.

Creativity and imagination

So far in Step 3, we have explored lunar wisdom, played with dream images, meandered through our Labyrinth and allowed ourselves to play. Let's return now to the Persephone story to explore *creativity and imagination*. Persephone has now wed Lord Pluto and has discovered the riches of the underworld. She has become Queen and grown wise in the ways of the unconscious. She has adopted an attitude of receptivity to her own depths, she has explored lunar wisdom and she has meandered through her Labyrinth and allowed herself to play. Now we come to the part of the story where Persephone is just about to return to her mother and the world above, but Pluto has one more demand. Before she can return and complete the life-death-rebirth cycle, Pluto hands her a pomegranate, which, if eaten, will keep her tied to Pluto forever.

Some people respond to the pomegranate part of the story with anger, as if Persephone was tricked once again and became a passive victim. I choose to see it as one of Persephone's most dynamic and powerful acts. I like to imagine that Persephone opened the pomegranate, saw the red flesh, recognized the instinctive power contained in the fertile seeds and promptly bit into it. Rather than another act of innocence, this is Queen Persephone willingly participating in her instinctive development by consciously affirming her own sexuality and creative capacities. By eating the pomegranate, *she ingests the seeds and internalizes her fertility*. She takes the Underworld fruit into her body and psyche and begins to assimilate the seeds of instinctual knowledge. In doing so, she discovers her own creative juices.

By handing her the pomegranate, Pluto ensures that Persephone stays connected to her instinctive soil. When she eats and ingests the fruitful seeds, she demonstrates her ability to hold her own ground. Now she is permanently, consciously and solidly connected to her Underworld.

When we can hold our own instinctive ground and when we have embodied our creative capacities, we can activate our great powers of imagination without the anxiety that we are going to lose our ground. The more we trust our instincts, the further out we can allow our imagination to go because we trust that there is a strong and sturdy base to return to.

As a therapist, I work with many people who have not eaten their pomegranate and do not feel connected to their fertile seeds of imagination. Some people feel afraid to explore the wisdom of their unconscious. They have a difficult time playing and a difficult time accessing their inner world. When we have experienced instinctive trauma, we often close down the gateway between the world above and the Underworld, between the conscious and the unconscious. When this happens, we feel cut off from the rich underground source of fantasy and imagination. If we cannot access the fecund images and symbols that bring life to the whole psyche, life can feel dry and parched. We feel unable to enter the lunar dance, which loves mystery and the subtleties of shadow.

To access creativity and imagination, we must find an inner voice that encourages fantasy and play. If we are in tune with our own instinctive rhythms, we can play, tell stories and move easily into the realm of dream and myth. These rich images are a gift from the unconscious, a gift to work with, write poetry with and dream our dreams with. We must develop a poetic imagination to feel juicy and moist.

As we become more technological and television-oriented in our culture, we forgo our own ability to imagine, and forgo our ability to tell stories. The computer revolution has given us synthesized images, where someone else is creating our images for us. This means that we are far more aware of and stirred by collective, popular images than we are by our own personal, unconscious images. Modern advertising, film, television and computer game images mesmerize us, and we fall asleep to the richness of our own internal image world.

If we are caught in the grip of collective images only, we only ingest what our culture is feeding us. So if we do not want to be spoon-fed all our images, we need to turn off our televisions, go on a media fast, and start paying attention to our own dreams. If we do this, we will be amazed at the creativity that we can generate ourselves, and amazed at the wisdom that springs forth from our own depths.

Step 1: Flow with cycles of change
Step 2: Honor your instinctive rhythms
Step 3: Explore the unconscious
* Step 4: Trust the Great Mother *
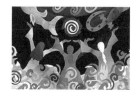

After becoming Queen of the Underworld, eating the pomegranate and recovering her creative capacities, Persephone is filled with a fruitfulness that leads to conception and the eventual birth of a child. Persephone finally leaves the Underworld and returns to the world above with her newborn baby to be reunited with the Great Mother Demeter, who has arranged for her return. Because she ate from the pomegranate, Persephone is obliged to stay one part of the year with Pluto in the Underworld, thus ensuring the continual circling of the life-death-rebirth cycle. In completing this passage, she is learning to reintegrate into conscious life all that she learned and embodied in the Underworld.

For you and me, this process is a life-long journey of forging a healthy relationship between conscious and unconscious life. We spend seasons dipping into the Underworld, retrieving lost parts of the self, and incorporating them into our normal life and relationships. Persephone shows us how to bring renewed consciousness and vitality back into the conscious psyche. She is no longer stuck on the wheel and therefore no longer abandons herself at one part of the cycle, for she has gained knowledge and experience of the entire wheel. She has gained lunar wisdom of darkness, death, transformation and rebirth, and now understands the importance of surrendering to the total life-death-rebirth cycle. She is reunited with the Great Mother, incorporating the Mother's powerful archetypal nature into herself. This means that she is now able to be a good mother to herself.

The final step in the second initiation is to *reunite with the Great Mother* as Persephone reunites with Demeter in the myth. The Great Mother is a powerful archetypal force that is constantly steering us back to our natural rhythms. When we have a positive relationship with the Great Mother, our instinctive body is strengthened and our ego is stabilized; this builds a sturdy psychological foundation that forms the bedrock for all further development along the path of initiation. Trusting the Great Mother also allows us to be in our child energy without anxiety or fear. We can rest, flop, relax, and play happily in the Mother's lap. We can dip courageously into lunar awareness because the Great Mother gives permission for us to do so. We can let our creative imagination explore the farthest reaches of inner space because She is providing the support.

I cannot overemphasize the importance of trusting the Great Mother in these ways, especially for those of us in Western culture. In the West, we tend to value the Father archetypal energy over the Mother by encouraging our children to grow up quickly, get an education and be independent. Dependency on the mother is often discouraged and devalued, and instead we encourage our children to leave the arms of the archetypal Mother long before they are ready. When children feel forced out of the arms of the Mother too soon, both culturally and personally in a dysfunctional family, the consequences are devastating.

Without a good mother in our lives to hold us physically, emotionally and spiritually, it is difficult to dip into our child energy to play, let go of control, explore and experiment. Without the good mother, we can feel isolated, anxious and unable to contain our feelings. We can feel abandoned with little or no extended family or community to hold us in a loving embrace where we can rest and relax. We then expect our spouse or child or therapist to be our only good mother, which puts far too much pressure on individual relationships. When a whole culture feels bereft of the good mother, there can be widespread abuse of alcohol, drugs, sex and materialism.

The second initiation requires us to retrieve our instinctive power, emerge from the Underworld, reintegrate with conscious life, and reunite with the Mother in a trusting relationship. Step 4 maps out five ways to build a healthy relationship with the Great Mother: *internalizing qualities of the good mother, healthy emotional digestion, positive attachment, positive mirroring and healthy narcissism*. In developmental psychology, these stages describe the process of healthy ego formation.

1. Internalizing qualities of the good mother

The first source of food for a baby is the breast. That is where the primary pair or dyad is formed, between baby and breast. This language from developmental psychology is helpful because the mother's breast is our first opportunity to take in the qualities of the good mother. The dyad of the baby and breast offers a nourishing source of good food, both physically and psychologically. If we can take in this good breast and take in the good food offered by the mother, it enables us to eventually internalize a loving mother within ourselves. This gives us the ability, in the future, to comfort ourselves and meet our own needs when necessary. It also gives us a healthy template for relationships and intimacy.

The baby and the good breast form the image of a healthy and nurturing dyad that becomes the foundation of an internal image of a loving baby/mother pair. In order to internalize this good mother, we must have the ability to conjure up an image of a healthy dyad. We can do this by imagining ourselves as both the child and the adult mothering that little child. In doing this, we set up a sacred dialogue between the mother and child parts of ourselves.

What are the qualities of the good mother that we want to internalize? Over the years, with the help of my clients and students, I have compiled a list of some of the most important qualities of the good mother. I have also compiled a list of qualities of the negative mother so that we can compare them and assess what kind of mothering we received as a child, as well as the kind of mothering we are giving ourselves today as an adult.

Qualities of the good mother:

Encouraging

Holding

Enthusiastic

Listening

Inclusive

Welcoming

Affectionate

Containing

Present

Allows interdependence

Protective

Kind

Initiates contact

Safeguards intimacy

Draws appropriate boundaries

Maintains generational boundaries

Tolerant

Patient

Holds our attacks and rage

Holds our anxiety

Does not rush in to fix things

Allows some frustration

Willing to make sacrifices

Does not retaliate

Aware of her potency and impact

Aware of her power to nourish

Loving

Open

Creative

Thankful

Appreciative

Encourages our unique expression

Encourages play

Honors our instinctive rhythms

Provides direction

Supportive

Guiding

Reassuring

Normalizes

Trustworthy

Consistent

Enduring

Strong

Satisfies our needs

Gentle

Sticks to it

Generous

Sensitive

Addresses fears

Instructive

Aware

Non-judgmental

Qualities of the negative mother

Withholding

Invalidating

Preoccupied

Attacking

Disapproving

Critical

Rivalrous

Envious

Jealous

Hateful

Chaotic

Neglectful

Indifferent

Pushing towards independence

Pushing towards dependence

Excluding

Angry

Suffocating

Smothering

Narcissistic

Penetrating

Invasive

Intolerant

Tries to fix everything

Does not allow frustration

Shaming

Persecutory

Disempowering

Diminishing

Controlling

Retaliating

Anxious

Depressed

Aggressive

Contemptuous towards our needs

Powerless

Not protective

Not vigilant

Not present

Abandoning

Manic

Violent

Vengeful

Resentful

Vicious

A martyr

A victim

Unable to communicate

Unwilling to communicate

Smashing

Shredding

Punishing

Judgmental

Distracted

Exercise 9: Internalizing the good mother

1. Referring to the list of qualities, write down the good mother qualities that **you have received** in your life and put initials by those qualities shown by your own mother (M), by a grandmother (GM), or by any other significant other (SO). Do the same with the negative mother list. Sum up your findings with several words that best describe the kind of mothering you received from your own family and extended lineage – Kind? Enthusiastic? Loving? Generous? Abandoning? Indifferent? Chaotic? Distracted?

2. Go through both good and negative mother lists again and write down the mothering qualities – both good and bad – that **you show to yourself** when you are needy or feeling small. Sum up your findings by naming the kind of mother that you carry inside yourself.

3. What negative self-mothering would you like to stop?

4. What positive mothering would you like to incorporate into your life? How are you going to get it? Who can help you?

If you feel overwhelmed by the number of negative mothering experiences you have had, please be gentle, kind and responsible and find a loving therapist who can help you to repair these wounds and restore a loving mother to your internal world. **Internalizing a good mother is the best emotional investment that you will ever make.** Once you have embodied these qualities, the good mother will be present and accessible for the rest of your life.

5. Try to find a picture of yourself as a little girl or boy and put it on your altar next to a picture of yourself as an adult. If you can't find a picture of yourself as a child, then find some representation of a mother/child pair and place this on your altar. In your daily meditations, imagine the little child and your adult self in a loving embrace. In your everyday life, attentively listen to the needs of your child, needs for comfort, security, and reassurance and needs to be seen, heard and witnessed. Try to acknowledge the child's needs whenever they arise. Use the photos to help you conjure up your loving adult/child pair as often as you can.

Being a good mother to yourself in daily life

After we have learned to conjure up the mother/child pair, another way to internalize the good mother is to *find someone older and wiser on whom we can depend*, someone who has already been initiated and demonstrates qualities of the good mother. We must find someone to trust who can facilitate our development through this stage. We learn to conjure up an internal dyad by experiencing a real, loving connection with a trustworthy person who is reliable. It is very difficult to conjure a loving internal mother/child dyad if we have little experience of a loving attachment in real life, so we need to seek out a loving relationship with a dependable person in order to learn, step by step, to trust our heart to another.

When we can imagine a loving pair inside, the internal mother then needs to *actively listen* to the child within us, without judgment or problem solving. Active listening opens up a space inside for repressed feelings to come up out of the ground like little green shoots. The good mother understands that the little shoots of feeling need constant care and nurturing. The inner mother must actively listen to the potentials that come from the child within us, because that is where new life originates. Active listening prepares the soil and becomes the holding, womb space. The good mother must listen to what is emerging – rage, joy, envy, curiosity, hatred, love, grief – and listen without judging the feelings. Her job is to actively hear and actively accept with unconditional love.

Once we identify what it is that the child within us wants and needs, it is important to prepare for shame to come up, because shame is usually attached to a repressed need. So when a need shoots up from the ground, shame often shoots up with it. The good mother needs to know how to deal with shame non-judgmentally. She can respond to the shame neutrally by saying, "Yes, here is that feeling of shame again, let's hold that." This helps to neutralize the shame and clarify what we want and need.

In some families and in some religious cultures, what "I" need is put last on the list and is seen as selfish. I have worked with many clients who were taught that what God wants is first, what others want is second and what I want is third on the list. That is not a helpful hierarchy when we are seeking the second initiation, because it is contrary to building a healthy ego foundation. We cannot form a healthy ego by listening to what other people want first. Completing the second initiation depends on our ability to know what we need and our ability to ask for what we need.

2. Healthy emotional digestion

After identifying the qualities of the good mother and working to internalize Her, the next step is to learn about the good mother's role in *healthy emotional digestion*. The physical digestive system is a helpful analogy to explain how emotional digestion helps to internalize the qualities of the good mother. Let's follow the cycle of digestion.

Imagine that you are eating an apple. You take a bite and begin to chew. Your body begins breaking down the fibers of the apple into smaller bits that the body can use for energy and storage. The apple is broken down further when it reaches the stomach. The broken down particles of the apple now move into the intestines, where the nutrients are absorbed and distributed to the cells. Another part of the digestive system separates out the parts of the apple that the body does not need and they are eliminated from the system.

This is exactly what happens psychologically. If our emotional digestive system is functioning properly, we take in a big bite of good emotional food, like when a loved one expresses warmth, affection or gratitude. Then we chew it over and it goes into our emotional container, the "womb space" we developed during the first initiation. Then we hold that good feeling for a while and bathe in the warmth of the love or compliment. (This may sound easy, but next time a compliment comes your way, hold it for as long as you possibly can. See how long you can sustain the good feeling inside without pushing it away.) After taking in the good food, we digest it and distribute the good feelings to the cells of our psychological system. This results in feeling seen, witnessed, heard and valued. This boosts our self-esteem and we walk around feeling confident and loved. Healthy emotional digestion builds strong psychological bones.

If the system flows correctly, we should have a mechanism to separate out and eliminate any emotional toxins that enter our system. *An internalized good mother has the ability to process the toxins, discriminate between what is good and bad for our system, and eventually eliminate what is bad for our emotional body.* If bad food comes in – like an attack upon the self-esteem – a healthy ego (good mother) will process this, chew it over, and invite the bad food to exit the emotional system because it discerns that it is unhelpful and unhealthy. Emotional toxins include negative feelings, voices of doubt or criticism, and many of the qualities from the negative mother list. If our digestive system is faulty, emotional toxins are not being released and there can be a tremendous build-up of poison in the emotional body.

Imagine what happens to our physical body when it fails to eliminate the waste products. Now imagine what your emotional body looks and feels like when you take in criticism or disapproval and keep these toxins in your system. The good mother inside can push toxic feelings out into the periphery of our psychic life where they can no longer take center stage. If we can do this, we have a healthy emotional digestive system.

There are many ways, however, that our emotional digestion can be faulty. For example, some people have trouble getting the good emotional food in their mouth because they spit it out, immediately pushing it away – the nourishing words do not get a chance to sink in. Others take the emotional food in, but have no holding space inside – the food does not get absorbed and the nutrients exit the system immediately and never have a chance to permeate the emotional body.

For instance, if we have a conversation with someone and experience it as nourishing, but the next day the other person has forgotten the conversation, intimacy cannot develop because the other person lacks the emotional holding space. They are not receiving our concerns or feelings, and therefore closeness cannot be established. We can imagine the situation for a child when the caretakers cannot hold a space for emotional food, or if they cannot help the child build his or her own emotional digestive system. A dyad for intimacy cannot form properly, and the inner holding capacity of the child cannot develop.

Exercise 10: How is your emotional digestion?

1. What state is your emotional digestive system in? Are you able to ingest, digest, absorb and integrate good emotional food into your system?

2. In your life right now, what good emotional food are you ingesting? Compliments, praise, gratitude, appreciation? Where is the good food coming from?

3. Once you have taken in the good emotional food, what happens? Can you make use of it? Does it nourish your self-esteem? Can you take in and digest love? Does it nourish your cells? Do you spit it out?

4. How is your elimination system? Can you discriminate between good and toxic food? Are you able to push emotional toxins into the periphery of life so that they do not take center stage?

3. Positive attachment and bonding

Most psychological and spiritual traditions would agree that we are relational beings, created to be in relationship and to form loving physical and emotional bonds with our caretakers and community. *Positive attachments* are essential ingredients for developing a trusting relationship with the Great Mother. Successful early attachments – either with mother, father or significant caretakers – are created when we are held, cared for, touched, respected, mirrored and seen. Healthy bonding provides the foundation of healthy ego development, and later, healthy soul and spiritual development.

Healthy attachments depend on the *maturity of the adult* and on the *child's ability to be open and receptive*. A newborn child is naturally open and receptive, and desires to attach and bond and have intimacy. Its life depends on it. When the child is held long enough in a safe atmosphere, it learns to feel comfortable and confident in the "dependent" position. Whenever I teach this to my students, I inevitably get the horrified response; "feel comfortable in the vulnerable, dependent position? Are you crazy?"

Many people have difficulty imagining that being in the receptive, open, vulnerable position could be anything but a set-up for betrayal or disappointment. The fact is, *positive attachment does require us to open ourselves to trustworthy people who are also open to relating and bonding in a healthy, positive way.* This means attaching to someone who is developed enough to set aside their own needs for a time in order to care for ours. If we can get into the receptive position, being open is not a set-up for betrayal, but an opportunity to receive love, care and intimacy. Healthy attachment is the backbone of true and lasting intimacy.

Cultures that value the Great Mother – such as India, Thailand and Indonesia – allow their children to be held in the maternal matrix far longer than our culture does. I noticed this especially when traveling in Southeast Asia and Africa. These cultures value holding children in the family and communal container, creating a pattern that fosters positive attachment and bonding. It seems to be far easier for these children to stay in the dependent, receptive position.

For example, a few years ago my husband and I led a workshop in Gambia, West Africa. We stayed in a family compound hosted by dear friends. In the compound lived an extended family that included a small, nine-month-old child. I never saw her touch the ground for the entire time we were there, because she was always being held by mother, aunt, sister, brother, cousin or friend.

In Western culture, we raise children differently and seem to produce adults who suffer from severe attachment problems that lead to feelings of isolation and alienation. We complain of negative self-esteem and a fundamental lack of core ego strength, which should be naturally woven when a child experiences healthy attachment and the culture allows the child to be dependent for a longer period of time. Most of my work with people in therapy focuses on fostering healthy dependency and bonding, which in turn creates a trusting relationship with the Great Mother and opens the door to the second initiation. When attachment has not been successful, rips and tears appear in the ego foundation that can create havoc for the psyche as a whole. Successful attachment is crucial.

Dependency needs have to do with what we want and need at a very basic, personal comfort level. Dependency needs are often not encouraged in our culture; rather, we are taught to be heroes and heroines striving for independence. Successful initiation at Stage 2 demands that we recognize our needs and our dependence on others. We are created to be inter-dependent beings, yet we have tremendous defenses against recognizing our dependence. Often our solution is to pretend that we are independent, not needing others or the Great Mother. Why is it so difficult to be in a dependent position – to be the child, the student, the underling, the novice? Why is it so difficult to be held in the arms of the Great Mother?

One reason that it is so difficult to recognize our dependence is that we are tremendously vulnerable in the child position. If we had a negative or toxic experience being in this dependent, child position, we are going to feel bad or frightened when we get into that position again. It is far easier to be in the mother position, to be the adult, the teacher, the one-who-knows. In the child position, we are wide open. On the one hand, we are wide open to the mysteries of love, relationship and life. On the other hand, we are also wide open to heartbreak, betrayal and abandonment. The memory of betrayal when we were wide open embeds itself deep in our flesh at the cellular level. This makes us suspicious of life to care for us, unable to trust that others will come through for us. Somewhere very early in life we said to ourselves, "I'm not going to be dependent and vulnerable again. I'm going to grow up and take care of myself and pretend to be independent, not needing anything or wanting anything from anyone."

These are the seeds – however they form in our child mind and heart – that grow into a myth of self-sufficiency. Although this is an understandable reaction to real experience, it leads us down a path of what I call "replacing the mother" or "killing the mother." To avoid feeling the wounds of the needy child, we jump into the mother position to feel big and powerful. Then we can fool ourselves into believing that we are independent. When we get rid of the mother in this way, we actually destroy the maternal values inside that can heal the wounds of heartbreak, betrayal and abandonment.

Pretending that we are self-sufficient has dire consequences and keeps us in a vicious cycle of deprivation. The wounds of the child within cannot be attended to because we devalue and destroy the mother within who could help, hold and heal. The myth of self-sufficiency prevents us from being initiated at Stage 2.

Exercise 11: Positive attachment and bonding

1. What kind of bonding did you get in your original dyad when you were an infant and child?

2. What kind of bonding and attachment patterns did you experience in your family of origin? How much capacity did the caregivers have for bonding, holding, touching? Were there any breaks in your early bonding experiences, such as mother/father being emotionally unavailable, depressed, hospitalized, you being hospitalized, a death in the immediate family, etc.?

3. Are you able to get into the receptive, open, child position in any of your relationships? Name the people with whom you can be receptive and name the people with whom you cannot. Why is it difficult to receive?

4. Make a commitment to yourself to find a trustworthy person and practice being open and receptive. Let them fix you dinner, help you with something, listen to you talk about something.

4. Positive mirroring

Successful bonding requires mirroring. Mirroring is the act of holding up a mirror to the child so that when the child is expressing something unique, the mother is able to acknowledge it and reflect it back. *Healthy mirroring depends on the mother's ability to acknowledge what comes from the child and to acknowledge the child's unique expressions.* This requires that the mother (or maternal figure) has been initiated and mirrored herself, so that she can differentiate her own needs and wishes from those of the child. The mother's ability to distinguish this is crucial in her role of providing proper mirroring. When the mother cannot mirror back the child's needs or expression, the child does not get affirmation for her own true self and eventually creates what is called a "false self." It is essential to get somebody in the family or tribe to mirror us and truly see our authenticity so that we can be true to our own self.

Mirroring from the mother or father helps the child to honor his own instinctive rhythm. If the parent is narcissistically focused on her own rhythm rather than being open to the rhythm of the baby, there can be major problems for the child. Parents must be deeply responsive to the child as a completely separate human being who has come into the world, or it will become difficult for the child to get in sync with his own body and emotional rhythms. Being out of sync with our natural, instinctive rhythms means that we are lost without the internal knowledge of how to care for ourselves at a basic level. We have not yet found the internal mother who intimately knows our particular rhythm. Some people, for example, take a long time to digest things. They need a lot of quiet space by themselves to work through a problem. Other temperaments digest more rapidly or need others to help them solve the problem. If we do not know our temperament, the internal mother is far away. Repair is made when we get the appropriate mirroring, learn our own rhythm and then honor it.

Some emotions are more difficult to mirror. For example, most adults find it difficult to mirror rage, sadness, depression and grief. But the fact is, children and infants feel these emotions often and quite profoundly. In Western culture, we find it easier to mirror the upbeat feelings of joy, confidence and happiness. What do we try to do with children when they are sad? We try to cheer them up. Failing to mirror the deeper and more melancholy emotions creates one of those rips in the ego foundation. In order to initiate the next generation, we must be prepared to tolerate and mirror our children's pain, depression and rage as well as our own.

Negative mirroring - the myth of Medusa, the stone mother

The myth of Medusa is a powerful myth of negative mirroring. The Medusa story reveals the secrets of the stone mother, the dark side of the Great Mother archetype. I use this myth often when I work with people therapeutically, and find that many of my clients and students can relate to having a stone mother inside.

Medusa is a terrifying Gorgon who has hair of snakes, sharp deadly claws and a deathly stare, which, if you look directly into her eyes, turns you to stone. In Greek mythology we are told the story of the hero Perseus who faced a battle with Medusa. He knew that it was deadly to face Medusa directly so sought the advice of Athena, who was wise enough to think of a plan. She suggested he play a trick on her with mirrors. So Perseus made his way into the swamp where Medusa lived and when he found the great Medusa, he held up his shield that acted like a mirror. In doing so, he was able to avoid direct contact with Medusa's gaze, thus averting his own death and slaying the Gorgon.

Here we have a myth about mirroring. All the ingredients are present: we have *the mother, the mother's gaze, the mirror and Perseus, the second half of the dyad*. But the Medusa mother paints a rather dismal picture of the loving gaze needed for us to be seen and acknowledged. The Medusa mother lives in a dark swamp, an uninviting environment where she is hidden and unavailable. The Medusa mother has writhing snakes for hair. She radiates negative "snake" energy, instinctive energy that is uncontrolled and therefore deadly. The Medusa mother has a toxic gaze, a look that could kill. What do these eyes see? Are they competitive eyes that want to kill off the child/rival? Are they narcissistic eyes that cannot see the other? Are they bitter eyes that resent the life force in the child? Everything about this mother will turn us to stone, if this is the kind of mother that we carry internally.

This is exactly what does happen if there is a Medusa mother lurking around inside us somewhere. Think of the Perseus character as you, trying to relate to this kind of mother. You try to find her but she is unavailable, buried in a swamp. You want to be mirrored and show her something that you have accomplished, but when you need her loving gaze to look upon you with kind eyes, she looks at you with a cold and stony stare.

When our feelings need to be mirrored, when we need the unconditional love and non-judgmental gaze, when we need our instinctive rhythm to be honored and the Medusa mother is around, these tender parts of us turn to stone. This is what happens inside the psyche when we have a stone mother gazing at us with stony eyes - we go rigid and want to run and hide.

When I ask people to think of a part of them that has turned to stone, they can typically think of something right away and can easily locate this stony feeling in the body. Then I ask them to imagine what kind of mother they have inside that is turning that part to stone. Usually it turns out to be a Medusa-like mother whose voice is critical, shaming, abusive, judgmental, silent or indifferent.

Imagine what happens every time a new part of the personality wants to emerge and grow and Medusa wants to turn that new life to stone. Imagine the depression of energy and the subsequent underground grief that grows. This means that we have tremendous pockets of unconscious energy where the ego has been wounded. This energy can either implode into chronic grief and depression or it can explode into rage. Each time we give ourselves a stony message or an unloving gaze, we must try to identify this as our inner stone mother and recover the feelings as quickly as possible. The Medusa mother needs to be tackled and, as Perseus demonstrates, defeated.

5. Healthy narcissism

So far, we have looked at four of the five ways to build a healthy relationship with the Great Mother: internalizing the good mother qualities, healthy emotional digestion, positive attachment, and positive mirroring. The fifth and final suggestion for connecting with the Great Mother is to embody *healthy narcissism*. To illustrate the difference between healthy and unhealthy narcissism, let's turn to the character Narcissus himself.

Narcissus was the young boy who, while left alone one day, stood over a pool and, upon seeing his reflection for the first time, fell in love with himself, his mirrored reflection. If we are left alone with no one around to mirror us, we are like Narcissus, abandoned to staring at our own reflection. We have no experienced elder around who can return a loving gaze. Without enough mirroring from a wise elder, we are left to either build a grandiose ego or a deflated ego, two extreme sides of the same coin, the coin of the false self. This scenario produces unhealthy narcissism that prevents us from building a trusting relationship with the Great Mother.

Healthy narcissism is developed when a mirror is held up to us by someone who can see our natural talents and abilities, which in turn enables us to see ourselves as we actually are. Each time this is mirrored and taken in, we get a clearer and clearer picture of who we are and what we are capable of doing. Rather than being grandiose or deflated like Narcissus, we can embody healthy narcissism and become *ordinary*, *adequate* and *capable*. The mirror needs to be held up, truth spoken and truth heard. If a parent is holding up a mirror and the child sees the parent's face on the mirror rather than his own, then the child senses an expectation to mirror the parent.

Narcissus was left with no elder holding up the mirror, and so what happened? He fell in love with his own image. We all know people like this, who are preoccupied with themselves. They spend enormous amounts of energy enlisting us to mirror them. This is a sad but compulsive attempt to get the good mother inside them and to get the good mirroring. The narcissistically fixed person is stuck in a monologue with their own reflection that leaves little room for dialogue. This kind of relating can be incredibly draining.

The goal of healthy narcissism is to allow oneself to be the child once again and bathe in the praise and attention from all the mothers, fathers, wise elders and friends who love us. For these lovely and important moments, we can embody healthy narcissism and all life can revolve around us. In this way we can truly internalize the good mother and get her into our bones. We must dare to be mirrored for our gifts and talents and take in "job well done," "that was a wonderful meal," "you have a good voice," "you have a way with kids."

In conclusion, Step 4 has offered us ways to build a trusting relationship with the Great Mother. We have learned to internalize her, develop healthy emotional digestion, attach and bond in positive ways, receive mirroring, and embody healthy narcissism.

Exercise 12: Meditation - Being held in the arms of the mother

One of our greatest challenges in this second initiation – trusting our instincts – is to fully allow ourselves to be held in the sweet arms of the mother, however she may appear in our lives. The following meditation is a powerful way to access the good mother. Many of my students and clients have used it as a daily practice to help internalize and trust the good mother more and more.

Imagine, in your mind's eye, traveling to a place of great comfort. This could be a beach, a cave, a garden with a fountain. Imagine a place that brings solace and comfort. Rest and relax. Breathe deeply. In this quiet and restful state, you look up and see the figure of a woman. She is the Great Mother, beaming love, admiration and respect towards you as you look her in the eyes. She gently picks you up in her arms as if you were a small baby, light as a feather. She rocks and cradles you in her arms. Allow yourself to deeply rest. Allow yourself to feel her big, strong, capable arms around you. What is this like for you? What feelings do you experience? If you feel fear or mistrust or anything negative, tell her, surrender it to the Mother.

Think of what is burdening you at this time in your life. What worry or concern or burden can you give to the Mother? Let her hold it for you. Trust her to help you. Be aware of your feelings for her. Be aware of her feelings for you. After some time, she gently places you back on the ground and you bid each other farewell. You leave the sacred place and return on your journey back into normal time and reality.

After this meditation, reflect on what happened. How is your trust level? Can you surrender? Does any anger, suspicion or fear emerge? Can you imagine a maternal figure who loves you unconditionally? Keep practicing daily, for as long as it takes for you to trust the Mother completely and take in her unconditional love for you.

Conclusion – Initiation 2: Trusting the Instincts

The second initiation has involved rooting our Tree of Life into healthy instinctive soil. We are now connected to the great instinctive cycles of life and have the flexibility to flow with cycles of change, evolving and developing around each turn of the cycle. We have retrieved our instinctive power and are capable of honoring our own instinctive rhythms. We are able to explore and value the wisdom of the unconscious and trust the Great Mother.

As the second initiation is completed, we should feel alive to our instincts and intuitive wisdom, able to comfort and nurture ourselves, aware of what we want and need and able to ask for it, able to form attachments and emotional bonds and open ourselves to play, creativity and imagination. We are now ready to cross the threshold to Stage 3 and complete initiation into our root system by forging a healthy connection to ancestors, tribe and community.

Chapter 3

Totem Lineage
Robe 3

Initiation 3 - COMMUNITY

Chapter 3 inspires us to connect in a healthy way to family and community, so that we experience a deep sense of belonging and support for our life's journey. Through stories of my African travels, we will learn to flow with the rhythms of community. Using myths about family blessings and curses, we will come to terms with our ancestral inheritance and heal the roots of our ancestral Tree. When initiation is successful, we no longer blame family or tribe for our problems in life and have transformed our negative family patterns into something positive and life-giving. We are connected to our ancestors and are proud of our cultural inheritance, having compassion for what they have been through.

To activate the third initiation, we call up the **Storyteller** within us, who gathers the ancestral stories and weaves the various strands of our life together in a masterful way. The Storyteller makes sense of all the functional and dysfunctional material that tumbles down our ancestral line. The Storyteller sits around the crackling fire, telling our story in a new and creative way, weaving our ancestral inheritance into a meaningful whole.

Qualities if initiated:

Healthy self-esteem

Deep sense of belonging to community

Proud of one's cultural heritage

Cooperative team player

Connected to family lineage and stories

Shares personal resources with the group

Constructive with negative family patterns

Feels support for life's journey

Feels valued for contribution to the group

Knowing our place in the community

Problems if initiation is not complete:

Needs other's approval

Feels isolated and alone

Blames family for problems in life

Unable to cooperate as part of a team

Disconnected from family lineage and stories

Shunned, shamed in the family or group

Stuck in negative family patterns

Involved in a dysfunctional group

Defined solely by our role in the group

Swamped by group influences

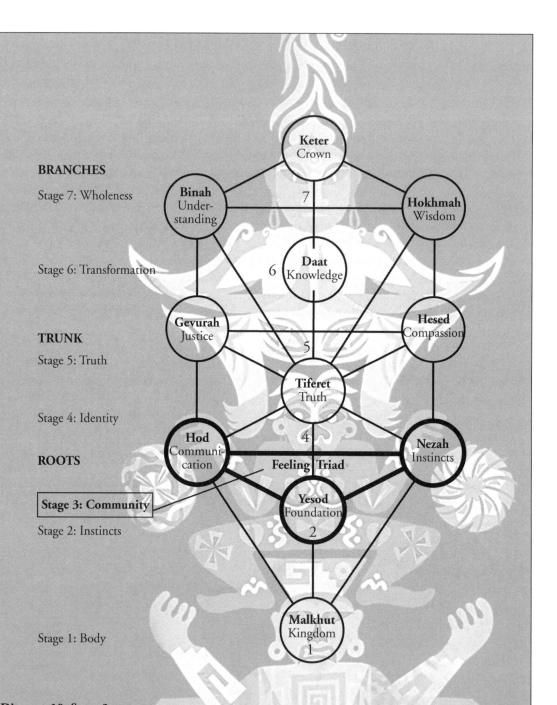

BRANCHES

Stage 7: Wholeness

Stage 6: Transformation

TRUNK

Stage 5: Truth

Stage 4: Identity

ROOTS

Stage 3: Community

Stage 2: Instincts

Stage 1: Body

Keter Crown

Binah Under-standing

Hokhmah Wisdom

7

Daat Knowledge

6

Gevurah Justice

Hesed Compassion

5

Tiferet Truth

Hod Communi-cation

4

Nezah Instincts

Feeling Triad

Yesod Foundation

2

Malkhut Kingdom

1

Diagram 10: Stage 3
In the third initiation, we connect with our ancestral roots, the community into which we were born. This includes our cultural, intellectual and emotional inheritance. Our communal roots provide us with a village, clan, race and cultural milieu that supply the ancestral soil for our Tree of Life. Without this connection to our tribal roots, our Tree would wither and die.

Chapter 3 - Connect with Community

The third initiation marks the final stage in strengthening the root system of our Tree of Life. In the first initiation, we set down conscious roots into nature and into our bodies, helping establish our sacred ground. In the second initiation, we nourished our instinctive body by flowing with the great cycles of life and trusting our own instinctive rhythms. Now in the third initiation, we connect with our ancestral roots, the communal matrix into which we were born. This includes not only our cultural and intellectual inheritance, but also our inherited emotional patterns. These roots reach back to the beginning of our ancestral lineage, back to the land and culture of our foremothers and forefathers. Our communal root systems vary in flavor and spice, but they are similar in providing us with a village, clan, race and cultural milieu that are the ancestral soil for our Tree of Life. Without this connection to our tribal roots, our Tree would wither and die.

Sometimes our ancestral roots are magical and colorful, filled with stories of heroism, triumph over adversity and successful relationships. Sometimes our lineage is filled with tragedy, violence, betrayal, and abandonment. It is probably fair to say that most of us have ancestral roots that contain a mixture of good and bad, magical and tragic. We possess some healthy tribal roots and some roots that are damaged, toxic, rotting or dead.

The fact is that we cannot escape our ancestral roots. We can weed out the rotting and dead ones and replant our roots in a more nutrient-rich soil, but we cannot get away from our tribal inheritance. These inherited patterns arrive in our cellular system when we are born, a combination of the psycho-physical gene pool of our collective lineage and our own karmic contribution that we bring with us to life. The trick in the third initiation is to be honest and realistic about our collective heritage and to do something creative with the unfortunate, tragic or more destructive aspects of our lineage. The good news is that, despite some rotting roots, our lineage has survived and trees have been sprouting in our family forest for many generations. We can have confidence that our Tree of Life is able to thrive and flourish, no matter how toxic our ancestral roots have been.

In order for our Tree to thrive however, we must pay steadfast attention to our ancestral inheritance, extracting every bit of nourishment we get can out of our tribal soil. We may need to re-pot some roots. We may even need to do some work around forgiveness, and learn to show gratitude to those who have gone before us and provided us with this interesting and unusual root system. Even though we may have grown up in an impoverished or toxic environment, there is still time to re-stabilize our ancestral roots.

Exercise 1: Meditation - Rooting your Tree into the ancestral soil

Imagine once again your own great Tree of Life. Focus your attention on the roots, and imagine yourself underground in the rich earth that surrounds the root system. Look around for the roots of your Tree that connect you to your ancestors. As you look around the root system, you eventually find your ancestral roots. Suddenly you are aware of a great crowd of ancestors who provide you with a rich mix of soil that surrounds and feeds your roots. See the men and women who have gone before you, working hard to survive and to continue this family line. Imagine what they have gone through from the beginning of your lineage. What land did they originate from? What kind of work did they do to survive? What religion did they practice? What is the mood of this great crowd of ancestors?

Become aware now of the great strengths of your tribe, the triumphs that are carried down the generations to you. See how this feeds and nourishes your roots, making them strong.

Now become aware of the weaknesses of your tribe, the wounds that are perpetrated down the generations. Notice what this does to your root system. During this initiation, you will be able to repair some of these damaged roots so that your root system can thrive and feed the rest of your Tree. Bring yourself back now into the present and, when you feel ready, open your eyes.

Write down what you noticed about your ancestral roots. Write down the strengths and weaknesses you perceived. Write down your hopes for this third initiation. What healing would you like to see happen? How would you like to feel at the end of it?

* Step 1: Build self-esteem *
Step 2: Feel the rhythms of community
Step 3: Gather your family stories
Step 4: Heal the ancestral roots

Security and belonging

The third initiation is concerned with the communal roots that wrap us in a blanket of belonging. This blanket provides the warmth of human contact and a soothing sense of togetherness. On the Kabbalistic Tree of Life, the third initiation corresponds to the "feeling triad," consisting of Yesod, Hod and Nezah (see Diagram 10). When the feeling triad is initiated and working properly, it stabilizes our emotional life because we feel securely held and rocked in our village, clan or community. Emotional belonging brings tremendous comfort, and when a child senses deep in his bones that he is wanted and that a special place has been prepared for him in the tribe, the child's psyche is stabilized in a profound way. The child can know his place with confidence and security because he can locate himself somewhere in life as part of this group or that clan or this village. Although a child must eventually grow beyond relying on the tribe for its self-esteem, it is imperative he begins by rooting into a stable communal environment.

When this happens, the part of us that longs to be a part of the human family can relax. If we do not stabilize this way in our family of origin, including our extended family, the *longing to belong* propels us to search and search until we find a community that provides a sense of comfort and home. We can spend tremendous amounts of time and emotional energy trying to find a community atmosphere where we feel held and rocked in the safe arms of a group. Every child longs to belong in a family. This helps to explain the appeal of cults: they exert a tremendous pull on the tender psyche of a person longing for a place to fit in.

A positive experience in community also provides the growing psyche with feelings of acceptance within the group. In a group, you can be acknowledged for the unique contribution only you can bring to the overall functioning of the community. You can be seen and appreciated for the particular part you play. This means that you will be encouraged to develop the talents and gifts that enhance the group. When a child finds her place and understands that she can make a difference in her human family, it forms the backbone of future self-confidence and feelings of potency in life.

For many years I did youth work with teenagers. For the smooth running of the youth group, many things needed to be organized and coordinated. It was like a family in many ways, and certain kids would, over time, emerge to fill certain roles that helped to keep the group running smoothly. Someone who was naturally organized would help set up the room or stay afterwards to clean up. Those who were naturally gifted musicians would help out with the music and singing, playing guitar and even writing songs. Others who were the enthusiastic extroverts would invite new people and think of enjoyable outreach events. Those who liked to cook and bake would help whenever food was involved. I was always amazed at the diversity of talents in the group and the kids' willingness to play a role that they knew would help the community. In exchange, each person received praise, thanks and status for the role that he or she played in the life and growth of the group. This often provided the kids with a great source of confidence and a sense of belonging and security.

Exercise 2: Security and belonging in your community of origin

The following are questions to help you assess what your family, extended family and early community offered you in terms of belonging, safety and security.

1. Did your tribe make you feel special and welcome?
2. What kind of stability did it offer?
3. What place or role did you occupy?
4. What confidence did it build within your being?
5. What gifts did you develop specifically because the tribe needed them?
6. Write out the pros and cons of your early community, in terms of security and belonging.

The community as our source of self-esteem

The other crucial role that the community plays in the life of the growing soul is the establishment of self-esteem. Our first sources of self-esteem are our family of origin, extended family and early community. In community, we begin to get a sense of where we fit, what we can contribute, what roles we play well and what kind of power we have in the world. This emotional umbilical cord has a two-way nourishing system. When we contribute to the communal group, the group then mirrors back how valuable a resource we are. This builds confidence in the growing child.

We spoke in the second initiation about the formation of the ego when the child feels secure in a primary dyad, especially between mother and child. Self-esteem is enhanced further in the third initiation when the child senses its place in the group. The group can be represented as the primary archetype of the family: the mother, the father and child. This need to belong to a primary community of three – a happy family where there is warmth, security and belonging – can be met in many ways: by the presence of stable grandparents, extended family, guardians or even older siblings. Any combination of relationships can form the stable triad for the child.

The triangle as a sacred shape and symbol is found in most mystical traditions and is often referred to as the "trinity." For our purposes here, let's look at how the sacred triad represents the **archetype of the happy family**, of a mother and father who relate lovingly to each other, maintain their generational boundaries, and adore the child who is a representation of their union, a product of their love and mutual respect. When the child comes into this kind of communal holding environment, he feels special, adored and loved.

The triangle is energetically very different from the dyad we spoke of in the second initiation. The dyad energetically creates a straight line, where energy flows directly from one person to the other, whereas the triangle creates a circular flow of energy (see Diagram 11).

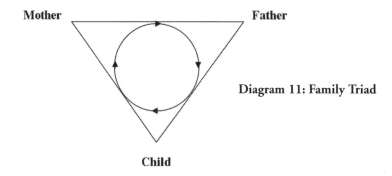

Diagram 11: Family Triad

The triangle creates community and greater possibilities of communal holding and belonging. Unfortunately, the triangle also creates more possibilities for dysfunction.

For instance, the triangle can turn into "triangulation," where two members turn against the third, shutting the third party out through blaming or scapegoating. Another dysfunction can occur if the parents are self-absorbed or preoccupied and do not cherish the child or see the child as special. The child then does not feel like an equal part of the triad, the community. The triad can also be destabilized when the parents are separated, divorced or conflicted. This can pull the child into an inappropriate involvement, trying to keep the parental unit together.

The best-case scenario for the child is when the parents are taking care of adult business and relating lovingly to each other so that the child can get on with her own development. Then the child can feel like the divine child, somehow special and kissed by the gods, occupying an important place within the family and community. If we are fortunate enough to experience some form of this happy family scenario in our childhood, it is easier for us to internalize the happy family and carry this circular flowing energy inside our being.

A child who has a happy family on the outside is well on her way to internalizing this and securing a happy family on the inside, forming the bedrock for self-esteem. Securing a happy family inside requires that the mother, father and child archetypes *within the individual* be in a proper relationship. This is when the child aspect of the personality feels free to play, create and express feelings, secure in knowing that the parental archetypes are intact and working together. The parental aspects of the personality must be inclusive of the child rather than exclusive, and must carve out a place for the child to belong. This brings feelings of internal security and stability, rooting the self-esteem in the internal landscape and freeing us from being solely dependent on the outer community as the source of our self-esteem.

If the parental aspects of the personality are not functioning properly and we possess an overly critical parental voice or an over-active super ego that is punitive or restrictive, the child within us does not feel safe to express and grow, making it difficult to internalize self-esteem. This process of internalizing a secure and happy family inside us takes time.

Connecting in different types of community

There are many different types of communities that offer members various ways to connect with each other. Our early family system sets the pattern for the way we learn to connect and how we come to feel a sense of belonging in a community. All communal systems fall on a continuum, ranging from "extremely **enmeshed** systems," where there is too much connection, to "extremely **disengaged** systems," where there is too little connection (see Diagram 12). The extremes of this continuum typically create dysfunctional systems because too much or too little connection affects our ability to grow and develop, and hinders the third initiation. The **flexible** system falls somewhere in the middle of the continuum, and is more functional because it offers its members a deep sense of connection and belonging without requiring too much sacrifice of self or pain.

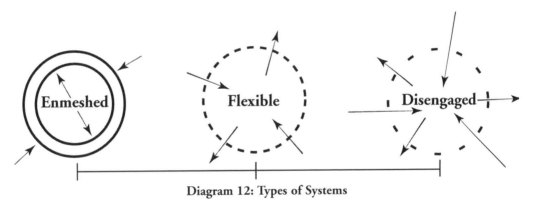

Diagram 12: Types of Systems

Growing up in a dysfunctional system greatly affects the way we learn to connect with others – either in an overly close or overly distant way – and affects how we belong in communities now, in our adult life. As I describe the different systems, think about your own family of origin and your early community. This will give you helpful insight into the way you presently connect with others and how you define belonging. Knowing this will give you the power to change unhealthy patterns and move towards connecting to a healthy community and finding a way of belonging that does not require you to sacrifice your true self.

The **enmeshed** group system can be pictured as a tightly knit, closed circle that is very difficult to penetrate from the outside or break out of from the inside. Energetically, it is closed and could be depicted as a double circle, where the membrane around it is quite impermeable, with little exchange of energy, ideas or thoughts from the outside world. Connection with others is made by being "the same as" everyone else. People who grow up in enmeshed systems often report feeling swamped, suffocated, trapped, coerced and controlled. Within an enmeshed system, there is a great deal of pressure to conform to certain norms, rules and regulations.

Although adequate structure does provide children with protection, belonging and feelings of security, too much structure and the pressure to conform can curb a child's development and sense of freedom to explore. Without a permeable membrane around the circle, there is little chance to be fertilized by new ideas; there is little room for innovation. A feeling grows of "the good is in here and the bad is out there."

The danger of this kind of primal psychological state is that it creates a situation ripe for a "shadow projection". A shadow projection occurs when the group collectively agrees that the way we think, believe and act is exclusively right and that anything outside the circle is exclusively wrong or bad. This places the bad, wrong and evil onto "others", and those inside the group are allowed to escape the difficulties of owning their own shadow aspects.

The **disengaged** group system can be pictured as a very loosely knit, open circle that is very easy to penetrate from the outside and easy to break out of and leave from the inside. Energetically, it is wide open and could be depicted as lines approximating a circle but not touching, so that the membrane is very permeable. In a disengaged system, outside influences can come right in, and there is little "glue" within the system to keep members engaged or focused on anything solid. There may be a lack of warmth, so that personal connection is very difficult to make. People who come from disengaged families often report feelings of loneliness, isolation, lack of guidance or supervision, feeling lost, lacking a sense of belonging and security.

In a disengaged system, there is little pressure to conform, little guidance, and few rules and regulations. Without adequate structure, a child does not feel protected, secure or feel that a place has been carved out for him in the group. With a membrane that is too permeable, too many outside influences invade the sacred "home" space, which can disrupt the secure container. A feeling can grow of "the good is out there and the bad is in here" or "the good is out there, there is emptiness or not enough inside this family circle." The danger of this kind of primal psychological state is that it creates deep internal poverty and a fantasy of always searching out there to get our needs met. It also creates the possibility of swinging to the other side to find an enmeshed system, in order to feel a sense of belonging.

In both the dysfunctional systems, we have to sacrifice something in order to connect and belong. In the enmeshed system we often must sacrifice a sense of individual identity, difference and uniqueness. Sometimes we must sacrifice the adventurous child within us who wants to explore beyond the village boundary. Often people must sacrifice their true self and develop a false self that conforms in order to belong. In the disengaged system, we are often forced to seek belonging elsewhere, and must sacrifice ties to the family. This can create feelings of guilt and deep grief and loneliness. We may also have to sacrifice warm and loving connection altogether if we cannot find it outside the system, and this causes the heart to ache.

There is another kind of system that is somewhere in between the enmeshed and disengaged system, which offers a balanced approach to healthy group functioning. It is called the "flexible group system."

The **flexible** system can be pictured as a circle, broken by small spaces, creating a semi-permeable membrane around its perimeter. This creates room for an energetic flow into and out of the system, opening the group to some outside influences and yet stabilizing it with common values, love and a core sense of belonging. In the flexible system there is a central belief that each member has a different, yet important part to play in the functioning of the whole. Therefore, difference is accepted. Conformity is de-emphasized, and members are not required to believe, think or act in the same way according to rigid rules. In a flexible system, there is adequate structure, protection and guidance, but also freedom to explore beyond the boundary. There is a belief that both good and bad exist within the members and within the group, and that both good and bad exist outside the group.

A flexible system has good cross-fertilization, and members can leave and return to fertilize the community with new growth, new ideas and new possibilities. A flexible system maintains appropriate generational boundaries between the adults and children. A flexible system has a flexible membrane that closes ranks into a tight structure to accommodate small children and opens the structure when the children are older and grow into teenagers. Its membrane becomes pliable and flexible depending on the life stages and transitions of its principal members. The flexible system has a responsive feedback loop and listens to the various needs of its members. The roles that people play are defined, yet interchangeable between parents and children when necessary. The rules are defined and structured, yet flexible, so that people know what they should be doing and what the consequences are if they break the rules. Connecting and belonging in a flexible system causes the least pain and asks for the least sacrifice. In a flexible community, we can connect and also explore the parts of us that are different from the norms of the group.

Exercise 3: Connecting in different types of community

1. What kind of membrane encircled your family system? Draw a picture of how it felt to you.

2. People who grow up in enmeshed systems often report feeling swamped, suffocated, trapped, coerced and controlled. People who come from disengaged families often report feelings of loneliness, isolation, lack of guidance or supervision, feeling lost, lacking a sense of belonging and security. What feelings did your family system produce in you? (You may have feelings from both lists.)

3. How did you learn to connect with others? How did you learn to define "belonging"?

4. Did you have to sacrifice anything in order to connect and belong?

5. How can you create community now in your life that is more healthy and flexible?

Hazards of community

We have seen how community is necessary for group survival, and we have discussed its role in building confidence and self-esteem. We have also looked at different types of communities and how they affect our ability to connect and belong.

One of the hazards of community – especially in an enmeshed system – is that a person can feel trapped within the confines of the group, *forever seeking approval from the family or tribe*. In this scenario, a person becomes tied to the community or group in an unhealthy way, dependent upon others to provide self-esteem. In a flexible system, we can internalize this source of self-esteem as a matter of course, naturally ingesting a strong sense of ego-self because we are surrounded by this nourishing source. When this does not happen, we do not develop a separate identity beyond group norms and "group think." This keeps us trapped and enslaved to our role identifications, and limits us to developing only the gifts that benefit the group. In the worst-case scenario, a person can get stuck developmentally, identifying themselves solely by the roles they play to ensure group survival and to ensure a return of self-esteem through the umbilical cord of the group. It is important here to contemplate what roles we play in our life and whether we are dependent upon these roles to gain our self-esteem.

Many people experience a loss of identity when their roles are taken away. When I suggest to people that they unplug their umbilical cord from the group, many experience anxiety, fear and panic. They have no idea that they can develop a far deeper identity that is based on individuality and rooted in their individual nature. If we remain plugged into "group think," enslaved to other people's approval as the basis of our identity, we will also remain tied to the timing of group karma, which means that we can only develop as fast as the least conscious person in the group.

Another hazard of being caught in the communal mind is *falling under the spell of conformity*. Many groups require their members to conform to certain norms. Some families, gangs, and even religious groups have their own agenda for survival and push for consensus and "sameness." There is very little room for deviance in thought and opinion, and often there is a threat of being ousted by the group if we stray outside the boundary. For the tender growing psyche, this threat can be extremely powerful and frightening. The threat of being kicked out of the tribe, without a "home" or the support of a group, however dysfunctional, can sometimes be too much for us. If the root foundation of our Tree feels shaky or underdeveloped, and cannot sustain the blow of being thrown out, the internal pressure to remain and conform will force us to stay. This is especially excruciating if we belong to a dysfunctional family or group and we can see how unhealthy it is.

The need for initiated elders

A dysfunctional system is a group without the guidance of initiated elders. Initiated elders understand the powerful pull of the group on the growing psyche and they know how difficult it is to break free of group influence, no matter what kind of system a person comes from. Initiated elders understand that the community system is designed to hold us in the matrix for a time, not all time. They know when a person is ready to develop beyond the family and group and have the wisdom to release these members when it is time for them to go on their own journey of discovery. They can see when the group has served its purpose in providing a stable root system for a growing soul and when an initiate is developmentally ready to move on. This is why, in many cultures, the elders initiate youth at the onset of adolescence, recognizing their need for appropriate separation.

Initiated elders in the community recognize that the membrane around the border of the village should be permeable – providing security and belonging, but allowing the exchange and flow of different ideas and influences. They are not threatened by new ideas or differing opinions because they know that the root foundation is solid and nourishing and from time to time needs an injection of fresh air from the outside. They know that in order for individuals to grow and thrive, they need to feel deeply connected and appreciated for their contribution to the group, but not tied to those roles with a ball and chain. People need to be encouraged to express their true selves, not sacrifice them.

In my therapeutic work with families, churches and clients, I have seen many groups with impermeable membranes. I have witnessed the psychological damage often done to the members of these communities and families. They have difficulty thinking for themselves and are frightened to step outside the tight parameters prescribed for them by the group, which can have a crippling effect on individual development. Without the presence of initiated elders encouraging individual development beyond the group, people get stuck never leaving home, tied to other people's approval and swamped by group influences. It is so important, at this stage of initiation, to spend the time and energy it takes to find a healthy community with initiated elders. If we want to build our confidence and self-esteem, and if we want to stabilize our root system so that we can walk further along the initiation path, we must find a nourishing community with conscious elders.

Step 1: Build self-esteem
* Step 2: Honor communal rhythms*
Step 3: Gather your family stories
Step 4: Heal the ancestral roots

Dancing to the rhythms of community

When I lived in London, my English friends teased me because, as an American, I was preoccupied with finding my roots and my "village." This was an enigma to my English friends who felt all too rooted in their island land, struggling to lift up out of a rigid, age-old class system and unbending ancient customs. "But we've always done it this way!" was a favorite British expression.

I will never forget my encounter with a village woman on the Isle of Skye, far in the north of Scotland. I was traveling around the island and ended up at this lovely woman's house as a bed-and-breakfast guest. After supper one night, everyone had gone to bed and I stayed up late asking our hostess about her life.

"Did you grow up here?" I inquired.

"Ach, no! Oh, my dear, no! No. I don't come from here at all!"

"Oh," I said, "where are you from then?"

"Ach, whell, I grew up about a mile down the road, in the next village."

It was then that I understood something of island sensibilities. In her experience, this epic move had totally uprooted her Tree and she faced the challenge of adjusting to a new community and village rhythm one mile up the road.

Most Americans have a different experience. Few of us remain in the village where we grew up, and even fewer of us know much about the land of our foremothers and forefathers. I meet people frequently who never knew their grandparents or even the names of their great grandparents. Tragically, the songs, poems and dances of the ancestors are lost. Stories are lost, and the rich ancestral soil of memory is largely unconscious. When this happens, we are left with vague impressions from the past and neuroses from family patterns whose antecedents we can only guess at. Many people in the West feel uninitiated and therefore isolated, wandering aimlessly without community and forgetting the instinctive communal rhythms that reverberate within our body.

As the third initiation progresses, it is crucial to somehow honor the rhythms of our ancestral community.

The rhythm of each village or tribe is unique and, according to the Tree of Life, is

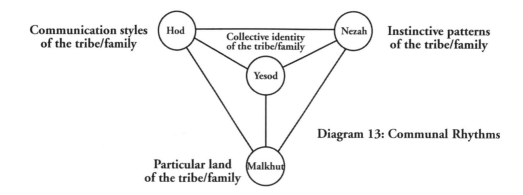

**Communication styles
of the tribe/family**

Hod

Collective identity
of the tribe/family

Nezah

**Instinctive patterns
of the tribe/family**

Yesod

Diagram 13: Communal Rhythms

**Particular land
of the tribe/family**   Malkhut

generated by the Nezah, Hod, Yesod and Malkhut aspects of the community (see Diagram 13). Each tribe has its unique communication styles (Hod), instinctive patterns (Nezah), collective identity (Yesod), and is rooted into a particular land (Malkhut).

The Hod rhythm of the tribe reflects the **communication** styles. Some tribes talk loudly and gesticulate with their hands, getting into heated discussions with everyone talking around the table at the same time. Other tribes have a communication style where members talk softly or use silence, where only elders are allowed to speak and dinner conversation is cold or intellectual.

The Nezah rhythm consists of the **instinctive** patterns of the tribe. Some tribes are hot-blooded and affectionate, and sexuality is approved of and expressed. Other tribes are restrained and sexually repressive, lacking affection or physical demonstration.

The Yesod rhythm is the **identity** of the tribe and the traditions that keep the wheel of life turning. Some tribes identify themselves as religious and celebrate particular religious seasons. Other tribes identify themselves as agrarian and celebrate the seasonal cycles of sun, moon and the growth of crops. Still other tribes identify themselves as counterculture groups and create their own celebrations.

Finally, the Malkhut rhythm is the rhythm that arises from the particular **land**, landscape and weather conditions where the tribe or community is based. The Malkhut rhythm also depends on the physical **body type** and physical energy of tribal members. The rhythms in North Africa, for instance, are very different from the rhythms in Indonesia or Norway. Even the musical instruments and drums that are made in each land create unique sounds and beats that reflect something of that particular land.

With each seasonal turn, each repeated custom and each ceremonial dance, the disparate strands of the village are woven together into a unique tapestry, according to each cultural blueprint. In Western culture, many of us have lost connection with the particular pattern and beat of our ancestral village. We need to reconnect with our ancestral variety, vitality and color. In our ancestral village, when each member learned the communal beat, the dynamic instinctual heart of the community came alive.

Exercise 4: The rhythms of your tribe

If you want to discover and learn the rhythms of your community, observe your tribe of origin and feel what kind of rhythmic patterns surrounded you. If you feel disconnected from some part of your ancestral rhythm, it can feel very healing to get back in sync with your ancestral beat. Begin by answering the following questions:

1. In your tribe of origin, what was the weekly rhythm? Did you congregate in any regular way with a synagogue, church, mosque, home meeting, worship or communal dinner? What was the seasonal rhythm? Was your community focused around natural seasons or religious holidays?

2. Referring to Diagram 13, describe the instinctive patterns, communication style, collective identity, body type and land of your tribe?

3. For a creative exercise, pick any strand of your ancestral inheritance that you wish to reconnect with and dedicate a period of time – either a season or one year – to celebrate the seasonal cycles of your ancestors. Do some research into the celebrations, traditions, holidays, special food, symbols, music and dances that made up the total rhythm of your ancestors. Celebrate the seasonal cycles and make them your own.

Rhythms from an African village

The Sacred Robe that represents the third initiation – "Totem Lineage" – was completed after traveling extensively in Europe and Southeast Asia and staying for a time in a West African village. In my travels around the world, the different sacred customs and rituals that arise from each culture have fascinated me. The indigenous wisdom that originates from different parts of the globe has something new and important to teach us. On the robe, each totem signifies the ancestral wisdom influenced by the land, the plants, the terrain, the weather, the animals, and the spirit of a particular place.

It is crucial to understand and tune in to the communal rhythms of our lineage. We may also need to align ourselves with the rhythms of other sacred traditions to fill in the gaps where our original community was lacking. It can be healing to our root system to experience an entirely new rhythm, one that holds and rocks us as a part of the greater human family.

I experienced this healing when I spent some time living in an African village. My husband and I led a group on one of our "Sacred Journeys" to the Gambia in West Africa to stay with dear friends in their family compound. These friends invited us to experience the communal and cultural rhythms of their homeland and village. We were treated to beautiful Gambian music, spectacular drumming, dance performances, village customs and family rituals. It became clear very quickly that the people there are in tune with the instinctual rhythms of the land and feel part of a thriving communal life. The family compound we stayed in consisted of an extended family of brothers, sisters, cousins and their children. They had a gated and protected plot of land with small homes, trees, a donkey we named Gerry-Jim, some chickens and some huts for guests.

Rhythms of communal crafting - drumming, singing, cooking, sewing, buying, selling

During this time in Africa, we awoke each morning to the sounds of the donkey braying, chickens clucking and scurrying around the compound, and the Muslim call to prayer. Dogs barked in distant places around the village, roosters crowed and birds began to sing their particular rhythm in song. Then a deliberate rhythmic sound would arise from the chaotic cacophony of morning sounds. The cook and the young girls of the compound would begin crushing the daily cooking spices with a huge wooden mortar and pestle – beating out a heavy *thump, thump, thump, thump*. Soon the cooking for the day would begin and this might last hours and hours while chicken stew simmered in Senegalese spices or fish sizzled in its deep-fry. Delicious, sweet-smelling, freshly baked bread was fetched each morning wrapped in newspaper, still warm from the local bakery down the main dirt road.

As the morning lumbered on, a steady stream of foot traffic would come in and out of the family compound to conduct business of one kind or another. Trades were made, drums were skinned, bargains struck and deals made.

Predictably, around five o'clock each evening, as the light of the day began to wane, five to ten people, mainly men, would arrive in the compound and the drumming would begin. The pulse beat of their songs and rhythms permeated the atmosphere. The young children gathered in a tight circle around the drummers, watching with wide eyes. If we were lucky, one of the women would break into the circle of drummers with a wild, enthusiastic dance, received with cheers, yells and peals of laughter. The women danced, the men drummed.

One day, we ventured into the capital city of Banjul, across the Gambian River, to wander through the various bazaars and markets that crowd Banjul's busy streets. As we wandered in the labyrinthine marketplaces, the sights, sounds, smells and boisterous atmosphere of the Gambian merchants accosted us. One of my favorite memories is of the indigo marketplace, where I witnessed the rhythmic beating of the indigo fabric against the ground as two kneeling women worked in perfect harmony, one beating while the other swung back, and then the next whack as they switched back and forth *whack, whack, whack, whack*.

As I approached the indigo market from far away, I could hear only the sounds of these strange "drums". As the square came into view and the drumming continued to dominate the landscape, my eyes were drawn to the huge vats of dark liquid, steaming around the square like dense, hot fog. Following the rising steam upwards, I could see yards and yards of deep indigo fabric hanging over clotheslines that crisscrossed the square in a haphazard manner. When I finally saw who was behind the mysterious drumming, I was amazed at the skill and accuracy with which these women delivered their perfectly synchronized blows to the fabric. Some women stirred the dark purple vats with large wooden rods, creating a great swirl of steam; other women hung the fabric on the clotheslines to dry and still others were inside the hot enclosure, sewing the hand-dyed cloth into dresses and shirts.

Kinship with nature's rhythms

The rhythms of this West African village began to slow my whole energetic system down to a pace where I could deeply appreciate the breathing in and out of the natural cycles of this land. I relaxed to the daily movement of the sun and the tides along the Gambian River.

One experience is etched upon my memory. One afternoon we set off walking through the village, through the mango groves, to the shores of the river to take the longboat across the river to shop in the market. The night before, the boat crew had forgotten to move the boat out with the tide - we were very close to the mouth of the river where it meets the tidal Atlantic Ocean - and the boat was severely landlocked. "Fifteen minutes. Only fifteen minutes and the tide will be in!" said the head of the boat crew confidently. So we piled into the boat with no water in sight and began talking amongst ourselves, sharing stories, drinking an occasional beer, and picking up the drums to play this rhythm or that. As the afternoon passed, slowly the tide crept around the boat, inch by inch by inch. Time passed. More time passed as we shared our stories and enjoyed hanging out. Over two hours later there was just enough water to attempt a sailing. All the men jumped out of the boat, stood in the shallow water and – "One, Two, Three, Whoa!" - they heaved and pushed and shoved the boat out of the sand and off we went. This was one of my favorite afternoons in the Gambia, waiting for the tide to come in.

The rhythms of life here are completely different from life in frenetic California. The slower African rhythm is life giving, nurturing and supportive to the soul. When a person feels genuinely connected to a thriving, vital community, initiation into Stage 3 is activated. Not only do we feel rocked by the cultural web of the human rhythms formed over generations, but we also feel rocked by the natural rhythms of the land, rivers, sea, mountains, flora and fauna surrounding our particular tribe.

To activate initiation into the communal rhythms, we must slow down our pace enough to be held in the arms of the community. When I slowed down enough, I was able to recognize that the rhythms of the West African drumbeats are based on the rhythms of the bird songs and the noises arising from the land and village life. I also noticed how the tide of the Gambia River affects the pace of life, like a giant Water Being breathing in and out, pulled by the great ocean.

One thing that I really came to appreciate was the West African kinship with nature. One late afternoon, a group of us decided to walk down to the edge of the river with our drum teacher, Samba, to drum together in our small group of seven or eight people. We loaded the *djembes* (the large drums indigenous to West Africa), onto the donkey cart and Gerry-Jim, the donkey, pulled our heavy drums while we walked through the mango groves. We arrived in a hot, grassy field near the shore of the river, set up some chairs in a makeshift circle on the bumpy and uneven ground, and began to drum. The sun was setting and seemed to be dropping directly into the river itself when, in the distance, a solitary man in a small fishing boat slowly glided by. I will never forget the feeling in my body as I clutched the wood base of my drum between my legs and hit my *djembe*, heard the deep sound on the large goatskin head and witnessed the silence of the man on the great Gambian River, moving across the orange disc of the sun as it sank gracefully into the water. The sky was darkening into tones of red, and the sounds of the drums carried on the hot breeze. The great river was quietly breathing in and out with its tidal flow as fishermen were bringing in their catch after a long day. As we drummed by the riverside, I felt a kinship with nature as never before, beating the rhythmic patterns of West Africa in the heat of the setting sun.

Cooperation - The circular rhythm of abundance and resources

As I observed the people in the family compound, I also noticed that each member of the community had his or her unique and special place. There was the taxi driver, the cook, the drum maker, the master drummer, the tailor, the money changer, the artist, the head of the boat crew, the dancer, the wheeler-dealer, the organizer, the boss, and so on. Each person had a sense of belonging to the clan and each person had found a place. It was clear that when there was a need within the community, everyone knew whom to turn to. If we feel like an integral member of a village, it satisfies and stabilizes our emotional roots. *We can experience a sense of purpose when we know our place in the group and can see the tangible effects of our contribution.*

In this African community, if someone needed transportation, the youngest brother – who was the taxi driver – would jump to the rescue. He could drive you anywhere you needed to go. He was also the one who made the exchange and flow of goods come into and out of the family compound. A car was a great commodity, which he generously shared. He was also the local DJ, traveling around, and setting up music for local parties.

In terms of cooperation and team playing, there was an amazing coordination system among the brothers, cousins and boat crew whenever we made a journey on the boat, either to venture up or down river or to cross the great river to Banjul. We could not simply walk to the shore of the river and step onto the boat. Because of the great tides, the boat had to sit off-shore about 100 yards, so that it had enough water to take off. This meant that luggage, food, drums, beer and whatever else we took on our outing needed to be carried to the boat on the heads and shoulders of the strong brothers, most of whom stood six and a half feet tall. It was truly a sight to see their sinuous silhouettes against the backdrop of the river as they handed great packages from one pair of strong arms to another, loading the boat and returning to shore for another package or even the odd person who needed transporting. After wading the length of a football field thigh deep in the water, we would arrive at the side of the boat and would be lifted up by the arms of the crew onto the deck to begin our journey.

The other aspect of cooperation that allowed for the smooth running of the community was the fact that if there were any needs among the community, someone would know someone who could provide the service or the good. If someone did not have enough money to pay, a service would be exchanged so that the need could be met. The extensive network amongst the members of the community ensured that if there was an emergency, help would arrive and things would get done. This became a reality for me one day as our group, our hosts, and the boat crew traveled up-river for a day of sightseeing and adventure. As we were getting into the boat to return home, one of our group members slipped and had a serious accident that required emergency medical attention. The boat was our only means of transportation, which meant a two-hour journey back to the village.

When our boat finally arrived near the village, one of the crew jumped out and ran to the small village clinic, but the doctor was nowhere to be found. Our messenger knew this doctor to be a Christian and guessed correctly that he would be in church. So the doctor was summoned and came quickly to the clinic where he could perform an emergency procedure for our brave group member. The generator at the clinic was off and the man who operated it was away, so we all gathered around and held candles in the darkened clinic and sang softly while our doctor performed his surgery without electricity. The doctor did not want any money for his follow-up visits in the days to come. He was willing to help and give what he could, and it took much convincing for him to accept our money for his services. In the days following the accident, the brothers of the compound carried our injured member everywhere she needed to go. This difficult situation turned out to be a beautiful example of cooperation in the village and a demonstration of the circular rhythm of abundance and resources that the people of the village were willing to share.

In order to accomplish a successful circular rhythm of abundant resources, each member must be willing to dance the rhythm of cooperation. Each member must learn to be an "ordinary" member of a community and be able to cooperate in a team. This means giving up any sense of grandiosity, or need to be more special than another person. Successful cooperation means that we must each take our own place and each person's place must be equally valued. This is impossible when people are unwilling to give up being special, thinking "I don't need community" or "I am better or more valuable to the community than the next person."

"Special" people often stir up trouble within the community. But more importantly, they find it extremely difficult to successfully complete initiation at Stage 3. They will not submit to elders, will not do their ordinary task, refuse to be a team player, and want to be in charge. When this happens, the ancestral root system of their Tree never stabilizes because they will not be held and rocked by the arms of the community.

The rhythm of humor

We took many lengthy boat rides in the Gambia, as the great river is the main mode of transportation. On these journeys, it was the humor and laughter that made an otherwise routine and perhaps dull boat ride a time of fun and adventure. This rhythm of humor – shared generously and often among our Gambian brothers and sisters – added much to the quality of life. A typical boat ride would begin with one of the men picking up a *djembe* and choosing a rhythm and maybe a chant, which would then be followed by the others. Inevitably, some mistake would be made or the drumming would get incredibly fast and someone would begin laughing. This would soon become contagious, and all on the boat would be smiling and laughing.

One time, one of the cousins decided to try a new dance step on the bow of the boat while others were drumming. His brothers and cousins would point, laugh, joke, and poke fun at his awkward movement or funny dance step. It was all done in good humor and no one felt shamed. I came to the conclusion that laughter was one of the staples of their diet, a necessary ingredient for the smooth and natural functioning of their community. It helped time flow in a non-linear, circular fashion and helped bind members together in a kind of "participation mystique," where they could fall into a pool of infectious laughter, sharing and reveling in the moment together as a group.

"Participation Mystique" is a term used for the kind of togetherness that is shared by a group when they feel a sense of merging, oneness and common purpose. When we actively participate in community, we can experience feelings of merging, floating and rocking, where the boundaries of self dissolve and we no longer feel separate or alone. Many people in the West never experience this in community and suffer from feelings of deep isolation. This is largely due to the fact that our tribal identifications have become smaller and smaller, and have narrowed down to the nuclear family. We have moved away from tribal living, putting far more pressure on the small family unit. We do not live in extended families or villages anymore and suffer from epidemic isolation. In a village, the sense of isolation is virtually nonexistent. We are much more apt to regularly experience participation mystique during celebrations, rituals, ceremonies and communal gatherings.

From my African experience, I came away with a deeper understanding of the communal rhythm of life. I experienced profound holding within the rhythmic joy of the natural surroundings and the African pace of life, which placed me into the rocking arms of the communal mother. I became much more aware of how life rolls on within the larger rhythms of land and sea, night and day. My internal clock slowed down enough so that I could sustain this healing rhythm even upon my return to America. I was also able to connect more profoundly with the tribe that I come from and appreciate the stories, rhythms, music, and dances of the cultural heritage that undergirds and feeds my root system.

Exercise 5: Engage in the rhythms of community

In many villages and communities, the main aspect of life that binds members together is the crafting circle where people drum, sing and dance together, where they cook and grind spices together, where they sew, knit and quilt together. There is also a rhythm of buying and selling that moves around a circular rhythm of exchange of goods and services.

What circle of crafting have you experienced? What kinds of crafting circles did your particular ancestors do? How has this informed your connection to community rhythms?

To facilitate a crafting circle, get a group of companions together and do a cooperative activity. Sing together, create something together on the floor or cook together. It helps if you have drumming, music or chanting while the crafting is going on.

Step 1: Build self-esteem
Step 2: Honor communal rhythms
* Step 3: Gather the family stories *
Step 4: Heal the ancestral roots

So far in this third initiation, we have looked at various ways to connect with community in order to gain confidence and self-esteem and engage in the rhythms of community so that we feel held and rooted, rather than isolated and alone. In Step 3, *we will gather our own family and tribal stories* and discover our true ancestral inheritance, including that which is noble and exemplary and that which is hidden, unstable, wounding and perhaps treacherous. All family inheritance includes the good, the bad and the ugly. If we are open and consciously seeking to know and understand, we can reconnect with our ancestral memories, uncovering hidden talents, gaining strength, and also releasing secrets that have bound up energy for many generations. When we gather the family stories, we give voice to all those who have gone before us.

Totem Lineage - calling the ancestors

Looking back at the Sacred Robe, "Totem Lineage," I can see that I tried to capture the different dynamic rhythmic beats of cultures from around the world. Embodied in each totem lies the ancestral lineage of a place, a land and culture.

In most indigenous wisdom, it is the ancestors who hold a focus of cultural values and hold the history of the tribe. They represent the collective body of wisdom, tested through the ages, that lays down a matrix of rich ancestral soil into which we can sink our roots. It is the ancestors who preserve the rhythms arising from the local territory and weave them into the songs, dances and stories of the people. They recite the ballads of survival, tragedy and bounty.

They tune into the instinctive rhythms arising from the land, the plants and the animals, and teach us how to stay connected to the land. Meeting the ancestors forges a link with the past and gives us stability in the present, connecting us with our colorful, cultural heritage.

Look closely at each Totem on the robe and discover the rhythm, spice and flavor of the people and the land it represents.

At the base of the robe, we meet a Central American ancestor, a warrior strong and fierce. His coloring is that of the fiery sun. Supporting him is an angular web, symbolizing the ancestral soil, the web that undergirds all of life. In his chest, an orange labyrinth shines and vibrates, drawing us into the mysteries of the heart. What passions pour forth from his heart? Try to imagine the sounds that would come forth from his bone-shaped mouth. What kind of dance would he do? How would his costume flow to the beat rising from his hot land?

Next we meet an African ancestor in rich, deep blue tones. Her expression is one of surprise, or perhaps she is in song. Beside her are two wheels that she commands. Each represents a wheel of life, spinning to her particular rhythm and showing the interconnectedness of all things. She is clothed in a repeating pattern of conch shells and mysterious symbols, gathering power and magic. What sort of sounds and dances will emerge from her? What stories can she tell of her magical African land? What drumbeats turn the wheels and reveal the sacred language arising from this culture?

Next we meet our Asian ancestor, a Buddha-like figure in a prayer position, reflecting and contemplating. A pair of all-seeing eyes emerges from his loins. What do they see? The greens and yellows of the Asian jungles clothe this ancestor, leading us into wild and unknown places. Dragons guard his heart chakra, and from his crown, an outpouring of his prayers reach to the sky. Does he hear sounds or silence?

To his left, we meet an Egyptian ancestor who wears the headdress of a priestess, and at her third eye sits the proud cobra. What Mysteries does the cobra impart? She brings a focused knowing with her mesmerizing eyes and draws us into a hypnotic inner chamber. How would her costume flow and jingle to her swaying movement?

To her left, we meet a totem from our North American lineage. Her animal totems of spider, elk and wolf protect this ancestor. She roams the land and weaves her tales of spirit, animals and power. She sees with the eye of wolf and runs like the elk in the wind. If she catches you in her web, will you allow her to teach you the ways of the spider's weaving? Can you imagine her animal dance opening your powers of intuition?

On the right side of the robe, we meet our ancestor from Oceania. Experience the fierce ocean waves carved into his flesh, the smell of ocean spray spread over his strong body. The rhythm of his land is the rocking of the ocean and the crashing of the waves against rock, cliff and coast. Listen to his oceanic music. What has the foam, spray, and salt of the great seas etched upon his imagination? What great sea adventure has he to tell, and what island wisdom can we learn from him?

The final Totem on the robe imparts to us the wisdom of indigenous South America. His all-seeing bird-of-prey eye brings our mind, body and spirit into a single focus. With his imagination we can fly high above the ground, gaining the perspective of Spirit. With his sight, we can dive down to an exact focal point on the ground, snatching our destiny. What sound does his song bring? Do you hear the rush of the wind, the screech of the bird of prey? Glide with him over the vast landscape and sharpen your focus of character. See what you came here to see. Enjoy the fresh, clear air and his song of the rushing wind.

Meeting your ancestors

The ancestors on the Totem Lineage robe have interesting stories to tell. Now it is time to connect with the intellectual, cultural and emotional patterns from our own lineage. If we can imagine reaching back in our imagination to the beginning of our ancestral lineage, back to the land and culture of our foremothers and forefathers, we might be able to glimpse what our own totems look like. What colors, patterns and facial expressions would convey the energy of your lineage?

Meeting our ancestors can fill us with powerful emotions: dread, sadness, joy, pride, confusion. Many people know very little about their inheritance and feel lost when asked to recite their tribal myths. The best place to begin is to make a **family genogram** - a family tree - going back generationally as far as you can. There is a very simple technique to map out your relationships on the family tree (see Diagram 14). Put yourself near the bottom of the tree and try to go back generationally as far as you can. Draw in the relationship lines of connection, conflict, distance and enmeshment as best you can. When answering the questions in the "mapping out your genogram" exercise, you can write them directly on the genogram paper or on a separate sheet of paper.

Getting it down on a piece of paper is powerful because we can see so clearly the patterns coursing through the generations. What we will find is a mix of functional and dysfunctional patterns – some that are colorful, magical and spicy and others that are tragic, depressing and bland. The important thing about working with our family genealogy is to learn about our own tribal myths as deeply as we can. This means that we must dig and search and ask the

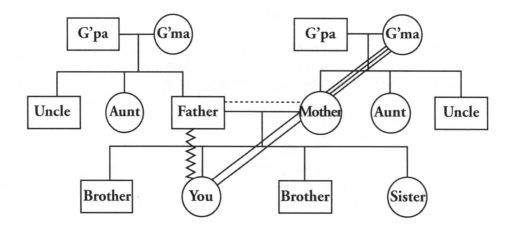

Two lines = connection
Three lines = enmeshment
Broken line - distance
Zigzag = conflict

Diagram 14: Family Genogram

right questions to get the whole story. When activating the third initiation, I suggest getting a tape recorder and asking the eldest family members to recount their memories of old. Getting the whole story means gathering the truth - the good, the bad and the ugly.

Exercise 6: Mapping out your family genogram

Get a large piece of white poster board or paper and map out your genogram according to the above instructions. Extend your relationships as far and as wide as you wish, to include important cousins, great aunts and uncles and great grandparents. Then, with your family tree before you, bear these questions in mind as you trace the patterns. Write down important facts next to relevant people for easy reference. Make symbols to represent the patterns in your family, like "D" for doctors in the family or "C" for those who have/had cancer.

1. What parts of the globe are your ancestors from?
2. What kind of cultures and climates do they come from?
3. What religious affiliations did they have and for how many generations?
4. What tribal customs and what religious holidays were celebrated?
5. What values were placed on education and intellectual pursuits?
6. What kinds of emotional relationships do you find as a pattern: close, distant, enmeshed or disengaged? Between whom - Fathers and sons, mothers and daughters, husbands and wives? What is the pattern?
7. What kinds of professions are prominent?
8. What classes or social strata do they come from?
9. How large are the families?
10. What are the triumphs and stories of heroism? What are the tragedies?
11. What kind of mothering and fathering patterns are present?
12. What are the attitudes towards money?
13. How does your tribe handle child rearing?
14. What diseases flow down the generations, both physically and psychologically? Is there depression, alcoholism, emotional breakdown or cancer? What particular addictions flow down in the line?
15. What are the patterns of intimacy? What are the marriages and relationships like? – Conflicted, loving, distant, violent or warm? How many divorces are there?
16. How do people overcome adversity? – Do they run away, face it, go numb?
17. How does your tribe handle anger?
18. How does your tribe handle grief and loss?

As you can see, this inquiry can go on and on. The most important thing is to gather the stories and fill in the tree as best you can. If your family tree looks bare, this also gives you information and may help explain your inner feelings of loss or disconnection. As you place yourself within this vast lineage, you become a vessel, a container for the patterns that tumble down the generations, gaining speed and force with gravity. This can feel empowering with regard to positive patterns, overpowering and daunting with regard to dysfunctional ones.

Storytelling around the communal fire

After gathering the stories and doing the family genogram, it is helpful to learn the art of storytelling. To do this, we can imagine meeting the **Storyteller** from our ancestral tribe, who sits around the crackling outdoor fire, creating a wonderful story out of our family inheritance. Storytellers can make the best out of a bad situation, reframing negative family patterns into useful material for a good story.

Meeting the creative Storyteller inside us is the key to activating the third initiation. How many times have we heard someone tell and retell his or her "story" in the same old boring way? Many people get stuck on the tragedy of their family roots because they tell their story the same way every time, with no variation - nothing is learned, no new insight is gained. They get stuck in the victim's perspective of the story, or in the pessimist's viewpoint, or get lost in denial.

It is the Storyteller in us who has a wider perspective than the narrow view of the victim. It is the Storyteller in us who can pull all the various strands of our life into the larger tapestry of the tribe and make sense of the tragedies, mistakes, bizarre events and personal violations. The Storyteller is the weaver, weaving our ancestral inheritance into a vast and colorful whole.

One effective way to contact the Storyteller in us is to sit in a sacred circle with others, sharing family genograms. The sacred circle forms a loving container where our "story" can be witnessed. I have found time and again that when I sit in a circle to witness the unfolding of people's family stories, tremendous healing occurs. With the use of the genogram, people spontaneously find new ways to tell their story of incest or their story of betrayal or of the loss of relationship. The larger dysfunctional patterns unfold before us and often can be traced back to a person or event. It becomes obvious why our grandmother had a breakdown or why our own mother was unable to mirror us properly or unable to show affection. It becomes obvious why a family member suffers from alcohol addiction, when we can see that the only way family members have dealt with anger is by numbing their emotions with alcohol. It becomes easier to see our individual dysfunction within the larger cauldron of the family, which may have been bubbling away unchecked, unprocessed and unconscious for several generations.

Within a storytelling circle, other people notice patterns that we have never seen. Somehow it is comforting to know that what feels like our personal pathology is really a larger thread running through the entire ancestral tapestry, shared by many others in the group. When others witness our pathology and when the antecedents are seen in the context of family patterns, it lessens our shame. Being witnessed can also break the spell or the hold some of these patterns have on our lives. Hearing other stories can also help put our own story into perspective.

Gathering the bones of the ancestors

As we gather the bones of our ancestors, we open the Pandora's box of our lineage, which brings into relief both the blessings and curses of our ancestral line. Some bones belong to the honorable skeletons and some bones belong to dreadful skeletons in the closet. The trick in the third initiation is to accept and honor our heritage no matter how dysfunctional or toxic. The other trick is to dig as deeply as we can into the collective pool of memory to recover what is lost. There will be many unanswered questions and many unsolved mysteries. Sometimes we will find clear antecedents to the family dysfunctions and other times we will not have a clue. Recovering what is lost takes great courage and fortitude. The following is the tale of a courageous woman who gathered the bones and survived.

"The Woman Who Honored the Bones"

Once upon a time there was a beautiful woman with long eyes and almond lips and the taste of wild blackberries on her skin. She was called Mpongo and lived in the forest where rain glistened and bright feathered birds drank from the leaves.

She fell in love with a son of the forest. He was a large lad with brown limbs and a free way of moving. When he danced to the drums, his body shone in the firelight. There was the fragrance of xchongl berries about him, and he was named for the bloom of the xchongl berry tree. It is a soft pink bloom of many petals, and in the tropical forest it graces the viridian jungle all year long.

Mpongo and Xchongl lived quietly in the secret forest. Each year a child was born to them. Mpongo bathed them and cared for them with love. They grew strong and beautiful.

One would believe that with such a fine beginning all would be well, but it was not to be so. One night as Mpongo slept, Xchongl was taken from her. When she woke, his sleeping mat was empty beside her. He was nowhere to be found.

Some say that he was carried off by the ghosts of the village. Some say he was eaten by Ntongo, the long snake that carries the past of everyone's tribe. Some say he was bewitched by a wicked maiden who cooked small creatures for breakfast and picked her teeth with their bones. Some say that he was injured in a fall and the jackals came; the jackals who lick the forest clean, living off the land and the lives of others.

Some say it was the mishwatoro world that took him away; the mists and winds that lay themselves over the minds of men and make them forget where they come from.

Oh, these were sorrowful days for Mpongo, and there were more to come. One morning she sent her eldest daughter, Natongi, to gather wood in the forest and she did not return. The next day it was her first-born son, Mboro, and next her silken-skinned second daughter, Iktari, who never came back.

So it went that all twelve children disappeared into the forest. Then Mpongo could not stop weeping for the ones she lost. Her tears became the creek that trickled by her feet, and still she could not stop. Then her tears became the rushing stream that followed beside her, and still she could not stop. Her tears became the deep river in the gorge, and still she could not stop. Her tears became the wondrous waterfall that flings itself over the mountainside, and she too felt like flinging herself over the mountainside. But still she could not stop weeping.

It was her tears that flung themselves over the mountainside and formed a bridge of spray. It was from this bridge of tears the butterflies burst upon the world. For it is said that the Great Creator carries the magic of just return, and from so many tears there must yet come hope.

It was these bright messengers that flew across the bridge, down to the xchongl berry trees where Mpongo stood. Sudden and bright, they swarmed around her shoulders, and before flying into the forest they whispered in the language of butterflies, "Suera, suera, suera... call them home, call the lost children home. Whisper to them in the forest, for the lost children only hear whispers."

From then on Mpongo rose early and stood above the waterfall by the xchongl berry trees, whispering the names of her children, "Natongi sueroyo, Mboro sueroyo, Iktari sueroyo…" For each child she whispered their name and called them home. And finally she would call to Xchongl, "Sueroyo, Xchongl."

Then she dropped a pale pink blossom from the xchongl berry tree over the waterfall, where it was torn to shreds in the violent rush of water.

Afterwards she returned to her quiet forest home where the rain glistened and bright-feathered birds drank from the leaves. It took all her day to gather food and fuel. It took all night for sleep. She waited for the dream of the Great Lover, but the dream did not come.

For seven years she whispered to the mishwatoro, "Suera, suera, I am calling you."

But no dreams came, only early morning songs and flying words she tried to catch. One morning when she woke, a strange light fell across the glistening leaves. She shivered with foreboding.

The bright-feathered birds rose up through the mist with a whirr and a whoosh. "We are leaving to search for the lost children everywhere, to tell them to come home. We are leaving to find the place where Xchongl rests with his children. And until we find them we will not return. You have grieved too long and loved too little. Now you may grieve for the loss of our bright songs."

"No!" cried Mpongo, but the birds had flown away. Now there was no one to join her in the early morning light. And now Mpongo found herself truly alone in a soundless forest, where the only movement was the flashes of color from the butterflies who flittered in and out of the phthalian shadow.

It was now she stopped crying.

Some say it was because she had no tears left. Some say she was too tired. Some say she was crazy. But when all the birds left the forest, Mpongo left too and wandered in the swamps and grasslands until she came to the great desert.

It was there she found the bones of her children and her beloved Xchongl with their wedding conch shell clutched in his bony grasp. It still shone with the shine of the sea and was filled with the sound of the ocean's roar. For a moment, seeing it, Mpongo was stunned, for she saw him suddenly once again, standing at the open door of their wedding hut, his body shining in the moonlight as he lifted the conch shell and blew his long wail into the night, before coming to her sleeping mat.

She gathered the bones tenderly and placed them in her bag with the conch shell. She brought them home to the forest. She buried them quietly in the earth and used small stones and twigs to form a beautiful pattern around them.

She planted a xchongl berry tree nearby and sang her early morning song, "Suera, suera, suera, I am calling you." When the song was finished she stood up beside their grave. It was at that moment that the birds returned to the forest, and when she saw their bright feathers and once again heard their songs, she laughed with joy.

As she stood there, a waiting warrior stepped out of the forest shadows. "Woman," he called, "Stop a moment. I am Dolabi, he who is filled with compassion. I have watched you for seven years. I have seen you in the morning as you sing your morning song above the waterfall. I have seen you drop the xchongl berry bloom into the water, and always it is torn apart, day after day, by the violence of the rushing water. Always you are weeping. Though I have wondered at your comeliness, I was afraid to approach because I thought you were possessed by a curse or that you might be an evil one who casts spells and bewitchments on the men who love them.

"But now I see you were only seeking the bones of your loved ones in order to say good-bye, so their ghosts will not be angry or sad or dishonored; so they could rest in peace.

"I hold this to be a good thing in the forest, and as it should be. Now that this is done, I should like you to bring your comeliness and your sleeping mat to share my forest home. We will marry as is done in the forest. You will bring your sleeping mat to the hut I build, and I shall play the conch shell to the moon on our wedding night."

And Mpongo agreed.

They lived together many years. Mpongo's name was honored and remembered for generations as the woman who brought the butterflies into the forest with her tears, and the one who caused the birds to leave the forest with her grieving, and the one who brought them back again by her suffering and her search and by the care and honor she brought to the bones of the ones who loved her.

Her story was told again and again. The children came to hear it and told their children, and from that day to this, the forest people still gather the bones of the ones they have loved and circle them with beautiful designs that sink into the forest floor, until finally they too fade away into the forest earth, and all rests in harmony.[1]

Grief and the loss of our ancestral connection

What does this story tell us about the journey of collecting the bones of the ancestors? In the story, Mpongo's husband, Xchongl, was a son of the forest and attuned to the instinctual rhythm of the land and the beat of his communal drum. Somehow, he tragically disappeared. When we apply this tale to the modern psyche, our instinctive, communal connection has disappeared within us; it has fallen into the unconscious and is nowhere to be found. Perhaps Ntongo, the long snake that carries the past of everyone's tribe, has eaten our ancestral connection. Or perhaps the mishwatoro, the mists and winds, have covered our vision, laying themselves over our minds and making us forget where we come from. Either way, we have forgotten the stories of the ancestors.

This powerful story informs us of the sorrow and grief that accompany this loss of the collective memory. We grieve the loss of ancestral wisdom in our lives and the loss of initiated elders. We weep for the pain and suffering our ancestors have endured. We grieve all the abandonments, betrayals, violations and lost loves. Sometimes we cry tears that form a deep river and a waterfall that flings itself over the mountainside. Gathering the bones can bring out a deep ocean of unexpressed grief and feelings that have remained unconscious for generations.

Grieving has a purpose – it has a powerful, healing effect on those of us in the present and those who have gone before. It propels us on a search to recover what has fallen into the unconscious. Grieving releases something in the collective unconscious of the tribe, bringing relief and lifting dysfunctional emotional patterns. Grieving is a powerful healing tool and can, in some cases, release the most tenacious and treacherous negative patterns.

Calling the lost children home

It is the butterflies in the story that encourage us to search for the bones by whispering in our ear, "Call the lost children home." It is often up to us to gather and settle the lost remnants of our ancestors and put them in some kind of order and pattern that makes sense to us. The story tells of the rewards gained when we go on a search for the bones, find the bones, and return to bury them in home ground. We search for the bones of our family to rectify the losses and to recover memory. We do it to keep the stories alive. Remembering the ancestors means remembering the good and noble things that come from them, but it also means learning from the disasters and mistakes that were made.

We call the lost children home because this healing aids those in the past and those of us in the present, and lays down healthy soil for future generations. Attending to the ancestral inheritance also ensures the continuity of communal life and preserves our sense of belonging to the great circle of life. Gathering the bones helps us to weave our own story into the fabric of the ancestral tapestry. Like Mpongo in the story, we need to set our will and intention on retrieving what has been lost in the unconscious, uncovering all we can and not giving up. Mpongo called for seven years, called, waited, and cried. Finally, she walked into the desert and found the bones of her beloved family. We must do the same.

Exercise 7: Gathering the bones of the ancestors

As you gather the bones of your ancestors, write down the answers to these questions. What you uncover here will be the material you can use in the next exercise, which is a grief ritual to honor and release emotional patterns in your ancestral line that have been constricted or blocked.

1. What has been lost in your family line? What has been buried and forgotten?
2. What skeletons in the closet need to be freed? What secrets need to be revealed?
3. What feelings need to be retrieved? What feelings need to be released?
4. What pain and suffering did your ancestors endure? What abandonments, betrayals and violations need to be grieved? What sacrifices need to be honored and acknowledged?
5. What truths need to be voiced and spoken?
6. What accomplishments need to be brought to light?
7. Who needs to be forgiven? Who needs to be released?

If you do not have any clear answers and do not know what the toxic and dysfunctional patterns are or where they came from, or what the hidden secrets are, sit down with your family tree and do some meditation or active imagination. Ask for guidance.

Reconnecting with the ancestors

When Mpongo discovers what has been lost, she is tender in her gathering of the bones. She gathers them up in her special bag and brings them home to the forest. She ritualizes the burying by gathering stones and twigs in order to surround the bones with a beautiful pattern.

We too must be tender with ourselves when we learn the truth of our heritage. We often spontaneously ritualize these moments as we are making peace with the past, as we say good-bye to an age-old pattern, as we mourn for our grandfathers or honor the sacrifices made long ago. Ritualizing and beautifying provides a container for the grief we hold inside. When

Mpongo makes a pattern around the bones, it is like us when we order and make sense of our generational patterns.

What Mpongo does next is interesting. She plants a tree near the circle and sings a soothing song to the bones, "Suera, suera, I am calling you." This calls to mind how we sit near the remnants of our past and tenderly plant new vegetation, new life, to replace what has been lost. We might literally go into the garden and plant to relieve the suffering. We might find ourselves making a small shrine in our home to honor and remember our ancestors. Perhaps we write a poem, thanking our ancestors for their fortitude and survival. As we sing a sweet song to all the people who have gone before us, we might find ourselves spontaneously forgiving even the most unlovable people in our tribe. Small gestures that help us honor, thank and remember can become healing rituals, soothing to body and soul.

When we have made peace and have recovered lost collective material, we, like Mpongo, are given a new lease on life. Birds return to our forest and dormant characters come to life within the psyche.

In the story, this is when Mpongo meets Dolabi, a warrior who steps out from the shadows. His name means "filled with compassion." Developing compassion is one of the tools gained in this third initiation, and it will be invaluable as we awaken further along the path. Feeling compassionate towards the ancestors means that we are no longer running away from our roots, but have come to terms with even the most toxic and unhealthy roots growing under our Tree. As we sit now in our ancestral circle, we have come full circle by making peace with the ancestors and bringing harmony to the communal soil.

Exercise 8: Grief rituals to honor and release

Begin by setting up a sacred ritual space in a very intentional way. The most important focal point of the ritual should be an ancestral shrine, some kind of special altar that can be set up either inside or outside. Gather photographs, memorabilia, anything you've written about your ancestors in the previous exercises, along with your family tree. Like Mpongo, you may want to gather natural materials and arrange them in the shrine. Flowers and candles are also helpful and beautiful. I recommend doing a grief ritual at night because the darkness helps the tears to flow and is conducive to emotional release.

Once you have set up the shrine, be intentional about exactly what you want to honor and what you want to release and grieve. If you are working in a group, have people answer the questions in the previous exercise (Exercise 7) and share what it is they want to grieve and what pattern they want to release. Sharing it and having it witnessed is a profound experience.

When people feel clear with their intention, begin the ritual. Remember to invoke the Divine so that the highest good can come out of the experience. If you are doing this by yourself, put on some music or drumming and light the candles and sit up at your shrine in the darkness (don't forget a box of tissues). Allow the grief to come. Talk to your ancestors. Tell them you are here to grieve and release for them. Listen to what they may be saying to you.

If you can, let the tears flow and try to put sound to the tears. Open the floodgates, open your vocal cords, wail. I cannot over-emphasize the importance of this kind of release.

A mysterious alchemical process happens within the body when we allow ourselves to cry, wail and give voice to grief, however strange or eerie it may sound. Grieving releases water from the body - locked up emotion - and releases primal sound from the body - locked up energy. A grief ritual can provide the structure, safety and sacred space we need to release blocked emotion and energy that can be loosened no other way.

When you feel finished, thank the Divine and thank your ancestors for all the hard work they have done over the generations. Pray for cleansing, healing, forgiveness and compassion to fill your being. As you close down the ritual space, be mindful of all that occurred.

Step 1: Build self-esteem
Step 2: Honor communal rhythms
Step 3: Gather your family stories
* Step 4: Heal the ancestral roots *

Ancestral blessings and curses

After gathering our family stories, grieving what has been lost, and reconnecting with our ancestral inheritance, we can now concentrate on healing the ancestral roots. In Step 4, we will look at the *blessings and curses* that tumble down our family line, and discover some creative ways to heal the specific negative patterns that affect the root system of our Tree.

When we look at the family genogram of a particular tribe, we can begin to see the kinds of blessings and curses that are passed down through the collective psyche. Ancestral **blessings** that come down our family line give us confidence and strength. They give us the skills we need to move forward in our initiation. The following are blessings you may have received from your tribe or clan: "I believe in what you are doing", "You are capable of success", "You are powerful/beautiful/intelligent/resourceful", "Being a man is empowering", "Being a woman is empowering."

Curses, on the other hand, hold us back, making development slow and initiation difficult. Curses take hold of us where the psyche has been wounded in some way. In order to complete the third initiation, we must learn to dance creatively with our wounds and curses. If we can acknowledge our wounds as healers and wisdom-bringers, we are well on our way to completing initiation and becoming that master Storyteller who can reframe destructiveness into useful material for a good story.

To find where we have been wounded, we must discover the curses that flow down our family tree. A "curse" could be a negative voice playing like a tape within our psyche that is mysteriously shared by other members of our tribe. A curse can manifest as a voice that gets under our skin and into our bones. A curse can feel like a choking vine growing up and around our beautiful Tree, threatening to invade our root system. This voice sends us negative messages, such as: "You don't deserve to be successful" or "Nobody takes you seriously." Someone in our young life could have spoken these words to us, but often we do not know exactly where the curse or negative message originated. In fact, it could very well come from the psychological "gene pool" of our tribe.

A "curse" is a psychological complex, a pattern of behavior that clusters around certain subjects such as power, sex, money, nurturing, success, intimacy, self-sufficiency, dependency and domination. If the Storyteller in us cannot help us come to terms with the curses, we get stuck developmentally, using up enormous resources on the lower part of our Tree. As a result, we never leave home and never develop beyond the roots – Stages 1, 2 and 3 on the initiation path.

The following is a meditation to meet the ancestors, in order to get a clearer picture of the blessings and curses that we have inherited from both our father's and mother's tribes.

Exercise 9: Meditation - Meeting the ancestors around the fire

Become aware of your breathing, relax and follow your breath as it moves in and out. Today we will be walking deep into the interior landscape, to visit the forest of the ancestors. Follow your breath as you are led deeper inside. . . As you walk on your journey, you see in the distance a great forest. You travel many miles to reach the edge of this forest. Eventually, you begin walking through this great forest and as you walk deeper and deeper into the trees, the forest becomes more and more ancient, more and more primeval. The sun is now beginning to set and the light in the forest is growing darker and darker.

As you look ahead, you notice a circular clearing in the trees where a sacred circle has been made especially for you. As you approach the sacred place, you notice that a crackling fire has been lit in the center of the circle. You step into the circle and come near to the fire where you feel its warmth and light dancing on your skin.

Off to your right, you hear a sound and see a figure stepping into the circle. As you look more closely, you see it is your father moving slowly towards the fire.

To your left, another figure steps into the circle. As she approaches, you see it is your mother who has come now into the sacred circle near the fire.

Your father reaches out his hands, takes your hands in his, and looks you in the eyes. Suddenly you notice that behind your father you can see his mother and father and his grandparents and great grandparents and, behind them, the entire clan. You can feel the energy of your father's ancestors around you. Where are your father's ancestors from? What land do they come from, what culture, what religious tradition? What kind of people are they? Get a flavor of your father's clan. . .

Your father tells you one of the blessings that you have inherited from his ancestors. He speaks this blessing to you now and makes some kind of ritual gesture to accompany the blessing... Your father looks at you once again, but this time with genuine sorrow in his eyes, for he now tells you about one of the curses that you have inherited from his ancestors. He tells you the curse and makes a ritual gesture to clarify what it means. . . Your father now moves aside and invites you into his clan, the great crowd of ancestors. You find yourself in the middle of your father's ancestors. They want to tell you something about the clan, what is it?. . . Now they give you a sacred object from the clan, what is it?. . . You come back out of the center of the clan and stand near the fire.

Your mother now reaches out, takes your hands, and looks into your eyes. Again you can see that behind your mother is her mother and father and her grandparents and great grandparents and, behind them, the entire clan. You can feel the energy of your mother's ancestors around you. Where are your mother's ancestors from? What land do they come from, what culture, what religious tradition? What kind of people are they? Get a flavor of your mother's clan. . .

Your mother tells you one of the blessings that you have inherited from her ancestors. She speaks this blessing to you now and makes some kind of ritual gesture to accompany the blessing. . . Your mother looks at you once again, but this time with genuine sorrow in her eyes, for she now tells you about one of the curses that you have inherited from her ancestors. She tells you the curse and makes a ritual gesture to clarify what it means. . . Your mother now moves aside and invites you into her clan. You find yourself in the middle of your mother's ancestors. They want to tell you something about the clan, what is it?. . . Now they give you a sacred object from the clan, what is it?. . . You move out of her clan and back into the great circle near the crackling fire.

You thank both your father and mother and bow respectfully to each clan. You are aware of the joys and sorrows, the triumphs and the defeats that all your ancestors have faced. Despite the curses they have endured and passed down to you, they have managed somehow to thrive and carry on the generations. Even though you may feel pain from your inheritance, find a way now to honor your ancestors before you leave.

It is time to go. Your ancestors depart and you take your leave of the sacred circle, knowing that you can return anytime. The light of the sun is rising now as you walk out of the ancient forest, through the trees. You walk a great distance and eventually find your way home to this place and this time…Become aware of your breathing and the weight of your body as it sits, and when you feel ready, open your eyes.

At the end of this meditation, write down what you saw, heard and received.

"The Demon in the Tree"

The following is an intriguing Jewish story about the nature of curses, where they originate and how to work creatively with them.

It happened in the City of Worms, that the rabbi's son was playing hide-and-seek with a friend, and he was looking for his friend in the hollow trunk of a tree. All at once he saw a finger emerge from the tree and – assuming it was his friend's finger – he took off his own ring as a jest and slipped it upon the finger, pronouncing the words of the wedding vow. Suddenly the finger was pulled back into the tree, and a moment later the face of a strange looking woman with long black hair emerged. Her smile was so evil that the young man jumped away, and then she disappeared back into the hollow trunk. At that the young man turned and ran away as fast as he could. Nor did he tell anyone what had happened.

Years passed and the young man was wed. The night the bride and groom went to his home together for the first time, the bride lingered outside, looking around. At that moment, the demoness emerged from the hollow tree and pulled back a branch that struck her in the face, killing her.

When the year of mourning was over, the young man was betrothed again, and the same thing happened again when he returned home with his new wife, on the very first night.

Now the man was becoming afraid that he was cursed. So too did many fathers refuse to consider him as a husband for any daughter, causing great anxiety to his parents. What was worse was that no one could explain what had happened to the brides, and a cloud of suspicion hung over him.

His third bride was the daughter of a very poor man, who had been unable to give a dowry. This girl had always worked very hard to help her family get by. She was modest and yet wise in the ways of the world. This girl too took a walk around the house to explore it, and the demoness in the hollow tree came out to kill her, as she had done to the others. But this girl saw the branch that the demoness had pulled back, and quickly bent down, avoiding the branch. So too did she see the demoness run away and followed her until she saw her slip back into the tree.

That night she told her groom what had happened, and he was horrified. He recalled at once the demon in the tree, whom he had long ago put out of his mind. He turned very pale, and in a solemn voice he recounted the strange incident. But why would this demon harm only his wives, and not him? The girl understood at once: "Because she considers herself your true bride. Did you not, after all, pronounce the words of the wedding vow?" And the poor groom grew faint with fear.

All that night they debated what to do. When the young man recovered from his panic, he grew angry. It had been a jest, after all! And he wanted to take revenge. He insisted that they must burn down the tree. But his bride talked him out of it. She said, "That tree is her home. And if you deprive her of it, she might seek to deprive you of yours." And he realized that she was right.

Then the girl said, "Let me try to come to terms with her. It is said that demons love jam above all things. Let me take a plate of jam and leave it by the hollow trunk as an offering of peace." And because he could think of nothing else except to move away and abandon his home, the young man agreed.

The next morning, the young bride placed the plate of jam by the hollow trunk. All that day she stayed away from the tree, and the next morning she came back to see what happened. There she found a gold coin on the plate, gleaming in the sun. She hurried in and showed it to her husband, who sighed with relief to know that they had appeased the demoness - at least for a while.

Every day after that, the young bride left a plate of jam by the tree, and the next day she found a gold coin. The young couple were grateful for the gold, but they still lived in fear of the demoness.

The time cam when the young bride found that she was with child. She knew all the tales about Lilith and how she liked to strangle children. Nor did she doubt that the demon in the tree was a daughter of Lilith. Therefore she felt that her unborn child was in danger.

So it was that the bride one day went to the tree and called for the demoness to come forth. At first there was silence, then at last the unearthly voice of the demoness was heard, demanding to know what she wanted. "All I want is to come to an understanding, for I know about the ring, and therefore I know that you feel that you are my husband's true wife." "Yes, that is right," hissed the demoness. "In that case," the girl continued, "let me be brief. I am willing to share him with you, if you will vow not to harm anyone of our family, including any child. If so, I will let him come to you one hour a day, at sunset."

At that moment the head of the demoness emerged from the tree, still looking exactly as she had when the young man was a child. She looked directly into the eyes of the bride and nodded. Then she sank back into the trunk.

For seven years after that, the man was a free man all but one hour of the day, when he was the slave of his demon wife. And all that time, the demoness did not bring any harm to anyone, and it even seemed that she protected them from danger. At the end of seven years the man came to the trunk and there on the plate used for the jam, he found his ring, the one he had placed on her finger. And he knew at once that the demoness had taken leave of them for good. [2]

Unconscious complicity in marrying the demon

In the story, we witness the origins of a curse. The young boy in the story is "innocently" playing around and has no conscious intention that the words of his vow have any real or lasting effect. However, as the story unfolds, it becomes clear that he has called forth a frightening figure in the form of the tree demon, a figure that is deadly serious about this vow. The story warns us of our own unconscious complicity in calling forth these inner characters and in making some kind of deal with them; marrying them, in fact.

It is so easy to make a vow as the young boy does in the story – without considering the consequences of our actions or the effects that the vow or curse will have upon us or upon future generations. There are many reasons for making a vow: *to get away from a horrible situation, to protect ourselves when threatened with harm or to avenge a violation.* Sometimes these vows are spoken with full awareness when we are adults, and other times they are formulated during infancy or childhood, making them less accessible to our consciousness. Many of our family curses originate with a distant ancestor; some originate with us. The following are examples of vows or negative statements that turn into curses:

Vows we make that turn into curses:
"I will never go hungry again."
"I will never be betrayed again."
"I will never trust again."
"I will never make myself vulnerable."
"I will never reveal the family secret."
"I will never be shamed again."
"I must be perfect and show no flaws."

Statements said to us that turn into curses:
"You will never amount to anything."
"You're going to end up a shriveled, old maid."
"You're a tramp."
"You'll never change."
"You will never live up to your father."
"You're lazy."
"You're crazy."
"You're too intense/emotional/sensitive..."

"You're stupid."

"You have to be perfect."

"Do it right or not at all."

"You have to fight for what you want in life."

"Don't air your dirty laundry in public."

"It's impossible to do the work you love and support yourself at the same time."

Exercise 10: Vows and curses

1. Referring to above lists, make a list of vows that you have made over the years – both in your childhood and in your adult life. Have you vowed to protect yourself, and at what cost? What led you to make this vow? Were you just "playing around" like the boy in the story, or did it arise out of a dire or painful situation? Can you connect these vows to anyone in your ancestral line? What were the circumstances?

2. Now make a list of the statements that were said to you that have turned into curses when you hear them replayed in your own mind. Go down the list and write down the name of the person who made these statements. In your best understanding, why did this person say these things to you? What circumstances led them to say this?

Demons in your family tree

Another kind of curse is a *family complex* that lingers in the tribal collective and affects various members of the tribe. A family complex can be shared between the women of the tribe, the mothers, the men, the warriors, the children, or any subgroup.

For example, the women of the tribe could inherit and share what is called an "Amazon" archetype, also known as an inflated Animus (overvalued masculine energy). The Amazon archetype creates relationship dynamics where the women can be dominating and controlling, especially with their men. This pattern can play itself out in several ways. One scenario is that a woman repeatedly attracts passive men, and as a result, she feels lonely and frustrated. In this case, a *tribal curse* could be that the women in this clan feel doomed to be *disappointed in love*. They may not recognize their own part in pushing away their men or in choosing men who will not be able to stand up to their overactive Animus. With this kind of inherited curse, the women can feel trapped in a horrible, negative spiral. The only way to tackle this curse is to learn to let go of control in relationships and make friends with the Animus who resides on the inner planes.

Another complex may be shared by the men of a tribe, such as the pattern of the distant and work-driven father. The men in this clan may get stuck in a pattern of workaholism and stress-related diseases. They may suffer from high blood pressure or have heart attacks at young ages. These men may find their wives and families leave them or their teenage children act out. A man in this tribe may feel doomed and *compulsively driven, a slave to his work and lonely in love*.

Where do these curses come from? Where do they originate?

If you trace back your family inheritance, you may find, for example, that the women in your tribe were forced to survive without their men, who were away at war. Perhaps the women felt abandoned for generations and, over time, had to be the strong, masculine presence in the family. This could create a family complex around the inflated Animus.

Perhaps your family immigrated to America during the Irish potato famine and your ancestors vowed never to be hungry again, no matter what. They may not have considered the emotional consequences of this vow in that, as it tumbles down the generations, it may take the form of emotional abandonment or obsessive workaholism.

Perhaps your ancestors fled the Holocaust and vowed never to grieve again. That vow may tumble down the generations in the form of an emotional chill, a silent aloofness, which becomes a haunting secret locked in the hearts of the children or grandchildren. The vow never to grieve again may transform into an ocean of sorrow that is never addressed, that surreptitiously expands into all areas of life, and that may ultimately manifest as depression or physical illness.

There are many stories of feuding clans in Scotland, Ireland, Israel, Bosnia and elsewhere around the globe. If we are born into one of these feuding tribes, we inherit this particular family complex and have to choose how we are going to deal with powerful feelings of revenge lurking in the depths of our tribal psyche. The question we must ask ourselves is: will we become conscious of the complex and try to neutralize the curse with understanding and compassion? Or will we submit to the complex and create situations in which we repeat the feud/revenge cycle? We need to take seriously the actions of our foremothers and forefathers, because we are in a direct line, psychologically, to inherit these emotional patterns.

Perhaps you yourself have made some kind of a vow, for example, "I will never marry a military man because my father was a tyrannical officer" or "I will be wealthy and not suffer as my father did." Either kind of vow can bind us in a marriage that is not easily broken. When we make a vow, we devote tremendous amounts of energy to this marriage, this strange partnership. Often, the more unconscious the vow, the more energy it takes to feed the partnership.

Years pass

What is so fascinating about family curses, as the story informs us, is that time can pass without any manifestation or visible consequences of the unconscious marriage. Generations can go by before someone challenges the family complex, someone who has the inner resources to do so. Perhaps it is your own vow that is spoken early on and goes underground. For example, "I will never again be put in a vulnerable position and allow myself to be betrayed." This vow could have been made as an infant, but it pops up later in life when you marry or when you have your first intimate relationship.

It is the nature of inherited complexes to lie dormant in the unconscious until they are awakened into life and emerge into a living situation, enacted with real people. In the case of the story, the demon pops up on the man's wedding day. He has completely forgotten about the frightening woman in the tree and the vow that bound them to each other. We need to pay attention and think about when our family demons arrive on the scene.

The bride is killed

On the night of their wedding, the first bride of the Rabbi's son lingered by herself outside the house. In that short time, the demoness emerged from the hollow tree and pulled back a branch that struck the bride and killed her.

When a psychological complex remains dormant, unacknowledged and unprocessed, it can become deadly to the psyche. It has the power to kill off the new bride, who represents promises of new life, love and happiness. If, for instance, we vowed to never be betrayed again, this particular demon in the tree may sabotage our intimate relationships, creating distance rather than the closeness we need. If our demon remains unacknowledged, it will find a way to strike the new bride with a branch, killing off our possibilities for intimacy. Our vow never to be betrayed begins as a worthy protection, but it ultimately keeps us from being vulnerable and open.

The story of the Rabbi's son speaks to us of the death of the bride and the subsequent mourning period following the appearance of the demon. It is similar with us as we go into mourning when these ancestral or self-generated complexes kill off new potentials, keeping us stuck and unable to move on with life.

The second bride dies

If we remain asleep and unaware of the demons in our tree and the particular curses they bring, we will continue to re-experience their tragic consequences until we break the cycle. The second bride will die – as will the third and fourth – until the pattern is broken. The person who is besieged with an unprocessed curse is tragically caught in a cycle of grief, sorrow and anguish. The new life that the bride represents is continually cut short and thwarted. This can make us feel doomed, trapped, victimized and defeated by "life." Like the young man in the story, we can find ourselves in continual mourning, without explanation of the tragic events that keep "happening" to us.

The curse is revealed

To add insult to injury, not only is the Rabbi's son suffering his own personal losses, but he is also beginning to be exiled from his community because they recognize that something is wrong. A cloud of suspicion hangs over his head. He is losing his reputation and his status in the village.

When a curse or an unconscious complex is at work in our life, it usually affects our outer life in a noticeable way. This is designed to get our attention and to reveal the curse so that we can do something about it. The more public it becomes, the more pressure there is to tackle the problem.

For example, a man may suffer from the curse of an internal voice that says, "You'll never amount to anything!" Perhaps the curse manifests in the man's work life as he is mysteriously "let go" or made redundant in job after job. His friends wonder what is going on, since the man seems like a really decent guy and he always has plausible excuses for his job losses. However, the friends never know his secret self-loathing and how this contributes to the loss of his jobs. As time goes on, he becomes more and more isolated from the community as his friends begin to suspect that he is sabotaging himself and seems to have a kind of cursed life.

The third bride

So how do we break the curse? How do we access the inner resources to confront the demon in the tree? In the story, it is the third bride who comes to the rescue. Who is this third bride within the psyche and what are her characteristics?

According to the story, the third bride comes from a poor family and so has to work hard to get to where she is. She is wise in the ways of the world and she is able to see the truth about the demon. She represents a part of the psyche that is *hardworking, dedicated, wise and true*.

The first thing that this savvy young bride does is inspect the house – she takes a look around the psyche to check it out. Metaphorically, this third bride represents the part of us that is unafraid, and willing to explore the problem around the house of the psyche.

As the story continues, when the demon – the complex – is about to kill the third bride, she quickly bends down, dodging the deadly branch and avoiding the direct blow of the curse. But it does not end there, because the third bride decides to follow the demon back to her home in the hollow tree trunk, in order to get to the bottom of this threat. She models how we need to follow the curse back to its source.

The third bride uncovers the mystery of the ancestral curse, showing us when we made the vow and why. She helps us figure out what toll the vow has taken on the emotional development of our clan and ourselves. She helps ferret out the source of our need to control or our need to keep people at a distance. Like the third bride, we need to be brave and curious, to search for what is true, and to seek out the origins of the curses that come from the root system of our Tree of Life.

Reacting to the curse

When the Rabbi's son is confronted with the truth and origin of the curse, his first response is to grow pale with fear. He remembers with dread how he slipped the ring onto the finger of the strange and frightening woman. His next response, however, is anger.

It is much the same with us. When we face the truth of the family curse, or our own unconscious vow, we often grow angry and want to lash out. We may want to destroy the ancestor who made the vow in the past or destroy the demon who is taunting us in the present. The wise third bride, however, understands with compassion why the demon is claiming her territory in the psyche. The third bride understands how and why we have given the tree demon a home by unconsciously inviting it into our emotional landscape.

If we have vowed never to be caught in a vulnerable position, in order to avoid possible betrayal, we have called this tree demoness to be our protector, to keep us from the wounds of betrayal. In this way, the demon serves her purpose well and has taken seriously the vow to be our "true bride." She is killing off the other brides because they are potential betrayers. This may not make *rational* sense, but it makes perfect *emotional* sense to the part of us that has been deeply wounded by betrayal.

If our vow was never to be hungry again and we have called upon the "demon" of success in the world, this demon may have served us well if we have generated wealth and have accomplished much in the world. But our demon cannot let us rest, because she knows that we might collapse or become depressed – and she will not let that happen. Therefore, our workaholism makes perfect emotional sense to our demon, but we may feel angry or cheated out of relationships and fun.

If our ancestors vowed to never grieve or pass down to their children the dread of war or persecution, they may have called upon the demon to close the floodgates of grief and loss, to let the demon do the work that has helped the lineage survive and carry on. Yet as descendants, we may carry oceans of unresolved grief in our bodies. We may also feel rage and wish to release this energy, reversing the curse and opening the floodgates.

Appeasing the demon, finding the jam

The third bride knows that a little jam, something delectable and sweet, will appease the tree demon. She knows intuitively that an offering needs to be made. This means we must find within ourselves some sweet compassion, some understanding of the curse and of the person or people who originally made the vows.

We can offer the jam by lighting a candle to our ancestors and saying a prayer. We can do a ritual with symbolic objects, like enacting a cutting of the ties that bind us to the vow. We can be creative with our offering of jam, finding just the right flavor to appease our particular tree demon. Appeasing the demon may also mean taking some action to change our ways, asking for forgiveness or risking intimacy. As we offer sweet jam to the unconscious complex, it will respond within the psyche by returning some gold coins: new life, new treasures, and new attitudes emerging.

Begin a creative dialogue with the wounded part

As the story continues, the third bride discovers that she is with child. She is now at an important crossroad in terms of her relationship with the demon. She is aware that the demon is still present, although appeased. She is also sensitive to the fact that the demon has been around in the psyche for a long time, many generations perhaps. She understands that the demon feels entitled to its place in the psyche and feels duty-bound to uphold the vow she has taken so seriously.

The third bride approaches the demon with cautious respect, "All I want is to come to an understanding, for I know about the ring, and therefore I know you feel that you are my husband's true wife." Then the third bride does an interesting thing – she makes a bargain with the demon. It is like striking a bargain with that character in our psyche who is sucking our energy, sabotaging our relationships, and has the power to kill off the new bride, new growth within the psyche. The third bride offers, "I am willing to share him with you, if you will vow not to harm anyone in our family, including any child. If so, I will let him come to you one hour a day, at sunset."

What an interesting bargain – and one that was agreeable to the tree demon - committing an hour of her husband's time at sunset every day. Our offering will be unique to us and to our vow. After finding the appropriate offering, we need to strike a realistic bargain with the part of us that is carrying the curse. Most importantly, we need to follow through and make the effort to get to know our demon in the tree. In order to reverse the curse, we must be willing to spend the "one hour a day at sunset" sitting with the curse. This means setting aside time to talk sweetly to our wounded parts.

The reference to sunset is interesting because it is the time when the sun goes down and our solar consciousness is waning. The moon is rising and darkness is growing, a time when our rational mind quiets and the powers of intuition become prominent. The sunset time allows us to go deep inside to meet the curse face-to-face in the darkness of the unconscious. During this time, we move into the world where the tree demon lives, getting to know the inner landscape and the ways of the unconscious. During the sunset time we can become more familiar with our ancestral root system – and do what it takes to eventually break free of the curse altogether.

Accepting the length of the healing time

This process is not accomplished overnight. Like the young man in the story, it may feel like we are slaves to our demon wife or demon husband for a long time. Sometimes it is hard to believe that we will ever be free of our family curse. However, the story also tells us the good news, which is the eventual release of the curse after a seven-year period.

In Kabbalah, "seven" represents the number of fullness and ending, the completion of initiation. This is when we look down at the jam plate, the offering plate, to find that the ring has been returned. After we have served our time, worked on the complex, made our offerings and diligently waited out the "seven years," we can experience the release of the curse and the lifting of the destructive behavior pattern.

The lesson to learn here is that we are not in control of the "seven-year" period. In order to appease the demon in our tree, we must accept the length of time that it takes to heal the wound. No matter how hard we work on one of our curses, we must surrender to the timing of the unconscious.

Exercise 11: Breaking the curse

1. Spend some time contemplating your genogram and the particular **"demons" in your family tree**. Pick out the demons in the family tree that you yourself participate in.

2. **What "bride" is killed by your demon** - what new life is being thwarted by your curse? How long is the mourning period after each bride has died? How long does it take you to recover after a loss or blow from your curse?

3. **When does your demon come to life?** When does this curse manifest itself and under what circumstances? Does your demon pop up when you start a new relationship or when you are under stress or in a transition period?

4. After assessing the problem and naming the demon, **what jam offering will appease your demon?** What is something delectable and sweet that will be the peace offering and appeal to your demon's emotional position? What can you say to your demon that makes it understand that you recognize the dilemma and the demon's right to its position? Can you strike a realistic bargain with the part of you that is carrying the curse? Are you willing to spend the "one hour a day at sunset" sitting with the curse, setting aside time to be with yourself and to talk sweetly to your wounded parts? Be creative and devise a ritual to break the curse and heal the wound.

Conclusion – Initiation 3: Connect with Community

As we complete the third initiation, we have come to terms with our ancestral inheritance. We have transformed the toxic, damaged roots, and dealt with the curses that have tumbled down the generations, distorting and blocking the precious energy that we need for further psychological and spiritual development. We have come to appreciate the color, variety and vitality that spices up our family line and makes it the unique expression of community that it is.

Now that we have connected in a healthy way to our tribe, we have completed initiation in the roots, and therefore have the inner resources to cross the threshold to the fourth initiation, where we leave the tribe and venture out into the wilderness. Now we are ready to establish our own identity separate from the tribe.

The root system of our Tree is a complex, interwoven network, involving thousands of people from both the past and present. Out of this complex root system springs a single trunk, which is our individual identity that draws upon the roots for nourishment, but becomes something totally new and different from every other tree in the forest. In the next initiation, we will come to discover the nature of our trunk and the unique, individual expression that has sprung from the roots of our Tree of Life.

Part II - TRUNK
Stages 4 and 5

In Part I, we learned to effectively root our Tree of Life so that our instinctual body feels grounded and emotionally stable. The initiation journey began with anchoring the root system for obvious reasons: to prepare us with a sense of grounding, a healthy ego, a place of belonging, confidence and self-esteem. A healthy root system provides a strong foundation that will sustain the weight of our trunk and branches.

Part II focuses on building the trunk of our Tree of Life. In order to establish a strong and healthy trunk, we need to shift our center of consciousness from a communal to an individual focus of life. During **Initiations 4 and 5** we will leave the underground roots and push our way to the surface, discovering who we are away from the various family, racial, and gender roles prescribed by the group. Here we begin the journey of establishing a separate and individual identity, experiencing the joys and frustrations of individuation.

When we begin to awaken at Stage 4, we contact a powerful archetypal urge to rise up out of the underground roots and break free from the gravity of group conformity. Here we awaken to our true identity and the possibility, in Stage 5, of making an individual contribution to life. If we take the steps to channel the powerful energies necessary to separate and establish our identity, then we can shift our center of consciousness to the soul, which is concerned with individual growth and truth. The soul directs and empowers us to commit to an inner path of development and frees us to creatively express our own ideas.

In order to separate from our inherited family patterns and ego patterns that keep us bound to the roots of the Tree, we must awaken out of our village slumber and confront our resistances to evolving and developing. This means giving up our egocentricity and the childlike dependencies that keep us from emotional maturity. It means walking the path of honesty, facing the truth about ourselves, and learning to rely on our own inner resources with powers of self-observation. As we develop our trunk, we must call up the wild and adventurous spirit inside us that can sustain the pain of separation and the explosion of unconscious complexes that erupt when we leave the containment of the roots.

After completing **Initiations 4 and 5**, our trunk will be healthy and thriving and we can expect to feel emotionally separate from group expectations and free to follow the beat of our own heart. We will be unafraid of conflict and confrontation and will have the courage to stand up for our truth. We will be aware of our personal power and be able to internalize our own authority, accepting self-responsibility and living with integrity. These are the qualities of a strong and centered trunk.

Chapter 4

Into the Wilderness
Robe 4

Initiation 4 - IDENTITY

In Chapter 4 we begin a new phase of growing our Tree of Life by pushing up from the underground root system and establishing a trunk. Through the story of John the Baptist, we will be guided in the discovery of our own identity away from family and tribe. When the fourth initiation is complete, we can emotionally separate from group expectations and roles, can manage conflict and confrontation, and withstand disapproval from others. We can sustain solitude, take risks and explore new territory.

To accomplish this, we must call forth the **Adventurer** archetype, our wild spirit who helps us step out of the village boundary and search for our true identity. When we are alone in the wilderness, the Adventurer taps into inner resources we never knew were there. The Adventurer is unafraid of whatever opposition hinders our growth or stops us from separating from the tribe. The Adventurer transforms negative and destructive drives that keep us scattered, and focuses our energy towards an individual goal.

Qualities if initiated:	Problems if initiation is not complete:
Adventurous	Unadventurous
Strong individual identity	Lacks personal opinions
Able to emotionally separate	Unable to emotionally separate
Awake, alive, invigorated	Unable to be alone
Unafraid of conflict and confrontation	Avoids conflict and confrontation
Openhearted	Hardened heart
Assertive	Dominating, willful without care for others
Refrains from acting out desires impulsively	Impulsively acts out desires
Withstands disapproval and rejection	Unable to take risks
Self-motivated	Passive, lacking direction

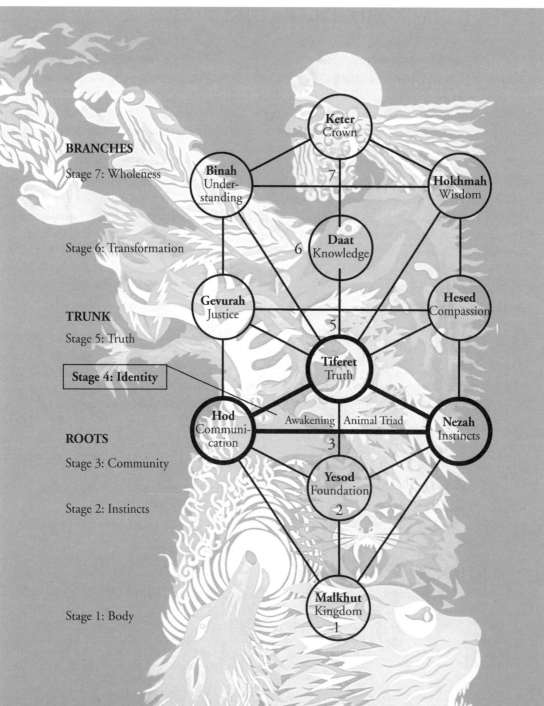

BRANCHES

Stage 7: Wholeness

Stage 6: Transformation

TRUNK

Stage 5: Truth

Stage 4: Identity

ROOTS

Stage 3: Community

Stage 2: Instincts

Stage 1: Body

Keter
Crown

7

Binah
Under-
standing

Hokhmah
Wisdom

6

Daat
Knowledge

Gevurah
Justice

5

Hesed
Compassion

Tiferet
Truth

Hod
Communi-
cation

Awakening Animal Triad

Nezah
Instincts

3

Yesod
Foundation

2

Malkhut
Kingdom

1

Diagram 15: Stage 4
The fourth initiation challenges us to move successfully from the roots to the trunk of the tree.
This means shifting from tribal consciousness to a more individual consciousness found in the trunk.
In Stage 4 we focus on stages of separation and establishing an individual identity.

Chapter 4 - Establish Identity

Exercise 1: Meditation - Growing the trunk of the Tree

Imagine back to the roots of your Tree of Life. Imagine yourself underground, in the darkness, amidst the rich earth surrounding the root system of your Tree. You feel contained in the warm, comforting earth, resting. Breathe deeply and allow yourself to be held by the roots of your great Tree. Rest in the darkness.

Now it is time to push your way to the surface of the ground to grow a trunk. Push your way through the thick and heavy earth. You are fighting gravity. It takes a great effort to push and push your way up and up until you finally penetrate through the surface and come out into the air and the light of the day. Begin to grow a trunk up through the air, staying connected to the roots.

As you grow the beginning of a substantial trunk, pull your full attention up into the trunk. How does it feel to be in the strong wood of your trunk? Look around you. You are now out in the air and sunlight. How does it to feel to be above the earth now? How is it different from being in the roots? What do you notice?

Bring your attention back now to ordinary consciousness. Become aware of yourself in your own human body and take some deep breaths. When you feel ready, open your eyes.

Take some time to write down what you found to be the most significant difference between the roots and the trunk of your Tree of life. For example, in the roots we often feel protected and contained. Once we push out of the ground and grow a trunk, we can feel unprotected and alone but also excited at our new freedom and new perspective.

The fourth Initiation

The fourth initiation challenges us to move successfully from *tribal* consciousness to a more *individual* consciousness, focusing on issues of *separation* and establishing an *individual identity* (see diagram 15). There is a powerful story from the Christian scriptures about John the Baptist that gives us specific and practical instructions about how to establish our own identity and build the trunk of our Tree of Life. The story of John the Baptist is found in all four Gospels, and the following version of the story is my own synthesis of John's life and work.

Open your heart and your inner ears and eyes and journey now with John the Baptist, this adventurous spirit who knows how to transform and harness your wild, untamed animal drives into the powerful, radiant soul that you are.

The story of John the Baptist

And so it was, 2000 years ago, that there lived a priest named Zachariah and his wife Elizabeth. Zachariah was a righteous man of the priestly cast, a descendant of Aaron. His wife Elizabeth was also a righteous woman and they followed the law in a humble way and were quite faithful. Elizabeth had always desired children but sadly, she was barren.

One day it was Zachariah's turn to go into the sanctuary to perform his priestly duties, keeping the incense burning, the candles lit and making sacrifices for the people. As he entered the sanctuary, it was suddenly filled with light and an angel visited him. The angel told him that he and Elizabeth would bear a child, even though they were well past childbearing years. The angel said, "Don't be afraid, your prayer has been heard. You will bear a son and will name him John. He will bring you much joy and gladness and many will be filled with joy at his birth. He is going to be great in the sight of God."

More prophecies were made about this remarkable soul who was coming to birth. One prophecy said that John was to be celibate and that he was never to drink wine or strong drink. It was said that even before his birth, he would be filled with the Holy Spirit. It was also foretold by the angel that John was going to turn the hearts of many of the people of Israel with the power of Elijah, who was a prophet with great powers. John will go before the people and will turn the hearts of parents toward their children. He will bring those who have been turning away from God back to wisdom and righteous living. He will make ready the people so that they can make straight the way of the Lord.

And so it was that John was to be a man of destiny. He was going to do something extraordinary. Zachariah the father did not quite believe what was being said, but the angel declared, " I am Gabriel, and you had best believe it, for I have been sent to you to bring you this good news." But Zachariah still did not believe and so he was immediately struck dumb. When Zachariah emerged from the sanctuary, the people thought he must have seen a vision. But he could not speak and so was unable to tell them what had happened.

Soon afterwards, Elizabeth conceived and for five months John grew in her womb. In the sixth month, the Archangel Gabriel once again appeared, but this time to Elizabeth's cousin, Mary. When Gabriel appeared to Mary, he told her that she was going to bear a remarkable child who would be the Christ. Mary put all of this away in her heart. Soon after Mary became pregnant, she came to visit her cousin Elizabeth, to stay with her for some time. As soon as Mary came into the room to greet Elizabeth, John leapt in Elizabeth's womb, for he recognized that Jesus, his cousin, was in his presence. From the very beginning, there was a deep recognition between them.

When it was time for John to be born, the whole community gathered. When all the neighbors heard that Elizabeth was to give birth they were amazed, because Elizabeth was getting on in years. And so the baby was born, and when he was eight days old, it was time for him to be circumcised. At the celebration everyone asked, "What is to be his name? Zachariah?" But Elizabeth said, "His name is John." There was much grumbling and disapproval. They said, "You can't name him John; no one in your family is named John. Why would you want to name him something different?" And they turned to Zachariah who still could not speak. The people asked him "What is to be his name?" So Zachariah wrote on a tablet, "His name is John" and the community began to grumble again. They did not understand why this son should be so special and have a name, a destiny so different from the clan. As Zachariah was writing on the tablet, he regained his ability to speak.

Then Zachariah opened his mouth and proclaimed a wonderful prophecy about his son. He thanked God and the ancestors for bringing such a son into their midst. He prophesied that his son John would deliver the people from the hands of the enemies and that he would bring holiness and righteousness. John would prepare the way and make straight the way. He would bring knowledge of salvation to the people and he would show the way for forgiveness of sins. He would give light to those who sit in darkness and in the shadows and guide our feet into the way of peace.

And so it was that John grew and matured and eventually left the village to venture out in the wilderness. It was in the wilderness that John grew strong and learned the way of surviving in the extreme environment. In the wilderness, he wore only a camel hair loincloth tied with a leather belt. He ate locusts and wild honey. It is under these conditions that John pares down to the bare minimum of life in order to become what he was prophesied to become: a bringer of light to the darkness, turning the hearts of many towards God.

After years of training in the wilderness, it was time for John to begin his teaching, preaching and baptizing. He came out of the wilderness and down to Jordan River, where he began baptizing people in the waters, urging them to repent for the forgiveness of sins. "Repent!" He would shout. "For the Kingdom of Heaven is at hand." Flocks of people began to come to the Jordan. Some asked, "What should we be concerned about besides forgiveness of sins?" John answered, "Share your wealth. Do not veer from your path of truth."

John knew very well that his job was to lead the people to the Jordan, to a place where they could cleanse themselves and prepare for the coming of the "Christ," which means "Anointed One." And John would tell the people, "I baptize you with water, but the one who is coming after me will baptize with the Spirit and with Fire. He will clear the threshing floor and will gather the wheat, and the chaff will be gathered and burned in a fire that will never go out." So John prepared the people to receive the spirit and the divine fire, which would soon come.

John himself was a fiery character and was known to have confrontations with the religious establishment. From time to time when he was baptizing and the people were flocking to him to receive the forgiveness of sins, the established priesthood and the lawmakers would come to the Jordan River to taunt and test him. John however, would have none of it. He would shout back at them saying "You brood of vipers, who warned you to fly from the retribution that is coming? But if you are repentant, produce the appropriate fruits, and do not think you are privileged just because you are sons of Abraham. For I tell you, God can raise these stones to become children of Abraham. Even now the ax is laid to the roots of the trees, so that any tree which fails to produce good fruit will be cut down and thrown in the fire." And so it was that John exposed the complacency of the establishment. Worthiness no longer rests on your lineage or ancestry. Worthiness depends on the good that you do. Any tree that is not producing good fruit is going to be cut down and thrown into the fire.

And so John carried on baptizing and crying out in the wilderness, "Prepare the way for the Lord, make straight his path! I am the witness to the Christ who comes after me." Again this provoked the priests and lawmakers who, in their frustration, began testing John's true identity. "Well, who are you? Are you Elijah, are you the Christ, are you the anointed one?" John answered, "No, I am none of these things. If Christ was right here in your midst you wouldn't even be able to recognize him."

One particular day as John was baptizing in the Jordan, he saw his cousin Jesus coming towards him. John then recognized that this was the one he had been waiting for - this was the Christ. Jesus waded into the water and asked John to baptize him. John looked at Jesus and was astonished, "I can't baptize you, I know who you are, you should baptize me." But Jesus insisted and eventually John agreed. And so it was that John baptized Jesus, dunking him into the waters of the Jordan. And when Jesus came up from the water, suddenly the heavens opened up and the spirit descended like a dove and came down upon Jesus. And then a voice spoke from heaven, "This is my son, the Beloved; my favor rests upon him." [1]

* Step 1: Leave the village *
Step 2: Survive the wilderness
Step 3: Transmute the power drives
Step 4: Open the heart

Why do we leave the village?

What kind of life would John have led if he had followed the clan's expectations and never ventured into the wild, away from the community? Could he have become the man he was destined to be? What would it be like to never leave the tribe, to never venture beyond the boundary of the village?

It is hard to imagine our own life lived completely within the root system of our Tree, to never actively develop the trunk of our Tree and to live totally within the expectations of the group. When our identity is defined solely within the group norms and expectations, it is difficult to even think our own thoughts or feel our own feelings, especially when the group grumbles disapproval as they did at John's circumcision.

When we are young, it is virtually impossible to leave the village because we need the community to hold us during important developmental stages. But there comes a time when it is appropriate to leave the village, to separate emotionally, to think our own thoughts and find our own voice.

The story of John the Baptist is an archetypal story for all of us. He represents an inner figure within us who carries the mystery of our **deeper identity**, helping us to forge a trunk out of the rich cultural inheritance of our roots. From the beginning of the story, we learn that John shoots from a priestly stock, reminding us that our true identity stretches farther than we usually imagine.

What is our true identity? From the story of John the Baptist, we learn that – in addition to our family identity – there lies another hidden identity that marks us from birth. We have a divine origin, a destiny that is special and unique. In the story, John's father Zachariah and his mother Elizabeth are connected to the sacred aspects of life and carry their divine lineage with consciousness and vigor. They prepare a place for John to inherit his divine lineage and they hold steadfast to John's true identity. "His name is John," they declare, "and he will be different from your expectations."

Finding and securing our individual identity requires leaving the village and the comfort and safety that it provides. This is no easy task and we need help. It is crucial to have some internal equivalent of Elizabeth and Zachariah who can encourage the search for our true identity.

From the very beginning of John's life, it is clear that he is not destined to take his father's name. Normally, it would be customary to pass down the father's name as a sign of respect. Taking on our father's name can also be seen as a metaphor for taking on group identity and complying with group norms. But rather than naming him Zachariah, as the community expects, the parents follow the lead of the Archangel Gabriel, who is the divine messenger encouraging the growth and development of his soul beyond the family and clan. With a new name, John is free to follow his own destiny and is not required to remain only within his ancestral inheritance. John represents that part of us which is destined to move out of tribal law and begin living under a different set of laws: the laws of individual fate.

Living as an individual apart from the tribe, requires us to embrace a paradox: *the paradox of living with more freedom through increased responsibility*. It requires maturity and individual responsibility to establish our own identity and to live with honesty, integrity and eventually, our own voice of authority. Our inner John the Baptist will lead us in this direction.

Besides discovering our deeper identity, another reason to leave the village is to **discover our own inner resources**. For some, it is imperative to cultivate inner resources because the resources we received from the village root system were insufficient. Others of us have gathered many resources from the roots of our Tree, but now it is time to rely on ourselves. Discovering independence from the group is a crucial developmental stage. There comes a time when we must honor the mystery of our deeper identity, and begin developing the trunk and following the beat of our own heart.

While living in the root system, we identify ourselves with certain prescribed roles - husband, mother, father, wife, daughter, teacher, grandmother, breadwinner and so on. While we are within the tribe, our imagination stops at the village boundary and we rarely think of who we might be underneath these roles. In the story, the community could only imagine John's identity being linked with his family and could not understand why in the world his parents would want to name him "John."

Here in the fourth initiation we are asked by life to find a clear, differentiated identity and to answer the question "who am I and what am I supposed to be doing with my life?" This requires us to clarify, sharpen and refine our individual identity. We must separate from our village attachments and expectations and experience freedom from this tribal pull. In Kabbalah, Stage 4 is called the stage of **awakening** because here we awaken our true self out of its village slumber, walk to the edge of the village and prepare to follow an altogether different path, one that leads towards our individuation.

Remember that in the third initiation we spoke of the need for initiated elders in the community who understand the process of individuation and know when certain members are ready to leave. These elders ensure that the boundary around the village is permeable enough to let people leave when their time arrives. The ease with which we leave the village depends on the attitudes held by the elders of our particular clan. If the elders understand that this is an archetypal movement away from the tribe in order to individuate, then they will allow members to leave. This is where our inner Elizabeth and Zachariah can watch out for us and encourage us to cross the threshold and follow our own path.

Exercise 2: Meditation - Leaving the village

The following is a meditation on leaving the village, to help you imagine what it feels like to have a sense of healthy emotional separation.

Imagine yourself in your home in your own village, in comfortable surroundings where everything is familiar. What kind of home are you in? What does your village look like? What kind of landscape are you in?

Today is a special day as you prepare to go on a journey by yourself to explore what is beyond the boundary of your village. You walk out of your home and wander through your village making your way to the outskirts of the village. On the way, you see all the people that you are connected with on a daily basis. You see your children, parents, friends and co-workers. Notice the roles you play with each person. What are their expectations of you? As you walk out of the center of the village, do people notice you are leaving? Do they say good-bye? Perhaps some in the village do not notice your departure. Others may be devastated.

You can now see the boundary of the village. Walk to the very edge of your familiar territory. At the edge of that boundary, you can see a narrow path that leads off into the far distance. This path is marked out especially for you. At the threshold of the path you see on the ground a bundle of clothing for your solo journey. If you choose you may take off your everyday, tribal clothes and put on this new set of clothes. These clothes have been set aside for you in particular as you cross over the boundary of the village and begin to move out on your own. What do your new clothes look like?

Step over the threshold and begin walking on the path. As you walk along, breathe deeply and enjoy the solitude. You are on your own. You are moving further and further away from the village. What landscape are you now walking in?

With each step, let go of the roles that you play in your everyday life. Let go of your role as mother, wife, girlfriend, and daughter. Let go of your role as father, husband, boyfriend, and son. Release your obligations and the roles that you play for everybody else. How does it feel? You may want to mark this in some way with a gesture or sound as you walk along. Who are you? Who are you really without any village identifications? Walk along for as long as you wish to refresh yourself and cleanse yourself of village clutter and expectations. You can return to your village any time or continue exploring along the path. If you choose to return to the village, notice how you feel after a refreshing walk in solitude.

How do we leave the village?

We have identified reasons why it is important to leave the village. Now we will look at how the leaving is accomplished.

Leaving the village is not age specific. Some people need to emotionally separate at age 18, others at 35, and still others at 65 years of age. There are basically two ways to leave the village: **voluntarily and involuntarily**. Either way, leaving the village is typically a turbulent affair.

John the Baptist shows us how to leave the village voluntarily. John represents the archetype within us who calls forth our wild, adventurous spirit, infusing us with the courage to explore beyond the boundary of the village. The Adventurer within feels an inner dissatisfaction and restlessness that propels our consciousness to the outskirts of the village and questions the various identities we have been given by our family, education, clan, religion, nation and race. The Adventurer manifests in voices such as: "This just isn't doing it for me anymore, I need a wider view of life. I want a fresh new perspective."

Voluntary leaving is propelled by an inner calling, by a voice that causes us to question our real identity away from the tribe. Some people feel a need to expand their horizons. They want to travel. They want to see, hear and experience things outside their own family and culture. Some people feel quite cramped by the tribe and need to break free. Others have not received the nurturing they need within the village and are painfully aware of their need to seek out nurturing experiences. Finally, we voluntarily leave because we feel ready inside to grow and develop.

On the other hand, many people do not want to leave the safety and containment of the village. These people have never considered developing beyond the tribe because of their family circumstances or their inner anxiety and fear. For them, voluntary leaving is out of the question, even though remaining in the tribe may take a great toll on their resources and limit their freedom. Inevitably, the archetypal urge to push up from the underground roots and sprout a trunk will surface, and those who cling to the roots are in for a difficult time.

Involuntary leaving can be quite traumatic because if we are consciously resisting the flow of emotional and spiritual development, the unconscious will usually set up a crisis to kick-start the fourth initiation and push us out of the village. Here is a scenario:

A young and lively minister of a popular church is deeply questioning his faith and trying to expand his knowledge of other spiritual traditions. He feels the need to keep it secret because this kind of exploration is not acceptable in his religious community. As time goes on, he feels a deepening conflict between the job that he loves and the deeper needs of his true self. He is also frustrated with the way things are handled within the church, the authority structure and the dysfunctional behavior that is part of any institution. The problem is that he never really allows himself to feel his frustration and anger because his particular church tribe says that it is wrong to be angry.

A situation begins to brew with his elders, those who oversee his job. He is increasingly irritable but not fully conscious of the source of his frustration. One particular elder becomes increasingly upset with him and openly questions his character, potentially damaging his reputation. Is the elder jealous of the lively minister's popularity and reputation? Or is he somehow picking up the minister's unconscious anger at the church? What is really going on in terms of the minister's relationship to his tribe?

Upon further questioning, it becomes clear to me that he is harboring anger at the church, which he is unable to process because, in his worldview, it is wrong and bad to have angry feelings. This minister is in a difficult position and seems to be setting himself up to be thrown out of his tribe involuntarily.

Often our aggressive impulses to break away and establish our own identity do not surface to the conscious mind and therefore remain unprocessed. Then our unconscious anger pops up in someone else and we precipitate an involuntary leaving. In this case, the minister's best option may be to take a good look at his anger at the church and see it in terms of another, more profound need to emotionally separate and establish his own identity. In this way, he could stay true to his inner yearnings to explore and expand his identity and still remain in his job if that felt congruent.

Sometimes people are propelled out of their tribe by becoming truants and outsiders. These are people who no longer fit within the limitations of the tribe. They do not want to follow the rules, but they do not know how to leave. They cannot find any space to breathe or be themselves, but they do not know where to go. So they remain within the boundaries of the village forcing the elders of the tribe to say, "Look, you no longer fit here and it's time for you to go."

Other people are content to stay within the village but are forced out unwillingly, as if life takes a crowbar and shoots them out of their stuck place. This can happen through life circumstances. They may lose their job. Or maybe a close loved one dies, forcing them to begin to think in new ways. Maybe a betrayal happens within their religious community and they are forced to rethink the spiritual and religious beliefs that they were given as a child.

It is a common occurrence for an individual within a group or community to test the tribal authority. Typically this happens in adolescence, but it can also happen at any age in relation to village rules and expectations. This is the voice that says, "No, I have a better idea. These tribal laws aren't expansive enough to encompass who I am and who I'm growing to be." When we awaken out of our village slumber, we are beginning to internalize our own authority. To do this effectively, we must confront the authority, test the authority, and then eventually internalize our own authority. In many groups, this kind of questioning will get you thrown out of the village.

Voices of opposition

We have looked at why we leave the village – to discover our deeper identity. We have looked at how we leave – either voluntarily or involuntarily. Now we will look at the **voices of opposition** that we must confront when we do leave. When we actually muster up the courage to emotionally separate and take a few steps outside the group, we are inevitably going to run into oppositional voices.

From the very beginning of John's life, there were oppositional voices that rose from Zachariah and Elizabeth's community. When they all gathered on the eighth day to circumcise the child and to name him, the community assumed that he would be named after his father. When Elizabeth declared that he was to be called John, the group was in a state of shock and disbelief, "But none of your relatives have this name." They began asking Zachariah what name he wanted to give him. Zachariah asked for a writing tablet and wrote, "His name is John." And all of them were amazed. Immediately, Zachariah's mouth was opened and his tongue freed and he began to speak, praising God. Fear came over the neighbors and all these things were talked about throughout all the hill country of Judea. All who heard them pondered them and asked, "What then will this child become, for indeed the hand of the Lord is with him?"

The entire community was following group law and expecting John to abide by the village rules. They had a stake in John being part of the clan, but his parents said "No, he's not going to be part of our clan, not in the way you expect." The oppositional voices began, the neighbors grumbled. They did not understand what it meant to live beyond the clan. This upset them terribly, "What? You're not going to follow the tribal mind?" The answer was "No, he's destined to be something different."

It is important when we do begin to leave home emotionally that we identify the voices of opposition that confront us when we move away from the village. We must identify the voices that prevent us from separating and from having our own thoughts and feelings. These voices come in two forms – **outer opposition and inner opposition**.

Outer opposition comes in the form of actual voices from members of our village. Family or community members may arrive at our doorstep with voices of *criticism, doubt, discouragement, collective opinion, indifference, disbelief, disapproval or anger*. The village is operating under the law of survival. Tribal law is designed, and rightly so, to ensure the survival of the community, so it is inevitable that we will threaten the group's survival if we move out of the tribe. Criticism is one attempt to persuade us to stay, "What? You want to become an artist? You'll never succeed, you're not talented enough." "You have never been good at school. What good would a college education be to you?"

Doubt is another favorite oppositional voice, "If you leave the tribe you're not going to survive out there in the wilderness, you'll need us to help you." Discouraging village voices may say, "You'll never find others to care for you the way we do." Collective opinion can be a powerful deterrent and come in a voice such as, "Every man in our family who has gone off on his own has failed in business." Some oppositional voices are cold and destructive, "If you leave or think differently from the group, you'll be cut off from your inheritance and never hear from us again."

Another form of opposition is indifference. This is when we cross over the threshold of our village boundary and people do not even notice that we are leaving. This could create a powerful compulsion to stay in order to get the village to notice us.

The community might also have disbelief in our divine origins, "What? Aren't you just John, from the parents of Zachariah and Elizabeth?" The same thing was said about Jesus, "Can anything good come out of Nazareth?" The village will most likely disapprove of our attempts to establish a separate identity, and we may even come up against anger and aggression for daring to recognize and assert our own opinions.

Oppositional voices can also originate from within. Inner opposition may take the form of self-criticism, self-doubt, fear or panic. The inner resistances are sometimes far more powerful than the outer ones. We may have a community that actually supports our emotional separation but we come up against our own fears of leaving the village.

These inner critical voices keep us in a child position and prevent us from leaving the village. Even if we have physically left our tribe of origin, we may still feel like a little girl or boy inside. In order to fight the inner opposition, we must be able to shift from the child position and find the adult position inside of us that can confront the authoritative voice that keeps us feeling small and disempowered.

Self-criticism is another powerful opposition that deters us from leaving the village. Maybe we say to our selves, "You fool, you're not strong enough to stand up to her, she's a faster talker than you and can run circles around you. Just keep things the way they are." Our self-criticism may also sound like, "he has such an imposing presence and I'm just a blithering wimp when I'm around him. I can't say what I really feel."

Self-doubt is another looming voice, " I don't think I'm good enough. I deserve to stay in this little place. I don't deserve to expand and try to find myself."

Inner fear can also arise to cripple our chances of emotionally separating. We may say to ourselves, "Oh no, I can't stand up to my spouse who drinks because if I do, she's going to become abusive. Everything in my life would change and that's too scary to think about."

Panic is another voice that can detain us, "What would I do, where would I go, how would I survive, what would people think? I can't do it, I'll stop thinking about it."

Dismantling the tribal worldview

Many of us have difficulty leaving the roles that are prescribed by our village. For example, if you were taught that women should stay home and raise children, you may feel tremendous guilt about doing something different. Perhaps in your village, men are supposed to spend their time working and you feel guilty or inadequate if you work less and spend time with your family in a more domestic way.

Every time we break our attachment to a particular role, we are questioning the tribal worldview and breaking its powerful hold on our lives. In order to access our deeper identity – the one that lies at the heart of us – we must throw off the mantle of the "tribal only" view of life. I call this **dismantling the tribal worldview**. It does not mean smashing it to bits or discarding the entire root system. It means breaking the emotional hold of the roles and expectations that hinder our growth.

From the story of John the Baptist, we learn one model of confronting the tribe and the established ways of doing and being. John uses the direct approach as he confronts the established religious leaders who come to the Jordan River, where he is baptizing. These leaders of the establishment test him and criticize him for being an outsider and moving outside the established boundary of the village. John penetrates right into the heart of their tribal worldview and exposes the false authority that they use to legitimize their status and power.

From the Gospel of Matthew 3:7-9 we read,

> *"So when John saw many of the Pharisees and Sadducees coming for baptism he said to them, 'you brood of vipers, who warned you to flee from the wrath to come. Bear fruit worthy of repentance and do not presume to say to yourselves, we have Abraham as our ancestor. For I say to you, God is able from these stones to raise up children of Abraham. Even now the ax is lying at the roots of the trees. Every tree, therefore, that does not bear good fruit, is cut down and thrown into the fire."* [2]

This is an incredibly bold confrontation. Imagine confronting the elders who are well respected, honored and powerful in the community. Imagine suggesting that their position in society means nothing. Within the psyche, this would be a confrontation with the well-established ego values concerned with conformity, fitting in and adapting. These ego/tribal values are unconcerned with our individual growth or with developing the trunk of our Tree. The John or Adventurer within us needs to confront these ego values head on, dismantling the limited tribal perspective and recognizing how false this authority is when we are trying to establish a more individual identity. John warns us that if we cling to the roots, define ourselves only by the tribe and fail to develop our own fruit, our Tree will be cut down and thrown into the fire. In other words, our potential for growth and development will be stunted.

John recognizes that these so-called leaders are not producing good fruit and are merely relying on their ancestral association with Abraham. They represent the dominant values of the ego, values lying at the heart of the root system that must be confronted and seen for exactly what they are. When we move out of the tribe, we come under individual law and it no longer matters what clan we are identified with, what tribal label we have, who we know, or how privileged we are within the clan. During the fourth initiation, we will only survive on the merits of who we are as individuals. John says clearly to the tribe, "Don't be complacent just because you have the right connections, for the path of initiation is open to anyone who rises up out of the roots and establishes an individual Tree. It is going to depend on the fruit you bear."

When we confront the voices that are hindering our growth and damaging our individual values, we must name them and break the power of their spell. We need to call upon our wild John the Baptist who can say, "No more! I have had enough! I am not going to listen to you anymore! I'm going to stop this unhealthy pattern!" Dismantling the tribal worldview means saying no to what everyone else may want and saying yes to individual growth. It means questioning external authority and following a more internal authority. This kind of confrontation helps us to establish our own authority and identity.

Exercise 4: Saying no!

The wildman or woman inside is able to say, "I will search for my true self. I will fight to discover who I am. I will take a risk. I am going to walk out there into the wilderness, into the unknown. I don't know what I'm going to find out there." The adventurous spirit follows our internal longings like, "I wonder who I am. I wonder who I'm going to be away from these voices." We need to come into contact with the wildness in ourselves, the wildness that can say "No!" or "I'm going to make a change!" or "I'm not going to follow that anymore!" Take some time to identify the following:

Who do you need to say "no" to?
What do you need to say "no" about?
What behaviors do you need to stop?
Fill in the blank - No more_____ I've had enough of_____!

Ask for Protection

We have gathered up the courage to leave the village, now it is time to ask for protection as we move away from the safety of the village into the wilderness.

Often in stories and myths, the hero is given protective clothing or a weapon such as a shield or sword to protect him as he embarks into unknown territory. Sometimes the protection comes in the form of a magic talisman, a guardian animal, or a word of power. (You may want to repeat Exercise 2 - the meditation on "leaving the village"-and ask for the particular protection you need as you cross the threshold. Note the form in which your help arrives and work with that symbol or figure as you move deeper into initiation at Stage 4.)

Years ago I had a dream about the tools of protection needed for this leg of the journey. The dream is called, "Learning the Art of Water Weaponry."

> *I am in a small group of women trainees. There is also another group of women elders who have been through a strenuous initiation and are training us. We are told to strip down to very little clothing and are taken by these older women into the heart of a thick forest. They lead us to a small clearing in the trees, which forms a circle about 30 feet in diameter. Here in the forest four initiates, including me, are instructed to stand in a semi-circle opposite the four initiated women. We are then given some kind of shield to hold in our hands. Each shield has a different design engraved on the outside, and I wonder whether they are particular symbols picked especially for each initiate. Silence pervades the clearing and, although we are given no verbal instructions, the initiation begins.*
>
> *Suddenly the elders begin to throw in our direction tightly packed balls of water that can fly through the air with great speed and accuracy. To avoid being hit, we must quickly put up our shields to duck the oncoming water weapons. As more and more weapons are thrown, we can hear the whooshing sound of the water as it rushes past our ears. With quickness of body and mind, we learn to dodge the water balls, for something terrible will happen if they hit our bodies. As the initiation continues, each woman seems to be passing the test. We are learning the art of water weaponry and the proper use of the shield.*

What exactly is the art of water weaponry? One interpretation is that I am being taught the skill of maneuvering in the emotional world, where dangerous "water balls" or damaging emotional exchanges can affect me. Sometimes in life, the forces of emotion that fly at us from others are like tight balls of water, packed with the intensity of their will, anger, expectations or emotional needs. It is tremendously helpful to have a visual image of these emotional exchanges and a tangible way that we can protect ourselves from their onslaught.

The forest in the dream reminds me of the wilderness we encounter when we leave the village. The water balls remind me of the damaging voices of opposition that could easily wound me and even pull me back to the village if I allow them to penetrate my body. I must quickly learn to dodge the water balls and protect myself with a shield, for if they hit me and penetrate me, something terrible will happen. And something terrible does happen when we are unprotected and a critical or disapproving voice penetrates our sensitive psychological body like a sharp arrow. This is how our emotional container can spring a leak.

The shield becomes our tool and ally in the game of water weaponry. The shield is designed to deflect the poisonous arrows and emotional attacks that are flung at us as we leave the village. We can hold up the shield against disapproval, doubt, negative projections and village grumbling. We can also shield ourselves against our own oppositional voices. Each time we hold up our shield, we can imagine ourselves saying, "No. Enough of that! This does not serve me any longer. I am not going to feel guilty. I am not going to take your criticism. It is not my job in life to do whatever you want me to do. I must discover who I am."

Step 1: Leave the Village
* Step 2: Survive the Wilderness *
Step 3: Transmute the power drives
Step 4: Open the heart

In Step 1, we began the journey of establishing our own identity by leaving the village. We discovered why we leave, how we leave, and the importance of confronting the voices of opposition when we leave. We learned how to dismantle the tribal worldview and to ask for tools of protection. In Step 2, we cross the threshold of the village boundary and follow the path that stretches far into unknown territory. We walk out into our psychological wilderness where we must discover ways to survive in the extreme environment.

Calling the wild spirit

Imagine the feeling as you step across the village boundary and begin traveling alone down the path that leads far into the distance, into uncharted wilderness.

The first thing we may want to do is to call for help. The initiating archetype for the fourth initiation is the **Adventurer**, the wild spirit within us who is willing to take risks and explore new territory. Our Adventurer is the pioneer in us who enjoys the challenge of investigating and searching. This spirit knows how to preserve a wildness of being, unafraid of what the oppositional voices say. The Adventurer is not easily thwarted from her goal and will take us into unknown territory no matter how much fear we have. The Adventurer thrives in the wilderness like John the Baptist, and finds our authentic voice away from family, clan and tribe. She follows individual law and knows how to seek out what is good for us as separate people from our tribe.

The wild one does not care what others think and will seek to discover our true identity. This archetypal energy also has the power to withstand disapproval, which we will confront many times as we begin forging an individual trunk out of the roots of our Tree.

Once we psychologically leave the village, it is the wild spirit who can be a pioneer in new territory, crying in the wilderness as John does, "Prepare the way of the Lord, make straight the path! I am the witness to the Christ who comes after me." John represents the archetypal energy within us that forges the path to the deeper and more profound parts of us. Only in the wilderness can this wild energy be found – when we are truly alone and finally listening to our own voice. This wild spirit is the pathfinder, hacking his way through the thick foliage of our wilderness to make contact with the higher self.

If John represents our wild, instinctive nature and Christ represents our spiritual nature, the path must be cleared for them to meet. In Kabbalah, this is called "the path of honesty" and it is the path on the Tree of Life diagram that travels between Yesod and Tiferet. This path

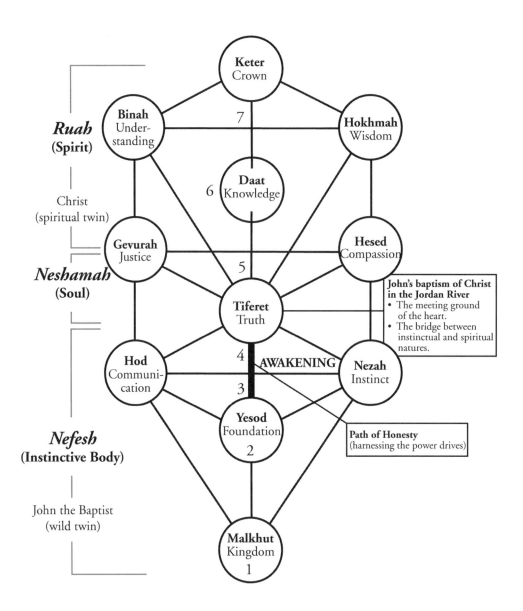

Diagram 16: Path of Honesty

In order to transform the *Nefesh* into the *Neshamah* we must walk the path of honesty (between Yesod and Tiferet) and continually return to the central pillar of consciousness, where we gain some detachment from our powerful *Nefesh* instinctive drives. Walking the path of honesty requires ethical responsibility, keen inner watchfulness and presence of mind to observe every situation.

can only be cleared with the sword of pure intention, self-scrutiny and honesty (see Diagram 16). This is such an important phase in our psycho-spiritual development that many stories depict these two sides of our nature as twins. In the story of John the Baptist, John and Jesus are the twin-like characters who, together, carry out the vital task of bridging our instinctual and spiritual natures.

John very much represents the wild twin. He is of the earth, physically strong, adventurous and able to survive extreme environments. He is the seeker, the one who prepares the way and forges a path to the other twin, who waits to be called. When our wild twin is developed and strong and we have prepared the path so that we can access our spiritual twin, a dialogue can begin between these two aspects of our self. The Shamanic tradition calls this kind of sacred dialogue "crying for a vision." After preparing for the vision quest in a wilderness place, the Shaman is supposed to cry for a vision, praying and asking for a sign from Spirit, from the spirit twin. Hopefully during the vision quest, the spirit twin reveals its nature through symbols given in dreams or visions, so that the initiate gains clarity about her future work and destiny.

John the Baptist is the Shaman within us, crying out in our wilderness, trying to discover our higher nature. John is well aware that he is preparing to meet his spirit twin. He is crying for a vision, crying for the "Christ" to come near; "The one who is more powerful than I is coming after me. I am not worthy to stoop down and untie the thong of his sandals. I have baptized you with water, but he will baptize you with the Holy Spirit and with fire." John understands the true nature of the spiritual twin and the power that can be experienced when we make contact with it; but there is much ground yet to be cleared, as we will see in Steps 3 and 4.

Transforming the *Nefesh* into the *Neshamah*

In Kabbalah there are special names for the twins: the **wild twin** is called the *Nefesh* and the **spirit twin** is called the *Ruah*. Our *Ruah* helps to humanize the *Nefesh* and move it to its next stage of development, the development of the *Neshamah*, the **soul** (see Diagram 16). Transforming the *Nefesh* into the *Neshamah* strengthens the trunk of our Tree and must be accomplished before we can fully develop the branches.

The *Nefesh* is the instinctive, "vital" soul that draws its energy from the body and the instinctive psyche. The *Nefesh* is also concerned with sexual and aggressive drives, the unrefined animal drives and the raw instinctive energies of the lower psyche. The *Neshamah*, on the other hand, is the "living" soul that God breathed into Adamah during creation, making Adamah a true human being with a heart and soul. The *Neshamah* occupies the soul triad at Stage 5 on the Tree of Life diagram.

The *Nefesh* represents our primal libido, having its energy base in the body. The *Nefesh* is concerned with the animal passions and desires, like the need to dominate, control and rise to the top of the hierarchy. I often imagine the *Nefesh* energy surging up from the ground, that powerful life force that comes from creation, the force that wants to grow and wants to push upwards. The *Nefesh* instigates our instinctive urge to push up out of the underground roots and thrust forth a trunk.

In an undeveloped state, the *Nefesh* is a wild tangle of chaotic energy without a focus. Without taming or transforming, these energies can wreak havoc within the psyche and can scatter our energy in all directions. It is said in Kabbalah that transforming the *Nefesh* into the *Neshamah* is a key step in our psycho-spiritual development. It is called the stage of awakening, and in order to wake up out of our village slumber, we must begin the task of harnessing the animal energies so that we are not dominated by our drives.

The key to transforming the *Nefesh* into the *Neshamah* is to harness the animal energies by steering them towards the positive goal of self-development, while simultaneously retaining the primal strength of the *Nefesh*. The *Nefesh* is our power pack, our super battery, our powerful fuel source that gives us bursts of vitality and long-term stamina for the entire path of initiation. We need to keep our *Nefesh* well fed, cared for and exercised because it is our fuel for getting things done in the world.

One of the difficulties in guiding the *Nefesh* to serve the *Neshamah* is that **the animal drives do not like to be tamed**. They prefer to be at center stage and to be gratified at will. One of the biggest stumbling blocks on the mystical path is getting waylaid at Stage 4 by getting caught in the animal drives. Kabbalistic teaching warns us of the dangers of getting locked into a position of always having to gratify the drives.

On the Tree of Life diagram, the animal triad consists of Hod, Nezah and Tiferet. There is a Hebrew phrase associated with the paths that connect these three Sephirot, which translates as "to lock in position." This means that we can easily get locked into a power struggle or a compulsion to follow our drives if the ceiling of our vision stops at the animal level. If John had confronted the religious authority just to be rebellious and did not have the vision of preparing the way for the spiritual twin, he could have easily become locked in a power struggle, compulsively spinning his wheels and not moving further in his development.

A few years ago, I witnessed a perfect example of the dangers of getting locked in position at the animal level. One day, during my travels in Southeast Asia, I was sitting on a beach on an island in the Gulf of Thailand. I had injured my leg and was unable to walk for a week, so my husband and I had plenty of time to observe the local color and discuss mystical things. This particular day, we were discussing animal drives and what the Kabbalistic teaching "locked in position" actually means. Suddenly, 50 feet down the beach, violent growling and snarling broke out between two puppies.

We had learned the previous day that they were from the same litter and were both male, making them as close to twin brothers as you can get. These little puppies would come out onto the beach every day, and we would watch their aggressive play. This particular day, someone had left a chicken bone in the sand, which was snatched up by one of the puppies. The other puppy saw his brother's treat and went after the chicken bone. At first, they locked onto the chicken bone, shaking their heads and trying to pry it loose from each other's toothy grip. At some point in the battle, they dropped the chicken bone and locked their teeth into each other's throats. It was no longer about the food, the hunger, or the original drive that had engaged them. Now they were locked into mortal combat, rolling around the sand, growling and battling to the death. They became fixed in position and neither animal was going to back down and break its lock. On and on it went.

It took the owners far too long to rescue the poor puppies and pull them apart; they had injured each other quite badly and I wondered if they would survive. What is etched in my memory from that day is the brutality of the animal level if there is no consciousness beyond the animal instincts. I understood that those who are caught here at Stage 4 without proper initiation could fight to the death, compulsively following their need to dominate. It is crucial for the wild and spiritual twins to unite in friendship, for *if the Nefesh has no contact or consciousness of the soul's morality or the spirit's vision, it easily becomes locked into position and therefore cannot transform.*

John the Baptist is a good model of an initiated wild twin because he truly understands the scope of his authority at Stage 4. He knows that the initiated *Nefesh* can only go so far and then the *Neshamah* – the true, internal authority – takes over. When confronted by the religious authorities as to his true identity – "Well, who are you? Are you Elijah? Are you the Christ? Are you the Anointed One?" John answers, "No, I am none of these things. I am, as Isaiah prophesied, a voice that cries in the wilderness: make a straight way for the Lord." As an inner archetype, John knows who he is, what role he plays in our development, and how to remain the wild twin without becoming inflated and thinking that he is the Christ. When John's disciples are worried that people are flocking to Jesus after his baptism, John replies, "A man can only lay claim to what is given him from Heaven. You yourselves can bear me out. I said I myself am not the Christ; I am the one who has been sent out in front of him." *John has a single-minded focus within the psyche: transforming the Nefesh into the Neshamah, helping us break the lock of the animal drives so that we can follow our Christ path.*

Facing the wilderness within

In order to break the lock of the animal drives and transform the *Nefesh,* we must learn to face the wilderness within. This means identifying: *1) our deep resistances to change, 2) our ego identifications that keep us from leaving the tribe, and 3) the destructive aspects of the power drives that keep our Nefesh enslaved and untransformed.*

When we step out into our inner wilderness, with only the Adventurer by our side, one of the first things we encounter is our **fierce resistance to change**. Whenever we enter therapy or put ourselves under strict spiritual discipline and meditate for any length of time – day after day or intensively on retreat – we will confront the parts of ourselves that are either afraid to grow up or unwilling to develop. These are the parts of our untransformed *Nefesh* that tempt us with every trick in the book, trying to convince us that we should run back home to the village and resume the quiet life we lived before all this wilderness nonsense began. If we are going to survive the wilderness, we must recognize our desires to return to the village where we feel safe, and experience how strong the pull is to go backwards in our development and fall back to sleep.

Facing the wilderness within also requires looking at the **ego identifications that keep us from leaving the tribe**. It is the ego's nature to become identified with various roles and power drives, because the ego does not have the capacity to envision our higher nature. For this reason, the ego tries on all sorts of identities and roles and becomes attached to the ones that provide some sense of self-worth and power. For example, a talented doctor may identify too much with the power his position affords in the eyes of patients and family. A business executive may have ego identification with the status she holds over others. A woman may over-identify with her powerful role as mother and become controlling with her children.

Often these ego identifications fill the hole inside us that was left by emotional abandonment and trauma. Although these role attachments bring immediate relief to the ego's sense of loss or low self-esteem, they are in fact false identities and part of an elaborate web of the false self that masks the original wound. Sooner or later on the mystical path, we must look underneath each ego identification, face the wound, and drop back into our real power and identity. The false identities that the ego loves to attach to drain us of enormous resources of energy and keep us bound to dysfunctional ways of living. For this reason, it is imperative that we break free of our attachments to being the all-important doctor, the powerful boss, or the Super Mom.

If we are not overly identified with our position, status or power, then a deeper and more solid identity can begin to take shape. In Depth Psychology, this deeper identity is called the "True Self." In Kabbalah it is called Tiferet, the soul, or one's truth, beauty and goodness. This is fully developed in Stage 5, but it is important to know now that this deeper identity does exist and is waiting to be revealed.

Finally, facing the wilderness within also requires **identifying the destructive aspects of the instinctive drives** that keep our *Nefesh* enslaved and untransformed. At this stage of initiation, we must be able to sniff out and recognize the parts of us that can be destructive to others and to ourselves. We must acquire the skills to recognize what those instinctive drives are and how, in their raw state, they are dangerous and destructive to our psychological and spiritual development.

The following is a list of some of the most destructive aspects of the instinctual drives when they are untamed and out of conscious control.

Destructive aspects of the instinctive drives:

Envy
Rage
Aggression
Possessiveness
Omnipotence (the illusion of being all powerful)
Hatred
Desire for power over others
Domination
A devouring nature
Ruthlessness (going after what we want without regard for others)
Control
Greed
Narcissistic entitlement (believing that we are entitled to anything we want)
Grandiosity (believing that we are superior to others)
Untamed passion

Recognizing our own potential to be destructive can be quite devastating. We may feel a deep sense of shock when we realize how often we engage in destructive behavior and how often these energies are exchanged between people. We begin to realize how unconscious we are of our capacity to divide and ruin relationships. So often we kill off the spirit of true intimacy by using relationships to satisfy our more primal drives – like the wish to dominate or the wish to gratify our own needs. Facing the wilderness within means recognizing when we feel envious, when we want to control or when our ruthlessness flattens or crushes another person. We may not necessarily act on these impulses, but the destructive energy is rumbling around inside us, affecting our health and the psyche of the other person we are relating to.

We may, for example, have deep feelings of envy towards someone in a place of authority because we long for recognition. Perhaps our tendency is to become inflated, desiring to get to a top position without climbing every rung of the ladder and gaining the experience necessary to build a solid container. Some people rise to top positions without the internal structures to hold the authority and responsibility required. Often these people become tyrannical rather than fair leaders, because their animal libido is running wild and untamed. Facing the wilderness within takes a lot of stamina and requires us to catch ourselves every time the destructive impulses surface.

The story of John the Baptist offers us some help in facing the wilderness within. At the beginning of John's life, Zachariah was given a vision of John's role in the life of the people. John was sent by God to "Save us from our enemies and from the hands of all who hate us; grant us, free from fear, to be delivered from the hands of our enemies; bring the rising sun to visit us; give light to those who live in darkness and in the shadow of death; and guide our feet into the way of peace."

From a Depth Psychology perspective, if we take John to be an inner character, John's job within the psyche is to rescue us from the "enemies" within our own being who thwart and distract our holistic development. John, as the awakened *Nefesh*, will help redeem our shadow aspects by shedding light on our internal darkness and guiding our feet into the way of peace. These rejected and repressed parts of the psyche have remained in our inner wilderness with little or no attention and have built up a powerful reserve of negative energy that keeps us from developing our true self. Without attention, these rejected shadow aspects degenerate into entropy, fear, anxiety, laziness, and the refusal to grow up and take responsibility. They threaten to scatter us in many directions.

If we can access our inner John, there is the hope that light will be shed on those parts that live in darkness, granting us "deliverance" and "peace." John will help us to raise the animal energies to their highest good, so that the *Neshamah* can use these powers to develop the soul. John moves us on the path of honesty so that we can arrive at Tiferet – which holds a special position on the Tree of Life, for it is the fulcrum point between Stages 1, 2 and 3 and Stages 5, 6 and 7 (see Diagram 16). If we can make straight the path and build a bridge to the spiritual twin, we can heal the split between our instinctive body and our spiritual body. For many people, the soul and spirit, developed in Stages 5, 6 and 7, remain unconscious for their whole lives, so the purpose of transforming the *Nefesh* is to make a conscious connection between the lower and higher natures.

Exercise 5: Identify your destructive drives

1. Go through the above list of the destructive aspects of the instinctive drives and assess if and when you have felt each one. What did it feel like when you experienced envy, for example? If you cannot relate to feeling any of these impulses, perhaps you are brave enough to ask a partner, trusted friend or therapist whether they have experienced any of these destructive drives in you.

2. Identify which power drives you feel enslaved to, which ones you would like to transform.

3. Where are they operative in your life? How are you destructive with these drives? Please be as honest as possible, for this list will assist you as we move into Step 3 – Transmuting the Power Drives.

Calling the animal allies

Preparing for surviving the emotional wilderness demands the very best of our animal nature: *strength, stealth, power, stamina, instinctive awareness, keen eyes, sharp ears and a nose to sniff things out.* My vision of the fully awakened *Nefesh* is the Adventurer on the fourth Sacred Robe. This is John, after years of training in the desert, calling up his animal powers and placing them, one by one, on his Shamanic cape. Let's look back to the "Into the Wilderness" robe and meet the animals on John's cape.

At the base of the Robe we meet Lion and Wolf. The lion is associated with the sun and holds the royal place of honor in the animal kingdom. Lion is placed at the base of the robe to guide the Adventurer's feet towards a goal, saving him from meaningless meandering. Lion holds solar values and will move us toward our true self, helping us individuate and reign as King or Queen of our own territory.

To the left of Lion at the foot of the Robe is Wolf, howling at the moon. She is often seen as the pathfinder, the one who is able to intuit the next step on the path. She takes her direction from the moon, having access to the unconscious and the dream world, and is able to pluck the fruit that sits right below the surface of consciousness. After a night of venturing alone and communing with the moon, she will return to the wolf pack and suggest where to go next. The wolf pack represents all the various parts of our personality that need to gather together and cooperate as a team. Lion holds the overall goal in mind, and Wolf knows where to take the next step.

Above the Lion is Wildcat – a fierce mountain cat, lynx, or bobcat. His open mouth generates a terrifying sound to counter any oppositional voices. Wildcat helps us find our own voice to say "no" or "go away" if needed. He reminds me of a totem mask that scares away any evil spirits along the path. There is a fighting energy here, ready to stand up for what we believe in or to throw off the enemy.

To the left of Wildcat is Elk. In some Native American traditions, elk medicine is said to bring stamina and strength. Elk sets the pace to go the long distance. This is very important for surviving in the wilderness. We must be able to sustain the transformation process over the long haul, and we need the courage to find our own path.

To the right of Elk is Hawk, who awakens us to perceive the truth. The hawk is also the messenger between spirit and matter and is aware of the messages that are coming from spirit, from a more conscious place. Hawk can see the overall plan because Hawk has keenly developed eyesight. When he flies high overhead, he can ride above the torrent of emotions and can see things from a much higher perspective. Hawk stays connected to the *Neshamah*, the soul, when the *Nefesh* is embroiled in the battle of transformation.

Directly above Hawk we have Horse. Horse is swift and strong, wild and free. Horse provides the drive to keep going, especially when we want to run back home. Horse will carry us to our destination against all odds.

The two creatures on John's arms are Lizard and Snake. They represent the primal and deeply unconscious instinctive drives that surface when we awaken our animal powers at Stage

4. They are the most difficult of the animal energies to reach because of their primitive nature, but once harnessed, they can provide a tremendous surge of energy for the transformation process.

The last animal on the robe is Raven, who is flying out of the small lamp held by John. In some traditions, Raven is the messenger who can open channels of communication between people or between parts of us. Raven can send energy to just the right place. Both Snake and Lizard are helping the wildman to focus the direction of the flying Raven, focusing the wild fire into a controlled fire

The wildman figure on the robe has gathered his animal allies and is now focusing all the powerful animal drives in a particular direction. He is sending Raven out to effect a particular occurrence. For example, if we set the intention to focus our ambitious drive into a creative project - like giving a workshop or setting up a business - we must remember to dedicate all we do to the highest good. Then we direct our intention towards the audience with whom we will be speaking or to the people who will benefit from our business services. We can focus our Raven message so that it touches the exact people who need it and awakens something profound in the people who hear the message.

Exercise 6: Calling your animal ally

One creative way to call up the best of your animal nature is to collect some magazines with photographs of animals. Get a large poster board and some glue and begin cutting out pictures of animals that attract you. Make a collage on the poster board by cutting and pasting your animals any way you wish. When you are finished, free-associate with the images as if you were looking at a dream. How is each animal protecting you, affecting you, helping you? What is each saying to you, demanding from you? Pick your favorite animal and work with that one, noticing what qualities the animal is imparting to you and what feelings it stirs up for you.

Preparing to transform the destructive drives

Facing the reality that we possess destructive drives is hard enough, but actually transforming them takes a tremendous effort that requires preparation. John the Baptist is once again our model of how to prepare the body, heart and mind for surviving the extreme emotional tension of transforming our power drives. Only a prepared sacred space can hold us as we change the power drives from their raw, potentially destructive state into something more refined and useful. When we can prepare a solid, sacred container, we can transform envy into personal success, hatred into love, domination into right use of power, control into right use of will, ruthlessness into healthy ambition, grandiosity into vision, narcissistic entitlement into leadership, possessiveness into protectiveness.

It was prophesied at John's birth that he would be a man who would fast, take vows of abstinence and dedicate himself to the service of God. These are precisely the preparatory ingredients for any psychological or spiritual transformation. Fasting, abstaining and dedicating ourselves to serve God are disciplines that create a heightened state of awareness and open us to the possibility of change and growth. Withdrawing for periods of time from the things that normally feed our *Nefesh* - food, drink and instinctual gratification - cleanses our physical body and emotional system. By not feeding the *Nefesh*, we are better prepared to tackle our negative drives head on.

Here are four ways to prepare for the transformation of the destructive drives: *seal the container, simplify, cultivate solitude and practice self-reliance.*

The first preparation is to make sure that you have a **sealed container**. We know from the first initiation that the Alchemists used a hermetically sealed container, an airtight vessel, to withstand extremes of temperature or extremes of emotions. In the Baptist story, the desert wilderness becomes the sacred and sealed vessel by virtue of its isolation and lack of food sources for the *Nefesh*.

Most traditions provide the initiate with some form of sealed container to act as the vessel or cauldron for the initiate in Stage 4. The Native American tradition of the vision quest is one where the apprentice Shaman prepares her sacred container by drawing a sacred circle in the ground. Then the circle is dedicated to the six directions of North, South, East and West, Above and Below, which create an individual medicine wheel for protection and preparation.

Kabbalah has a similar preparation of the hermetically sealed container. We can begin by imagining ourselves on the Tree of Life map standing at the central place of Tiferet. The six directions are dedicated by consciously acknowledging the North/South axis of the central Pillar of Consciousness and the East/West axis of left and right Pillars of Receptivity and Activity. Then we dedicate the Below by honoring the earth which grounds the transformation, and we honor the Above by dedicating the whole operation to the service of the Holy One and to our highest good.

The second way to prepare for the transformation of the instinctive drives is to **simplify**. John simplifies life by paring down to a camel hair loincloth and venturing out into the wilderness. He strips down to the bare essentials of life, cutting out normal distractions so that his mind and body can become clearer and cleaner.

It is interesting that John's loincloth is made of camel hair. This says something about the importance of the camel's nature in helping us prepare for the desert. Camels, of course, can travel for long periods of time and for great distances in the desert extremes. Their ability to store water means that they need nothing but the hump on their back. When John puts on the camel hair loincloth, he is signaling us to strip down and bring only ourselves to the sacred circle, not our television or computer or relationships or substances of addiction as well. All we need is our fierce determination to face our destructive drives and wrestle with them.

Another way to prepare for the transformation of the power drives is to cultivate **solitude**. In order to forge an independent identity, we must be truly alone. Solitude can feel utterly relieving for some people and utterly terrifying for others. Those of us who feel terrified, will need to learn to tolerate our own company so that we can contact our own thoughts, feelings, strength and will.

Imagine what it was like for John the Baptist to be alone in the desert, preparing for his mission. Out in the desert, he was forced to be with himself in a radically present way. When we learn to cultivate this kind of solitude, we begin to wake up. Our inner watcher develops a keen sense of inner sight, sound, smell and taste, and we begin to tune in to our inner landscape. Nothing escapes our vigilant eye.

The other benefit of cultivating solitude is that eventually we become comfortable with whatever comes up on the screen of our mind and heart. We will experience extreme thoughts, emotions, images and fantasies in our wilderness. Cultivating solitude expands our inner horizons so that we can explore states of mind and heart that we never could when we were confined by the formalities and restrictions of tribal living. When we become comfortable handling extreme states within ourselves, we will be able to handle outer situations of intensity, tension, conflict and confrontation with far more ease.

The fourth way to prepare for the transformation of the power drives is to practice **self-reliance**. When we practice self-reliance, we discover that we indeed can sustain intense swings of emotion, tolerate frustration, handle grief, or deal with rage. When we are out in the wilderness alone we must be able to dig deeply into our own well and mine our own resources. Outdoor wilderness training can be effective at this stage of initiation because it forces us to rely on our own instinctive knowledge and embody these principles in a profound and tangible way.

Step 1: Leave the Village
Step 2: Survive the wilderness
* **Step 3: Transmute the power drives** *
Step 4: Open the heart

Transmutation

The word "transmute" is used in Alchemy to mean the changing of one substance into another. For example, when grapes turn to wine, a transformation takes place that alters the original substance and chemistry of the grapes.

When a power drive is in a raw, instinctive state, it holds us in a kind of possession, as when a compulsive behavior locks us into a particular way of feeling and behaving. When that drive is transmuted however, the feeling of compulsivity or possession wanes and we are less reactive and more able to experience conscious control over the original drive.

For example, a woman (I will call her "Amy") feels a compulsive need to continue a relationship with a man who is unable to give her what she needs. She is conscious of his inability to nurture her and give her affection and she can see the way this hooks into her abandonment issues. Despite her awareness of this, she continues to pursue him in a compulsive way, hoping that perhaps this next time he will be different and respond to her needs. Whenever she thinks about him, it triggers feelings of loss and sadness that quickly convert into a compulsive need to call him and fill the emptiness in the pit of her stomach.

During our work together in therapy, Amy identifies the drives she is trying to transform as *rage* at being abandoned and *hungry greed* that drives her to fill her inner emptiness through relationships. The untransformed rage and greed have a particular emotional charge and a particular impact on her body that keeps her in the vicious cycle of disappointment and grief. She describes feeling possessed by these drives. Transmuting this energy means breaking the powerful hold that it has on her body, her feelings and her responses – so that she can stop compulsively picking up the phone, stop trying to solicit his tender feelings, and stop expecting him to change.

Each mystical path has its version of transmuting the energies. In the language of Kabbalah, we transmute the *Nefesh* into the *Neshamah* by walking the path of honesty, gathering the instinctive energies of our *Nefesh*, wrestling with them and placing them under the direction of the *Neshamah*. In the language of Alchemy, the Alchemist gathers the *Prima Materia* (the raw instinctive drive) and submits it to a series of operations for transmutation. The goal of these operations is to "turn lead into gold," to refine the instinctive energies into soul qualities, so that our devouring nature transmutes into generosity or our ruthlessness transmutes into healthy ambition.

The purpose of transmuting our lead into gold is to build a new vessel of the soul, one that is more tailored to our individual truth. However, the vessel of individual identity is not easily built. At birth we are supplied with a ready-made group identity from our roots. Building and maintaining this group identity or "communal vessel" is a shared responsibility with members of the tribe. On the other hand, the golden vessel of our soul, our individual identity, must be forged, built and maintained solely by the individual and cannot be built by the community. Often our individual vessel is built anew from the bricks and rubble that survive after our communal vessel has been damaged in some way or dismantled.

The *result* of consciously putting ourselves through such a rigorous transmutation process is healthy separation from the tribe and the building of a strong trunk to our Tree. The benefits of transmuting the power drives include: *better personal boundaries, sharper self-definition, and the ability to think our own thoughts, feel our own feelings, withdraw projections, grow a harder edge, and say "no."* Transmuting the power drives sharpens our individual identity so that we no longer serve the tribal identity, enslaved to inherited patterns and complexes. It is time now to move from bondage to freedom, breaking free of our false "adaptive" self and transmuting any destructive drives so that the emotional charge dissipates, the emptiness in the pit of the stomach disappears, the spell is broken, enslavement to the addiction wanes and we experience new internal boundaries.

The three main components needed for successful transmutation are: personal will, conscious reflection and, once again, a hermetically sealed container that can hold us through the process. We must have the will to change a pattern. Nothing will transform if our will is not involved. We must have the capacity to consciously reflect on the pattern or addiction that we are trying to change. This means diligently observing the pattern and becoming aware of our own participation in it, how we attract it and how we feed it. We must have the safe container that can hold the torrent of feelings that arise when we break the pattern. We are not in control of the timing of the transmutation process, so we must hold and wait patiently in a safe and sealed container until the pattern works its way out organically.

Starving the dragon

The first step in the transmutation process is to identify our dragon – be it a negative behavior, destructive energy, addiction, or whatever is hindering our psycho-spiritual growth. Once identified and named, we must take steps to stop feeding the negative pattern or addiction. This is what I call "starving the dragon."

Identifying our dragon is not easy, and sometimes the dragon is so unconscious and hidden that we cannot see it – but others usually can.

I worked with a man who was on a spiritual path and had a sense of his life direction and purpose, but he had not dealt with his *ambitious drive* and was unaware of the part of him that was, at times, *ruthless*. Without conscious control and transmutation, his ambition to succeed caused damage to others when he disregarded them and pushed them aside. At one point, he even attempted to steal another colleague's creative ideas and take credit for himself. This ruthless and omnipotent behavior severed his relationships time and time again. Despite my warning that his destructive behavior was cutting off his relationships and thwarting him from his soul path, he rejected my help because he was unable to acknowledge the ruthless part of himself. He was unable to own his destructive energy and therefore could not identify his dragon. Only when we can acknowledge our drives – such as ruthlessness – can we begin to starve the dragon and transmute this negative energy into something positive.

Here are some familiar dragons that my clients have identified and starved over the years: addiction to cigarettes, alcohol, drugs, sex, pornography, gambling, food and relationships, toxic rage, possessiveness, desire for fame, attention, status and power, ruthless ambition, co-dependency, the inability to say "no", envy, self-destructive thoughts and behavior, and attachment to unhealthy relationships.

Dragons are individual or family complexes that suck tremendous energy from us, pulling us into an emotional "black hole" that surrounds us with darkness rather than clarity, light and consciousness. When we feed the dragon by continuing the destructive behavior, it does not quiet down with satisfaction, but growls continually for more gratification. The untamed *Nefesh* energies fueling our dragons are tremendously resistant to being transformed because they want to flow with their natural energy, the energy that originates from the vegetable and animal natures. The vegetable nature wants to survive and be comfortable, and the animal nature wants to dominate. For this reason, *the key to transmuting the dragon is to starve it and refrain from gratifying it every single time it demands feeding.*

When we stop feeding our addiction and start to break the gravitational pull of the unconscious complex, what happens? The dragon's appetite intensifies and it begins to scream more loudly and thrash more violently. When the dragon increases its demands, you know that you are beginning to transmute the energy because you are getting to the root of the problem. Behind each dragon is a wounded part of the personality that needs protection. The dragon may have been useful as a bodyguard at one time, perhaps in early childhood, but it is no longer useful as we grow and develop. Unfortunately, dragons do not leave quietly or easily, but put up a fierce fight when threatened with starvation.

I worked with a woman (I will call her "Susan") who wanted to quit smoking. What she noticed immediately when she starved her "cigarette dragon" was the amount of anger that surfaced when she stopped gratifying her compulsive need to smoke. She also contacted deep resentment and pain at not getting her needs met as a child. All the feelings that she had been repressing when she fed the dragon popped up, including her unprocessed anger and her need for emotional nurturing and connection. Each time she wanted to reach for a cigarette, she was forced to confront these feelings. When she starved her dragon, she began facing more profound feelings of loss and abandonment, emanating from the original wound.

In another case, I worked with a man (I will call him "Robert") who identified his dragon as envy towards authority figures, both male and female, who could help him on his personal and professional journey. His envy would inevitably draw him to strong and successful people because they possessed something he wanted - power and position. He would then proceed to sabotage the relationship because part of him wanted to destroy the other person's power. When he finally identified his dragon as envy, he could pinpoint exactly when he needed to starve his dragon and could then abstain from doing something destructive to the relationship, contain his envy, and appreciate what the mentor could teach him.

Exercise 7: Starving the dragon

1. Identify your dragon and commit to starving it for one month. It will take longer, but start with a realistic goal. (For help, refer to your lists from Exercise 5.) Practice starving your dragon. Keep track of each time it breathes fire and demands feeding and you successfully starve it

2. What feelings arise when you starve your dragon? Keep a notebook with you at all times and track it for one month. You'll be amazed at how often you hear the compulsive voice to return to your habitual pattern. For example, if you are caught in an unhealthy relationship and wish to break your habit of picking up the phone to connect with the unavailable person, notice each time you have the urge and refrain from calling. Sit with whatever feelings come up when you starve your dragon. Write down the feelings.

Exercise 8: Creative visualization - Transmuting the dragon

The following is a creative visualization you can practice when you are wrestling with one of your dragons.

Imagine the "dragon" that you are trying to transmute, such as cigarette addiction or healthy separation from a toxic relationship. Imagine now the feelings that come up in relation to your "dragon," such as anger or betrayal. Imagine that this feeling intensifies and grows into a large dragon. Picture exactly what the dragon looks like. (**Make absolutely sure that you do not picture the other person as a dragon, just the feeling that comes up when you relate to that person.**)

Face the dragon and ask it what it wants… What does it say?

Tell the dragon that you are no longer going to feed it.

When the dragon breathes fire and thrashes about in protest, imagine the dragon surrounded in its own fire and cooking in its own flames. Now imagine intensifying this fire and see it as the fire of purification, burning away all the poisonous feelings and internal voices that the dragon produces. See the poisons and the toxins burning away. Let the dragon cook in the fire.

Now imagine that you have in your hand a magic neutralizing solution that you can pour over your dragon. When you feel ready, pour the neutralizing solution all over the dragon. Watch as the flames die down and the dragon begins to shrink and shrink. Keep neutralizing any fire or any poisons left. Watch as the dragon shrinks down into a small golden seed.

Pick up the golden seed and plant it into the ground.

Imagine now a beautiful tree sprouting up from the ground where the dragon once stood. Your tree is vibrant, green and leafy.

Cranking up the heat

Cranking up the heat is the active phase of energetic transmutation, the burning phase when the heat of the libido really cranks up and begins to boil. When we starve our dragon and stop gratifying it, the dragon begins to breath fire in protest over having our primal desires thwarted. The Alchemists call the fire-breathing stage Calcinatio. This is the burning phase when we are plunged into the fire of transformation for purification. The burning can be triggered in many ways, like when we have a passion for someone or something that is not available to us. Perhaps we are forced to go back to work after a divorce, which triggers tremendous fear and anxiety. Perhaps we long to have a baby, a home, a secure job, but circumstances prevent it and we cannot have what we so desire. All these scenarios can cause deep suffering because frustrated desire is so hard to bear.

The internal burning of Calcinatio may seem cruel, but sometimes the fire of transformation is required to burn away the dross and forge the way to true individuation. The goal of the transmutation process is to arrive at a more core experience of ourselves, which the Alchemists call the gold. In order to get purified gold, the impure materials must be burned away. Emotional burning, therefore, is a purification process that eventually leads to our inner gold.

Some power drives and dragons only transmute under intense heat. Remember what John the Baptist says about the importance of purification: "Any tree that does not bear good fruit goes into the fire." In other words, any part of our personality that is unrefined, dysfunctional, hindering our growth and not serving our whole self will be put into the refiner's fire for transmutation.

Building the vessel of the individual takes tremendous energy – energy that has been bleeding off to feed our particular dragon. During Calcinatio, this precious energy is withdrawn from the dragon, conserved and rerouted to stoke our creative inner fire, rather than being used to maintain an addiction or external demand. Withdrawing attachments from the outside and focusing our energy inward helps us to form an attachment to the Self. This is crucial as we build our individual vessel.

In the heat of my own Calcinatio purification process, I had the following dream.

> *I am acting in a play but do not yet have a part. It seems that the cast decides with me what part I will play. It is decided that I am in charge of the "precious baby" and my job is to carry the baby throughout the play. I am under the impression it is baby Jesus, but as the play begins, I am rocking in my arms not a baby but a beautifully carved wooden crucifix. I am struck by how exquisitely crafted it is. I'm so deeply moved by the beauty and craftsmanship of the crucifix that I ask who the artist is so that I can meet him and speak with him. Someone tells me that he is a student doing very serious study with a master craftsman, and he may not be available to see me. I insist on going to meet him anyway.*
>
> *I follow a man down some scaffolding, which turns into a ladder hanging over the sky. I feel frightened but determined to find the artist, because I feel deeply connected to him and must meet him. We finally make it to solid ground and are searching for the artist across a huge field. On our journey we come across an incredible sight. There are two bodies lying on the side of the road – a man and woman – that have been completely disemboweled,*

their organs placed neatly alongside the bodies. Their bodies are a blackish- brown color, as if they have been exhumed. As I get closer I can see that they have been burned, completely torched and charred. I notice that one of the bodies still has life in it because there is a faint color of red emanating from the heart region underneath the rib cage. My traveling companion wants to put this person out of her misery by killing her quickly, so she pulls the head and rib cage apart. I'm devastated by the violence of this act and torn between seeing it as a mercy killing and wanting desperately to try to save whatever life is left in this person.

Then I notice that behind the bodies are six lions guarding the site. Three lions are in a cage and three of them are not caged and are pacing back and forth behind the burned and disemboweled figures. The lions are also a blackish-brown color and have been torched by fire. Even more horrifying, the lions actually have no skin. They have been skinned alive. When I see this, I am devastated further and realize that something must be done. So I fly up into the air and put a protective circle of light around me. Then I spread a circle of light around the whole field, around the bodies and around the people who are now gathering in the field. I never find the artist but end up performing an important ritual of cleansing around the burned and dismembered couple.

There are many layers to this dream but I want to look at its significance to the Calcinatio process. The dream begins with a symbol of baby Jesus and the crucifix, which I associate with Jesus' life path of birth, suffering, death and resurrection – a reference to the life-death-rebirth cycle that happens during the transmutation process. In the dream, I agree to carry the baby and the crucifix – which signals my willingness to carry the suffering that is required to make it to the resurrection phase of the cycle, when the power drive is transformed and released into another, more useful form.

Many people believe that we can bypass this stage by meditation or spiritual discipline, but this is not so. It seems that suffering is the archetypal and unavoidable experience that we must endure when our negative patterns are unraveling. The disemboweled, torched couple reminds me of the horrifying and devastating experience of the active phase of transmutation, when the heat is cranked up and we are in the throes of the dragon's thrashing.

We learn from Depth Psychology, Shamanism and Alchemy that certain symbols appear when we are in the midst of the fourth initiation, often coming in dreams, waking visions or fantasies. *Dismemberment, burned bodies and skinned lions are familiar symbols that represent the dismantling of negative complexes, the burning of unfulfilled desire, and the stripping away of personal power.* This describes the death phase before emotional rebirth, and it is a crucial stage that must be endured, felt and embodied. While we are in the heat of it, it seems violent and heartless, like the scene in the dream where my companion kills off the tiny flicker of life left in the charred body. However, if this phase is endured, we can transmute and be free of the omnipotence, inflation, narcissistic entitlement, possessiveness and rage that keeps us trapped in destructive patterns.

Let's take a look at the lion symbol in the dream. The lion is the king of beasts and often represents the part of our conscious psyche that reigns supreme or feels entitled. It may be a part of us that is overvalued, inflated or grandiose. The lion within us is at home being the king of the jungle. So if the lion in our psyche is stripped of its power (skinned), feels diminished in some way (burned) or when our dominant way of being in the world collapses, we can feel extremely exposed, vulnerable, skinless and unprotected. It can feel shaming and humiliating when our power gets stripped away and we feel devalued or demeaned. This was certainly my experience and was depicted vividly by the burned lions.

Let's return to our third example, Robert, who identified his dragon as envy towards authority figures. During our work together, a series of incidents at his work resulted in a job demotion. Some of his responsibilities were taken away because his boss perceived him as competitive and trying to usurp his job. Indeed, upon reflection later in therapy, he was able to see how competitive he was with his boss. This demotion dealt a crucial blow to his grandiose self, his lion, and the part of him that wanted power and position even though he was not yet ready or worthy. This cranked up the heat and triggered a full-scale Calcinatio. With his grandiosity exposed, his lion skinned and burned, he encountered the intensity of his *powerlessness*, which had been hiding underneath his dragon. Now the envy was no longer taking center stage, and the *impotence* that he carried as a core experience of the Self could be acknowledged, felt and embodied. Active transmutation was in progress.

Sometimes the only way to burn off an inflated state of mind is to face the truth of the original wound, endure the subsequent suffering, and refrain from moving back into the grandiose position. Embodying our sense of impotence and powerlessness does feel excruciating, however, and is depicted vividly in the dream as bodies that have been burned from the inside out. During Calcinatio, as the heat cranks up, it is crucial to stay with the torrent of primal feelings coming from the original wound, feelings such as hopelessness, shame, despair, impotence, guilt, hatred, depression or rage. *Enduring the heat and embodying the real feelings are the keys to lasting transmutation.*

Our culture does not provide us with a strong container for holding and suffering through these kinds of feelings. We are not trained to suffer and to hold and wait and be patient. There is great social pressure to work through transmutation quickly. We hear things like "get on with it" or "stop wallowing in self-pity" or "get over the loss of that relationship" or "it's not worth suffering over."

Even in the Calcinatio dream, rather than staying beside the burned bodies and lions and *weeping*, I wanted to *fly* away, up into the air, and put a protective circle of light around myself. This seems to be one of my defenses against the excruciating exposure of having my power stripped during Calcinatio. I learned from this dream the importance of staying with the most difficult feelings of shame and not flying off into a spiritual or intellectual defense to get a higher perspective too quickly.

When Calcinatio is in full swing, the internal heat begins to dry out all of the unwanted water and we find ourselves shedding the long-forgotten tears of hurt, grief and shame. All the tears we have withheld begin pouring out of our body during Calcinatio. The heat acts like a sauna, pulling out the sweat and the toxins that have lain dormant in stagnant internal pools. It is appropriate to shed tears, to wail and to mourn, as if a huge iceberg of defensiveness and hardness melts into something more supple and pliable. During Calcinatio, our body and psyche become softer and warmer as the icy waters melt and pour out of our body as tears.

Eating locusts and wild honey

So far we have looked at starving the dragon, which triggers the transmutation process, and cranking up the heat, which actively transforms the destructive drives through fiery purification. Now we will learn to "eat locusts and wild honey," the food that John the Baptist ate in the wilderness, in order to neutralize the toxic effects of our particular power drive. In psychological language, eating locusts and wild honey means *emotionally metabolizing the most primal form of life we carry inside ourselves* - our raw, primitive energies. It means processing our intense feelings and making sense of our pain and wounds, neutralizing the acidic, burning toxins that affect the body and soul.

Eating locusts and wild honey forces us to drop even further into the body, rather than flying up into the air as I did in the "Calcinatio" dream. It requires staying beside the burned bodies and skinned lions within us, and experiencing our loss of power and thwarted desires. Eating the locusts means metabolizing the shame, humiliation and grief, observing it, shedding the light of consciousness on it, chewing it over, getting the full flavor and adding some wild honey. Digesting these primitive energies takes "guts." It takes guts to see how controlling we are or how much we want things our own way or how destructive we can be.

Let's look again at the example of Amy, who deeply desires a partner but attaches to lovers who cannot provide intimacy. This cycle produces intense frustration and disappointment. During the Calcinatio phase, she uncovers another layer and hits her grief head on, feeling the burning intensity of her sadness and loneliness. Now, during this third phase of transmutation - "eating locusts and wild honey" - she has more insight and perceives her own fear of intimacy. She metabolizes her fear and chews it over and realizes that underneath it all is her unconscious need to control her lovers, which pushes them away. She observes that her need to control comes from the abandoned child within her, and she is painfully aware of how dominating, controlling and destructive this part of her can really be. As she faces the terror and destructiveness that true intimacy triggers in her, she is eating her locusts and wild honey.

Eating locusts also means *identifying our trigger points and retaining our emotional composure during heated interchanges.* When some people are under extreme stress and heat, they lose their emotional composure and either explode or implode. When we can eat locusts and wild honey, we can hold our emotional composure and have a sense of detachment and consciousness about what is happening. When we eat locusts and wild honey, we can handle extreme emotional states so that if we feel triggered into a rage, rather than screaming, we learn to "eat it." This does not mean repressing the feelings but rather dealing with them, containing them and holding them inside our sealed vessel.

Back to our example of Susan, who fought the cigarette dragon; her biggest challenge was trying to retain emotional composure with her siblings, who triggered intense feelings of rivalry and competition. In her family of origin, emotional resources were very limited because neither of the parents was available for warmth or intimacy. So the five siblings fought for a very limited supply of love. Susan worked hard to eat her locusts and not fly into a rage at her siblings or fall into an old pattern of feeling undernourished and victimized. Over time, she was able to see how she herself stirred up rivalry and chaos in her siblings and among her peers by aggressively going after the biggest slice of emotional pie, trying to secure the resources for herself. This revelation helped curb her rages and aggressive attacks. Eventually, she was able to resist hurting her siblings emotionally and could see them as having been just as deprived as she had been. When she could eat locusts and wild honey, she no longer saw them as aggressive individuals fighting for limited resources, but imagined them as a group struggling for the very same thing – love and approval.

The wild honey metaphor reminds me that something sweet needs to be added to the process when we eat and metabolize our primal "locust" drives. I think of the wild honey as the neutralizing solution that we must pour over the toxic, burning, acidic feelings that get stirred within us during transmutation. When our blood is boiling or our emotions burning, we can pour on some neutralizing solution to help them settle and quiet down. We can find the right kind of honey to soothe the wound that is inevitably underneath. If we identify our locust drive as controlling others, we can have some sweet compassion for the wounded part of us that wants to control. If we identify our locust as envy and rivalry, we can pour some honey over the part of us that feels the need destroy those we envy. We can feed ourselves wild honey until we neutralize every drop of acid, toxin and poison.

Harnessing the transmuted energies

After actively wrestling with our destructiveness, embodying the feelings from the original wound and neutralizing their toxic effects, now we have a chance to redirect the transmuted energy into avenues more suited to our true Self. The image on the fourth sacred robe suggests this movement. The John the Baptist figure has transmuted the animal energies to the point where he can focus the fire flaming out of a very small oil jar in his left hand. Where we once had a wildfire of passions and chaotic animal forces – scattering our energy in a hundred directions – *now we can harness the wildfire into a controlled and channeled flame that has purpose and focus*. Think of the tremendous resource of energy that can now be redirected from our dragon. This is the next step in establishing our own identity: learning to harness these powerful drives towards a goal that takes into consideration our growth, development and higher purpose.

So how do we do this? We know from the story that John the Baptist appeared in the wilderness of Judea proclaiming, "Repent, for the Kingdom of Heaven is near. This is the one of whom the Prophet Isaiah spoke when he said 'the voice of one crying out in the wilderness, prepare the way of the Lord, make his paths straight.'"

John once again embodies the Adventurer archetype who teaches us how to make our path straight, how to harness the transmuted instinctive drives and focus them in a particular direction, the way a chariot rider must take the reigns of his horses and steer them down the path with a strong and steady hand. Now that we are no longer impulsively gratifying our drives and dragons because we have survived the refiner's fire, we must stay on the straight path toward our truth. In Kabbalah, we teach of walking the path of honesty (between Yesod and Tiferet) and continually returning to the central Pillar of Consciousness, where we gain some detachment from our powerful *Nefesh* instinctive drives (see Diagram 16).

Preparing the way and making straight the path, means *checking ourselves, cleaning up our act, practicing honesty and being ethical*. As we do this, we are developing keen inner watchfulness and presence to observe every situation. We learn to watch our envious drives, our destructiveness in relationships, our rivalrous or victimizing behaviors. We learn to wait with patience as our lions grow back their skin and are restored with a new kind of power – a power without the grandiosity but rich with ethical responsibility that can truly serve our development and facilitate our individuation.

With this shift, our energy is no longer drawn inward into compulsive or co-dependent behavior. It is no longer drawn outward into entanglements and projections. We therefore have more energy to harness and direct towards a new goal of personal truth and growth. We are now clearly shifting our attachment from the tribal/communal self to the individual self.

Another way to harness the transmuted energies is to *resist being swayed by external events*. This means steadying our chariot and steering it through whatever circumstances life brings our way. It does not mean railroading through life, but holding tight the reins and staying focused on the straight path. To do this we must have some sense of the long-term vision of our development, a vision that is absent in the "instant gratification" state of mind that can only see the short-term vision of getting the need met. A long-term perspective helps us gather and galvanize our energy when crisis or tragedy happens, not scatter our energy with panic and anxiety. If we get fired from our job or rejected in a relationship or lose money in the stock market, these external events no longer suck tremendous energy from us because we can see them as a stepping stone of learning on the way to our goal.

Back to our examples: when Susan was able to transmute the energy that once fueled her cigarette dragon, she had the energy to train as a counselor and was able to harness tremendous gifts of healing into a counseling practice that was fulfilling to her both personally and professionally. The rage and resentment that had previously entangled her was changed, freed and harnessed into healing others with similar dilemmas.

Amy was able to transmute her unhealthy relationship pattern and resist the pull to find men to rescue her from her emptiness and sadness. She broke the hold that this old pattern had on her body and soul and felt a tremendous surge of new energy that she could use to think about herself and build proper boundaries around herself. She used the chariot analogy to describe how she now felt like the driver of her own chariot, taking charge of her horses and the direction her chariot was going. This enabled her to sustain some solitude and spend time doing things just for herself – such as a spiritual practice, yoga and reading books. Now she was truly carving out space in her life to grow the trunk of her Tree.

Acts of Power

Now that we have harnessed new resources of energy and are focusing it toward a constructive goal, how are we going to manifest this in the world? How will this new identity be expressed? There comes a time in our development when we can no longer remain hidden or mute and must find our own voice as John does when he cries out in his wilderness. This entails moving out from a position of fear to a position of *actively risking the unknown, following the beat of our own heart, hearing our own voice, forming our own opinions, aligning with our own energy, and manifesting our identity in the world. At this stage we are ready to create acts of power.*

Once again, John the Baptist offers valuable suggestions. The first act of power that John models for us is "crying in the wilderness." This is when we practice hearing our own voice, testing out our own opinions based on our own experience. After separating from the tribe, we have a greater capacity to think our own thoughts, form our own opinions, and come to our own conclusions. As we perform this powerful act of speaking out in our own voice, we are building the base of the trunk of our Tree. Every time we take risks in the world, begin a new direction, take on a new job that directs us towards our passion and bliss, we lay a solid foundation to our trunk.

After crying in the wilderness, John returns to public life, baptizing and teaching his disciples who are ready for further initiation. They ask John what they should do, now that they have harnessed their energy and focused their lives in the direction of truth. How can they manifest their new identity in the world? John suggests some acts of power that will help them solidify their identity in the outer world, "whoever has two coats must share with anyone who has none and whoever has food must do likewise." Even tax collectors come to be baptized and they ask him, "Teacher, what should we do?" And he says to them, "Collect no more than the amount prescribed to you." Soldiers ask him, "What should we do?" And he says to them, "Do not extort money from anyone by threats or false accusations, and be satisfied with your wages."

The first act of power that John recommends to his disciples is to share their coats and food. From the psyche's perspective, this means sharing our wealth, sharing our abundance, sharing who we are. An act of power actually feeds other people in the world and makes a tangible difference. Now we can share our personal "wealth," gifts from our own storehouse of experience.

The next act of power that John recommends is to collect no more than the amount that is prescribed to us.

The tax collectors may have been tempted to collect more money than was actually due and to keep it for themselves, hoarding resources to make them feel more abundant. But John tells them to be exact and clear and honest. From the psyche's perspective, this means that we must not steal another person's resources – be it emotional abundance or creative ideas - for in order to build a solid trunk to our Tree, we must energetically develop and rely on our own resources. Being honest, exact and clear with who we are – limitations and all – is an act of power.

The next act of power recommended by John is to not extort money from anyone by threats or false accusations and to be satisfied with our wages.

Here he is speaking to the soldiers – the warriors within us who have a tendency, if not checked, to use force and intimidation to get what they want. "Extortion" means literally to wrench out or twist through torture. So an act of power is getting our soldiers in line and refraining from entangling them in other people's business. This saves tremendous energy. Again, it is an act of power to be satisfied with what we have and to not get caught up in the domination game of the animal level.

The whole arena of self-exploration – of actually having the courage to go out, take risks, and make new choices for ourselves – is clearly part of the hero's journey and involves acts of power from our Adventurer. These courageous acts in the world - standing up to our father, our mother, unhealthy relationships, saying "no," defining our personal boundaries - help us experience our true Self more tangibly in life. These deeds of courage strengthen our individual identity and our ability to stand under pressure.

Exercise 9: Commitment to acts of power

At this stage in the transmutation process, we have an abundance of energy that we can now use to express our new identity in the world. Make a commitment to performing these acts of power in the world. Set your intent in each of the following areas and take some risks. Write down exactly what you are going to do, and do it.

1. What gift or talent am I going to share with the world? When and with whom?
2. How will I be exact and honest, practicing self-honesty?
3. How will I refrain from entanglements?
4. What risk do I need to take in my life right now? When am I going to do it?
5. What do I need to say and express that I have been holding back – In my work? In my family? In my partnership? When will I express it?

Step 1: Leave the Village
Step 2: Survive the wilderness
Step 3: Transmute the power drives
* Step 4: Open the Heart *

The waters of the heart

So far, our fourth initiation has included leaving the village, surviving the wilderness and learning the art of transmutation. The final step in our initiation at Stage 4 is to follow our John the Baptist out of the desert and into the cooling waters of the River Jordan, where we arrive at the shore of the waters of the heart.

Opening the heart is the culmination of the fourth initiation. We have experienced the alchemical Calcinatio – the fiery, burning stage. Now we can bathe in the alchemical Solutio – the watery, heart-opening stage that brings cleansing and forgiveness of self and others, releasing us further from the bondage of dysfunctional patterns.

The River Jordan can be seen as a symbol of the healing waters of the heart. After the parched, arid wilderness experience, we finally arrive at the quenching waters of the heart, where healing can occur between body and mind, instinct and reason, intuition and intellect.

When John begins his teaching after his long desert training, he is a fully initiated wildman. In the psyche, he represents the awakened *Nefesh*: vital, powerful and alive. This is the part of us that has triumphed over the instincts, yet still retains the wild, instinctive spirit. When we reach this state of being, our heart is open and strong and we are awake enough to witness the *Ruah*, the spiritual twin. This is exactly what occurs to John when he is in the River Jordan and sees his cousin Jesus coming towards him into the water. This is not ordinary seeing but extraordinary seeing - seeing with an open heart - and recognizing with a great gasping "A-ha!" that it is not merely his cousin approaching him but the "Christ." Here is his beloved, the spiritual twin he has longed to meet.

Waiting for this blessed meeting, when the heart opens and we finally have some hope for inner healing and integration, can seem like an eternity. It often feels as if we are struggling and struggling all alone, hacking our way through the thick jungle of the tribal psyche. What we may not realize, however, is the tremendous amount of work that is being done on the other side of the jungle path. As we have been struggling, suffering, enduring and crying out for Spirit, the Spirit - or the spiritual twin within us - has been forging a path of connection as well.

In the story, not only has John been preparing and searching for the Christ but the Christ has been searching for John, for he needs John to baptize him and initiate him into the next phase of the journey. It is as if the Christ has been on the other side of the jungle path hacking away the obstructing vines and plants and suddenly bursts through on the day that he walks into the Jordan River and reveals himself to John. The spiritual twin has found the instinctive twin and there, in the waters of the heart, the twins are reunited and the possibility of internal integration begins (see Diagram 16).

Now John and Jesus – the instinctive and spiritual natures within us – can work together as a team helping us complete the fourth initiation and cross the threshold to the fifth stage. This important meeting happens for us on an internal level when we feel a deep inner awakening of the heart. This is when we contact an aspect of our deeper self that brings the promise of greater fulfillment in life, and our heart feels pierced with love.

Reuniting the twins

There is another story in the Jewish scriptures of twins, their separation, and eventual reuniting and heart opening, which is found in chapter 25 of the book of Genesis. This is the story of Jacob and Esau.

Esau is the first-born twin and Jacob the second-born. Esau is the wild twin – named because of his thick, wild, red hair. This links Esau with the earth and with the primal energies of nature. Esau is a skilled hunter of wild game and a man of the open country. Clearly he has physical strength and is connected to the instinctive world of the *Nefesh*.

Jacob, on the other hand, enjoys staying close to home among the tents and is clearly the more refined twin. His preference for quiet and for staying indoors connects him to the inner life and to our capacity for reflection and introversion. Jacob represents the spiritual twin. Although undeveloped at the beginning of the story, Jacob as our spiritual twin carries our capacity to journey deep within the heart to access our interior truth. This is the twin that carries knowledge of our purpose and destiny. Jacob develops and grows, but only through trials and great suffering. As the story progresses, Jacob steals his brother's birthright and his father's blessing and flees his home to escape the wrath of his wild twin who means to kill him.

During his exile on the way to his uncle's home, Jacob dreams of a great ladder extending from earth to heaven. After this powerful experience, he realizes that he has been given a vision of Spirit, an image of the ladder of initiation that bridges the two realms that the twins represent. This ladder of initiation represents the path that is forged so that earth and heaven can be bridged externally and our instinctive and spiritual natures can be integrated internally. *This is why the twins must work to reunite – because they work as a team within the psyche to build the trunk of our Tree of Life and to create a bridge between the roots and branches of our Tree.*

After receiving the knowledge of the Ladder vision, Jacob's eyes are opened to the reality of Spirit and he is transformed into the spiritual twin. On the way back to the land of his father, Jacob wonders whether his brother Esau is still embittered with the intent to kill him. Jacob hears from a scout who has traveled ahead that Esau is coming to meet him with 400 men, and Jacob braces himself for a violent confrontation. But when the twins finally come face-to-face, Esau runs to meet Jacob, takes him in his arms, holds him close and weeps.

What a beautiful ending to the story. Despite all the betrayal and heartache, Esau meets Jacob with an open heart and with tears of joy.

When the heart opens in this way, all wrongdoings melt into the distant past. When we can hold true to the primary values of the heart – such as love, forgiveness, compassion, and heartfelt desire – any chasm can be bridged. There is no misdemeanor of the heart that is too awful to repair. Within our own being, our "twins" often get separated, and it may take years of wandering in the wilderness and running from our real or imagined enemies to prepare us for the eventual reuniting and reconciliation that finally brings them back together again.

The caged heart

The emotional heart is one of our most tender and sensitive "organs." It is a painful fact that – through the experiences of life – our once open and vulnerable heart becomes wounded in some way, and we begin protecting and shielding our heart from further damage. Although this helps us at the time of the wounding, it prevents our heart from further opening, bonding and loving. Soon a cage begins to grow around our heart.

What experiences build a cage around a person's heart? What experiences do we personally endure that make our heart retract, shrink or hide? Some of the most common experiences have to do with abandonment, betrayal and rejection. When these experiences are repeated, the heart begins to shut down, freeze and withdraw. The heart loses its suppleness and juiciness, and it can dry up and harden.

On our initiation journey, we cannot complete the fourth initiation with a hardened heart. The heart must be opened, cultivated and made ready to receive the Neshamah, the soul, which blossoms in Stage 5.

So what keeps our hearts hardened? There is a famous story in Jewish history about Moses and the Egyptian Pharaoh, who was said to have a hardened heart. Pharaoh had enslaved the Hebrew people, and when Moses asked Pharaoh to let his people go so they could be free from bondage, Pharaoh refused to let them go because his heart was hardened. Pharaoh was using the Hebrew slaves to build his ever-expanding kingdom and therefore had great selfish motivation to maintain the status quo. He wanted to keep the slaves serving him and his desires.

The lesson here for us as initiates on the path is to recognize when we are being like Pharaoh and hanging on to the status quo, refusing to release the parts of us that need to develop. If we keep our heart hardened, we will not be allowed to cross the Jordan and begin the next initiation. When we fear leaving familiar territory or refuse to leave old karmic patterns, our heart remains caged and we cannot cross the threshold. If we continue to blame family, clan, tribe, religious upbringing, and other external circumstances, the cage around our heart tightens and we remain trapped. When we are unwilling to let go of the rage and disappointment over our needs not being met by the tribe, our heart remains hardened. When we refuse to forgive ourselves or refuse to forgive others, then we cannot cross the threshold.

If we are unwilling to surrender to the higher levels of authority – as John did to Christ – then we cling to our need for grandiosity and miss the chance to loosen the cage around our heart.

Exercise 10: The caged heart

The following is an exercise to assess whether there is a cage around your heart and to see how this cage is affecting your emotional openness or thwarting your healing process.

You will need to gather some supplies for this exercise. First, find a small box (shoe box or smaller and must be cardboard or something you can cut into), some masking tape, scissors, and paper and pen. You will also need an object that symbolizes your tender heart, an object that fits into your box so that you can close the lid. Place your heart object into the box. Then write down the answer to each question below with as much honesty as possible. (This will be your "caged heart list" for the next exercise.)

After you answer the first question, cut a long piece of tape, enough to go around the whole box, to represent each fear – and, one by one, begin taping up your box. Do the same with each question, using a piece of tape for each person you still blame, each disappointment you still hold on to and so on.

1. Do you fear leaving familiar territory? What fears exactly? Write down each fear and cut a piece of tape for each one and wrap it around your heartbox.
2. Do you refuse to leave old negative patterns? Which exactly? Tape your box for each answer.
3. Are you still blaming others – such as family, tribe, or religious upbringing? Who exactly and why? Tape…
4. Are you unwilling to let go of rage or disappointment that your needs were not met by_____? Who exactly and for what? Tape...
5. Do you refuse to forgive yourself for…? What exactly? Tape…
6. Do you refuse to forgive others for...? Who exactly and for what? Tape…
7. Do you hang onto betrayals perpetrated by others? What betrayals exactly do you hang on to? Tape...
8. Are you unwilling to surrender to your higher conscience, a higher "knowing" within yourself? How exactly? Tape...

When you are finished, behold the cage that surrounds your tender heart. How does it feel now to experience your tender heart inside this box bound with fear, blame, unwillingness, refusal and clinging? Keep the box wrapped and taped until the next exercise where you will dismantle the cage around your heart.

Repentance and forgiveness

How do we unbind and dismantle the cage that has grown like armor around our heart? How do we soften and melt our hardened heart?

To dissolve the cage around our heart, John leads us into the emotional waters to "repent" and "receive forgiveness of sins." "Repent" comes from the Greek word *"metanoia"* and it means literally "to turn around." Various scripture references were helpful in filling out the meaning of this word. From texts in both the Jewish and Christian scriptures, "repent" means:

to turn to God; to listen to God's will or voice; to seek God with all our heart and soul; to become humble; to seek the ways of God; to turn from unproductive ways; to not harden our heart; to forsake the foolish ways and to go in the way of understanding; to live in truth, judgment and righteousness.

The main message to be found in "repent" is the encouragement to turn around and open our heart. From the psyche's perspective, this means that we must turn around from all the ways that keep our heart closed and move into the emotional waters to open our heart. This means embracing what we have split off and banned from consciousness and turning around. Now we are free to move in a new direction.

The second half of John's message is "receive the forgiveness of sins." The word "sin" comes from the Greek "*hamartia*," which means, "to miss the mark." So if we have been living our life in a way that has nothing to do with our own truth, we need to turn around and adjust our aim so that we can stop missing the mark. Asking for forgiveness of sins means getting back on the path of honesty, rather than missing the mark by staying on the wrong path.

Repentance and forgiveness are crucial to our psychological and spiritual development. If we do not turn around and open our heart, it is extremely difficult to have empathy for others, to see our own destructiveness in relationships, and to initiate repair when damage has been done. Without the capacity for repentance, we remain like Pharaoh with a hardened heart, possessing no empathy for the slaves that we keep in bondage. Pharaoh was unable to contact his feelings of remorse, guilt or grief at their plight. Because Pharaoh refused to open his heart – which would have enabled him to see his wrongdoing – Moses was forced to send the Angel of Death, the tenth and final plague that hit Egypt and killed Pharaoh's beloved son. It was only after this terrible tragedy that Pharaoh contacted his grief, which then allowed his heart to soften so that he could let the Hebrew slaves go free.

We must be able to see how we have constructed the cage around our own heart, for only then can we contact the grief and remorse that will release us from this terrible trap. This is the stage of initiation where it is appropriate to feel guilt and remorse, for only through these feelings can we truly open our heart to empathize with others. Repentance and self-forgiveness are crucial if we are to make a true heart connection with others and with ourselves. Without repentance and the forgiveness of sins, we never step into the Jordan and flow with the waters of the heart.

Exercise 11: *Dismantling the cage around your heart*

First, place your caged heartbox on a low altar that you can comfortably sit next to. Light two candles on either side of the box and sit down. Look once again at your "caged heart list" and reflect on the ways you keep your own heart caged. Take as much time as you need to reflect on the questions below. Acknowledge each clearly and cleanly without "beating yourself up" or getting bogged down in remorse. Sit with each experience for a while. (It is very helpful to have soft chanting, music or drumming during this exercise.)

1. See how you have been destructive to self and others.
2. Ask forgiveness of self and others.

3. Let go of blame and disappointment.

4. Find your willingness to turn around from your unproductive ways and go in the direction of your truth.

5. Allow grief, remorse and tears to flow.

When you feel you have finished, take your box and your scissors and cut through the tape that binds your heartbox shut. Cut all the tape and, as you do, imagine the cage dismantling around your heart. Open your box and retrieve your heart symbol and place it on your heart. When you are ready, place your heart symbol on the altar. Rest and meditate on your emotional heart and the freedom you feel when your heart is released.

Living with the beat of your own heart

When the cage around our heart is dismantled, we can finally hear the beat of our own heart. This brings a tremendous sense of freedom; for now we can finally follow our heart's true desire and choose a life that is in sync with our own rhythm. When the cage is dismantled, we also have more access to the powerful emotions of the heart - love, compassion, forgiveness, empathy and desire. Not only can we follow the beat of our own heart, but we can also live our life with openheartedness, embracing others and ourselves with a contagious sense of freedom. When the heart is free of cages, defenses, walls, fortresses and debilitating wounds, we feel a tremendous release and a sense of being cleansed.

Most spiritual traditions have sacred rites and rituals that mark this stage of initiation. Most rituals that acknowledge the opening of the heart and the cleansing away of old destructive patterns use the element of water. In the Christian tradition it is called the "rite of baptism." Any kind of "baptism" or ritual cleansing with water symbolizes an emotional rebirth of some kind – a dedication and commitment to live a new kind of life. This initiation marks the opening of the heart so that we are free to love in a new way and free to live with the beat of our own heart.

Baptism

One of my favorite scenes in the story of John the Baptist is when Jesus asks John to baptize him. What a powerful experience it must have been for John to finally meet his beloved twin and to initiate him in the sacred rite of baptism.

Baptism is an initiation of the heart, a rebirth of the heart into a new level of being. It involves sprinkling, dipping, dunking or submerging into the sacred waters, which helps the heart transform from a hardened state to a soft, supple and pliable state. Baptism consecrates the heart as a sacred vessel of healing. The heart has the potential to become our greatest asset in healing because it is big enough to accept the full spectrum of emotions from love to hate. It can grow to expand and embrace everything in life - good and bad, light and shadow. The open heart can genuinely ask for forgiveness, acknowledge fault and mistakes, and can hold the flaws of human experience. The open heart can become the greatest healer.

When Jesus asks John to baptize him, Jesus is affirming that John is now a suitable vessel to gestate and birth the *Neshamah*, the true Self. If John had not completed his initiation and was still a tribal self, he would not be a suitable vessel to embrace the Christ, for the seed of the Spirit can only take root in a person who has developed a separate identity with a sense of solidity and self-definition. The awakened *Nefesh* is the right kind of vessel because this robust, individuating self has the right kind of soil to receive, nurture, incubate and birth the *Neshamah*. The development and purification of the *Neshamah*, the radiant soul, happens in Stage 5, but this final step in Stage 4 is when the heart opens to accept the seed of Christ consciousness that will eventually grow into a beautiful, unique, individuated soul.

This seeding and rebirth occur in the landscape of the heart because the soul speaks the language of the heart. When the soul breaks in upon our mundane world and we experience a soulful connection, a soulful piece of music or a soulful dream, it is the heart that understands this language. It is the heart that breaks open, falls in love, gasps in awe and wonder, and sings with beauty. It is the heart that is able to receive "the Christ," for only the heart is able to humanize and personalize what comes from Spirit. The heart is where the Spirit is made concrete in an individual life, where the transpersonal meets the personal. When we invite the Christ, the spirit twin, into the meeting ground of the heart, we invite the seed of our true Self to grow within the heart until we can eventually cultivate our heart's true desire.

The heart (Tiferet on the Tree of Life) is the emotional organ where the roots, trunk and branches of our Tree of Life meet. Only the heart can bind together all three parts of our Tree in its magical, healing waters. When John initiates Jesus in the sacred rite of baptism, he activates a rebirth, a second birth. The first birth is our physical birth and the second is the psychological birth of the individual soul. During this baptism, we experience the watery alchemical Solutio that binds the *Nefesh* and *Neshamah* together in the chalice of the heart, where the magnificence of our true Self can grow and flourish.

Conclusion – Initiation 4: Establish Identity

The fourth initiation has taught us to lay a solid foundation to the trunk of our Tree of Life. We have learned how to leave the village and manage healthy separation from our tribal voices and expectations. We have established a deep connection with our own identity away from the tribe. We have successfully survived our wilderness and we feel adventurous, awake, alive and invigorated. We are now able to transmute the destructive aspects of our power drives and harness that energy to work for us rather than against us. We feel confident of our inner resources so that we can handle conflicts, confrontations, disapproval and criticism. We can take risks and we can venture into unknown territory with excitement and curiosity. Our heart is open and we are ready to cross the threshold to the fifth initiation.

It is time now to step to the other side of the Jordan River, where we begin the next phase of our training: developing the chalice of the soul.

Chapter 5

Soulflare
Robe 5

Initiation 5 - TRUTH

In the fifth initiation, we solidify the trunk of our Tree of Life, finding the true center of our personal power and living out our personal truth. During this initiation, we develop and manifest the qualities of the soul, which are: integrity, justice, love and compassion. The ancient Greek myth of Theseus, King Minos and the Minotaur will guide us to complete initiation so that we feel courageous, confident, responsible, potent, passionate and focused.

In order to activate this initiation, we call upon three powerful archetypal forces: The **Hero**, the **Warrior** and the **King**. (The feminine versions are the **Heroine**, the **Warrioress** and the **Queen**.) The Hero claims our authority in life, the Warrior focuses the will, and the King acts courageously with compassion. Together they create a dynamic team, helping us to find our own voice, stand in our own power and speak our own truth. The Hero, Warrior and King set our passion alight so that life is infused with meaning and we are able to follow our heart's true desire.

Qualities if initiated:	**Problems if initiation is not complete:**
Courage	Lacking courage
Self-responsibility	Irresponsible
Internal authority	Authority and power seen in others, not within
Self-confidence	Feeling impotent
Passionate about life	Life lacks meaning and passion
Able to speak our truth, take a stand	Unable to speak our truth
Focused will	Lacking will power
Aware of personal power	Drive to perfection, need to be extraordinary
Integrity	Dishonest, false-hearted
Developed conscience, inner morality	Lacking compassion and moral strength

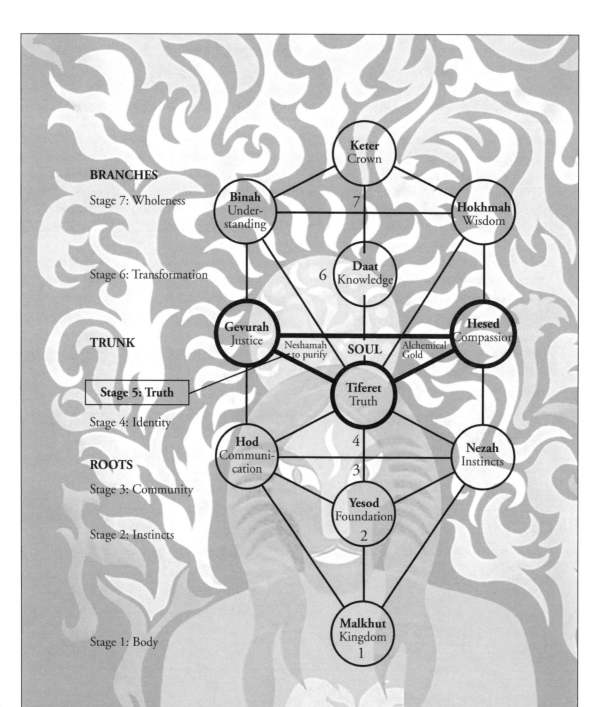

BRANCHES

Stage 7: Wholeness

Stage 6: Transformation

TRUNK

Stage 5: Truth

Stage 4: Identity

ROOTS

Stage 3: Community

Stage 2: Instincts

Stage 1: Body

Keter Crown

Binah Under-standing

Hokhmah Wisdom

7

Daat Knowledge

6

Gevurah Justice

Neshamah to purify

SOUL

Alchemical Gold

Hesed Compassion

Tiferet Truth

4

Hod Communi-cation

3

Nezah Instincts

Yesod Foundation

2

Malkhut Kingdom

1

Diagram 17: Stage 5
The fifth initiation involves solidifying the trunk of our Tree. This is the stage of true individuation, as we commit ourselves to our own path of truth and awaken the soul. What follows is a process of purification, as the soul is tested, refined, sculpted and shaped into the unique vessel or trunk that will bear the branches and fruit of the Tree.

Chapter 5 - Live your Truth

In the previous initiation, we left our root system to establish our own identity away from the tribe. We discovered the beginnings of a strong trunk, separate from the roots and different from all other trees. Now in Stage 5, our trunk grows in stature and strength, making itself known in the big forest of life. The fifth initiation is the place of true individuation, where we are able to embrace our roots (Stages 1, 2, and 3) and withstand the wilderness (Stage 4) so that we can commit ourselves to our own path of truth.

One of the differences between this stage and Stages 1 through 4 is that our needs in the first four stages center on the instinctive needs of the *Nefesh* for security, relationship, comfort, sexual gratification and animal survival. In Stage 5, we are initiated into the *Neshamah*, the soul proper, which has very different needs. The soul has a need to express its unique and individual contribution to the collective. The soul needs to feel connected to its heartfelt desires and deep passions. The soul needs to find purpose, without which it will wither and die. Life has little meaning unless we are in touch with some aspect of the soul.

In the fourth initiation, John the Baptist prepared the way for the *Neshamah* by going out into the wilderness, grounding the energies of the instinctive psyche and leading us to the waters of the heart. Now we have crossed the threshold to Stage 5 – where the *Nefesh* and *Neshamah* engage in an alchemy of the heart, stirring us to passionately live our truth, centered on the heart and will.

Exercise 1: Meditation - Strengthening the trunk of your Tree of Life

Imagine once again your Tree of Life. See the sturdy root system and the beginning of the trunk of the Tree. Focus your attention on the trunk and imagine being inside this good solid trunk you have established.

Next, focus your attention on where you are going. What is your destination? Your main destination is to continue to grow up towards the sky and the light so that you can eventually sprout branches and grow fruit. Your destiny is to move up and out, becoming more and more visible to the world, sharing your fruit with others.

To do this, your trunk must be centered and strong, focused and steadfast in purpose. As your trunk grows in height and thickness, find the true center of your trunk so that you can find your balance. Stand strong within this place. Feel confidence in your ability to draw from your roots. Stay centered in your power and direct the further growth of your Tree. Breathe deeply into this center of power. When you feel balanced and centered, draw your attention back to the present and bring this sense of your trunk into your awareness now as you read on.

* Step 1: Ignite the Soul *
Step 2: Claim your Authority
Step 3: Focus the Will
Step 4: Act Courageously

Igniting the Soul

In the fourth Sacred Robe, we saw John the Baptist focusing his flame and setting out his intent as he cried for a vision, "Who am I and what am I supposed to be doing?" This question was infused into the Raven, who flamed out of his hands to seek the answer. The Raven is like a flaming arrow launched towards the soul. When it is directed with accuracy and passion, it pierces the soul and sets it alight, igniting the *Neshamah*. The Raven in Robe 4 is the messenger, the scout – and the radiating figure in Robe 5 receives the message, is pierced by the flames and ignites into a great flare of the soul – whereupon the soul then responds "This is who I am. Initiate me. Ignite my soul. Bless me. Help me to birth my true Self."

It reminds me of the Genesis story that describes the birth of Adamah. In Genesis 2:7 it says that God breathed into Adamah a "living soul," a *"Neshamah"*. This is when Adamah became conscious of the soul and therefore fully alive. It is in this moment of self-consciousness and self-reflection that our *Neshamah* is set alight by the breath of God.

This is exactly what happens to us during the fifth initiation: we awaken the soul and become conscious of our true Self, our true humanity. *What follows after the soul is ignited, is the long process of purification, when the Neshamah is tested, refined, sculpted and shaped into the unique trunk that will bear the branches and fruit of the Tree.* On the Tree of Life diagram, the soul triad is traditionally associated with the word "purify," indicating that the soul moves through a series of purifications and refinements over the course of its initiation (see Diagram 17).

This chapter will cover the steps of purification that refine the *Neshamah* to transform it into the beautiful chalice of the soul. In mythology, the refined and sculpted soul chalice is often referred to as the Holy Grail, the beautiful goblet of the true Self that receives the breath of Spirit and the spark of divine fire that sets it alight. In the Christian tradition, Mary, the mother of the Christ, is a good example of what the awakened *Neshamah* looks and feels like. She represents the purified soul in a state of openness, ready to receive the spiritual impulse. Mary built her internal soul vessel or chalice into a Holy Grail that was ready, worthy, and sturdy enough to birth the Christ. When our own soul is purified and in a state of openness, we too can birth the Christ child within ourselves and begin to manifest our individual purpose. When the true Self is born in the stable of our open heart, this newborn consciousness is free of ego identification and is open to the impulse of Spirit.

Radiating our own Light

Let's look more closely at the figure on the fifth Sacred Robe – a figure that inspires us to live our truth in a unique and individual way. This figure represents an initiate of the "Solar Mysteries" who has awakened the heart and will and has developed the soul. The Solar Mysteries of Stages 4 and 5 help us to connect with Tiferet on the Tree of Life diagram, which is where the sun resides. The ancient Solar Mysteries were designed to help people *access their inner sun in order to radiate their own light and heat and be conscious of their true essence.* The Solar Mysteries ensure the continuity of soul and soulful life and help us shape our contribution to the collective life of humanity. (For more on the Solar Mysteries, see Appendix D.)

As we look at the robe, there is a sense of solar radiation that we can see in the eyes, in the forehead flame, and in the sun disk above the figure's head. The other important images on the robe are found at the base where we see two tender hands holding the chalice, which in turn incubates a heart. This reminds us to build a sacred vessel strong enough to incubate our heart, while our soul muscles are developing. After we declare, "Initiate me. Ignite my soul," what follows is a period of softening of the heart, holding of the heart, strengthening of the heart, centering of the heart and a time of finding the heart's true desire. During the fifth initiation, we move into a time of deep soul searching.

On the fifth Sacred Robe, the hands holding the chalice can be seen as the hands of the true Self, providing a safe container while we incubate and dream our heart's true desire. When our tender heart or brave heart is held in the hands of the chalice for long enough, then we can slowly manifest our desires in the outer world. When this happens, we begin to radiate our own sun, sending out a solar flare or a "Soulflare" to the world. When we live radiating our own light and doing our soul work, we begin to draw people towards us. A sacred dialogue begins with the outer world that attracts the attention of the collective heart or the divine heart, which, on the robe, is descending to meet the personal heart of the figure.

This sacred dialogue at Stage 5 is often called "synchronicity" – when events occur in the outer world to confirm the soul's development. This is when things seemingly fall into our lap, the right person shows up at the right time, we are in the right place to make just the right connection, the right door opens and we walk right through. This is not just luck, but the perfect synchronization of universal laws. It is said that when we reach this level of consciousness, we call out to the universe and the universe responds.

The Chalice of the Soul

Let's return to the image of the chalice on the robe. The chalice shape has three basic points: the base and the two sides of the cup. To locate this soul chalice on our body, imagine the base of the chalice around the heart, chest and lung region. Then imagine the left and right shoulders forming the two sides of the cup, with a line connecting them through the throat region. This means the chalice of the soul embodies both the heart and throat energy centers.

On the Tree of Life diagram, we can see the chalice shape quite easily by looking at Tiferet, Gevurah and Hesed, which make up the soul triad, also called the "Chalice of the Soul" (see diagram 18). Tiferet translates as "truth, beauty and goodness", Gevurah as "justice or discipline" and Hesed as "mercy or compassion." Astrologically, Tiferet, Gevurah and Hesed correspond to the Sun, Mars and Jupiter. From an archetypal perspective, they correspond to the Hero, Warrior and King. When all three archetypal points of the chalice are developed and coordinated together, they manifest the powerful soul qualities of commitment, conviction and courage – commitment to our truth, conviction to fight for our truth, and the courage to take action in order to manifest our truth. This describes the ignited soul – **committed, full of conviction** and **courageous**.

In order to build a strong soul chalice, we need to combine the leadership of the Hero, the discipline and determination of the Warrior and the fierce compassion of the goodhearted King.

The **Hero**, who occupies the Tiferet position of the chalice, is the part of us that seeks after truth and claims individual authority in life. The Hero commits us to our own path of truth and takes the helm as captain of the great ship of the soul to guide our heart's true desire.

The **Warrior**, who occupies the Gevurah position, generates the passionate conviction

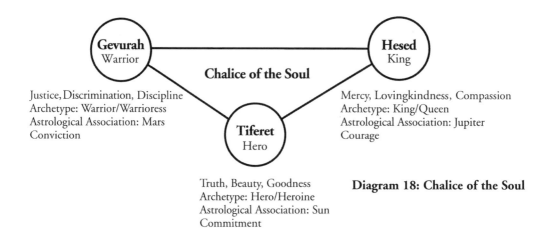

Chalice of the Soul

Gevurah
Warrior

Hesed
King

Tiferet
Hero

Justice, Discrimination, Discipline
Archetype: Warrior/Warrioress
Astrological Association: Mars
Conviction

Mercy, Lovingkindness, Compassion
Archetype: King/Queen
Astrological Association: Jupiter
Courage

Truth, Beauty, Goodness
Archetype: Hero/Heroine
Astrological Association: Sun
Commitment

Diagram 18: Chalice of the Soul

that helps us fight for our truth and generates the discipline needed to focus our will. The Warrior also wields the sword that creates boundaries *to protect our truth and defend our heart's true desire.*

The **King**, who occupies the Hesed position, has the courage to make sacrifices and take positive action to manifest our soul's dream. The King *initiates the heart's true desire in the world.*

Together, these three powerful archetypes create a dynamic team to help us develop a truly individual focus, take full responsibility for ourselves and become the true author of our own life. When our chalice is strong, our personal power is well developed and artfully balanced between the heart and the will. The fifth initiation involves first igniting the soul and then training the Hero, the Warrior and the King. When initiation is successful, we will be able to manifest the qualities of the soul, which are *commitment, conviction, courage, love, justice, mercy, integrity, self-responsibility, inner authority, individuality, and authenticity.*

Exercise 2: Meditation - The chalice of your soul

The following is a meditation to envision the chalice of your soul and anchor it inside your body.

Close your eyes and imagine a beautiful chalice, the chalice of your soul. What does it look like? What is it made out of? Is it decorated with anything? Are there symbols or jewels around it? Once you see this chalice clearly in your mind's eye, imagine the chalice moving towards your chest and melting right into your heart, chest and throat region. Feel the strength and beauty of your chalice radiating within you.

Focus now on the three main points of the chalice. At the base of the chalice feel the Hero within you who knows your truth. Stand your chalice firmly on your truth. Make a commitment to yourself and your own path in life. On the left side of the chalice cup, near the left shoulder, feel the Warrior within you who fights for justice. Feel the strength of your conviction and the strength of your will. And on the right side of the chalice cup, near your right shoulder, feel the King within you who can take right action in the world and who can show great compassion to yourself and others. Feel your courage.

Now activate and energize the chalice of your soul by acknowledging your commitment at the base of the chalice, your conviction on the left side of the chalice, and your courage on the right side of the chalice. Commitment, conviction, courage...commitment, conviction, courage... commitment, conviction, courage... See your chalice glowing, beaming and radiating within your being.

Imagine now your chalice holding the beauty of your soul. Allow your soul to rest comfortably in this beautiful chalice. Breathe and allow the wondrous qualities of your soul to unfold before you – love, justice, compassion, integrity, self-responsibility, inner authority, individuality and authenticity. Relax and breathe. Bring your consciousness back now to the present and allow the beauty of your chalice to come into real time and your real life. Come back fully into the present and when you feel ready, open your eyes.

Who is ruling the Soul Kingdom?

How do we develop all the beautiful qualities of the soul? How do we find our own voice, stand in our power, and speak our truth? How can we develop the commitment, conviction and courage needed for a strong chalice of the soul? There are certain conditions that must be right in order to build the chalice of the soul and purify the *Neshamah*.

First, we have to know that the kingdom of the soul exists somewhere deep within our being. We must have a belief or hope that there is something greater than the *Nefesh* and something more satisfying than gratifying our instinctual and animal desires.

Next, we must make sure that the ruler who sits on the throne of this inner kingdom is our true Self. If the ruler on our throne is not looking after our best interests, then we must adjust this inner situation and put a good ruler on the throne. In order to build our chalice into the Holy Grail, we must know with certainty who is ruling our soul's kingdom.

In order to understand the makings of a good ruler, it is sometimes helpful to look at stories about a bad ruler. The following is an ancient myth from the Mediterranean about a corrupted ruler and a hero who overthrows the king and redeems the kingdom. This is also a story about individuation and the making of a true soul. It will guide us through the Hero, Warrior and King training and will help us rule our soul kingdom with a strong will and compassionate heart.

The story of King Minos, the Minotaur, Theseus and Ariadne
Part 1: King Minos and the Minotaur

Once upon a time, there was a man named Minos, who was the son of Zeus and Europa. He was contending with his two brothers for the throne of Crete and was seeking divine affirmation from Poseidon, god of the sea. When Minos asked for a sign to bless his Kingship, Poseidon looked favorably upon Minos and sent to him a pure white bull from the sea. But in return, Poseidon demanded that the bull be sacrificed back to him. "A small price to pay," thought Minos to himself, "For what would I, as King of Crete, need with another white bull?"

But when Minos saw the beautiful white of bull of Poseidon emerge from the sea, greed grabbed his heart and he decided to keep the bull for himself, substituting another white bull from his royal herd to be sacrificed.

Poseidon was not amused and decided to take revenge for this act of hubris and disrespect. He enlisted Aphrodite, goddess of love, to cast a spell on King Minos' wife, Queen Pasiphae, a spell that would cause her to be consumed with passion and desire for the white bull from the sea. And so it was that Queen Pasiphae became inflamed with passion for the bull and to satisfy this passion, she enlisted Daedelus, the king's master craftsman, to build her a hollow cow to tempt the bull.

The product of this fated union was the monstrous Minotaur – a fierce creature with the body of a man and the head of a bull, whose devouring hunger could only be satisfied with human flesh and blood. Now King Minos was horrified that his greed and disregard for Poseidon's demands had led to the birth of the Minotaur. How could he have made such a terrible mistake? To hide his shame, he enlisted Daedelus to construct a great labyrinth in the deepest, darkest bowels of the palace. And at the center of the labyrinth, he kept the Minotaur, whose bellowing and groaning was a constant reminder to the king that the Minotaur needed to be fed.

King Minos arranged to enslave seven maidens and seven youths from mainland Athens so that he could feed them to the Minotaur. But before going to their doom, these maidens and youths were taught the sport of the bull dance, which became the entertainment of the king's court in Crete. In this way, the young men and women had a sporting chance to live – for if they could avoid the bull in the ring, they would be kept out of the winding path of the labyrinth and the waiting jaws of the Minotaur.

The ritual of the bull dance was presided over by Ariadne, daughter of King Minos and Queen Pasiphae. Now Ariadne was the high priestess of the royal court, and in her role as high priestess she would watch the sport of the bull dancing, week after week, month after month and time after time. And never once did any man stir her heart or her loins until one day she laid eyes on a powerful bull dancer who had come to the royal court. His name was Theseus.

Part 2: Theseus and Ariadne

Theseus was a man with two fathers, one earthly and one divine. On the night he was conceived, his mother, Aethra, lay with a kingly stranger. On that same night, she was told in a dream to wade through the waters to a small island shrine where Poseidon also lay with her.

During his childhood, Theseus knew only of his divine father, Poseidon. But at the age of sixteen, his mother told him that by moving a large stone and revealing what lay underneath it, he could find the identity of his earthly father. With great effort, he moved the stone, which revealed the sword and sandals of Aegeus, the King of Athens. Theseus donned the sandals, which were a perfect fit, and he took the sword, leapt onto a chariot, and headed for Athens to reveal himself to his father, a father who as yet did not even know that he had a legitimate heir to his throne.

On his journey, Theseus faced many life-threatening trials. But his desire to know his royal father drove him on to finally reach Athens, where he presented himself to Aegeus, his father. But the king's mistress was the witch Medea who wished to secure the throne for her own son and convinced Aegeus that Theseus was an impostor. She suggested that Theseus be poisoned for posing as the king's heir and Aegeus agreed. Theseus was saved in the nick of time when he revealed the sandals and the sword that proved his legitimacy as heir to the throne. Aegeus then welcomed Theseus as the rightful heir to his kingdom, and the Athenians grew to love him as well.

But one day, all of Athens was plunged into mourning at the sight of the Cretan ships approaching the harbor, for everyone knew that seven maidens and seven youths would be taken from them for the bull dance on Crete and as a sacrifice to the Minotaur. Hoping to put an end to Crete's power over Athens, Theseus volunteered to be one of the seven youths who would go to Crete to learn the bull dance.

On the long sea voyage, Theseus became a leader to all the young men and women. He encouraged them and united them together as a team. When at last they arrived on Crete, they were not a group of frightened children but a band of young warriors and warrioresses. For many weeks, Theseus led his team to learn the art of bull dancing. Soon they were ready to face the bull. As they entered the ring of the bull dance for the first time, they raised their eyes to honor the high priestess of Crete. It was then that Theseus first laid his eyes on the beautiful Ariadne. His heart was stirred and his loins burned. He found new motivation to survive the bull dance.

As the dance began, the bull charged. Theseus grabbed the bull by the horns and pulled himself to somersault over its head and onto its back before leaping into the waiting arms of his teammates. Theseus' skill in the ring drew the attention of the audience who had never before seen such a skilled bull dancer. But no one's attention was more drawn than that of the high priestess Ariadne, who felt an unknown stirring in her heart.

As time went on, their secret passion for one another grew. Ariadne finally sent for Theseus and he was brought secretly to her chamber. Knowing that they were in love, they also realized that they came from two different worlds – Athens and Crete, sun and moon, god and goddess.

Ariadne introduced him to her world by showing him the magical tools of the high priestess: the snakes used in the snake dance, leading the priestesses into states of ecstasy, and her snakelike bracelets that coiled around her forearms and were used for divination during the rituals and ceremonies she performed. Next, she showed Theseus the sacred labrys, the double-headed ax which guarded the entrance and the exit to the labyrinth. The labrys and all the secrets it held, was crucial for the journey to the center of the labyrinth. Lastly, Ariadne showed him the ball of white linen thread, the tool that could lead Theseus through the labyrinth, through the twists and turns of the dark path to the center and back.

Theseus then introduced her to his world. He came from a world where Apollo was worshiped, the solar realm where heroes were revered for their accomplishments in battle, sport, and hunt. Rather than the snake dancer, Theseus was the bull dancer. His success depended on skill, wit, strength and courage to face the bull and grab it by the horns. He told her that this is what it would take to defeat the Minotaur, his purpose in coming to Crete.

Ariadne knew that whoever ventured into the labyrinth would not come out alive, so she vowed to help him. She gave him the sacred labrys and the ball of white linen thread, and led him to the entrance of the labyrinth, which sat in the depths of the darkness below the palace. As she held securely to one end of the thread, Theseus unraveled it as he traveled into the coils of the labyrinth. Holding the labrys and feeling Ariadne at the other end of the thread, he sensed the presence of the goddess who gave him second sight, enabling him to penetrate the secrets of the labyrinth.

As he drew near the center, he heard the great bellowing of the Minotaur. Turn after turn, he drew nearer and nearer to the beast. He knew that the Minotaur smelled and sensed his approach. Now these two sons of Poseidon would do battle.

Theseus turned the final corner, and in the darkness was upon the beast. There was a great battle - flesh against flesh, man against beast. After much struggling, Theseus emerged victorious. Having slain and defeated the Minotaur, he picked himself up from the scene of the battle, still holding the end of the linen thread and still sensing Ariadne's love at the other end of the string.

Theseus wound his way out of the labyrinth and as he returned to the light, he and Ariadne were reunited. In slaying the Minotaur with bravery and strength, Theseus redeemed the whole kingdom from the curse and sin of King Minos. He saved not only himself, but also freed Athens from their enslavement to the demanding King.

It is said that after the Minotaur was slain, a violent earthquake destroyed King Minos and his palace so that never again did the Athenians have to sacrifice their children to a bad King. Theseus and Ariadne escaped the earthquake and were free to follow their own destinies. As the story goes, when Theseus and Ariadne stopped at an island on the way to mainland Greece, Ariadne met Dionysus and there remained with him, creating a fruitful partnership of ecstatic dancing and worship. But Theseus was destined to return to Athens, and in time took his place on the throne as rightful heir and fair ruler of the Kingdom. Thus ends the story of King Minos and the Minotaur, Theseus and Ariadne. [1]

Sin, redemption and sacrifice

This is a powerful story about the state of a kingdom when a corrupt ruler is sitting on the throne and about the redemption needed to release the curse and restore the kingdom. The story also tells us of the consequences if we have a bad ruler on the throne.

How did King Minos become corrupt in the first place? What was his sin?

At the very beginning of the story, Minos was fighting for the kingship of Crete. When Minos asked Poseidon for help in securing the throne, Poseidon agreed to help him because he saw in Minos the potential to be a good ruler. Minos had access to his power and showed much promise in his ability to rule his own life as well as the life of the kingdom. Based on this, Poseidon agrees to help, sends him the pure white bull from the sea, and asked that Minos return a blood sacrifice back to him in acknowledgment of the gift. At first Minos agreed, but when he saw the beautiful white bull, something grabbed his heart – greed.

King Minos had great responsibility because he was the ruler of the whole land. Within the psyche he represents the soul, which rules the entire landscape of the psyche. The good ruler's job is to sit on the throne, survey the kingdom, and make decisions based on the good of the whole – not based on self-gratification. *Minos' sin was to gratify self rather than the whole kingdom.* He wanted to keep the lovely white bull for himself, instead of sacrificing it back to the collective, back to the god who gave it to him in the first place. We too commit a similar "sin" when we receive a gift from the gods, from Spirit, and either ignore it or keep it for ourselves.

In terms of the Tree of Life, rather than ruling consciously from his soul triad of Tiferet, Gevurah, and Hesed, Minos dropped down to the animal and vegetable levels and said, "I'm going to keep this for myself. This gift from the gods is to gratify me." King Minos lost consciousness of the *Neshamah* and dropped into his *Nefesh* passions for self-gratification.

When we have developed to this stage of consciousness and transgress the laws of soulful living, willingly going against the laws of the *Neshamah*, it has grave consequences not only for the individual, but also for our family and loved ones, and for the generations to come. The laws of the soul are the laws governing someone who has reached the level of individuation and has attained mastery over the *Nefesh*. Therefore, at this stage of initiation, we are required to take more and more personal responsibility for our choices. *Minos' sin is a transgression against the soul and therefore warrants a specific kind of redemption, an act that will redirect the soul back to its original course, back into alignment with its true heart and will.*

Redemption is the act of freeing from captivity by payment of ransom, freeing from the consequence of sin or releasing from blame or debt. Unfortunately, Minos is unable to perform an act of redemption to save his kingdom. He is unable to free himself from his crime and instead compounds his debt by building the labyrinth and hiding the Minotaur within. As the beast continually screams for food and further karmic payment, the Minotaur reminds Minos of the depth of his crime, which hits at the heart of his kingdom and is aimed against his very soul.

If we look back at the beginning of the story, we can see how a bad decision on the part of our ruler (positioned at Tiferet) has serious consequences. For it was directly after Minos' transgression in failing to carry out his promise, that Poseidon arranged to have Minos' wife cursed and gave Queen Pasiphae a longing for the bull. When our ruler "goes bad" and makes inappropriate choices, it has a direct effect on our "heart" and we long for the wrong thing.

Furthermore, when we understand that the bull represents the *Nefesh* – our animal drive – and the Queen represents the *Neshamah* – our heart and soul – it becomes clear how this longing for the wrong thing cannot result in a sacred union of human-to-human, or soul-to-soul. Rather when we "miss the mark" or "sin" as King Minos did, our heart's desire becomes misdirected, and we begin desiring things that are incompatible with our spiritual journey. It is for this reason that it is often very difficult for people to know what their heart's desire truly is, because it has been misdirected into something that ultimately does not satisfy the soul.

The result of this misdirected heart is a union that can produce a Minotaur, a creature who is half animal and half human. This union produces not a sacred child, but a child of shame, resulting in feelings of humiliation. The Minotaur also becomes an entity within the psyche that is devouring and consuming and must be constantly fed, and the food is the horrible sacrifice of the seven maidens and the seven youths.

What King Minos does to hide the shame of his actions is to build a labyrinth underneath his palace. The Minotaur is like a psychological complex hidden and buried in the unconscious that the individual pretends is not there but, of course, it comes bellowing down the generations. Eventually, somebody has to deal with and redeem the sin of the ruler who transgressed the laws of the soul. In the end, Minos inflicts suffering on his wife, on himself, on his kingdom and on the children of Athens, who represent the new and vital potentials surging up from within the psyche. Rather than feeding Minos with vitality and new life, these "maidens" and "youths" are instead sacrificed and fed to the devouring complex of the Minotaur so that all forms of new life within the psyche are aborted and life remains unredeemed and in a state of continual suffering.

In order to redeem this transgression, an appropriate sacrifice needs to be made by someone who possesses the *purity of heart, purity of will and purity of intention* necessary to free the kingdom from Minos' sin. In Steps 2, 3 and 4 of this initiation, we will see how Theseus has the heart, will and intention to redeem the kingdom and how we too can do the same for our own kingdom.

Staying in alignment with the soul

In the story, Poseidon required that a sacrifice be made and although Minos agreed at first, something happened to make him forget his promise. In the language of Depth Psychology, an autonomous complex took control because his *Nefesh* was not yet under full command of the *Neshamah*. If Minos had sacrificed the bull, he would have stayed in alignment with his soul.

When Minos kept the bull for himself, however, he went radically off course. When our motivation is "impure," when our heart is not true, when our will is aligned with the power drives and not in service of the heart, *we move out of alignment with our soul*. The sacrifice of the appropriate bull back to the gods is a symbol of the sacrifice we must make to stay in alignment and to keep the vitality of the *Nefesh* under conscious control of the *Neshamah*.

When Minos refused to make the necessary sacrifice to surrender his *Nefesh* to the higher will of the *Neshamah*, the result of this karmic choice was the birth of the Minotaur and its devouring need for human sacrifice over and over again. In this scenario, there is continual grueling sacrifice but no redemption, continual suffering both to self and to others, but no renewal. The blood sacrifice of the maidens and youths never redeems Minos' sin. True redemption comes from a sacrifice of a different nature, an inner sacrifice. The kind of sacrifice that will end the suffering is the sacrifice that is made by the Hero, Warrior and King within us - the Theseus figure - who is willing to risk his life-blood to save the whole kingdom.

There are many types of sacrifices that we may need to make in order to **stay in alignment with our soul**. They include:

- The soul taking the bigger picture into account by stopping, reflecting and thinking about what is happening, rather than acting impulsively.
- Refraining from using others for self-gratification.
- Refraining from manipulating situations to get what we want.
- Accepting differences in a radical way.
- Loving others with a compassionate heart regardless of how they treat us.
- Being compassionate with our complexes and neuroses.
- Being compassionate with our children, loved ones, parents, students, clients.
- Loving our enemies.
- Holding our anger and frustration and not retaliating when people hate or envy us.
- Loving and caring without promise of personal reward or affirmation.
- Giving without strings attached, or expectations of getting in return.
- Opening our heart and continuing to open it even in the face of rejection.
- Sacrificing personal concerns to a far larger picture and purpose.

When we continually practice making these kinds of "sacrifices" on a daily basis, we are, in fact, purifying the soul. This psycho-spiritual practice moves us in the direction of the ignited and awakened soul depicted on Robe 5. You see how open her heart is – and in this state she is free of shame. She is in the active process of redeeming her inner soul Kingdom. She has released herself from the vicious cycle of shame and hiding and killing off potential new life, and has opened her heart and committed herself to purifying the soul and practicing the soul sacrifices to stay in alignment with the Neshamah.

Exercise 3: Staying in alignment with your soul

1. What kind of a ruler is sitting on your throne?
2. Have you made any mistakes like King Minos – sold yourself short, tried to take something that was not yours, refused to make the appropriate sacrifice or to thank those who gave you a gift of power?
3. Is your heart being untrue? Are you inflamed with passion for the wrong thing?
4. Is your soul out of alignment? How are you off course right now in your life?
5. Referring to the above list, what sacrifices are you willing to make to get your soul back in alignment?

Step 1: Ignite the Soul
* Step 2: Claim your authority - training the Hero *
Step 3: Focus the Will
Step 4: Act Courageously

Now let's look at the second step of Stage 5, where we redeem and purify our soul by training our Hero. This will enable us to *claim our individual authority in life* and *commit to our own path of truth.*

The focus of this particular step of initiation, training the Hero, is located at Tiferet on the Tree of Life diagram (see Diagram 19). The main quality developed at this stage is commitment – **commitment** to our own path so that we can claim our own authority in life. As we learned in Stage 4, we must leave the roots or tribal level of life at some point in order to establish our own identity and build a trunk to our Tree of Life

In the story of Theseus, his mother recognizes that he is ready at age 16 to leave the tribe and go on the hero's journey to establish his identity and claim his truth, his rightful inheritance. The mystery of his true identity lies with the father. According to the Tree of Life, the Mother archetype rules the roots of the Tree and the Father archetype rules the trunk. Now it is time for Theseus to actively move towards his father, towards his Tiferet or individual self. The story emphasizes that Theseus already has a strong connection to the mother, indicating a deep and intact root system to his Tree. This prepares him to leave the tribe safely, with an intact maternal container.

It is important to remember that when we individuate to go on the hero's journey and develop the relationship to the father or our inner sun, this departure takes a toll on the

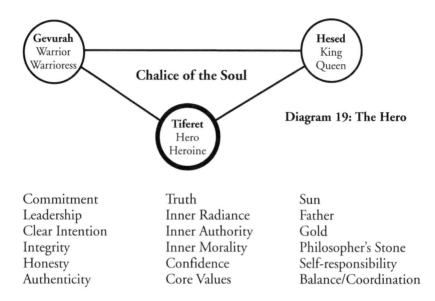

Diagram 19: The Hero

Commitment	Truth	Sun
Leadership	Inner Radiance	Father
Clear Intention	Inner Authority	Gold
Integrity	Inner Morality	Philosopher's Stone
Honesty	Confidence	Self-responsibility
Authenticity	Core Values	Balance/Coordination

community. When we leave the tribe to develop our individual gifts, it creates a gap, a hole in the communal structure, where once we contributed and gave vitality to the community. Although it is right and proper to leave, it is important to not become inflated, forgetting the root system and cutting ourselves off from instinctive life and the emotional stability that we have received from the community. As we develop our individual truth, we must honor our roots – the grounding, the maternal container, the community, the support and the belonging that we have gained from the roots of our Tree. Remembering this blesses the solar journey of Stages 4 and 5.

Claiming inheritance from the father

In order to develop the Hero archetype within us so that we may claim our own authority in life, we must first recognize that we have an inner Tiferet – an inner "father" principle – and we must claim our rightful inheritance to it. *This means recognizing our right to have our own truth and to live our life according to it.*

Theseus was unable to claim his rightful inheritance before the age of 16 because he was unaware of his earthly father's existence. He had known Poseidon as his heavenly father but remained unconscious of his earthly father, Aegeus. Within the psyche, this corresponds to those times when we have an inkling of our Tiferet – of the soul and its truth – but we have no way of establishing that royal inheritance in real life. We have not yet developed the capacity to rule our soul's kingdom in a practical and tangible way and thus manifest the qualities of our Tiferet in real life.

When we have not yet developed our truth, it is as if the ship of our soul is being directed from some far and distant place. Events and people come into our life at seemingly random times and places. When Tiferet is not yet developed, we are still subject to group law and group karma and the seemingly random winds of life toss our ship this way and that. Only by developing the hero and claiming our rightful inheritance to be the captain of our ship can we establish and rule our soul's kingdom according to our own inner truth.

We can imagine Theseus' surprise, excitement and perhaps even fear when his mother tells him about the possibility of meeting his earthly father. With all his might and skill, Theseus lifts the stone, which reveals the sword and sandals of his real father, King Aegeus. He dons the sandals, takes the sword, and sets off for Athens to claim his rightful inheritance. Theseus, as the inner Hero archetype, is that part of us who enthusiastically and boldly presents us to the father saying, "Here I am. I am the rightful heir. I am your son/daughter." Theseus knows what inheritance is coming to him and he claims his right to it. He goes to the father, to the Tiferet place, and says, "I am your son. I wear your sandals on my feet, and I wield your sword."

An example of recognizing one of our soul qualities could be realizing that we have an affinity for art. Then we find a mentor who sets us on fire and present ourselves to them enthusiastically saying, "I would be honored to sit at your feet and learn from you." Or we might recognize our passion for cooking and take a course with a creative chef and say, "Teach me all you know." When we acknowledge our soul's desire, we can follow our passion with enthusiasm and vigor and have the confidence to claim our rightful place in the line of artists or chefs or web designers or teachers. Then, like Theseus, we go through the apprenticeship of proving ourselves as the rightful heir, proving ourselves capable of sitting on the throne.

When Theseus first presents himself to the King, the father shows one obvious weakness in his ability to rule his kingdom with balanced power. King Aegeus listens to his mistress Medea, who desires her own son to be heir to the throne and suggests that the King poison this "Impostor." Her motivation is neither pure nor true, her heart is not open to the good of the whole kingdom, and she almost persuades the King to kill off the good and true developing soul. In the end, however, Aegeus is able to see the truth and recognize his legitimate son, that part of us that is the authentic Self. Here we have an inner situation where the father principle within us can truly see the authentic Self and will not allow the inauthentic or illegitimate parts of the personality to sit on the throne and rule. So not only do we need to claim our rightful inheritance from the father, but the father must be able to recognize and make room for the authentic Self in the kingdom.

Consolidating the self

When Theseus jumps into his chariot and goes to Athens, he activates the next phase of the Hero training – *consolidating the self.* Prior to this, Theseus is growing and developing, but he does not yet have a focused mission or purpose to his life. With this new information about his royal inheritance, he can gather all the various parts of himself together and without reservation or hesitation, point all of his energy in one direction. He is so determined to reach his goal that he fights his way through various trials and dangers without harm, as if blessed by the gods.

As Theseus goes on his hero's journey to consolidate his true Self, he is developing what the Alchemists call his "Philosopher's Stone." This "stone" refers to an inner experience of our rock-solid core Self and signals a stable and consistent contact with our Tiferet, our place of truth. The Philosopher's Stone conjures up an image of solidity and strength and describes the core, indestructible self that is realized at this stage of initiation. This is when the whole personality – including the ego, the true Self, and the various internal archetypes or subpersonalities – unites and takes on solid form. When consolidated, we feel a sense of inner self-definition and inner permanence.

There is a story from the Jewish scriptures that exemplifies the consolidating of the Self and has a clear reference to the Philosopher's Stone. This is the story of David and Goliath. The following version is my own synthesis taken from various parts of I Samuel, chapters 16 and 17. The story informs us that

David is a skilled harpist, a brave man and a fighter, prudent in speech, and a man of presence, for Yahweh is with him. During the reign of King Saul, the Israelites are fighting the Philistine army and are facing a losing battle because one of the Philistine warriors, Goliath, is intimidating the entire Israelite army. Goliath is a giant of a man, with full armor of bronze and a spear in hand. He shouts at the army of Israel, "Come out and do battle. Choose a man and let him come down to me. If he wins in a fight with me and kills me, we will be your slaves; but if I beat him and kill him, you shall become our slaves and servants to us."

All the Israelite army is afraid and runs away in terror. The Israelites say, "The King will lavish riches on the man who kills Goliath and will give him his daughter in marriage and grant his father's house the freedom of Israel."

When David sees the army running away in fear, he cannot believe his eyes. Without hesitation, he volunteers to face Goliath. But King Saul is worried because David is young and inexperienced. However, David is an experienced shepherd and he tells King Saul, "I have killed both lion and bear. Yahweh has rescued me from the claws of lion and bear and will rescue me from the power of Goliath." Then David picks five river stones, puts them in his bag and with sling in hand, he goes to meet the giant.

David then declares to Goliath, "Today Yahweh will deliver you into my hand and I shall kill you." No sooner has Goliath started forward to confront David than David leaves the line of battle and runs to meet Goliath. Putting his hand into his bag, he takes out a stone, slings it, and strikes Goliath on the forehead. The stone penetrates his forehead and Goliath falls to the ground. Thus David triumphs over the Philistines with only a sling and a stone. [2]

David, although young in physical age, has nevertheless consolidated the Self to the point where he confidently knows that he can defeat Goliath. We know from the story that he has "killed lion and bear," which signals to us that he has championed the fourth initiation and has become a master of his *Nefesh* and animal drives. And now David is ready to face Goliath, a giant in the world of the *Nefesh*. David's advantage over Goliath is that he is a man of the *Neshamah*, a man of soul, a man of presence, whose God is with him.

When David picks up the river stones as his weapon, this signifies that he is consciously accessing his Philosopher's Stone, his Tiferet, which far surpasses the *Nefesh* weapons of Goliath, such as animal power and intimidation. With the sling and stone, David slays Goliath with one swift blow. This speaks to the power that a skilled Tiferet can wield without raising the sword (Gevurah/discipline) or negotiating and compromising (Hesed/mercy).

The skill and accuracy of the consolidated Self can achieve incredible things: it can deliver a piercing and life-changing insight during a therapy session, make a life-saving diagnosis during medical treatment, or influence a board meeting with one level-headed suggestion.

When developed, our Tiferet can knock out a Goliath with a single accurate blow from the Philosopher's Stone, the part of us that has confidence and knowing.

Exercise 4: Consolidating the self

1. Focusing first on the past, can you recall a time when you did something or said something without reservation, when you jumped into your chariot with clear intention and purpose? Gather up that feeling now, that sense of solidity, inner self-definition and inner permanence. Write down what it feels like to be in this emotional place.

2. Can you remember a time when you hit your Goliath right between the eyes? How did you do it, with penetrating insight, verbal accuracy, wise counsel, correct diagnosis, level-headed suggestions?

3. Focusing now on the present, who or what is the Goliath right now in your life? What do you need to tackle head on in your life right now? How does your David want to tackle this problem or challenge? When will you do it?

Coagulatio

The alchemical stage that helps us consolidate the Self and become the true Hero is called "Coagulatio." Coagulatio is the process of coagulating, congealing and solidifying. This is the phase we go through during the fifth initiation because there is a crystallizing action that happens to the trunk of our Tree. During Coagulatio, the true authentic Self becomes embodied and fixed in position. We no longer live in fantasy or hope of "maybe someday" or "wouldn't it be nice if". During Coagulatio, we actually live out our truth.

Theseus had an inkling of his potential, his powers and his abilities, but it was not until he claimed himself son of the king and began to prove himself through heroic deeds that he began to manifest his Hero in the real world and consolidate the Self. Our other Hero, David, was a man of presence, but his real Coagulatio occurred when he took the stone and did something with it. He aimed his stone, his solid, true Self, and hit the target.

When we are moving through Coagulatio, we do not just talk about what we are going to do; we do it. We are no longer caught in illusion – we are able to follow through and act. Coagulatio means making things real, fulfilling desires and dropping into a deeper level of incarnation - coming into our own skin.

Coagulatio also means accepting our limitations – I can do *this*, but no more than *this*. Thus, sometimes Coagulatio can feel like an imprisonment, entrapment or bondage. For some people, making things real in the world can feel limiting because it cuts off other possibilities. They avoid growing up and taking responsibility because it feels frightening to be committed. Many people resist coagulating, but the fact is that coagulating and solidifying brings a great relief to the soul because finally the authentic Self can be expressed. There is a sigh of relief as finally the energies of the personality are directed to the proper place, towards a goal that can embody the whole personality, not just parts here and there.

Commit to your own path

One important way that our Hero claims authority in life is by making a deep and lasting commitment to our own path. With the help of our consolidating self, our Philosopher's Stone and the Coagulatio process, we can gather ourselves together and commit wholeheartedly to our truth.

Committing wholeheartedly to our path requires that we spend time soul searching for what our core values are so that we can become more definite, solid and confident when we present our truth to the world. Core values are those values that undergird and give substance to our soul, those values that steer our life in a particular direction. Core values determine the essence of who we are. So we need to know what our core values are so that we can *commit to our own path, find our voice and speak our authentic truth.*

As we find and speak our truth, we begin mirroring ourselves and no longer need to rely on others to mirror our core self. This frees us in a profound way to become the author of our own life, free of village voices, group karma and familial restrictions. At this stage of initiation, we begin taking full responsibility for our own life, no longer blaming others for our shortcomings, failed commitments, wounds or lost chances. We no longer say to ourselves: "I can't do this or that because of my family background. I can't have happy relationships because my mother was so toxic and unloving. My father wounded me too much for me to have healthy self-esteem." Although these things may have happened, when we make a commitment to our own path and become author of our own life, we are able to say: "This is what I will do with what I have been given."

Internalizing our own authority in this way frees us to express our individual rhythm because we no longer spend energy worrying about others. This frees us to become alive to ourselves and express our originality in our life, our work and our relationships. As we commit to our own path in life, we infuse the world with uniqueness, adding our own spice to the great soup of life. We begin living creatively with honesty, integrity, inner morality and authentic Self-expression.

Exercise 5: Core values

The following exercise is designed to help you define and choose your core values. It is an invaluable exercise to activate initiation and help you claim your authority. Read through the words and descriptions and ask yourself whether you ALWAYS, SOMETIMES or NEVER value that particular value. Write down the ones to which you said ALWAYS. Make a list of them and then narrow it down to your top ten.

Variety - I value activities that provide change
Stability - I value a lifestyle that provides stability either emotionally or physically
Risk - I value having opportunities to take risks
Creativity - I value having the time and space to create
Help Others - I value being of service to others
Solitude – I value opportunities to be alone and have limited interaction with others
Routine – I value set routines and a life of predictability
Knowledge - I value pursuing information and truth that leads to knowledge
Innovation - I value developing new ways of thinking/doing that have not been followed by others
Artistic Expression - I value expressing myself through some artistic form

Communication - I value communicating my values to others (verbally or in writing)

Familiarity – I value being in familiar circumstances in my work and relationships

Wisdom - I value opportunities to apply my life experiences, insights and wisdom

Status - I value being respected by my family, friends and community

Exploration - I value activities that allow me to explore and discover new things

Team Work – I value working as a team toward a common goal

Beauty – I value being in beautiful surroundings

Nature – I value spending time in nature

Thrill – I value work, relationships or activities that provide a sense of thrill

Fast Pace – I value a lifestyle with a fast pace of activities

Leisurely Pace - I value a lifestyle with a relaxed pace of activities

Purpose - I value engaging in activities that bring me a deep sense of meaning and purpose

Organizing – I value opportunities to organize activities, work or people

Quiet – I value a lifestyle that provides inner and outer quiet

Promoting – I value promoting my own or others' ideas/work

Travel – I value experiencing life through traveling

Physical Fitness and Health – I value the importance of keeping my body physically fit and healthy

Truth – I value striving for truth in my life and relationships

Recognition - I value being publicly recognized for who I am or what I do

Loyalty - I value being faithful to a person, group or cause

Persuading - I value having influence over others

Security - I value a lifestyle where I can feel safe and secure

Teaching - I value teaching people new information or skills

Emotional Well-being - I value handling inner tensions and feel emotionally at peace with myself

Courage – I value showing firmness of heart and will in the face of adversity

Friendship - I value a lifestyle where I can develop and maintain close friends

Adventure - I value a life of excitement and remarkable experiences

Competition - I value engaging in activities where I can prove myself against another

Physical Challenge - I value situations that test my physical abilities

Emotional Challenge - I value situations that test my emotional abilities

Consideration - I value being thoughtful and doing things that make others happy

Entrepreneur - I value starting projects/businesses and setting up new endeavors

Conviction – I value fighting for a cause I believe in

Motivating – I value motivating others and instilling them with incentive and drive

Relationships - I value working towards deep connections to family/partner relationships

Belonging - I value being a member of and accepted as part of a group

Compassion – I value empathizing with others and trying to help their suffering

Leisure Time - I value plenty of time away from any obligations or commitments

Expertise – I value having expert knowledge in some field

Integrity – I value honesty and a firm adherence to a code of moral values

Intelligence – I value using my skills of reason in new or trying situations

Commitment – I value pledging or entrusting myself to a definite purpose

Education – I value the pursuit of knowledge and learning to acquire new skills

1. When you have your list of top ten core values, sit with them and evaluate whether your life, your work and your relationships are now reflecting these values in a truthful way. If not, how might you make some changes so that you can live in a way that reflects your truth and so that you can make a deep and lasting commitment to your soul's path in life?

2. **Write a mission statement.** Narrow down your list to your top three or four values and write one or two sentences that incorporate your top core values, your beliefs and your life mission. For example, if my top three values were the last three on this list (intelligence, commitment and education), I might formulate a mission statement like this: "My mission is to educate others, encouraging their pursuit of learning and knowledge and training them to use their intelligence." Try several different versions and pick one that best fits your life mission.

3. Practice speaking your truth - Once you know what your core values are, practice speaking your truth and practice hearing your own voice. You can do this privately or with a trusted friend. Notice if you find tightness in your throat at this stage of initiation. Remember, the throat chakra is the energy center of the fifth initiation, so we are learning to open our throat in order to speak our truth. Do you have any fear or hesitation about speaking your truth? If so, follow the fear to its source and recognize what happened to you when you did speak your truth. Practice listening to the sound of your voice while you are speaking your truth. Does it sound different than when you are being accommodating or not standing up for yourself?

Purify your truth

Once our Hero puts our core values and truth on the line and begins living with honesty and integrity, our truth gets tested. Remember, the fifth initiation is where we develop the soul through purification. So when we put out our truth for the world to see, our truth – in all its aspects – comes up for purification.

It is said in Kabbalah that the universe is interested in souls who are developing because these people are becoming worthy and conscious vessels for Spirit. Therefore, when we are developing our soul we put through the fire of purification and are tested on our honesty. Surviving this fire requires us to have impeccable integrity and tell the truth. We can no longer live with what is untrue.

Returning now to the image of the Sacred Robe for Stage 5, the Soulflare robe, one of the most powerful aspects of the main figure is that it resembles the Sphinx. In Greek mythology, the Sphinx was known for killing anyone unable to answer its riddle. The Sphinx made heroes out of those who knew the truth and destroyed those who spoke out of "untruth." The Sphinx did this by posing a riddle that was extremely difficult to answer. If you knew the truth and answered correctly, you could become ruler of the kingdom.

From a psychological perspective, the Sphinx is an archetypal "tester," whose job it is to test our truth. So the Sphinx-like figure on the robe tests us to see whether we speak truth or whether we deceive ourselves, a test designed to purify our truth. If we confront the archetypal tester and are able to understand the riddle of our life and tell the truth, then we pass the test and strengthen the Hero. As we speak our truth, we are more psychologically prepared to internalize our own authority and become ruler of our kingdom.

What would it be like to face this figure if we were lying to ourselves in some way? Surely this powerful figure would know immediately if any untruths were within us and would shine the intense light of the sun into all our dark places. In order to withstand this confrontation, we would need a strong sense of our own power and truth, and access to our solid core. It is easy to imagine that facing this figure could induce a tremendous amount of anxiety and fear – as we would expect when we face the unadulterated truth about ourselves. We might have to be truthful about how selfish we have been in our relationships or how deeply we have hurt or betrayed a loved one. For example, an alcoholic would need to face the truth of his destructive, addictive behavior, and the internal rage that has never been addressed. It takes courage to look into the Sphinx's eyes and see the naked truth about some of the choices we have made.

Facing this kind of truth can generate tremendous anxiety because, as we confront the Sphinx's power to see all truth, we may feel exposed and penetrated. It may feel as if our inner container will fragment under such an extreme fire of purification. However, if our Hero can stay with the anxiety and fear and not run away, we will be forged into a more solidified state of being. The more truth we face, the more integrity we have, and the more we can embody our power.

So what sustains and contains us during the process of purification? Step by step, little by little, as we tell the truth *we gain a sense of mastery over our own lives* – and this is what sustains us. We encounter our own power and can, over time, meet the Sphinx face to face, giving us direct experience of our own strength. Holding our own power and feeling the solidity of our own soul is something that no one can take away from us. It allows us to say to ourselves, "My soul is mine. This is my truth. This is who I am." Now it no longer feels terrifying, penetrating, or uncomfortable to face the Sphinx. Now we can feel seen, mirrored, matched and honored, one Hero to another.

Shine like the sun

When we can hold our own truth and confront the blazing figure on the robe, a transformation occurs within the soul. We realize that this blazing figure is not separate from us, but is the reflection of our true, authentic Self. Understanding this, we can withdraw our projection of this as an "external" figure and experience it as an "internal" aspect of ourselves. When this happens, we internalize and fully embody the Hero. We can sit upon the firm foundation of Tiferet, and shine our own "sun" – with all of the sun's ability to be *self-sufficient* and *generate its own light*. This "inner radiance" cannot be hidden, and others will notice this new brightness coming from us so that we will be able to see our "inner light" shining onto those we love and those around us.

During an active imagination with the Soulflare robe, I imagined the sun beginning as a flame in the belly of the figure. Then the sun began to rise slowly through the chest, throat, face and came blazing through the top of the head as the halo or sun disk that casts its light in all directions. As I reflected later about this image, it occurred to me that there are both wonderful and painful aspects to shining our own light. On the one hand, when we raise our sun disk and shine our own light, we become leaders of our life and rule on our own throne. We experience our own inner radiance and are connected to our true center. On the other hand, this place of individuation is where we stand truly alone and we can feel extremely lonely at times. Shining our own light also requires personal changes that can feel uncomfortable and irritating.

To get to this place, we must be willing to sacrifice our attachments to people and things that have kept us from shining our own light fully. Sometimes shining like the sun means sacrificing obligations to friends, family and loved ones for a time. Some people may have to go against the wishes of partners, family, group or collective opinion in order to follow their own star. This is not an adolescent rebellion, but rather a conscious choice to sacrifice for the sake of creatively expressing our truth and taking responsibility for this choice.

When we do finally shine our own light and feel that sense of embodied, inner radiance, we have reached what the Alchemists called the "alchemical gold," the metal of the sun. Gold is called the sun metal not only because of its golden color, but also because of its lasting brilliance over thousands of years. Ancient golden treasures have been uncovered the world over – jewelry, goblets and sacred objects – that have retained their original beauty. Like the authentic Self, once polished and worked into a delicate shine, gold can withstand the test of time. Pure gold never tarnishes. (For more on the Alchemical metals on the Tree see Appendix F.)

The alchemical gold therefore describes the soul quite beautifully. The soul is like a golden nugget, buried until it is searched for and found. When found, we then submit our golden nugget to a series of ordeals, in order to transform it. *Our gold is our gift, our talent, or our treasure that must be purified and refined over time.* We offer it to be heated, melted, hammered, molded and shaped into a beautiful and elaborate work of art. As our gold is refined and purified, these tests to our soul are designed to hammer us into an authentic Self. The wonderful paradox about gold is that it is both strong and malleable, sturdy and flexible at the same time. It can be hammered but not broken. No matter what happens to it, pure gold always retains its essence.

Shining our own light of purified gold can be risky, for when we shine brightly, it attracts others and arouses envy in those who wish to lessen or extinguish our light. These people do not as yet have access to their own power and radiance and can be destructive to our development. On the other hand, the rejection from others forces us to handle criticism, rejection, disapproval and envious attacks. When our Hero has mastered this, we are able to retain our gold's purity and brilliance and not become entangled in attachments that lessen our light. When we do then form attachments from the soul, they are not attachments out of need as they are from the roots of the Tree. Rather, soul connections are based on mutual giving and receiving, one individual to another.

Coordinate and unite

So far in our Hero training, we have claimed our rightful inheritance, consolidated the self, committed to our own path, purified our truth and allowed our golden light to shine like the sun. The last step to embody the Hero is to *coordinate and unite* the crew of the psyche, so that all parts of the soul are moving in one direction.

Theseus demonstrates this beautifully in the story. After he makes a daring commitment to redeem Minos' sin, he arranges to be one of the seven youths who travel to Crete to face the bull dance and the dreaded Minotaur. On the long sea voyage, Theseus unites his group of seven maidens and seven youths together so that they feel like a team, preparing to fight together as a united front. When they arrive in Crete, Theseus also coordinates the group together as a bull dancing team, increasing their chances of survival in the bullring. As the

Hero, *we take command of our soul and unite our various inner characters, steering them towards the same destination.*

We must also coordinate all the various systems, organizing and harmonizing the heart, mind, will and emotions so that we can move towards our goal. Only when we have a Hero to keep everyone in line can we hope to exercise free will, a choice that is open to us at this point in our initiation. Remember that the Hero as Coordinator is placed at the very heart and center of the Tree of Life at Tiferet, where all systems can be *observed, adjusted, harmonized* and *united.*

For example, we can imagine Theseus as Coordinator of his bull dancing team, and how he must have a pulse beat on the physical stamina of his team, their energy level, athletic ability and emotional mood. He must also be aware of the bull and his energy and mood, the strategy of their "game" and the execution of their moves. In our own lives, the Hero/Coordinator should have a pulse beat on what we are doing, whether it is in line with our destination, what steps we need to take and what inner characters need to get in line and cooperate. The Coordinator should know which parts of our life need adjusting, where we are off course – in our work, relationships, spiritual practices – and how to steer ourselves back on course.

Exercise 6: Training the Hero

1. Referring to the list of qualities in Diagram 19, what **Hero qualities** have I developed and what qualities would I like to develop more fully?

2. Have I **committed to my own path**? How is that manifesting?

3. What are the major **choices** I have made to get to where I am now in my life? How conscious have I been with these choices? How many choices have I made out of free will and how many were made for me because of my own passivity? Why did I make the choices I made in terms of my relationships, my career, or other aspects of my life?

4. **Declaring my truth**. The following is a "free writing" exercise to help you see more clearly what is true or untrue in your life. A free writing exercise allows your thoughts to flow freely and helps you to avoid editing yourself in any way. With pencil and paper, write without stopping, punctuation or capitalization, addressing the question, "What is true in my life?" When you have exhausted your thoughts and feelings on this subject, then address the question, "What is a lie or untrue in my life?" Then address the question, "What do I need to tell the truth about?" When you are done, read over your unedited pages. What changes would you like to make in order to live out what is true in your life?

Step 1: Ignite the Soul
Step 2: Claim your Authority
* Step 3: Focus the will - training the Warrior *
Step 4: Act Courageously

So far in this fifth initiation we have been following the myth of King Minos and Theseus, a myth about a corrupt leader and a Hero/Warrior/King who redeems the corruption and becomes a truthful, passionate and courageous ruler of the kingdom. In Step 2, we learned to develop our Hero so that we can claim our authority in life. Becoming the Hero of our own inner kingdom establishes the base of our soul chalice.

The next step of the fifth initiation is to train the Warrior to focus our will. Warrior training is located at Gevurah on the Tree of Life diagram and builds the left side of the soul chalice (see Diagram 20). The main quality developed here is **conviction** – holding steadfastly to our truth by focusing the will and learning the right use of power. The archetype of the Warrior fits very nicely at Gevurah, where the planet Mars is also placed. In Step 3, we will discover how to develop and focus the will of the Warrior or the Warrioress.

Conviction	Strategy	Strength and Might
Taking a Stand	Focus of Will	Observing and Waiting
Setting Boundaries	Holding Power	Right Use of Power
Discipline	Defending	Steadfast Resolve
Sword	Discerning	Conserving Energy

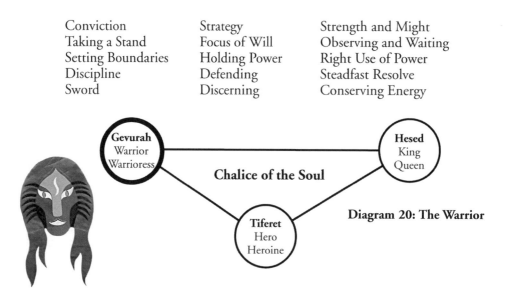

Diagram 20: The Warrior

Focusing the will - discernment

After Theseus has developed the Hero by committing to his truth and claiming his authority, now the question arises: Where is Theseus going to direct his will? What kind of Warrior will he be and what is he going to fight for?

This question is answered one day as the Cretan ships pull into the harbor of Athens to collect the seven maidens and youths for the deadly bull dancing, where they will become objects of sport for the Cretan court and possible food for the Minotaur. As Theseus sees the ships and hears the cries of the Athenians, he realizes the plight of his people. Suddenly his Warrior is engaged and his will has a specific target. Now he can focus his inner Warrior towards a specific goal; he will go to Crete, survive the bull dance, and defeat the Minotaur. By focusing his will, he will release the curse of King Minos and free the people of Athens.

In order to focus the will as Theseus does, we must have a specific goal in mind that inspires and motivates us. Without a goal, the Warrior's will power becomes diffused and scattered. One of the ways to gather and focus our will is to *discern what our will actually is* as opposed to the tribal will, our spouse's will, or our parents' will for our life.

According to Kabbalah, there are several kinds of will. There is **vegetable will** – which is "will-lessness" that simply keeps us going around the wheel of daily routines. There is **animal will** – which is "willfulness" that pushes us out of the vegetable state so that we can survive and dominate. Then there is **free will** – the "will" that is generated from the *Neshamah*, the human soul, which allows us to freely choose the direction of our life without being driven by the vegetable will-lessness and the animal willfulness.

During the fifth initiation, we are developing "free will," which reflects individual consciousness, follows individual law and expresses individual choice. According to the laws of the individual, no one should impinge their will on us, as if they know better than we do what our soul's purpose is. The Warrior says "I will not follow tribal will" or "I will not allow your will for me to define my individual reality or stop me from making my own choices." When we stop to look at how much we actually exercise free will, it is surprisingly little. It is also very rare that we direct our will towards a goal that is good for our whole being. Directing our will takes intense focus, and if our Warrior gets distracted or dissuaded easily or is a corruptible character, we are in for a rough time.

I once worked with a woman who was in a continual battle with her husband over the way he treated their children. From her perspective, the husband was neglectful and was not "fatherly" enough. She had a list of criteria and expectations that he did not meet and probably would never meet. She was continually frustrated and angry, and this energy permeated the household and affected the children. When we talked about her Warrioress, she experienced this part of her as refusing to put down the battle sword, for this battle seemed a cause worth fighting for! But as we talked over the weeks and months, she became aware of how much energy this "battle" was draining from her life and how it was negatively affecting her children.

Her Warrioress was being fueled by expectations coming from the little girl inside her who wanted a "daddy", rather than the grown woman, who held her true values. In her case, the Warrioress was taking orders from the little girl, rather than aligning with her individuated adult self. Eventually, she discerned that this was a battle she could let go of, and she began to lay down her sword and change some expectations of "what a father should be." Letting go of this battle had a profound effect on the atmosphere of the household; and although she still felt some disappointment, she no longer wasted energy feeling enraged. Her Warrioress was now free to choose more relevant battles.

One of the most dangerous aspects of the Warrior is when he or she is an autonomous figure within the psyche, fighting battles indiscriminately or ones that happen to appeal to a momentary passion.

I have seen many different examples of this in my experience as a therapist. I saw one client whose Warrior was like a sniper out of his conscious control, sneaking up when he least expected it and taking down the "enemy" with one fatal blow. This is a Warrior with focus but no direction from the true Self at Tiferet. I have also seen Warriors who are just the opposite – unfocused or unable to muster the energy to fight. And I have seen over-zealous Warrior types that are ready to fight at a moment's notice. Other Warriors are aggressive, manic and over-stimulated; some are tricksters.

I once worked with a woman who described her Warrioress as incredibly focused and determined, but she would get stuck on minute details, fighting with her partner over choices of restaurants, movies or trivial decisions of little consequence. She had an over zealous Warrioress who enjoyed sinking her teeth into battles that were quite petty and irrelevant. Once she locked onto a cause – no mater how trivial – her Warrioress had difficulty letting go. So when the important battles came along, her Warrioress had little reserve left.

Another man that I worked with described his Warrior as reluctant and had difficulty rousing him into action. Even during a crisis, his Warrior would get over-stimulated and become paralyzed, unable to take orders from his true Self. He felt that his Warrior was both lazy and fearful.

Exercise 7: Developing your Warrior -Focusing the will

1. Referring to the list of qualities in Diagram 20, what **Warrior qualities** have you developed and what qualities would you like to develop more fully?

2. What kind of Warrior do you have inside? What is your Warrior's nature? Stoic, lazy, aggressive, over-zealous, mercenary, a Lone Ranger, a sniper, passive, enraged, vengeful, quiet...?

3. From whom does your Warrior take orders? Does he obey your voice of truth and core values or is your Warrior autonomous and mercenary, following his own agenda? Take some time now and discern whose will you are under.

4. What inspires and motivates your Warrior to focus your will? What distracts your Warrior from focusing your will?

5. Make a list of the battles that your Warrior is fighting at the moment. Pick the ones that are important to you and the skirmishes that you can let go of. Stop wasting energy on the battles or causes that you cannot win and the ones that are not in alignment with your truth.

6. What will it take to focus your will? Set realistic goals to engage your Warrior. (For example, "For the next six months, I will focus my Warrior on project X and will not get distracted on projects Y and Z.)

Purifying the will - right use of power

Discerning our will, focusing our will, and making free will choices are the first steps of developing the Warrior. When we are exercising free will, the universe becomes very interested in our development and we may soon find ourselves being tested. Our Warrior will likely be put through a series of tests to purify our will and to see if the Warrior can exercise right use of power, which is the Warrior's greatest weapon.

In the story, Theseus embodies the archetype of the Warrior when he passes the tests of purification. But before we learn from his example, let's first look at how Minos *fails* the test of the Warrior and is unable to demonstrate right use of power. Watching Minos' mistake, we discover the consequences of our Warrior failing this particular test.

When Poseidon sends Minos the white bull from the sea, it is a test – a test of will power to see if Minos will sacrifice the bull back to the god. Poseidon was testing him to see whether he was the kind of Warrior whose will power would serve his higher nature or his lower nature of greed. During our Warrior training - our "Poseidon" - the part of us that is concerned with our highest good and encourages us to serve our higher nature, also tests us. The test is to see whether we are going to align our will power with the *Neshamah* or whether we will align our will power with the *Nefesh* and serve the ego and self-gratification.

Minos is an example of someone who gets tempted by the seductive nature of power. The white bull from the sea is a perfect test, for the bull symbolizes many desirable things – beauty, fertility and potency. How tempting for Minos to keep it for himself. When Minos was grabbed by a wayward *Nefesh* drive he succumbed to temptation, failed the test and aligned his power with his animal nature.

The power base of the instinctive *Nefesh* is centered on the ego at Yesod and takes its orders from this place. The power base of the *Neshamah* is centered on the true Self at Tiferet (see Appendix B). It is essential that the true Warrior at Gevurah take orders from the Hero at Tiferet, for only our deepest truth, integrity and honor can provide a stable power base for the Warrior (see Diagram 20). So *right use of power occurs when the Warrior aligns with the soul's purpose and truth and fights only those battles that are in accordance with our truth*. When Minos failed to exercise right use of power, the consequences were grim, and a corruption occurred within his soul that brought down a curse upon the entire house of Minos, eventually destroying his entire kingdom.

Let's see now how Theseus successfully embodies the archetype of the Warrior and how he passes the tests of purification. As Theseus makes his way to Crete, he is committed to purifying the corruption in Minos' kingdom. Because one of the most difficult tests during the purification of the will is facing the "dark side" – our shadow aspects at the level of the soul – Theseus must pass the initiation test of the Warrior by facing his shadow and wrestling both the bull in the Cretan sporting ring and the bull in the form of the Minotaur. If Theseus can wrestle the untamed passion of the bull and pass the Warrior's test, then he can set the kingdom free.

In the end, Theseus successfully wrestles both the bull in the ring and the Minotaur. He faces the bull, exercises right use of power and aligns with his higher nature.

In order to counter our destructive tendency to align our will with our lower nature, we need to call up the best of our Warrior who can stand up to a corrupting character like King Minos. King Minos reminds me of Darth Vader in the Star Wars story, who fails to purify his will and turns to the dark side. Luke Skywalker is like Theseus, the Warrior, who must face his own shadow/father to redeem the curse on the house of Skywalker. Only the Warrior who is in alignment with the highest good will not be corrupted and will remain true to the cause, to the "Force."

During our Warrior training, we are asked to face the shadow side of our soul and we will be tested to see whether we will take a stand for what is right and true or whether we will denigrate the power and potency generated from the higher self and use it for our own self-gratification. If we have misused our power and find a stream of corruption running through our kingdom, it is possible to initiate a purification process that helps realign our power with our higher truth and will. During my own Warrior training I had the following dream.

> *My husband and I are the King and Queen of a vast land. It has come to our attention that there is a vein of corruption running throughout our kingdom. We call all of our*

servants and subjects together into the palace and assemble them before the court. My husband and I sit on our thrones and – with the Chief Priest at our side—we survey the subjects to decide what to do. Without speaking, my husband and I look at each other and know what we must do. Then together we declare aloud, "Sack the lot of them!" The Chief Priest stands beside us looking smug, as he believes he has avoided the purification. "You too must go," we say to him. The only subject to remain is the Royal Cook.

It seems from this dream that my only hope in purifying my will, with a true Warrior's stance, is to perform major surgery within my psyche, banning some aspects that have become like King Minos and have refused to align with the will of my inner King and Queen. I had to replace all of my subjects with the exception of the cook, whom I see as the inner Alchemist of my psyche, who can cook up another version of the kingdom. The cook takes charge of the alchemical cauldron and knows the alchemical recipe to purify whatever elements have been corrupted and are hindering the alignment of my will.

Galvanizing the will - conviction

So far in our Warrior training, we have learned to *focus our will* by exercising discernment and we have learned to *purify the will* through exercising right use of power. Now our Warrior must conjure up the necessary conviction to *galvanize the will*.

Galvanizing the will enables us to take a stand for what we believe in and defend that with passionate conviction. But in order to remain steadfast and act or speak with resolve, the Warrior needs a cause worth fighting for – he needs to be engaged with important and satisfying soul concerns, not petty squabbles. The Warrior functions best when he finds a cause that arouses deep conviction. When the cause is linked to our personal truth and individual purpose, the Warrior can muster up the crusading spirit necessary to do the job effectively.

The Crusades began with such a force, as a group of Warriors volunteered to secure passage for pilgrims traveling to the Holy Land. This idea appealed to their sense of personal truth and honor. It appealed to their spiritual truth as well, for they provided safe travel for a physical, emotional and spiritual journey that would transform people's lives and gift them with a taste of the Divine. Unfortunately, much of the Crusades went terribly wrong and the Warrior archetype was corrupted, as King Minos was. However, the concept of the Crusades rallied brave Warriors with the conviction and steadfast resolve to fight for the truth.

In order to develop the kind of deep conviction that it takes to fight for something with our whole heart and soul, the Warrior must galvanize the will with the help of Gevurah (discipline, strength and might). On the Tree of Life, the alchemical metal associated with Gevurah and the Warrior is iron, and iron is the principal ingredient in making steel. So the Warrior can make use of this symbol by aligning with the power of steel.

When we want to invoke the conviction of our Warrior, we can do so by calling up the image of steel – as in a steel blade or shield. Or we can imagine "steeling" ourselves with the armor of strength, honor, integrity and discipline. When we "steel" ourselves in this way, it does not mean becoming emotionally rigid, hardened or tight. There is a difference between someone who is overly defended and impenetrable and someone who is healthily defended and protective of their sacred truth. Aligning with the energy of steel must be balanced, as we shall see later, with the compassionate heart of the good King.

When our Warrior becomes like steel, it means that we do not give up. When we galvanize our will, we have the stamina to keep going and to keep fighting for our cause. We can endure and suffer hardships, knowing that the end result is extremely rewarding. There are times when it is appropriate to hang in there with minimal rations, to do without and to delay gratification so that the goal can be reached. Galvanizing the will and "steeling" ourselves forges the conviction that we need to stick with something no matter how difficult or challenging.

Tools of the Warrior/Warrioress

On the ship to Crete, the small band of seven maidens and seven youths must have felt terrified as they contemplated their fate. They had probably heard nightmarish stories about the Cretan bull dancing ring and the horrific accidents, mauling and death that befell the bull dancers. On the ship, Theseus must have acted as the Warrior, understanding their fears and rallying the frightened group together and teaching them the essential tools of the Warrior – tools to help them survive the bull dancing and the ordeals to come.

We have already spoken of the Warrior's tools of discernment, right use of power and conviction. The following is a list of the essential tools that the Warrior can also develop: *the ability to strategize, set boundaries, defend those boundaries, ensure discipline, conserve energy and demonstrate strength in battle.*

Tool #1. The Warrior's Ability to Strategize

The Warrior is a master strategist who looks at a situation and analyzes the best course of action, carefully weighing the pros and cons. In the Minotaur myth, as Theseus approaches Crete and the inevitable bull dancing, he realizes that brute force will not save them. The only way for Theseus and his companions to survive is to use an alternative strategy. Just as Theseus knows that one person is no match for a huge and powerful bull, our own Warrior knows when it is not appropriate to meet an opponent head on with animal force. The true Warrior can develop a plan with his/her intelligence and will. For example, Theseus forms a strategy to outsmart the bull by using his teammates to distract and confuse it. Using the chaos in the ring, Theseus can then exercise his gymnastic skills to leap over the charging bull and onto his back and then leap off into the arms of his teammates. Rather than focusing on what they lack – muscle strength and battle experience – Theseus realizes their strengths, which are youthful energy, agility and teamwork. The Warrior, therefore, is resourceful in his strategy, using what is on hand and focusing on strengths and talents to get the job done.

We can use those same skills when we face situations in our lives that require solution or resolution. Rather than dwelling on how or why we *cannot* solve the problem, we can focus on what skill or talent we do have that could bring about a resolution. We can invite our Warrior to form a clever strategy to outwit or outsmart the dilemma by being resourceful.

Tool #2. The Warrior's Ability to Set Boundaries

Another crucial tool for the Warrior to develop is setting appropriate boundaries. The Warrior's function is to defend the core values and concerns of the soul, so we must become crystal clear about *the boundaries that will create a safe and sacred space around our soul in order for it to thrive.* To set these kinds of boundaries, we need to discern, discriminate and clarify what and whom we allow into our sacred soul space. The Warrior identifies what situations drain us of precious energy and deplete our resources, and what situations bring us joy, creativity and increased reserves.

I have worked with many people who need to set clear boundaries with their loved ones – spouses, children, mothers, fathers – because they all too easily get swept up in others' concerns, forgetting themselves and becoming exhausted or resentful. The Warrior has the insight, strength and fortitude to say NO and, when appropriate, to say YES. The Warrior is able to say, "This may be good for you, but it is not good for me." The Warrior can draw the boundary and not buckle under the pressure of guilt or succumb to the pleas of others trying to move and manipulate the boundary. The Warrior holds steadfast to the boundary by willpower and strength.

We can establish and strengthen our boundaries by imagining our Warrior setting up camp and defining the perimeter, posting guards, and securing a safe environment for himself and those under his command. The perimeter of our boundaries can be different, depending on the situation. In one case, we may wish to include our children within our boundaries, so that our Warrior protects the whole family. In another case, we may want to set up a boundary perimeter that excludes our children, so that we can protect ourselves from them when their behaviors toward us are destructive or dysfunctional. Our Warrior can help us set up and define a boundary that consistently helps us in our dealings with friends, family, spouses, and co-workers. When our Warrior has helped us create a safe internal environment for our authentic soul, we can work from that space to become better partners, parents and friends.

Tool #3. The Warrior's Mission to Defend and Protect

The Warrior's main job is to defend and protect. Once we have set appropriate boundaries around our truth and core values, we then employ the Warrior to defend and protect those boundaries. The Warrior shields us from those people or things that try to penetrate, upset or destroy our sacred space. Like a mother bear whose primary purpose is to protect her cubs, our Warrior protects us from both external and internal saboteurs.

One very effective exercise that develops the tools of boundary setting and defending/protecting is what I call the sacred circle meditation.

Exercise 8: Meditation - The sacred circle meditation

Begin by standing in your room or outside in nature and extend your arms sideways as far as you can, drawing an imaginary circle around you.

Imagine yourself as the very center of your own circle, this circle that creates a sacred space around you. Imagine this circle with you and around you for the whole day. Imagine as clearly as you can that you occupy the center of your circle wherever you go.

Conjure up a clear image of your Warrior. Imagine the way that he or she would defend your sacred circle.

Notice how it feels to have people come into this space. Clarify whom you want and do not want in your space. Clarify what emotional boundaries you should protect. Can you allow positive affirmations into your circle? Can you defend and fight off negative voices, attacks and destructive emotions? Notice how empowering it is to know that you are the center of this space. Notice that only you are responsible for protecting and defending your boundaries. Notice what it is like to make decisions from this place and to relate from this place of centered power and strength. Remember to spend energy only defending and protecting boundaries that are good for your soul.

Whenever you need to re-establish your sacred circle during the day, simply stretch out your arms and recreate your circle with a sweep of your arms.

Tool #4. The Warrior's Discipline

There is no way around it, sooner or later we have to use discipline to get the Warrior's job done. Nothing is accomplished in terms of soul growth without discipline. No challenging goal is reached without discipline.

Theseus' main goal in going to Crete is to defeat the Minotaur, but the only way that he can do this is by first practicing his discipline and perfecting the art of bull dancing. It is the same for all of us – we must practice discipline in order to reach our goals or expand psychologically or spiritually. Discipline gets us in shape, sharpens our skills, and prepares us for known and unknown situations.

Each new skill requires practice before it is ingrained. We may have to remember to re-establish our boundaries 10 or even 20 times a day until we get the hang of it. Our Warrior can help us by using his willpower to conjure up the discipline necessary to consistently set boundaries – or to pursue some other personal goal, such as consistently doing a spiritual practice.

The Warrior also uses discipline to focus the will and direct our intention to where we want it. This takes determination and integrity. When we have zeroed in on a goal for our soul, then we must orient the energies of our life solely to that purpose and move towards the goal. It takes great discipline to stay on target and not get side-tracked. If we want to write a book, establish a business, adopt a baby, get sober, end an unhealthy relationship, or survive cancer, the Warrior ensures discipline and streamlines our energies so that we can reach our goal.

Tool #5. The Warrior's Ability to Hold Power and Conserve Energy

After Theseus learns the art of bull dancing and disciplines himself to perfect his Warrior's art, he must hold and wait for the precise moment to enlist Ariadne's help to enter the labyrinth and defeat the Minotaur. Here Theseus exercises another aspect of the Warrior: he becomes a keen watcher and a vigilant observer. He holds his power because he understands the importance of right timing. Theseus realizes that he cannot reach his goal by himself – he must partner with Ariadne because she knows the mysteries of the labyrinth, she knows how to go into and out of the maze without perishing. So Theseus waits for the precise time and picks his moment to ask Ariadne for assistance.

The Warrior within us is on vigilant watch – staying awake and alert, observing what is happening. In this way, when the door opens and the opportunity arises to act – whether it is to fight and take a stand, to make a point, or even to stay silent – the Warrior is ready.

It is a continuing fascination to me that Gevurah, the Warrior, is placed on the left or "feminine" pillar of the Tree of Life. The feminine pillar is concerned with reserving and conserving energy. We usually do not associate the Warrior with the feminine because most often the Warrior is depicted as masculine and as pro-active and initiating, rather than receptive and holding. But the feminine way of watching, waiting and holding power actually depicts the most refined kind of Warrior.

The Samurai Warrior depicts this type well. The Samurai practices mindful power – which is connected, refined and purified personal power. The Samurai Warrior makes an art out of conserving and reserving energy, only expending it when absolutely necessary. A Samurai needs only to show up and be present and to make his or her presence known. When people recognize the intensity of this kind of embodied power, they obey and show respect.

A dangerous Warrior is one who has not done the feminine work of creating the internal container, what I call the "holding space" for personal power. Only with this conscious interior space can we learn to hold our power, face our inner demons, and do the necessary shadow work to use our power wisely. A dangerous Warrior, who is disconnected from the feminine, overly expends energy. A dangerous Warrior projects inner demons onto others and blindly fights an external enemy that really comes from within. A dangerous Warrior cannot discern this and becomes an aggressor, destroying others rather than holding on to their power.

The sacred Warrior has a very different focus and is dedicated to the feminine principles of preservation and conservation of life rather than destruction. In light of this, the true Warrior can be imaged as a pregnant woman – full of life force, holding space for the mysterious and powerful life energy. She has the power of presence and does not need to expend energy to command and get things done.

As we put this tool into practice, we might want to imagine holding our power within the body, containing and reserving our energy. We might imagine having a sword but not using it, or fighting a battle with as little energy expended as possible. We may want to practice waiting, watching and carefully observing, not acting indiscriminately. And finally we may want to practice formulating the exact word or phrase that will get our point across and carefully calculating the one blow from our "sword" that will affect the situation. Holding, watching, waiting, reserving and conserving are valuable tools of the true Warrior.

Tool #6. Strength in battle - pulling it all together

Theseus is now ready to face his greatest challenge and slay the Minotaur. As true Warriors we are aware of the precise moment when we are called to face a challenging situation that could change the course of our life. This is when our Warrior must be fully prepared and must pull together all of our skills. This moment might be a life-threatening illness, a confrontation that changes our life direction, or a work situation that requires complete integrity because people's futures are at stake. Whatever the challenge, our Warrior must pull it together and remain wise and strong in battle so that we can persevere even when we are scared, bored, uncomfortable, weak, depressed, angry, hot, cold or exhausted.

When the moment arises, Theseus enlists Ariadne's help to guide him safely through the labyrinth and to the Minotaur. Ariadne gives Theseus the ball of white linen thread to help him stay connected to his Warrior's task and purpose as he is facing the challenging situation. So often, our Warrior goes into battle and, in the heat of the struggle, forgets what we are really fighting for.

I worked with a woman who went into a difficult divorce negotiation and could not hold on to her Warrior's purpose. We had spoken ahead of time about her need to draw her boundaries and remain firm, strong and steady – asserting what she needed to protect her soul. But in the heat of the negotiation, she could not hold on to the white linen thread and got lost in the labyrinth. She felt victimized by the lawyer and her husband and forgot to fight her battle. But she was able to learn from her tactical mistakes, and the next time she went into negotiation, she kept the Warrior in the forefront of her consciousness and protected herself with more strength and resolve.

The Warrior can use many tools to help us protect and defend our authentic self. Tools could include weapons like the labrys, for those times that we need to – metaphorically – behead the mighty Minotaur. Or they could be tools of strategy – like right timing. Regardless of their form, all the Warrior's tools serve to *defend and protect, and embody honor, integrity, and authenticity.*

Exercise 9: Using the tools of the Warrior

Using the tools enumerated above, let's look at how your Warrior is going to assist your Hero in fighting for your core truths. Look back at your mission statement from Step 2, Exercise 5, then make a specific action plan as to how you are going to carry out your mission. Try to add dates and times so that your Warrior has specific instructions to follow.

With your mission statement in hand:

1. Strategize – What strategy does my Warrior propose that will effectively accomplish my mission?

2. Set boundaries – What boundaries need to be set in order to assert my truth?

3. Defend and protect – How will my Warrior defend and protect the boundaries?

4. Discipline - How is my Warrior going to impose the proper discipline to get the job done?

5. Hold and conserve your power – In what ways can my Warrior reserve and conserve energy to reach my goal?

6. Strength in battle – When do I withdraw out of fear in battle? How can my Warrior help during the heat of the battle when I need to fight for my truth?

Step 1: Ignite the Soul
Step 2: Claim your Authority
Step 3: Focus the Will
* Step 4: Act Courageously - training the King *

So far in our fifth initiation, we have been developing the soul by calling forth *commitment* from our Hero and *conviction* from our Warrior. Now in Step 4 we call upon *courage* from our inner King/Queen so that we can take decided action to serve our soul kingdom and its primary objectives.

The King archetype is located at Hesed on the Tree of Life (see Diagram 21). The main quality developed here is **courage** – the courage to live with compassion and offer up the heart for service to the greater good.

Courage   Destiny   Feeding the Kingdom
Generosity   Purpose   Forgiveness
Right Action   Meaning   Mercy
Initiating   Inspiration   Openheartedness
Expansion   Service   Compassion
Self-love   Sacrifice   Gratitude

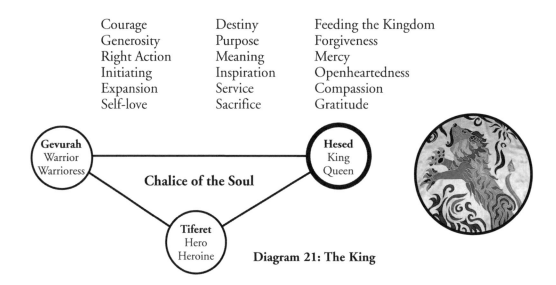

Diagram 21: The King

The power of voice

We move now to complete the chalice of the soul by developing the archetype of the King/Queen. When the three archetypes of the soul are strongly developed and functioning, they help to open the throat chakra so that our voice can be heard. The Hero gets us centered where we connect with the voice of the authentic Self. Then the Warrior draws protective boundaries around the soul and strengthens our will, helping us to take a stand for the authentic Self. Finally, the King *strengthens the powers of the heart, bringing the passion and compassion necessary to speak our truth in the world.*

The King's focus on love and compassion brings a needed counterbalance to the Warrior's intensity of conviction and steadfast resolve. Where the Warrior anchors us by activating discipline and standing firm to ground the energy of the authentic Self, the King *enables us to move and expand our heart and vision.* Now that our personal power and will have been firmly established and grounded within the body and psyche, we can safely and powerfully speak our truth in the world. When this kind of power – balanced between the heart and will – is vocalized and vibrated into life, it can become a powerful force to get things accomplished and change people's lives.

Just as when the benevolent King or Queen makes a decision for the good of the people, speaks the decree, and so is it done, this action of *"deciding, speaking and doing"* is the job description of our archetypal King or Queen.

The words of the King, spoken with integrity and with heart, are a powerful tool that can influence a person, a group, a nation or an entire generation. However, this tool of words can easily be misused as a weapon. I have heard many stories from students and clients over the years as they recall crystal clear memories of when mother, father, sibling or lover had pierced their tender heart with harsh words. On the other hand, others recall when a gentle truth was spoken and it opened their heart or altered the direction of their lives in some way. Charismatic leaders have used their voice and the archetypal energy of the will and heart to rally whole nations into war or into peace. Whether on the world stage or in the privacy of our own homes, the power of words, for good or for ill, is undeniable.

Purify the heart through compassion

So much responsibility comes with the King/Queen archetype because our voice and our words are so powerful once we manifest them in the world. For this reason, those of us on the initiate's path encounter periods of purification of the heart. These are experiences that test us, *to see whether our heart will remain true with purity of motivation and purity of intention*. If our motives are pure and our intentions honorable, then the words we speak in the world will ring true with integrity, love and compassion. Most importantly, we will be aligned in our truth, in our will and in our heart. When this happens, the truth is spoken with great conviction and tempered with love, which produces the kind of great King or Queen that people trust, obey and follow.

How do we cultivate this kind of inner King or Queen? We know from the Kabbalah that the King archetype is placed at Hesed on the Tree of Life, which translates into mercy, loving kindness, and compassion. It is also placed on the right-hand pillar of force, expansion and outward movement. Cultivating the King, therefore, involves expanding the boundaries of the heart as much as possible. This means actively loving others and loving ourselves far beyond our perceived capacity.

Cultivating compassion first begins with self-love – and often this is much more difficult to manifest than we expect. Some people find it hard to give self-affirmations and are blocked from giving themselves the compassion necessary to heal. I have worked with so many who, when we discuss the pains of their childhood, lack a primal and basic compassion for the little boy or girl they once were. Without the balm of compassion to love ourselves fully, we cannot cultivate the King or Queen to full capacity. Because we cannot give away what we do not have, a good King can only give love to the whole kingdom out of a storehouse of abundant inner love. So we need to extend the deep love of Hesed to ourselves first so that we can expand out of any constriction and tightness around our heart and soul.

We spoke in the fourth initiation about the cage that grows around our heart. This cage is built to defend the precious authentic Self that was attacked or ignored, or to protect our tender emotions when we opened our heart and no one was there to receive our love or return it. When love, warmth, mercy and tenderness are missing in our early environment, the cage is assembled around our heart so that it will not be broken again through betrayal, cruelty or absence of the Beloved. *Cultivating self-compassion means actively beaming love to all the parts of us that feel wounded in some way.*

With clients, I recommend beginning this process of purifying the heart through compassion by focusing love to the little child within them. I suggest that they may want to get a picture of themselves as a child and put it on their altar, and that during their meditation time and during the day they consciously remember their child and listen for what he or she wants and needs. I ask them to give that child a voice, to allow that child to state his/her will and desire, and to take some form of compassionate action to give that child what it needs.

King training begins with self-love, because loving ourselves unconditionally creates the internal container we need to give or receive any kind of love and in any kind of circumstance. This includes that love that we give to friends, enemies, and God – as well as the love that we receive from others and from God. Loving ourselves in a deep, compassionate way builds a connection to the parts of us that need love, creating a circular flow of love between our King and our inner child. We must make this relationship conscious and learn to diligently respond to our own needs for love – for when we offer ourselves unconditional love and compassion, we can heal past wounds, respond to our current needs, and care for our soul in a radical way.

When we know how to love ourselves, then giving and receiving is done from the core Self, the *Neshamah*, rather than from an undifferentiated, needy self. When the true King's inner container for love is fully developed, he gives love freely with no expectation of return. This constantly replenishes the good King's storehouse of compassion.

If we have been wounded around giving or receiving love, then we may move into the shadow aspect of the King. This is the classic co-dependent stance, where we generously "give" to others out of our own woundedness. The result is that we unconsciously expect something in return, and others feel the strings that are attached. This is not freely given love, but love given out of neediness. So the shadow of the King involves an emotional complex around loving, giving, receiving and feeling worthy and deserving of love.

Many people show compassion to others and bypass self-compassion as a defense against the wounds of love. In some cases, they move away from their inner emptiness or broken heart by loving others excessively. Others bypass self-love by inviting what they call "transpersonal" love - the love of God or a guru - to fill the emptiness inside. Although this might seem to be a healthy solution – and it does give temporary relief – if the circular flow of **self-love** is not in place, then we cannot make full use of transpersonal love when it is offered. Often, it creates an even deeper hunger and we are compulsively drawn to prayer, asking to be filled with the love of God. The solution is to develop the good King whose first responsibility is to give abundantly to the *inner kingdom*, because when the kingdom's resources of love are full and replenished, loving others is the easiest thing in the world.

Tests to purify the heart

Practicing self-love is one way to purify the heart. Another way is to *question our soul intentions and motivations*. What is really in our heart?

For example, a friend of mine is writing a book, and he related to me how his heart's true intentions were tested while he was writing. He found himself at a crossroad, asking himself: "Why am I really writing this book? What is my intention? What is my motivation? Is it to be famous and rich? Is it to help others?"

As soon as he asked himself these questions honestly, some motives arose that were not in true alignment with his heart. Yes, it might be nice if he could make some money and become known for his work, but he wanted to align his energies with what he really felt in his heart. He found himself consciously letting go of his fantasy of being rich and famous. He just let it die. He would rather give up the whole project than have commercial motives influence the quality of his work. Soon after this surrender of his heart, he had an image of himself in meditation standing in a church with a tray of food to feed others. This is a beautiful image of the King who feeds his kingdom with a big plate of food, feeding and nourishing and giving to his kingdom.

Other tests to purify our heart come in the form of life circumstances that *challenge us to expand the boundaries of our compassion*. As we actively love from the King/Queen position, our heart grows to include people who are different, difficult and downright impossible. There is a beautiful saying from the Christian tradition that tells us to "see the face of Christ in each person." This encourages us to beam transpersonal, Christ-like love to each and every person regardless of his or her personality or circumstances. Each person deserves transpersonal love and it is not our place to judge who should and should not be loved. In Kabbalah, it is said that Hesedic love knows no bounds, and with it we can circle the whole world with compassion and loving-kindness.

Another way to purify the heart is to practice acts of indiscriminate generosity. Part of our King/Queen training is to practice spontaneous and planned acts of love – like giving more hugs and warm handshakes, helping someone who looks lost, taking our difficult mother out to lunch, giving to charities, taking time to listen to others and opening our heart to their pain. The heart is strengthened by acts of generosity and mercy.

Active decision-making and courageous action

During the Warrior training we looked at how the Warrior reserves and conserves energy. The King functions in the opposite way by *expending energy and initiating right action in the world*. The King does not just think about the kingdom and evaluate the things that must be done, he also actively decides and takes action, sometimes courageously, when it goes against what is popular within the kingdom or in the subculture to which he belongs. We can talk about doing something for years, but the King decides and gets it done. The kingdom will not thrive with a weak King or procrastinating Queen.

At the level of the soul, many decisions must be made responsibly and decisively, taking the entire kingdom into account. In our inner kingdom of the *Neshamah*, the soul is in a critical position between the *Nefesh* and the *Ruah* – the instinctual needs of our roots and the spiritual needs of our branches. The soul sits in the center of our trunk and can sense what is needed above and below (see Appendix B). The King, therefore, must consider the broadest view of the whole kingdom and decide what will further our evolution and ultimately civilize our kingdom.

For example, when we enter therapy – especially in-depth therapy that may require a huge amount of time, energy and money – the inner King must be part of that decision to coax our inner subjects to cooperate. The King must realize that the regressions and frustrations during therapy are necessary for the overall healing process. The King must courageously encourage every part of us to show up and resist the temptation to leave or check out emotionally when painful memories arise or anger comes up. The King has the courage of heart to keep going through a healing process no matter how difficult and painful.

Sacrificing and serving

The mark of a true King is his ability to serve and to make sacrifices for the good of the whole. These sacrifices are made in service of our growing consciousness and expanding kingdom. Although Kingship comes with the development of great personal power, this power is *always secondary to the power of service*. The King, because of the archetype's placement at Hesed on the Tree of Life, is able to focus upwards towards the Spirit (*Ruah*) and receive transpersonal love that he can then impart to the kingdom. This is true service.

The best analogy to the way a King serves the kingdom is the relationship between a parent and child. When this relationship is functioning at its best, the parent/King/Queen – with the greater consciousness and capacity – serves the child by generously giving the child anything that could possibly aid his or her growth and development. Great sacrifices must be made of the parent's time, energy, and resources, but all seems worth it when we see the smile on the child's face or hear his laughter or see her developmental progress. Somehow, the sacrifice of setting aside our needs – getting up at 3:00 a.m., cleaning dirty diapers, driving them to their lessons, and spending countless hours nurturing them – seems worth it, knowing that we are furthering our children's evolution. This sacred relationship of giving and receiving, serving and being served is mutually satisfying to both parent and child, but only when the King's storehouse of Hesed is full and flowing. In order for the King to sacrifice and serve without resentment, he must be conscious of the greatness of his own character. He must be conscious of his gifts, talents and personal power.

The good King also knows which are the appropriate sacrifices that will civilize the kingdom and bring greater consciousness, and which sacrifices will stir up feelings of deprivation and scarcity within the inner kingdom.

If we go back to our story of Theseus and King Minos and the Minotaur, we can see an example of how a good king knows the difference between an appropriate sacrifice and an inappropriate sacrifice.

King Minos offers us an example of an inappropriate sacrifice. He made a deal with Poseidon – a kingship in return for the sacrifice of a specific white bull. Minos however, reneged on the deal and made an inappropriate sacrifice by substituting a bull of lesser quality and value in place of the "authentic" white bull. The consequence of that inappropriate sacrifice was a devouring beast that, in turn, led to many, many more inappropriate sacrifices. Had Minos' heart not been hardened by his greed or lust for power, he may have been able to see that, in returning the gift that had been given to him generously from Spirit (Poseidon), he would have been granted a kingdom full of great bounties instead of one ravaged by shame.

In contrast to King Minos, Theseus offers us an example of an appropriate sacrifice. Theseus risks his own life so that he might redeem Minos' sin, free the kingdom from the shadow of the King's shame, and save future innocent victims of the Minotaur. Theseus models how a good King serves the people, rather than making the people serve him. And this serving spirit that comes from an authentic King does not originate from weakness or meekness. *True service from the heart and true sacrifice from the heart come from a place of great strength and courage* – so that when Theseus makes his commitment to offer his own life in order to free the land from the Minotaur's shadow, he does not offer to sacrifice himself as a victim, but as a redeemer.

One of my favorite stories from the Christian tradition is the story of the "Last Supper" – the final Passover meal that Jesus shared with his disciples before his death. At a crucial point in the Passover ceremony, Jesus demonstrates true kingship by kneeling and washing the feet of his disciples. This simple yet powerful act of service allows the disciples to experience what it is like to be given to unconditionally from a truly individuated and realized Self. Here was their true and great King, willing to serve them in a tangible and embodied way. What a profound lesson in Kingly service that is for all of us.

Becoming a source of inspiration

So far in our King training, we have learned about the power of our voice and how to purify our heart through compassion. We have learned about active decision-making, courageous action and the necessity of sacrifice and service. *The good King is also a source of tremendous inspiration.*

The film "Braveheart" is a wonderful story illustrating how a good King can become a source of inspiration for the people and can rally a whole nation to fight for their own freedom. The main character in "Braveheart," William Wallace, is a charismatic leader who infuses his followers with bravery and perseverance. He motivates them to act courageously and to have hope when all hope seems to be lost. He inspires loyalty and trust and remains true to his cause until the end. This kind of King can produce a thriving kingdom where the people are encouraged and inspired to do their best and strive for excellence. When our inner King is developed, he can inspire us to great works and great acts of generosity and creativity.

An inspirational King can expand us in many ways - in thinking and feeling and in our life experiences through travel, adventure and imagination. He can extend our horizons, allowing innovative ideas to permeate our inner Kingdom. He motivates us to experiment with new ways of doing and being and to speak words we never dared say before. When we become inspired in this way, we can overcome tremendous adversity, both internally and externally, and can break through to new life and new possibilities. The inspirational King brings hope, anticipation and the fuel to make our dreams come true in the world.

Exercise 10: Developing the King

1. Referring to the list of qualities in Diagram 21, what **King qualities** have you developed and what qualities would you like to develop more fully?

2. **The power of voice**. Does your King or Queen have a voice? Do you feel blocked from speaking your truth? With whom and in what situations does your voice constrict? With whom and in what situations can you release your voice? How would you like to increase your power of voice?

3. **Intentions and motivations of the heart**. In order to test your intentions and motivations, review different aspects of your life - Why are you really in this relationship, this job, or this community? What are your motivations? Do they align with your heart? Notice what motivations arise that are not in alignment with your heart. Let them go. What life circumstances are challenging you to expand the boundaries of your compassion?

4. **Commitment to courageous action**. What kind of courageous action do you need to take now in your life? Are you actively making decisions to further your evolution? What decisions are you avoiding? Look back to your mission statement from the Hero training in Step 2 and write down the courageous action that needs to be taken, the next step towards your destination.

5. **Serving my Kingdom**. Who does your King serve – your own truth, or the truth from someone else's kingdom? What sacrifices has your King made for the benefit of your further development? Are you overly generous in serving others, failing to serve your own kingdom?

6. **Calling upon the inspiration of the King**. Who in your life is a source of inspiration? How do they encourage your expansion? How are you an inspiration to others? How would you like your own good King or Queen to expand your horizons? What encouragement would you welcome right now in your life?

Meaning, Purpose and Destiny

According to Kabbalah, the King at Hesed is said to be the jumping-off point into the next initiation, as we shift our attention from the soul to the spirit, from the personal to the transpersonal aspects of life. The King initiates experiences of expansion to prepare the soul for the sixth initiation where we develop the branches of the Tree. *The fifth initiation has helped us to ground, develop, and expand the soul so that it becomes the Holy Grail, the chalice strong enough to be filled with Spirit during the sixth initiation.*

The King's job is to prepare the soul by opening us wide to transpersonal love. This orients us towards the upper part of the Tree. When we near the end of the fifth initiation, we can truly open our soul to the Divine unconditional love that is beaming towards us in a constant, warm stream of light. When we are pierced by this warm transpersonal love, it activates an inner search for higher meaning. We are drawn to seek our higher purpose and destiny. We ask: "Why was I born? What was I born to do? What is my higher purpose? What am I supposed to remember about my destiny?"

The King helps us to make the leap into the next initiation as he encourages our gaze upward and outward, in order to prepare us for the next major transition as we move from the trunk of the Tree to the branches. As we shift our focus, the *Neshamah* must now be placed in service of the *Ruah* (see Appendix B).

If we go back to our mythological story to see how this plays out, we see that, once again, it is Theseus who sees the larger plan and the part that he can play in the unfolding of destiny. He must slay the Minotaur of Crete in order to fulfill his destiny and free the people of Athens and reign as their King, bringing peace and abundance back to the kingdom.

Within the psyche, our King – like Theseus – has the ability to free us, redeem us and make the appropriate sacrifice that restores our internal peace. When our good King restores the inner kingdom to a state of flowing abundance, it allows the soul to reap its bountiful harvest of great talents and gifts. With the good King's help, we see our greatness and our confidence grows until we are ready to offer our magnificence to the world. As we give of our soul to the world and offer our service for the betterment of humankind, we can connect with something larger than ourselves – and life becomes infused with meaning.

Although the issues of meaning, purpose and destiny will be covered in depth in the sixth and seventh initiations, the King is the aspect of our soul that opens us to these larger spiritual dimensions of life. The King is interested in these larger issues because he knows that for the kingdom to thrive, we must be seeking meaning and purpose – we must be interested in fulfilling what we were born to do. When we begin to get a glimpse of what that is, the King integrates that new vision into our personal life by making decisions and taking the courageous action that moves us towards our destiny.

Conclusion – Initiation 5: Live your Truth

As we conclude the fifth initiation, our Chalice of the Soul has grown into a strong and shimmering Holy Grail. Our soul container should be strong enough now that we can confidently move from the trunk to the branches of the Tree, shifting our center of life from the *Neshamah* to the *Ruah*, from the soul to the spirit.

Let's review the three aspects of our soul chalice:

• *The Hero* holds our core values of truth and provides leadership, balance and coordination of the soul's efforts.

• *The Warrior* supplies the will power, discipline and determination to defend our truth.

• *The King* expands our boundaries of compassion and takes courageous action to manifest our truth in the world.

At the end of this initiation we should be able to confidently embody the qualities of the soul, which are: love, compassion, justice, mercy, integrity, commitment, self-responsibility, inner authority, individuality and authenticity.

Take some time now to reflect on your chalice and ask yourself whether you can contain and manifest these soul qualities in your life. If the answer is yes, then you are ready for the sixth initiation – opening to the mystery of Spirit and transforming whatever is hindering you from living out your true purpose and destiny.

Part III - Branches

Stages 6 and 7

In Part I we developed the roots of our Tree of Life and in Part II we developed the trunk. Now in Part III we widen our vision to a spiritual perspective of life, which requires another shift in our focus of consciousness, this time from the trunk to the branches of the Tree.

During **Initiation 6**, the branches of our tree grow outward and upward, expanding our horizons and shifting our worldview from an individual/personal view to a transpersonal view of life. When we climb up into the branches, we gain access to our higher purpose and how our particular gifts fit into the much larger spiritual plan. This shift in consciousness occurs only if we are willing to risk further transformation and shed whatever is keeping us from fulfilling our life purpose.

This kind of radical transformation and spiritual awakening requires commitment to a spiritual path that connects us with a living tradition and guides us into the realm of Spirit. As we awaken spiritually and spread out our branches, we become part of the greater collective family, fulfilling our human destiny to be stewards of creation and to be involved in the evolution of humankind.

Sometimes, serving Spirit means that we need to make personal sacrifices – like giving up personal desires, surrendering control, letting go of behaviors, patterns, relationships, careers, possessions or ego attachments that do not serve our own spirit or the universal Spirit. Opening to Spirit also has its great rewards, as we gain wisdom, understanding and knowledge. We find meaning, deep satisfaction, contentment and ecstatic joy.

During **Initiation 7**, the branches of our Tree of Life begin to flower and fruit. Here we make direct connection to the source of all life – God, the Beloved, and the Sacred Ground of Being. Opening to the divine consciousness in Stage 7 gives us access to the mysterious force pulling all opposites, all fragmentations, all dualities into a unified whole. When the seventh initiation is successful, our instinctive, psychological and spiritual selves experience mystical union, oneness with all of life, wholeness and well-being. Here we receive powerful healing as we tap into a permanent source of renewal and rejuvenation.

At this point of culmination, all three systems of our Tree of Life come into alignment. The roots, trunk and branches are working together as a holistic system that is generative and bountiful, resulting in the budding and ripening of our particular fruit. Now our fruits of wisdom, understanding and knowledge become the nourishment for other souls along the path. When initiation has been successful, our Tree of Life can be a powerful healing sanctuary for others, with bountiful branches and fruit offered for rest, refuge, refreshment and blessing.

Chapter 6

The Gatekeeper
Robe 6

Initiation 6 - TRANSFORMATION

In the sixth initiation, we face the challenges and joys of opening to Spirit so that we may glimpse our life purpose and transform any obstacles blocking us from living our destiny. Through the myth of Dionysus, we will learn how to surrender to the transformation process, which brings not only death and loss, but also ecstasy and new life. When this initiation is successful, we can trust our innate spiritual knowing and feel inspired to practice our creativity.

In order to activate this initiation, we call upon the **Visionary** archetype, which widens out our vision of life from the personal to the transpersonal. We begin to see the vast interwoven tapestry of life and understand how all things are interconnected. The Visionary stimulates our inner vision and draws us into states of ecstasy, joy, celebration and creativity. With this archetypal energy, we will meet our creative Muse who invites us to dance the sacred dance we were born to do.

Qualities if initiated:

Wise

Inspired

Objective

Spiritually open

Creative and innovative

Can release outmoded beliefs

Committed to a spiritual path

Able to endure suffering and hardship

Able to be ecstatic and joyful

Able to surrender

Trust in the unknown path ahead

Problems if initiation is not complete:

Unable to see the spiritual purpose for our life

Lacking inspiration

Stuck in personal concerns of life

Unwilling to surrender

Lacking creativity and innovation

Holding onto outmoded beliefs

Unwilling to commit to a spiritual path

Spiritualizing/intellectualizing as a defense against pain and suffering

Fear of chaos, madness, disintegration

Controlling

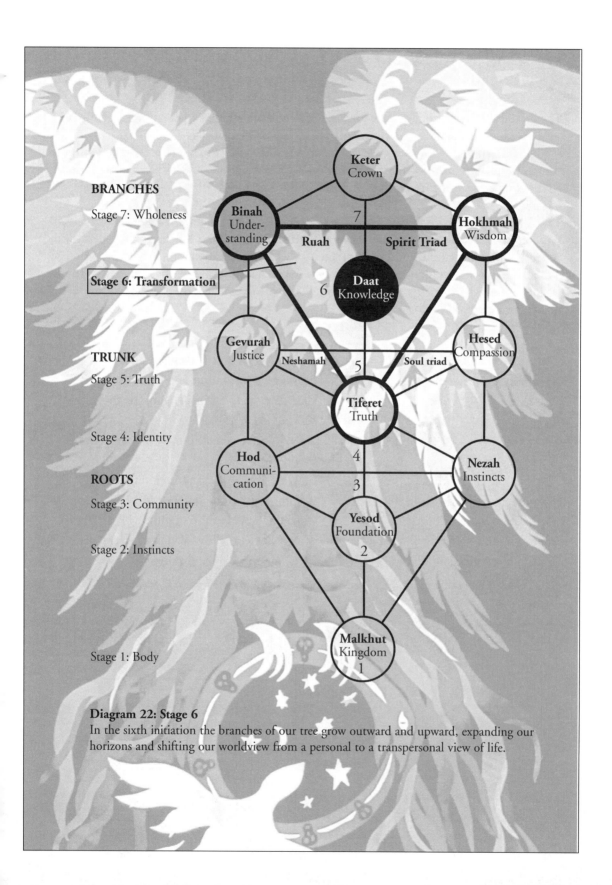

BRANCHES

Stage 7: Wholeness

Stage 6: Transformation

TRUNK

Stage 5: Truth

Stage 4: Identity

ROOTS

Stage 3: Community

Stage 2: Instincts

Stage 1: Body

Keter
Crown

Binah
Under-
standing

Ruah

Spirit Triad

Hokhmah
Wisdom

7

Daat
Knowledge

6

Gevurah
Justice

Neshamah

5

Soul triad

Hesed
Compassion

Tiferet
Truth

Hod
Communi-
cation

4

3

Nezah
Instincts

Yesod
Foundation

2

Malkhut
Kingdom

1

Diagram 22: Stage 6
In the sixth initiation the branches of our tree grow outward and upward, expanding our
horizons and shifting our worldview from a personal to a transpersonal view of life.

Chapter 6 - Open to Spirit

Exercise 1: Meditation - The branches of the Tree

Imagine yourself as the Tree of Life. Experience your deep and complex root system, and acknowledge the rich earth that anchors your great Tree. Move your awareness up to the trunk and affirm the strong and sturdy trunk that sustains your Tree.

Now shift your focus to the branches of your Tree. Experience how your branches thrust upward toward the sky and the sun. Let your branches grow as far and as high as they want. Allow the branches to grow leaves. Soak the sunlight into your thousands of leaves – feel them receive the sunlight, take in the carbon dioxide and transform it into the life-enhancing oxygen that sustains life.

What is it like to focus your attention upward and outward? As your branches reach outward, can you feel yourself touching the branches of other trees? What is it like to connect with other trees? Are your branches a home to any creatures? What is it like to experience life from this height? How is it different from the perspective of the roots and the trunk? How comfortable do you feel here in your branches? Do you want to make any adjustments?

Become aware once again of your whole Tree with its roots, trunk and branches. Then allow the image to fade, and slowly bring yourself back to the present.

* Step 1: Commit to a spiritual path *
Step 2: Rejuvenate your spirit
Step 3: Risk transformation
Step 4: Become a Visionary

Branching out to a spiritual perspective

The fifth initiation helped us to complete the trunk of our Tree by developing the Hero, the Warrior and the King. These three powerful archetypes of the soul develop our inner chalice that has integrity and strength, enabling us now to open to the Spirit.

As we learned in Stage 5, the King aspect of the soul is especially helpful in moving our gaze upward and outward, preparing us to grow branches to our Tree of Life and to eventually bear fruit. The King mediates the gifts and bounties of Spirit and feeds this to the soul.

Here in the sixth initiation, we will look at how the individual soul digests these gifts from Spirit and how, in turn, the soul feeds Spirit by returning its unique gifts and bounties back to the collective. This is accomplished when we branch out to a spiritual perspective and understand precisely how we can contribute to society, culture and the spiritual progress of humanity.

When we open to Spirit and grow branches on our Tree, we begin activating the Visionary archetype, which enables us to expand our field of vision, transforming life on many levels. In Kabbalah, the Visionary occupies the place on the Tree called the "Spirit triad" and it is where the *Ruah* resides (see Diagram 22). On the diagram we can see clearly how the soul is like a chalice, open to receive the gifts from Spirit. The soul and Spirit intersect in

Tiferet, where our *personal truth meets universal truth*. This is also where the heart, will and higher mind integrate within each person.

Let's look at the Spirit triad more closely to see what awaits us in the sixth initiation. The Spirit triad consists of Tiferet, Binah, and Hokhmah and is centered on Daat. The translations are as follows: Tiferet – truth, beauty and goodness, Binah – understanding, Hokhmah – wisdom, and Daat – transformation and knowledge from direct experience

On the body, the *Ruah* is centered on the face, focused on the third eye, the place of "gnosis," mystical knowing and spiritual awakening. The qualities that will be developed as we open to Spirit and open the Visionary's gaze will be qualities of universal truth, understanding, wisdom, knowledge (of spiritual realities) and the ability to transform our perceptions at will.

As we branch out to a spiritual perspective of life, the first thing we notice is the tangible difference between our soul and spirit, between the *Neshamah* and the *Ruah*. Our soul is concerned with developing our individual truth and unique personal gifts. Our soul is associated with water and with the world of emotions, deep passions and our heart's desires. Our spirit, on the other hand, is concerned with collective, global and cosmic concerns, oriented towards the transpersonal rather than personal aspects of life. Spirit is associated with the element air.

Looking out into the night sky extends our vision far beyond our small, personal perspective and gives us a perspective approximating that of Spirit. Whenever I fly in an airplane and my field of vision extends over a vast landscape or I can see the curve of the earth itself far over the horizon, it helps me to shift into a spiritual perspective. I have solved many dilemmas and let go of many petty, personal concerns while gazing out of the window of an airplane.

The world of Spirit can also be seen as the higher mind, the world of ideas, spiritual principles and universal truth in all traditions. These concerns – such as social justice, tolerance, equality, universal love and forgiveness – are at the heart of all spiritual traditions.

As we are being initiated into a spiritual perspective of life, something slowly transforms in our consciousness. In Kabbalah it is said that during the sixth initiation we shift from "living out our fate," where we are subject to individual law, to "living out our destiny." This is when we search wholeheartedly for how our individual gifts move us into the flow of destiny and how we can contribute to the larger collective, universal plan.

There are fascinating stories throughout history of men and women of destiny. These are people who are in the right place at the right time to play their part in the unfolding of historical events. St. Teresa of Avila and St. John of the Cross, who reformed the Catholic monastic orders in 16th Century Spain, were *religious* leaders of destiny and helped reconnect monasticism with Spirit. Rosa Parks and Martin Luther King reformed social law and called us all to justice and higher *spiritual* law. Marie and Pierre Curie were people of destiny in the *scientific* field, studying radioactivity and magnetism. They both won the Nobel Prize for Physics in 1903, laying a foundation for future studies in Nuclear Physics and helping to establish radiological work in hospitals. Another interesting person of destiny was a man named Philo Farnsworth, the son of an Idaho potato farmer, who, at 21 years of age, invented the first electronic television signal and catalyzed our modern television revolution.

Today and every day there are men and women who are working diligently in their particular fields of teaching, commerce, child development, banking, agriculture, science, spirituality, technology and every field of life imaginable – living out their destiny in countless ways.

The purpose of developing our spirit and finding our higher purpose is to *inject universal spiritual values into our field of work or sphere of influence, which in turn breathes new life into the culture*. When the breath of Spirit is breathed into the culture by those of us working to find our destiny, it can be powerful enough to renew a whole civilization – and we have seen these powerful renaissance or "renewal" periods throughout our history. The European renaissance of the late 1400's brought renewal on a number of fronts – art, music, architecture, astrology, and mysticism, to name a few. As this powerful wind of the Spirit breathes new life into the human community, it can civilize us and inspire us to live with more tolerance, social justice and care for the earth and its resources. It encourages reconnection with Spirit and with universal values that help humanity evolve in a life-giving direction.

Identify your spiritual path

In order to develop the gifts of the Spirit so that we may become men and women of destiny, our life must transform on many levels. It takes a tremendous effort to shift our center from the *Neshamah* to the *Ruah*. It also requires death to some old ways of being in order to make room for the new.

It is imperative during the sixth initiation to search for and identify the spiritual path that is right for us, because the support of a great spiritual path or mystical teaching can help us successfully transform into our *Ruah*, our spirit body. There are many paths that understand the universal spiritual principles and can support our awakening consciousness. I suggest finding a path that offers practical knowledge, a path that has been tried and tested through time with followers that you respect. I also suggest focusing on a living tradition - a spiritual path that has a dynamic connection with Spirit that can bring you rejuvenation and renewal. When we identify the right path, then we need to commit to that path of higher wisdom with all our heart, soul, mind and strength.

Many people find it difficult to commit themselves to a spiritual path – they dabble in many different paths, moving from one to the next when they reach a certain point in their development. This is different from the person who truly searches, perhaps trying several different paths to see which suits them. It is also different from the person who truly commits heart and soul for a period of time to a physical path of yoga, for example, but who then feels called to develop further on a more devotional path. The advantage of committing for a long period of time to one path is that it gives us an opportunity to face our psychological resistances to spiritual transformation. It requires commitment from our higher self, our *Ruah*.

Some people access Spirit and gain qualities of wisdom and understanding through a *physical* path like yoga or Tai Chi. Others access Spirit through the mind or by choosing *contemplative* or metaphysical paths. Others find engaging their mind a distraction, and they need a path of meditation that quiets the mind. Others are attracted to *earth-based* spirituality and follow seasonal Pagan celebrations or various Native American paths. Some seekers are people of the heart and seek a *devotional* path to Spirit. Some need a path of *solitude* offered by the monastic traditions.

So how do we find the right path that matches our sensibilities and fulfills the needs of our particular body type, soul type and spiritual type? The following are some questions to help us identify our particular path.

Exercise 2: Identifying your spiritual path

1. Do you feel moved by or connected to Spirit when you engage in **physical** practices such as Yoga, dance, Tai Chi or ritual of some kind? Write down the specific practices you enjoy.

2. Do you feel moved by or connected to Spirit when you engage in **emotional or devotional** practices such as singing, listening to music, reading or writing poetry? Write down the specific practices you enjoy.

3. Do you feel moved by or connected to Spirit when you engage in **contemplative** practices such as meditation, solitude, being in nature, reading sacred texts? Write down the specific practices you enjoy.

4. Commit to exploring a spiritual path that makes you feel connected to Spirit.

Open to spiritual guidance

Every path of knowledge or living tradition has initiated elders - dead and alive – who have paved the way before us. As we acknowledge our spiritual ancestors and open to them, they can become our guides. This means tapping into the collective wisdom of our foremothers and forefathers who have contributed to the particular spiritual path of our choosing.

On the Tree of Life diagram, the female and male ancestors of each tradition would be placed at Binah and Hokhmah respectively. These are collective archetypes of spiritual understanding and wisdom that have pooled over the centuries, becoming wells of living water into which we can dip our buckets and drink.

During a particular time in my own journey of opening to spiritual guidance, I received this simple, yet profound dream.

> *I am standing in the midst of what seems like deep space – and yet I am not floating, but standing on something quite solid. As I look down, I am standing on the shoulders of a woman. I look down further below her and can see that she is also standing on the shoulders of a woman who is standing on the shoulders of another woman, and so on, for what seems like infinity. Then I notice that there is a woman standing on my shoulders and many others above her. I realize I have taken my place in the long line of women mystics who have stretched out in time before me. I am also supporting those women who will come after me and take their place when the time is right.*

When I awoke from the dream I was reminded of the ancient idea of "the golden chain" of being. The golden chain is another name for the perennial teaching, the spiritual guidance that is carried continuously by people growing in consciousness and willing to "shoulder" the responsibility of transmitting the spiritual teachings and practices. It is comforting to know that the golden chain has existed as an unbroken connection of consciousness and enlightenment for thousands of years. Spiritual guidance from all traditions emanates from the source of the golden chain, offering a variety of psycho-spiritual practices for people of every spiritual persuasion. There is an abundance of available resources from Spirit, if only we have eyes to see.

Once you have identified your path of transformation and begun practicing it, then you can begin to call the ancestors of that line and follow the guidance of those who have gone before. So, if you are on a Sufi path and feel a kinship with the great Sufi poet Rumi, find some of his books filled with beautiful poems and stories and enjoy reading them. If you are a follower of Jesus, then learn about him, pray to him, and ask him to come alive in your life. If you follow Mother Meera, go and see her, get darshan, allow her to bless you on your spiritual journey. If you are interested in Kabbalah, find a teacher and learn the Tree of Life so that the principles can come alive in your everyday life. Learn some Kabbalistic chants and meditations to deepen your spiritual practice.

Get initiated by the elders. If the leaders of your ancestral line are not alive, there will always be people who are carrying on the tradition. Ask, seek, knock, search and life will bring you exactly what and whom you need. When the student is ready and willing, the teacher will appear.

Hearing the call

If we only develop the roots and trunk of our Tree of Life and nothing more, our perspective of life remains truncated. When the branches are not consciously developed, our vision remains stunted, revolving around a small range of personal concerns. Growing the branches and expanding our truncated vision of life is often initiated by a "calling." This calling is an invitation to grow bigger inside and take our place in the unfolding of destiny. A calling to develop our branches confronts us with the enormity of Spirit, which can be difficult for both the *Nefesh* and the *Neshamah*, as we are challenged to surrender our comforts and attachments to a purely personal life. To illustrate the process of calling, let's follow the ancient Jewish story of Moses and discover some of the challenges and rewards of following our destiny. The following story is my own retelling of the famous tale with excerpts taken from the Book of Exodus, Chapters 2 and 3.

The Calling of Moses

A long time ago, Moses was born in Egypt to Hebrew parents at a time when the Pharaoh of Egypt had issued a decree to kill all the newly born male children of the Hebrew slaves because they had grown too numerous. Moses' mother, desperate to save her child, hid him for several months. When she could hide him no longer, she put the baby Moses in a papyrus basket and sent him afloat down the Nile. As destiny unfolded, Moses' basket landed on the banks of Pharaoh's palace and Pharaoh's daughter found the child. She recognized that baby Moses was a Hebrew but nevertheless took him into her keeping and raised him as her son in Pharaoh's palace.

When Moses was grown, he set out to visit his countrymen, the Hebrew slaves, and saw what a hard life they were having. When he saw one of the Egyptian taskmasters cruelly beating a Hebrew slave, something awakened within Moses' heart. He saw the plight of his people and in a rage, killed the taskmaster. Moses was horrified and frightened and fled from the palace and from Egypt altogether.

Moses wandered in the wilderness until he arrived in the country inhabited by Jethro, the priest of Midian. Moses stayed with Jethro's family and his clan for many years, marrying

Jethro's daughter, Zipporah, and tending the flocks of sheep. One day while tending his sheep, Moses encountered an angel of God appearing in the form of a burning bush. He was curious that the bush burned but was not consumed by the fire, so he went to investigate and what follows is his encounter with the Divine in the wilderness.

God spoke to Moses saying, "Moses!" – to which Moses replied, "Here I am." Then God said, "Come no closer. Take off your shoes, for the place you are standing on is holy ground. I am the God of your father – the God of Abraham, Isaac and Jacob. I have seen the miserable state of my people in Egypt. I mean to deliver them out of the hands of the Egyptians and bring them to a land flowing with milk and honey. I send you to Pharaoh to bring the people of Israel out of Egypt." Moses asked, "Who am I to go to Pharaoh and deliver the people?" And God told Moses, "I will be with you." [1]

So here we have the archetypal calling of Destiny. It begins with Moses' remarkable birth and early infancy. From the beginning, the story foretells a remarkable soul who is protected against all odds, set apart for an important and sacred task. If we look at the story from an archetypal perspective, it tells us that we all have the potential to live a remarkable life – we all have a special task of destiny to fulfill and the forces of God are on our side, working against all odds to set up the best circumstances to ensure the fulfillment of our task.

The next part of the story tells of Moses growing up in a life of worldly privilege. His *Nefesh* and *Neshamah* needs are cared for, and he is comfortable and safe within the palace walls. His life revolves around his own personal concerns.

Then at a crucial point, he seems to awaken from his comfortable life of privilege. We are not told in the story how Moses knows his Hebrew lineage or why he leaves the palace one day to visit his countrymen, but he ventures to where the Hebrew slaves are working and witnesses the harsh reality of their daily toil. Something stirs in his heart and he awakens out of his comfort and ignorance and begins to see the true human condition – in others and within himself. Suddenly, his concerns widen out beyond himself and he grows in compassion. This awakening represents the archetypal awakening of the *Ruah*, when we recognize the parts of us that are oppressed and enslaved and in need of redemption. It happens to each of us in a different way. Moses' *Ruah* awakening seems to have been sparked by the shock of seeing his kinsmen so brutally treated.

Moses now realizes that he can never go back to his old life. Perhaps with nowhere else to turn, he flees into the desert, where he is stripped of his old identity, his status, wealth, power and worldly privilege. Out in the wilderness, far away from the palaces of Egypt, Moses leaves behind all that he has known and takes on a new identity. Here with Jethro's clan in a far-away place, Moses experiences a rebirth, which includes an expansion of values and an extended vision of life. Now he is ready to receive his "destiny papers."

God comes to him in the form of a burning bush, fire being a symbol in Kabbalah of the Divine Presence. God then goes on to describe what is needed – both collectively for the people of Israel and personally for Moses. According to Spirit, Moses is the man for the job. He is given a task for which he is perfectly suited, and yet Moses' immediate response is doubt. He asks, "Who am I to perform this task of destiny?"

It seems to be inevitable that when we are given our destiny papers, we cannot quite believe it. We experience doubt or we feel frightened. Even if we have been seeking our destiny or telling Spirit that we are ready, when the calling actually comes, we can feel unprepared.

Often the calling to a particular task is surprising or shocking – "You want me to do what?" It must have been like this for Moses too. "What? You want me to go back to Egypt and face my countrymen whom I betrayed and Pharaoh whom I abandoned? I am decidedly the wrong man for the job!" As outside observers to the story, we can see clearly why Moses was the perfect person to fulfill this task – and so it is with all of us. An outside observer to our life can sometimes more easily see that our calling does fit with our destiny, even if we may not be able to see it yet.

This happened recently to a friend of mine who had been avoiding her calling as a hands-on healer, even though she knew from a very young age that this was what she was born to do. After years of resisting, her life circumstances brought her to the point where she could do nothing else but begin her healing practice. People are now flocking to her office.

Once we hear the call, we must eventually respond by taking proactive steps to move towards our destiny. Sometimes we can only move one tiny step at a time. That is enough, for it is still moving forward. And though it is likely to be a time of challenge and uncertainty, we can rest assured that God will be with us.

Exercise 3: *What is your personal calling?*

In the Moses story, we are given the main components of the archetypal call of Destiny.

1. **Remarkable birth** - In order to receive the calling to our destiny, we must believe that we have a remarkable purpose, that we each come into the world to fulfill a remarkable task. It doesn't matter how big or small, it is a task for which we are uniquely suited. We must also understand that the universe is working against all odds to ensure the fulfillment of this task because it is needed in the grand design. Pretend now that you are your own spiritual guide. Get a piece of paper and write these three questions at the top, filling your name in the blank spaces.

What is remarkable about _____?
Why has _____ come into the world?
What is _____'s special task?

2. **Spiritual awakening** - Most of us go through life in a vague state of slumber. We are asleep, comfortable, innocent, going along, and then suddenly we wake up and our vision of life expands. We have a spiritual awakening. We see the plight of the human condition and we grow in compassion. We also recognize parts of us that are enslaved and oppressed.

When did this happen for you?
How did you perceive life differently?
Did you grow in compassion?
How did your life change?

3. **Calling to a new kind of life** - The purpose of a spiritual awakening is to call us to live a different kind of life, one with spiritual values and universal principles at the center. During this stage, we either flee the old life or are stripped of our old identity and our attachments to status, wealth, power or worldly privilege. In the wilderness we take on a new identity, or perhaps just remember our original identity and who we were called to be.

Have you experienced being stripped of an old identity?

What was this experience like?

Who were you when the old identity dropped away?

4. **Destiny papers** - After we show our willingness to live with the *Ruah* as the center of our life, at some point, at just the right moment, we are handed our destiny papers. They may not come to us in the form of a burning bush, but if we are awake, the papers will come.

What is your specific calling? It doesn't matter if it is only a small piece of the total picture; describe anything that feels like your calling.

How did this come to you? Through another person or organization? Was it an inner calling or prompting?

Why are you the perfect person suited for the job? Look at your background, personality, family, training, ancestral inheritance. If you can't see why you are the perfect person, ask a trusted friend and get their response.

5. **Doubt and fear** – Once we receive our destiny papers, we may doubt our ability to carry out our purpose.

What doubts and fears come up when you think about actually fulfilling this task? Are you tempted to walk away or ask for something else or give the job to someone else? Find a strategy for overcoming your fear and get on with your life task. God will be with you.

6. **Life Purpose Statement** - Now distill all you have written about your personal calling into a life purpose statement of no longer than three sentences. If you can, distill your personal calling in one sentence. Write it out on beautiful paper and put it up on your wall somewhere and look at it every day.

Step 1: Commit to a spiritual path
* Step 2: Rejuvenate your spirit *
Step 3: Risk transformation
Step 4: Become a Visionary

Rejuvenate the Kingdom

In the first step of this sixth initiation, we saw the importance of committing ourselves to a spiritual path, asking for guidance, doing our spiritual practices and listening attentively for a calling from Spirit. The second step involves opening ourselves to the powerful *rejuvenation and renewal* that comes from Spirit.

The purpose of spiritual rejuvenation is to allow the fresh wind of the Spirit to breathe into our lives so that our personal life is renewed on all levels and in turn, the collective life of the culture is rejuvenated. We also need the wind of the Spirit to help move and steer the ship of our soul towards its destiny or destination.

Allowing spiritual rejuvenation requires great personal strength because the wind of the Spirit can storm in like a tornado, turning our life upside down with change and destroying structures within the psyche that no longer serve our spiritual growth. At other times, the wind blows in quietly like a cool breeze, bringing new insights and understanding to our life so that we feel inspired, refreshed and enlightened. Both the destruction of old ways and the construction of new ways of living are needed for spiritual renewal. We must allow this flowing of Spirit to create both death and rebirth in our lives so that these transformative cycles can clear out the internal clutter and make room for spiritual growth.

To help us through this initiation, the mythic figures of Dionysus and Apollo will be our guides. They facilitate two opposite but essential experiences of spiritual rejuvenation.

Dionysus – the god of intoxication and ecstasy – brings a wild, free and ecstatic experience of Spirit, like that experienced at a charismatic revival meeting or during a lively Jewish circle dance. Apollo – the god of the arts and sciences – brings a more sober and refined experience of Spirit, characteristic of the feeling we get when we enter a gothic cathedral, see a great work of art, or hear a beautiful piece of classical music. Dionysus allows new inspirations from Spirit into life, and Apollo weaves these inspirations into refined and practical forms. Although opposite energies, these two powerful archetypes are both essential for the survival of civilization and spiritual renewal.

An important part of the sixth initiation is to value both expressions of Spirit and not favor Apollo over Dionysus or vice versa. When we learn to value and encourage both expressions of Spirit, we can invite both the ecstatic, chaotic wind to flow in and change things, and the focused, clarifying wind to breeze in and stabilize our spiritual life. This creates true spiritual renewal.

Spiritual rejuvenation involves the Spirit triad of Tiferet (truth), Binah (understanding) and Hokhmah (wisdom), and is centered on Daat (knowledge). We can superimpose Dionysus, Apollo and the Visionary on our Tree of Life by placing Dionysus on top of the right pillar with Hokhmah, and seating Apollo on top of the left pillar at Binah. The Visionary occupies the place of Daat, and stands between the Dionysian and Apollonian experiences of Spirit, helping to integrate both (See Diagram 23).

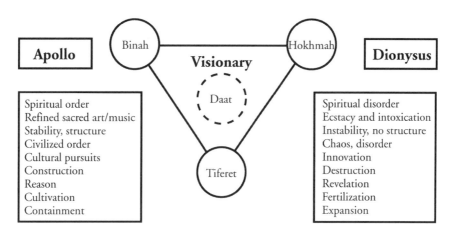

Diagram 23: Apollo and Dionysus

Let's look now at how Apollo and Dionysus introduce us to the ways of Spirit.

Apollo is the god who civilizes by stabilizing culture – placed at Binah, and representing our highest and most refined spiritual values. Apollo is the god of *spiritual order*. He is the god of light, truth, beauty, ethics, heroic excellence, science, medicine and math, to name a few.

I once worked with a man who felt akin to Apollo and this particular way of experiencing Spirit. He was a classical musician and had a deep appreciation for what he considered "highly refined music," especially church music that "shot him straight into the realm of Spirit." He loved to frequent the beautiful stone cathedrals in England, where he lived, and listen to classical concerts, which would put him into a state of calm and deep reflection.

Dionysus, on the other hand, is the god of *spiritual disorder* – placed at Hokhmah, and representing the dynamic primal life force. Dionysus is not concerned with existing structures or institutions; his Spirit does not want to be bound. Rather than stabilizing the civilized order of things, he destabilizes civilization and opens us up to innovation, new ways of doing and being. Dionysus is the god of wine, ecstasy, intoxication, liberation and abandon. He brings in new impulses from Spirit: ecstasy and creativity but also chaos, disorder and sometimes madness.

Another client I worked with felt more akin to Dionysus and this particular way of experiencing Spirit. She was a dancer and loved to connect with Spirit through many forms of dance: circle dancing, belly dancing, salsa, and especially dancing out in nature at large rave gatherings. There she felt a sense of wild abandon and freedom when she moved her body to music and rhythms. Without use of alcohol or drugs, she could feel "the intoxication and ecstasy of Spirit." It was important for her to find a spiritual practice that would get her out of her head and her "anxious thoughts and worries."

As we observe the function of these gods within the individual and within the culture at large, it is clear that both the Dionysian *fertilization* and Apollonian *cultivation* of spiritual impulses are necessary for new life and for true and lasting transformation.

Dionysus: Fertilizing the seeds of Spirit

The seeds of the Spirit are ever abundant and ever available – and there is infinite potential in an unfertilized seed. But for life to grow and for those possibilities to become real, the seed must be fertilized. So when we open ourselves to be fertilized by one of these spiritual seeds, we open ourselves to be infused by the primal life force. When this happens, our life can be transformed in wondrous and unexpected ways.

So it is with Dionysus, the god of the unpredictable life force who renews life by pulling us into experiences of death and rebirth. Let's look more closely at the story of Dionysus, who shows us the wild fertility of Spirit and also warns us of the consequences if we refuse to surrender to the great renewing force of Spirit.

The Myth of Dionysus

Dionysus was born of the god Zeus and the mortal woman Semele. It is said that Zeus' name means "shower of light," so Dionysus was born from this divine place, connecting him with the stars, the shower of light that fills the cosmos.

Zeus was so pleased that Semele was carrying his child that he granted her one wish, any wish her heart desired. So Semele thought of her heart's desire and asked to see her lover Zeus in his full glory as a god. Zeus knew he could not refuse her wish – and he also knew that if he revealed his full nature of light to the mortal woman, the intensity of it would incinerate her to death. And so he pleaded with her, "No, no. Don't ask that of me!" But in her love for him she insisted, saying "I want to see you in your full glory."

So Zeus was forced to keep his promise and reveal his true nature to her. As Zeus' light came into full power, Semele was tragically burned to death. But she had wrapped ivy around her belly, which protected the unborn Dionysus from the fire. Zeus quickly plucked Dionysus from Semele's protected womb, made an incision in his own thigh, and put Dionysus there for safekeeping until it was time for him to be born. When the time of his birth arrived, Dionysus sprang alive from Zeus's thigh.

And so it was that the extraordinary birth of this extraordinary child quickly came to the attention of the Titans – who were the first gods of the earth. When the Titans heard about this child, they were terrified of him and decided to take action. Their fear turned to violence and they dismembered the baby, tearing him to pieces and boiling him for good measure.

But Dionysus could not remain dead. A beautiful pomegranate tree sprouted from the earth where a drop of his blood had fallen. His grandmother Rhea saw this blood and the fertile pomegranate tree, and in mercy she decided to put him back together once again.

And so it was that Dionysus was born three times: once from his mortal mother's womb, second from his immortal father's thigh, and the third time from his grandmother Rhea, who resurrected him from the earth.

Now, Zeus was a married god. And his wife Hera was understandably angry that her husband had been unfaithful with Semele. So Hera unleashed her wrath by searching for Dionysus everywhere to destroy him.

During his childhood, Dionysus was taken into the wilderness and cloaked as a girl so that he would be hidden from the jealous Hera. And so he lived his early life as an androgynous figure, embodying both masculine and feminine energies. The fawns, the nymphs, the satyrs, and all the wild animals of the forest took care of him and raised him. The Muses were also his teachers – and they inspired him with poetry and music and the wonders of dance.

But it was his mentor Silenus whom Dionysus valued above all. Silenus was a satyr – half man and half goat – who taught Dionysus the wonders of the vine. An alchemical teacher, Silenus showed Dionysus the mysteries of transformation – turning water into wine, grapes into spirits. Thus Dionysus spent his childhood playing around the mountainside and reveling in the ecstatic mysteries of nature.

But Hera was undaunted in her desire to destroy Dionysus. So when he grew into manhood and became a god in his own right, Hera found Dionysus and cursed him with madness – and he roamed the countryside stark raving mad. Despite this – or perhaps because of it – Dionysus had a huge array of followers. There were satyrs, including his favorite Silenus. There were nymphs, centaurs and wood spirits that danced alongside of him. Dionysus also had a group of women followers called the Maenads who, when worshiping the god, would go into wild and ecstatic frenzies. During these states, the Maenads were known to tear people and animals to shreds, dismembering those who were not worshiping Dionysus, or simply destroying all who got in their way.

In time, Dionysus' grandmother Rhea came to his rescue again and cured him of his madness. After his cure and recovery, Rhea initiated him into the women's mysteries, and thus

Dionysus became the only male god in the Greek pantheon who was ever initiated into the female mystery cults. After this initiation, Dionysus gained more and more in power...... [2] (To be continued)

Open to the creative life force

The story of Dionysus speaks to us of the powerful nature of the Spirit that cannot die. No matter how hard they tried, even the gods could not kill him. No matter what was done to him, Dionysus continued to resurrect and even thrive – like a vine in the moist, fecund jungle, growing and blooming and blossoming, exploding with bright and colorful flowers in uncontained profusion. Dionysus is the god of the wild spirit that bursts forth with new life. He cannot be tamed, manicured, cultivated, bound, contained or stopped. His spiritual energy is in service of change and transformation. His spirit changes life through fermentation – adding the yeast that makes the juices of life bubble, heat and move. Initiated into the female mysteries, he is a male god who is intimately connected to the feminine, representing the joyous intercourse of masculine and feminine energies that create the multifaceted array of life that is birthed constantly from Spirit.

As appealing and as life giving as he is, the Dionysian spirit is not always easy to open to – especially in our Western Apollonian-structured society. It is difficult to contain the chaos, disorder and abrupt changes that Dionysus brings, and it is challenging to maintain the flexibility that this kind of Spirit demands. To truly open ourselves to the fertilizing wind of the Spirit, we must have the capacity to be intimate, open and receptive. Our inner King must be able to let go of the known ways of doing and being within the psyche.

Another chapter in the story of Dionysus gives us a vivid picture of what happens when our inner King is not open to spiritual renewal and refuses to allow Dionysus into the kingdom:

As his power continued to grow, Dionysus traveled from kingdom to kingdom – demanding that his form of worship be accepted as valid within the kingdom. Many kings accepted and tolerated these ecstatic and frenzied rites. But some kings opposed Dionysian worship in their kingdom because it was the antithesis of the spiritual law and order they preferred.

One day, when Dionysus and his followers invaded Thrace, the ruler there –King Lisergus – fought violently against Dionysus and captured the god's army. Dionysus in turn went into hiding deep under the sea. But once again, Grandmother Rhea defended Dionysus and struck King Lisergus with madness. In his madness, the king believed his son to be a grape vine and tragically, Lisergus hacked his son to death. As a consequence of this horrible act, the land of Thrace became barren, and the people likewise felt barren and bereft. This set the stage for Dionysus to emerge triumphantly from his hiding place deep within the belly of the sea. And he came to Thrace and told the people that the kingdom would not flourish unless King Lisergus was killed. The people listened to Dionysus and, in a state of frenzy, tied horses to the king's arms and legs and pulled him limb from limb.

In this part of the story, we can see that if the construction of our inner kingdom is too rigid or is overly concerned with order, control, structure or maintaining the status quo, then we resist the Spirit in its Dionysian form. If we have a King that adamantly resists growing bigger inside, opening to a higher perspective and to the creativity coming in from a higher level of consciousness, then the King becomes susceptible to madness. If the King within us is to remain sane and whole, he must serve the Spirit and have a higher guiding principle by which he makes decisions.

A King, such as Lisergus, who gets stuck in "order", lacks the humility to follow the superior wisdom of Spirit when it comes "calling." A stuck or rigid King does not allow himself to be dependent on something larger than his own limited perspective and resources and refuses to be reborn from that experience. In the language of Depth Psychology, a rigid King is open to Dionysian possession, where Dionysus shows up from the depths of the unconscious (the depths of the sea) in an unrefined and therefore destructive form.

We can see from the story that when Dionysus is shunned, he seeks revenge – through madness, dismemberment, destruction and death. It is therefore very unwise to refuse to incorporate the energy of Dionysus when it comes "knocking on the door" of our life. In the Greek myth, when the King of Thrace refused to allow this kind of wild, ecstatic energy in, the land became barren, the people bereft, life went out of the kingdom and things that were precious to the king – his son, his sanity, his life – were destroyed in a horrific and frenzied manner.

So how do we set up a good kingdom that is centered squarely on our soul values but also allows the influx and renewal from the Spirit? Our inner Kingdom must be able to tolerate the chaos and disorder that comes with the winds of change. We must be flexible enough to allow new ideas in, and we must be strong enough to let go of personal control. The bottom line with Dionysus is that we must be able to *surrender* to the great, wondrous, transpersonal energy of Spirit, whose consciousness extends far beyond our limited, personal awareness.

According to the myth, Dionysian worship always includes some form of ecstatic state – either through drunkenness, dancing, or sexual orgy. In symbolic terms, this means that Dionysus demands that we let go of control and open ourselves to be penetrated and fertilized by the seeds of Spirit. It invites us to be "drunk with the Spirit," in an altered state where we are more receptive to spiritual guidance or more open to the shifting of old energy patterns. It invites us to pay attention to how often we truly open ourselves to sacred "intercourse" with Spirit, where we receive an impulse to heal someone or travel to a war zone to sing songs for world peace.

The establishment often sees most visions or inspirations from Spirit as strange, impractical or downright crazy. These Dionysian impulses can feel that way at first – but it is important to remember that they are always in service of new life. These seeds of potential can allow us to be truly penetrated by the cares and needs of the world.

Baptism of the Spirit

We were first introduced to baptism in the fourth initiation, with the story of John the Baptist. John initiated us into the baptism of water, which brought us into deeper relationship with our heart and our true self, located at the trunk of the Tree. John was clear that there would be two more baptisms in the process of our development that would initiate us into the branches of the Tree. John said, "I baptize you with water, but the one who is coming after me will baptize with Spirit and with fire." According to the Kabbalah, the baptism of Spirit happens here in Stage 6 and the baptism of fire occurs in Stage 7.

The baptism of Spirit is associated with air, wind, breath and even wine, as wine is juice changed into alcohol or "spirits"- fermenting, heating and bubbling with transformation. The Dionysian myth offers many images of spiritual transformation, as we shall see in this next section of Dionysus' story, which shows what we can expect when we encounter the "wind and wine" baptism of the Spirit - the Spirit that cannot be bound, tied, controlled or stolen.

One day a pirate ship was sailing near Greece, and the pirates spotted a young man sitting near the shore. He was dressed in fine clothes and looked very well off, so surely he must be a nobleman and worthy of a large ransom. Filled with greed, the pirates captured him and brought him on board. They tried to tie him up to prevent his escape, but the ropes they used to tie him up would not hold their knots. Only one member of the crew, the helmsman, realized that they must have captured a god.

The helmsman begged the others to let their prisoner go, but the crew refused – and that's when extraordinary things began to happen. The wind blew and filled the sails, but the ship did not move. In a frightening yet wondrous moment, rivers of wine began to stream over the deck. Grapevines grew in wild profusion up the sails. Ivy, fruit and flowers twined up the mast. Dionysus transformed himself into a lion, and the terrified crewmembers jumped overboard and were changed into dolphins in midair. Only the helmsman was spared, for he had recognized Dionysus.

Here is a classic Dionysian scene, where the wind fills the sails of the boat, wine spills over the decks in abundance, and vines grow up the mast, flowering and fruiting in profusion around the ship. In order to receive this spiritual baptism, we must be like the helmsman of the ship who recognizes Dionysus and realizes that there is no choice but to surrender to his greater authority and wisdom. When we are ready to acknowledge and surrender to this spiritual life force, our sails fill with wind and wine spills over our deck and new life flowers in our lives.

Baptism of the Spirit brings feelings of *revival, excitement, promise, hope, clarity, wisdom and understanding*. Suddenly doors open, life changes – we may move into a new house, we may meet a new partner, make a helpful connection, get a new job. Life is renewed on all levels and we find that we are moving towards our true destination, towards what we were born to do. When the wind of the Spirit arrives, we must be ready to go where the wind blows.

Another aspect of baptism of the Spirit is *liberation*. As with Dionysus – who could not be held down by ropes or bound by knots – baptism of the Spirit unbinds us, releasing the parts of us that are enslaved. Our fears and anxieties lose their power to tie us down. As we truly surrender to this creative influx, we synchronize our Spirit to the dancing universe, the cosmic flow. Life blooms and flowers and becomes inspired and alive.

The story of Dionysus and the pirates warns us that if we attempt to control, bind or steal this Dionysian Spirit, we are in for a very difficult time. The pirates represent a common and often disastrous response to baptism of the Spirit. They recognize Dionysus' beauty, splendor and wealth but – because of their own limitations – they cannot see the kind of true spiritual wealth he can bring them. They are seeing with the instinctive *Nefesh*, with its power drives for self-gratification, rather than seeing from their *Ruah*, their spiritual center.

The pirates' fatal mistake is to believe that they can capture and bind this Spirit for personal use. How wrong they are! The purpose of spiritual baptism is not to gratify our personal power or heighten our status – but to serve the collective good and help manifest what is needed by Spirit. The pirates thought that they could steal the Spirit and tie it up. We cannot tie up the Spirit and we cannot own the spiritual wind when it comes.

Exercise 4: Baptism in the Spirit

1. Describe a scene when you feel you were baptized in the Spirit, when you experienced the dynamic, impregnating nature of Spirit. What were the accompanying feelings – revival, excitement, promise, hope, clarity, wisdom or understanding? How did this change you?

2. Write down some examples of how you would like to feel more liberated by Spirit.

Freedom from the past – what exactly do you want liberation from?

Freedom from the future – what worries do you want to let go of?

What parts of you feel enslaved and how might you imagine being liberated?

3. What outlet do you have in your life for Dionysian worship? Do you engage in any activities that activate altered, ecstatic states for you such as drumming, chanting, dancing, group ritual, or charismatic worship services? How might you let go of control and simply experience the ecstasy and loss of personal boundaries that the Dionysian spirit brings?

Apollo - Cultivating the seeds of Spirit

Dionysus blows new wisdom, new insight and new life into our being. He loosens the knots and liberates us from the chains that have kept us bound. The question now arises: what are we going to do with this newfound freedom? How are we going to *cultivate* these new seeds of Spirit? How are we going to *manifest* and *refine* these spiritual impulses that have blown into our lives? Once we have been infused with this creative life force, we need to cultivate the seeds of Spirit by incubating, gestating and giving birth to these powerful inspirations in a tangible form. This is the work of Apollo.

Apollo, as the god of civilized order, watches as the Dionysian wind breaks down structures that no longer serve Spirit. Apollo then boldly picks up the rubble and makes something of it, stabilizing life and encouraging *cultural pursuits* such as the arts and sciences. Dionysus values destruction and Apollo values *construction*. Dionysus values revelation and Apollo values *reason*, seeking to understand what these revelations mean. Dionysus brings us the drunken Spirit, where we lose our boundaries and participate in the Divine through direct experience. Apollo on the other hand, brings the *sober Spirit*, where the Divine is experienced through the beauty of the Catholic mass or through a carefully constructed symphony.

Dionysus brings the primal life force whereas Apollo, through much hard work, delivers the highest and most *refined spiritual values* of our culture. Dionysus is concerned with intercourse and fertilizing the seeds of Spirit whereas Apollo is concerned with *cultivating* and growing the seeds of Spirit. Dionysus is concerned with impermanence and change. Apollo is concerned with *permanence* and what is lasting. Dionysus is the erotic, embodied Spirit that expands our boundaries and opens us to new possibilities. Apollo is the great containing Spirit that *makes these possibilities into realities.*

Dionysus loves ecstatic inspirations because of the sheer joy of the sensual pleasure involved. Apollo's genius is that he can envision what this inspiration can be made into. Apollo can see in his imagination the already - constructed cathedral, the completed song, or the exquisite sculpture in an unformed piece of marble. He can see the order that will emerge from the chaos. He is the great *builder, refiner* and *tester.* A world without Apollo, with only the Dionysian spirit, would be a world of excess, destruction, drunkenness and compulsive gratification. Without Apollo we might dream our lives away and fail to manifest any of our ideas. On the other hand, a world that was too Apollonian would be dry, constricting, and overly structured. Culture would ossify and the once juicy ideals would crystallize into rigid dogma. We would be forced to drudge through hollow religious forms.

Apollo is needed to balance, temper and contain the wildfire of the Dionysian spirit. *When we befriend and use both of these dynamic spiritual energies, we will experience rejuvenation.* We will open to the creative life force and allow the wind of the Spirit to breathe fresh ideas and new possibilities into our life. Then we must spend whatever time it takes to refine, make, build, write, craft, formulate, choreograph and compose our great work of spirit, regardless of the discipline we come from. It is up to us to weave the fabric of our culture with enthusiasm, personal flair and dedication to spiritual values of beauty, love, integrity, justice, mercy, wisdom, understanding and joy.

Step 1: Commit to a spiritual path
Step 2: Rejuvenate your spirit
* Step 3: Risk transformation *
Step 4: Become a Visionary

Radical transformation

In Step, 2 we looked at Dionysus and Apollo (Hokhmah and Binah) on the Tree of Life and discovered how personal and collective life is renewed through fertilizing and cultivating the seeds of Spirit. Now in Step 3, we will focus on the center of the Spirit triad at Daat: the place of radical transformation, death and rebirth, and knowledge gained from direct experience (see Diagrams 22 and 23).

Step 3 will outline what radical transformation requires of us personally and will discuss in detail what it feels like to experience the *symbolic death and descent* that always precedes rebirth, ascent and ecstasy. The *descent* phase demands a deeper personal commitment to spiritual renewal, for it requires a willingness to *shed whatever hinders us from living out our higher purpose and following our calling.* During Step 3 we must risk transformation by actually stepping through the gateway of Daat and directly encountering the death-rebirth energies awaiting us as we cross the threshold.

Looking back at the Sacred Robe for Stage 6, we see the large Gatekeeper bird that holds open a circular "Uroborus" – the Alchemical snake eating its tail. This is the gateway that must be passed through during the sixth initiation. The Uroborus gateway on the robe is surrounded by death skulls, which emphasize the very real deathlike experiences we encounter as we move through the gateway. As with the chaotic Dionysian experiences, these symbolic death experiences are always in service of new and expanded life.

In order to achieve spiritual transformation, we are asked to die to our limited vision of life that centers solely on personal concerns, so that we can be reborn to a cosmic perspective of life. This shifts our center of consciousness from the roots and trunk to the branches of our Tree of Life. This shift and symbolic death awaken us to the bigger picture of life, giving us the ability to see the consequences of our own actions and collective actions that affect the future. This affords us true foresight and insight so that we can see how our decisions and choices affect our spiritual health for good or ill and affect future generations.

With this transformation, we gain deeper understanding of the human condition, wisdom and the courage to speak out against injustices. We gain the ability to shift our perceptions at will so that our neuroses and addictions no longer hinder us. From the branches of the Tree we can love more, serve more, and scatter more seeds of Spirit. Radical transformation means opening the third eye – the sixth chakra – to comprehend where we are, how we got here, and how we can move forward into our future with more consciousness.

Let's look now at what it takes to move through Step 3 and risk transformation, which will include *preparing for the descent, transforming negative core beliefs, gathering the tools of protection, facing the Gatekeeper at the threshold, surrendering control and, finally, sustaining the descent.*

Preparing for the descent: stories of death and rebirth

Sometimes it feels as if there is no helpful way to prepare for the death and rebirth that happens during the sixth initiation. "Why is this happening to me?" is often the phrase I hear in my counseling room. But when these same people examine why changes are happening, they can usually identify the time they sent out a prayer or made a commitment from deep inside to find the truth, grow spiritually, or find their destiny. In my experience, most people recognize that they indeed called for their own radical transformation.

Although nothing can take away the difficulties of this phase, our spiritual traditions do prepare us in many ways to move through the death and descent phase. The most important thing that our spiritual traditions offer us is hope – hope and assurance that there is *light* at the end of the tunnel, *ascent* after the dark night of the soul and the *Promised Land* after the wilderness. These images of light, ascent, joy and a welcoming spiritual home are crucial to hold on to when we are in the midst of the descent phase of transformation. Theses images are not simply idealized projections that defend against the pain and terror of the death phase. *They represent very real and possible experiences after we sustain the descent into the valley and emerge on the other side.*

These positive images of hope – the light, the ascent, and the Promised Land – describe the state of mind or the inner state of being that emerges when spiritual transformation is successful. If we have not endured the death-rebirth initiation, then these positive spiritual images remain idealized fantasies and can be used defensively. When someone tries to get to the resurrection without going through the crucifixion or tries to get to the Promised Land without going through the wilderness, it is often called a "spiritual bypass".

A spiritual bypass is evident when someone enters a monastery or lives in an ashram in order to avoid the difficulties of relationships or the difficulties of living in the real world, rather than to follow a genuine spiritual call. Another example of spiritual bypass is when a person wants to focus on spiritual love and light but does not want to see the darkness or the reality of suffering in the world. In order to transform, we must be able to endure the descent and all the challenges and difficult feelings that arise. Facing pain and grief and not pushing them aside prepares the way for the eventual meaning, acceptance and wisdom acquired at the end of descent.

Spiritual teachings offer stories and sacred art that address this archetypal journey of death and rebirth, showing us the value and necessity of both experiences. The traditions of Christianity, Judaism, Shamanism and Alchemy provide us with ample preparation for the personal journey of spiritual death and rebirth.

From the **Christian** tradition we have the death and resurrection story of Christ to lead us through the transformation process. The story of Christ's passion is one of the most vivid depictions of what is often personally endured during spiritual transformation. The story of Jesus' persecution, surrender, crucifixion, death, resurrection and ascension prepares us for the real experiences of initiation at Stage 6.

Often we must make a very real sacrifice when we dedicate our lives to spiritual growth. When we make a commitment to serve at the level of Spirit, we may encounter persecution from those who are opposed to what we are doing; or we may encounter persecution from within, from our own inner voices that do not want to lose their power. The Christ story reminds us to surrender attachments to the *Nefesh* and even the *Neshamah* as we commit to develop the *Ruah*. This story prepares us to let go into the unknown.

The Christian story tells us that Jesus descended into hell for three days and then arose from the dead triumphantly and ascended into heaven. Here is a vivid picture of the descent phase into the depths of "hell", which is experienced by anyone who journeys to this mythic realm as a place of pain, grief, terror or anxiety. Our place of hell is the experience of facing our deepest feelings of fear or grief head-on. If we can sustain ourselves through this time, the rewards will include our own spiritual awakening or triumphant ascent.

From the **Jewish** tradition we have many stories to depict the death-rebirth process of the sixth initiation. One of the most important stories in Judaism is the story of the Exodus, the journey of the Israelites out of Egypt after they have been enslaved for generations. The Exodus celebrates Moses leading the people out of Egypt, into the wilderness, and eventually to the Promised Land. In this story, the "death" phase is represented by the harsh desert wilderness, where there is little food or water and no distractions to lighten the journey for the people. We are told that the only way to get to the land flowing with milk and honey is to wander in a desert wilderness for forty years.

During the forty years in the desert, the people went through many trials and tribulations. They experienced fears, famine, betrayal, homelessness, hopelessness, despair, anger, frustration and stubbornness. These are many of the feelings that emerge during the death phase when we are letting go of old, familiar patterns that keep us enslaved.

To sustain ourselves during the wilderness transformation time, we must do as Moses did: gather the various parts of us that are untransformed and convince them to all move in one direction, towards the Promised Land. The hot desert wilderness is our place of purification and transformation. If we can endure the intensity of the frustration and let go of all our old habits of slavery, then we can make it to our spiritual home, the land flowing with milk and honey.

The **Shamanic** traditions also offer helpful images for death and rebirth. In many of the Shamanic stories, the apprentice who is undergoing initiation reports vivid experiences of death and dismemberment prior to rebirth. Many apprentices are instructed to meditate on their own skeleton and to imagine their flesh and blood being stripped away so that nothing is left of them but their white bones. This is designed to prepare them for the psychological stripping that occurs during the death phase of their initiation.

Other apprentices tell of dreams or visions in which their Shamanic teacher comes to them and dismembers their body – either by chopping off their arms and legs or by decapitating them and then placing "light" crystals inside their body and putting them back together again. Symbolically, this can be seen as an image of disintegration and eventual reintegration to a higher level of consciousness. Disintegration is a familiar state of mind in the descent and death phase because we feel disoriented, confused and even crazy – as if life is coming apart at the seams. Eventually, if we can survive the ordeal, we get put back together again and – in our reintegrated form – are more expansive, more "light" or enlightened.

Alchemy is another tradition that offers us vivid imagery of transformation through death and rebirth. In Alchemy, the Prima Materia – the power drive or the negative belief that we are trying to transform – is put through a series of Alchemical operations such as Separatio, Calcinatio, Solutio, Coagulatio, Mortificatio, Sublimatio, and finally Coniunctio. During these stages, a negative belief such as, "I don't deserve to be loved," undergoes quite an ordeal as it intensifies, dominates, collapses, dissolves, dies, and eventually is reborn into a new and transformed belief or inner voice. The Alchemical engravings depict this death-rebirth process in graphic detail, showing a wolf devouring a king, a salamander being burned in the fire, a lion eating a bleeding sun, and even skeletons in a mass grave. Alongside the decay and death images, there are also images of resurrection, of crows rising from open graves, figures rising from the waters in baptismal rebirth, and couples intertwined in blissful union.

Transforming negative core beliefs

Embedded within the body and psyche are negative core beliefs about ourselves, others, and life that hinder our spiritual transformation. These negative core beliefs need to be transformed so that we can live consciously from the branches of our Tree and embody spiritual qualities such as universal love, compassion, tolerance, justice, equality, wisdom and understanding. The following is a list of often-quoted core beliefs that my students and clients have wrestled with over the years.

Common core beliefs about **ourselves** that need to be transformed:
I am alone
I can't trust anyone
I am excluded
I don't deserve to be loved
I don't deserve abundance
I must do everything myself
I can't count on anyone
If I let go of my addiction/problem I will not survive
I can't be who I want to be

I am trapped
There is no room for me
I must accommodate in order to be loved

Common core beliefs about **others** that need to be transformed:
Others have more than me
Others are in competition with me
Others have it easier than me
Others don't see me or acknowledge me
Others don't support me
Others are a threat to me
Others have more power than me
Others have stopped me from being whole, fulfilling my dreams, etc.

Common core beliefs about **life** that need to be transformed:
Life sucks
Life is unfair
Life is out to get me
Life provides limited resources, so I must fight for my slice of pie
Life doesn't provide what I need
Life needs to be controlled

To activate the sixth initiation, we must confront these negative core beliefs and acknowledge the power that they hold over our lives. As we confront these beliefs that keep us enslaved and spiritually untransformed, we uncover the core Self that has been clinging to the beliefs as a defense and protection. It is crucial to understand the depths of primal terror and anxiety we come up against when the core Self is exposed during the sixth initiation. It requires bravery and courage to let go of these primal beliefs.

Transforming negative core beliefs is like dismantling an old, familiar house – pulling it apart stone by stone. This inner house or temple, built with the stones of "I am all alone" or "I don't deserve to be loved", has served us up to this point. But during the sixth initiation, these old attitudes fall apart, and as a result we can feel as if we are dying or being ripped apart stone by stone. *The purpose of dismantling the old "temple" of our negative core beliefs is to rebuild our inner life with a spiritual temple, a new container, whose stones consist of "I am not alone", "I can trust life to assist me", "There is room for me", "I deserve to be loved".* Imagine our inner temple built upon the foundation of these inner voices and experiences! This is an inner container that we can solidly rely on, one that is strong enough to support our true, radiant Self and to support the destiny that we were born to fulfill.

Exercise 5: Identifying negative core beliefs

1. Take some time and look through the above list of negative core beliefs. Pick out your beliefs that need to be transformed. Add to the list any other beliefs that you want to change. Write them down. How do these negative core beliefs impact your daily life?

2. Now take your list and place it on your altar with a candle. Light the candle and answer this question: Am I willing to risk transforming these beliefs? As the candle burns, imagine the flames of consciousness helping you surrender and transform these negative core beliefs. (There will be more exercises to help rebuild your new spiritual temple. The first step is to identify the core negative beliefs that you want to transform.)

Tools of protection during transformation

When our negative beliefs are being dismantled, some spiritual tools are available to protect us from the onslaught of negativity and destructive energy that explodes during the descent. Let's take the example of a woman (I will call her Dana), who is in the midst of a painful separation and divorce after many years of marriage. Even though she chose this path of descent and knows that it is the right decision, the death of her marriage triggers early infantile material related to loss that has been repressed and unprocessed. This crisis exposes her core Self and triggers deep abandonment anxiety and terror.

When faced with the change of a negative core belief, the primitive psyche experiences the transformation process as agonizing. For Dana, confronting the loss and abandonment is disorienting and frightening, bringing to the surface ancient voices within her that recreate her original trauma and core belief: "I am all alone". During this descent phase she hears the voices, "I will never make it on my own. I am not worthy of love. People abandon me." This causes her great anxiety, and she is seized by intermittent panic attacks.

Dana needs some *tools of protection* so that she can descend far enough to face the wounds and wait long enough to transform and heal the wounds. She has several tools of protection to choose from: *she can find a guide, she can practice her spiritual disciplines, she can shield herself from the destructive voices, and she can remain consciously awake through the experience.*

1. Find a guide

When transforming our negative core beliefs and descending into the primal wounds, it is recommended that we go through this with a guide who is an experienced therapist, a spiritual guide or a mentor. The death energy that must be endured at this level of initiation cannot be easily faced alone. In fact, some people do not make it through this phase without a guide. They remain stuck at this particular transformation crossing point – caught in their addictions; their depression, their anxiety or their confusion – and they never recover. They remain untransformed. Other tragic circumstances can also happen when the psyche gets dismantled and never reintegrates – like suicide, madness, paranoia and debilitating anxiety.

The transformation that happens in Stage 6 is different from the kind we spoke of in Stage 2, although there are some similarities. In Stage 2, we transform internal patterns that keep us from our natural, instinctive rhythms and cycles – the end result being that we awaken the Great Mother so that we know exactly how to nourish the *roots* of our Tree. Here in Stage 6, we are transforming deep core patterns that keep us from fulfilling our destiny. The end result is to awaken the Visionary so that we know exactly how to nourish the *branches* of our Tree. Because the gateway of Daat is filled with profound spiritual challenges, it should not be a journey taken alone. A qualified therapist or an experienced spiritual guide is an appropriate companion on this difficult portion of our spiritual path.

2. *Spiritual disciplines*

Spiritual disciplines are handed down to us for a very good reason – they are designed to strengthen, prepare and protect our body, soul and spirit as we awaken the *Ruah* and move into radical spiritual transformation. Every tradition has spiritual disciplines that can support us by giving us the tools we need to survive the rigors of the death and rebirth phases.

Whether they are prayer, meditation, daily breathing exercises, practicing yoga, chanting mantras or reading sacred texts, all spiritual disciplines and the rituals that accompany them are designed to create protection around us and engage us in very practical ways with the consciousness of Spirit. Building ritual shrines to the ancestors, the elements or the four directions, singing, chanting and taking communion all set up a circle of protection around our being. If we practice these spiritual disciplines faithfully, we strengthen our physical, emotional and mental bodies so that they are alert and resilient when we confront the anxiety, fear, grief or loss that comes to us during the descent.

3. *Athena's shield*

In Stage 2, we encountered the story of Medusa, the stone mother, and learned how the goddess Athena showed Perseus how to conquer Medusa with her protective shield. The shield acted like a mirror so that Medusa's destructive negativity was mirrored back to her – which meant that she herself was turned to stone. Athena bears a shield with the head of Medusa on it, for she has the wisdom and knowledge to move through the destructive swamp of Medusa and deflect her cruel and poisonous voices. Medusa's voices grow particularly loud during the descent as we are transforming our negative core beliefs. If we do not have a shield like this to protect us, then we get hit directly with **Medusa's negative voices**:

"You will never make it through this initiation."
"You will never cross this threshold."
"You fool, people will always betray you."
"This divorce/loss/tragedy is going to kill you."
"You don't have the strength to avert my gaze."
"I've caught you in my web."
"You are crazy." "People think you are crazy."
"You are going to rot in this descent and never see the light at the end of the tunnel."
"If you move into your grief, you will never come out of it."

These are some examples of voices we hear during the descent. These are the death voices that have no knowledge of the rebirth that awaits us on the other side. These destructive voices go against what the spiritual traditions teach us: "Persevere because the resurrection is coming. Rebirth always follows death." Within each of us is the wisdom of Athena that can act like a shield to protect us from Medusa's deathlike voices, saying, "Don't listen to that voice. Don't take that inside. Don't take that personally. That is only a trick to make you veer from your true path. Keep going. Hang in there. There is the light at the end of the tunnel."

4. The staff of knowledge

The staff of knowledge, our Sapphire Staff, which embodies all the knowledge contained in the Tree of Life, is probably the most powerful tool of protection as we move through spiritual transformation. The staff of knowledge connects us directly with Spirit and the Mysteries of transformation. Taking hold of the staff is our free will choice to *stay conscious* and use our powers of *observation, mindfulness* and *wakefulness*. This keeps us steady through the dismantling process and through the dark night of the soul when all light is extinguished and chaos is all around.

In the Dionysus story, the staff of knowledge manifests in the form of the ivy vine. It was the vine of ivy wrapped around Semele's womb that saved Dionysus's life in the face of tragic death. His mother Semele was unprotected from Zeus's illumination and did not survive the powerful transpersonal energies or higher consciousness that Zeus revealed to her. Dionysus had access to this vine, his version of the Sapphire Staff, which enabled him to stay alive and carried him through death to rebirth into his full power.

Facing the Gatekeeper at the threshold

Let's return to our example of Dana, who is in the descent during a painful breakup of her marriage. We have just seen that she has several choices in terms of the tools she can employ to protect her. But she also has another, more profound choice – *to voluntarily shed these old skins and leave behind her own destructive patterns that have kept her moving towards "death" rather than towards expanded life and spiritual awakening.* If she wills, she can stop at this threshold and consciously surrender control and free herself of all the excess baggage weighing her down and keeping her small and unawakened.

According to Kabbalah, few travelers enter the realm of Spirit because they are not ready to give up their addictions, their ignorance and their self-illusions. They are not ready to shed their old skins. As I worked with Dana, she was ready to transform her old pattern of regressive dependency that led to her expectation that her partner should "father" her. She wanted to shed this skin – and yet on another level, she did not want to give up the control she asserted in this relationship, because she desperately wanted to get her primal needs met. She was not quite conscious of this yet, but as she approached this threshold, she was tested and challenged to become fully aware of her destructive pattern.

The reason she arrived at this sixth threshold in the first place was because she was on a spiritual path and had asked to be spiritually awakened. "Whatever it takes," she would say. If this meant going to the depths of despair to get out of her destructive relationship and shift her depression, she was willing to risk everything – for underlying all of this was her vision to help other women in need. Though the details of the vision were not yet clear, she knew in her soul that this was her calling.

When we are really serious about spiritual awakening, we eventually come to this initiatory threshold, where a Gatekeeper guards the entrance to the world of Spirit. This Gatekeeper stops each initiate at the "gate," and tests us before we open to higher spiritual awareness. Gatekeepers stand at these initiatory thresholds to safeguard us from opening to higher levels of consciousness too soon, before we are ready. Looking back at the sixth Sacred Robe, the large Phoenix or Eagle character depicts such a guardian. When we approach the sixth threshold, the Gatekeeper is obliged to ask, "Do you know where you are?"

The Genesis creation story has God asking this very question of Adam and Eve in the Garden, after they have eaten the fruit of the Tree of the Knowledge of Good and Evil. In Kabbalah, we say that when Adam and Eve eat this fruit, they partake of the world of Spirit and awaken their *Ruah*. This gives them access to the powerful energies of creation and destruction (good and evil) and spiritual capacities such as wisdom, understanding and knowledge. As Adam and Eve now stand at this threshold, they realize that they are "naked" – in other words, they realize that they are exposed and unprotected in the face of the vast powers of Spirit. Then they hear the voice of God saying, "Where are you?" – or more precisely, "Do you know where you are? Do you know what level you are at? Now that your eyes have been opened to the world of Spirit, are you aware of the responsibility that awaits you?"

These very questions were also being asked of Dana: "Do you know what awaits you if you cross this threshold? Are you willing to give up controlling others to get what you need and shed this pattern of control? Are you ready to trust that your needs will be met? Do you truly want to understand the destructive patterns you cling to that keep you untransformed? Are you willing to step through the gateway?" By asking the right questions, Gatekeepers ensure that anyone entering this realm is a genuine seeker and that everything that has outlived its usefulness is left behind. Excess baggage *must* be tossed before crossing this threshold. It is crucial to name the thing that you want to die so that Spirit hears your intention.

Crossing the threshold of Daat is also called "the Abyss" in Kabbalah. At each initiation there is a gateway to be gone through, but the Abyss gateway at Stage 6 has some added features. When we voluntarily descend into death by letting go of our control patterns, we die to the past and move into the mysterious future. The light is extinguished and we have no idea what is to come, because our mind and heart have not expanded enough to see the specific rebirth that is coming. The Abyss is a gateway to the unseen and unknown and, because of this, the risk is far greater than with the other initiations.

Gateways and portals are archetypal passageways that open up at certain times in our lives. When the timing is just right, the portal opens, the Gatekeeper tests us and, if we are willing to risk transformation, we can move through. But we must be aware that the gateway is opening, and this takes wakefulness. In the example of Dana, she was aware that the portal opened during her painful divorce and she seized the moment, which enabled her to transform many of her old negative patterns.

Exercise 6: Meditation - Meeting the Gatekeeper

Think of when gateways have opened up for you. Did you step through? Did you hesitate and miss your moment? Were you asleep? Were you unable to take the risk of transformation? Perhaps the gateway is opening for you now. If it is, the following is a meditation to help you name what you need to shed so that you can cross the threshold and open to Spirit. Before you begin, write down the negative core beliefs or negative patterns that you want to transform in your life. What kind of spiritual awakening do you seek?

Imagine yourself walking through a forest, alone, pondering the threshold that you have come to in your life. As you walk slowly through the forest, think about what spiritual gateway is opening for you now. What threshold have you come to? Look deep within your heart; what do you need to transform in order to cross this threshold? What do you need to let go of in order to move through this gateway?

As you walk, you are aware of being weighed down by many bags strapped to your back and hanging off your arms. Big and small, heavy and light, each bag represents something that holds you back from awakening spiritually and following your true calling. Your load is heavy and you would like to get rid of these bags.

You come to a small clearing in the forest and up ahead you see an entrance to a tunnel that stretches far into the distance. As you approach the tunnel, you see that there is a Gatekeeper guarding the entrance. What does the Gatekeeper look like?

Behind the Gatekeeper, you can see a passageway that stretches away into darkness. At the far end of the tunnel, you can see a tiny pinprick of light. You also notice a kind of invisible veil drawn over the entrance to the passageway. As you observe all of this, the Gatekeeper draws your attention and asks: "Do you know where you are?" You answer truthfully.

"Do you know what awaits you if you cross this threshold? Do you truly want to understand the behaviors and attitudes that keep you untransformed? Are you willing to step through the gateway?" You answer truthfully.

As the Gatekeeper asks, "What is all this luggage?" you are suddenly able to let go of the baggage and everything drops to the ground. One by one, you pick up each piece and name it out loud to the Gatekeeper. It may be a behavior or a negative core belief that holds you back from realizing your full potential. It may be a negative family pattern or a fear that stops you from pursuing certain things in your life.

Finally, you have named each item. As you finish, you stand facing the Gatekeeper and realize that, in picking up and naming each piece of baggage, you have again become burdened with their load.

The Gatekeeper asks you, "Which of these bags has the most effect on your life right now? Are you willing to let it go?" You answer truthfully.

"Come with me," the Gatekeeper instructs. You are led off to the side where a fire is burning. You can see the metal frames and buckles left from many other pieces of luggage that have been burned in this fire by sojourners before you. "If you are ready and willing," the Gatekeeper continues, "take each piece of baggage off your back again and throw it in the fire. You must name each piece again to acknowledge what is being let go."

You begin removing each piece of baggage, again, naming each one and throwing it in the fire. As you do, you are aware of lightness in your whole being. You are gaining energy with each piece tossed into and consumed by the fire. When you have finished, take a deep breath and feel the freedom of having shed all that excess baggage.

"Follow me," the Gatekeeper says. You are guided back to the veiled entrance to the tunnel. The Gatekeeper turns and faces you, looking deep into your eyes, "You have done well. You should be proud of yourself. Many start, but not all finish."

As you breathe deeply, you become aware of a loving presence near you. A guide has come to help you cross the threshold. Who is it?

Your guide shows you the staff of knowledge he holds in his hand. He instructs you to take hold of the other end of the staff. The guide then motions to the Gatekeeper to draw back the veil. As the veil is drawn back, you and your guide cross the threshold and enter the long, dark tunnel.

As you walk slowly through, you are enveloped in total darkness. You can hear the great wind of the Spirit dancing back and forth between death and rebirth as you move through the passageway. As you walk through the darkness, imagine yourself like a snake shedding all of your skin, letting go of all of your burdens, surrendering control of all the things you hang onto that keep you from spiritual awakening. Let go. Let the old skins fall away – shedding, shedding, and shedding.

Breathe into it as you move closer and closer to the light at the end of the tunnel. Soon you approach the other end of the passageway. In the light ahead of you, you see a vision of yourself after you have shed all your burdens and excess baggage. Here you are, in your new skin, a vision of yourself in a transformed state. Look at yourself closely. How do you look? What do you feel in this new state? How are you different now from the person with the luggage before crossing the threshold?

Hold this vision of your transformed self and thank your guide for helping you through. He or she will be there for you anytime you need to let go of something and move through this passageway. Embrace this new, enlightened version of yourself and allow yourself to melt into your transformed state. Feel the lightness of being, the lack of burden. Breathe and relax into it.

Bring your consciousness back now to the present and become aware of your body as you sit. Breathe deeply and slowly and, when you feel ready, open your eyes.

Surrendering control

When we cross the Abyss, shed our old skin and risk death, the essential ingredient that sets true and radical transformation into motion is surrendering control. No matter which negative core belief we want to change, if our core Self cannot surrender control, we will get stuck in the tunnel and we will not be able to complete the initiation.

It is not easy to surrender control, especially for the pained and anxious core Self that believes it is alone, abandoned, persecuted, powerless, homeless, impoverished, disadvantaged, excluded, trapped, undeserving or doomed. If these are the beliefs at the core of our being around which we orient our life, base our decisions and behave in our relationships, it is no wonder that we have blocks to our spiritual awakening. In this state, most of our energy is spent trying to control the environment and appease the core Self so that we do not feel so alone or powerless. We control our parents, children, friends, lovers, bosses and co-workers to varying degrees in an attempt to get our needs met. When we are in an abandoned state of mind, it sounds utterly ridiculous to surrender control, because it truly feels like jumping blindly into the Abyss without hope of rebirth.

But something mysterious happens when we can consciously surrender control.

Returning to our example of Dana, she identified her core experiences as feeling abandoned and excluded. Eventually she could see that her negative core beliefs led her to control her husband, manipulating him into taking care of her primal, wounded self.

Although controlling him temporarily appeased her feelings of abandonment and exclusion, her excessive control of the relationship left very little room for her husband to move, grow or be himself. He became resentful and emotionally distant, which caused her to panic and increase her control. It was this need to control that Dana wanted to surrender during this time of transformation.

For years, this pattern had kept her in a state of suffering because the dynamic of the relationship consistently ripped open her core wound. She had been stuck in a state of unconscious suffering, unable to see her part in the relational dance and therefore feeling victimized and powerless to change anything. When she became aware of her own controlling nature, she also became aware of the power that she had to change it. *She made a choice to move from suffering unconsciously to taking on conscious suffering.* This is a profound shift that happens during the sixth initiation. For Dana, it meant consciously taking on her primal wounds of abandonment and exclusion. She shifted from abandoning and excluding others – which she had unconsciously done to inflict her wound on others – to taking responsibility for her own feelings. She began to withdraw her projection and started to carry the feelings of abandonment and exclusion herself. *Taking on conscious suffering in this way led to her healing.*

Surrendering control also means accepting our primal wounds, accepting the damage that we have done to others, and accepting the limitations that these wounds have created in our lives. Rather than seething with anger or being paralyzed with blame, we can consciously choose to take on the wounds and ask ourselves, "How have I created this situation? How have I attracted this into my life? How can I work with this? How can I move on from here?" Surrendering control means trusting Spirit, trusting in a higher power, a bigger plan, the transpersonal intelligence, to hold us and guide us and provide for us. It means trusting that there are enough resources to go around.

Sustaining the descent

So far in Step 3, we have prepared for the descent, identified the core negative beliefs that we want to transform, gathered the tools of protection, faced the Gatekeeper at the threshold, and surrendered control. Now we will explore the direct experiences and feelings of the descent phase.

The descent is triggered by either internal or external events that pull us down and in, so that we can attend to the explosion of feelings that erupt from deep within our being.

The purpose of descent is multi-faceted:

• to destroy false self-constructs and illusions that keep us enslaved and addicted.
• to help us awaken and live out our unlived life by giving us access to the unseen realms of our deepest nature.
• to help us confront psychological death head on, which releases the repressed terror, grief and anxiety that has been draining us of energy.
• to break our pride, our hubris, our narcissism, our petty self-interests, our narrow vision, our bigotry and intolerance.
• to break down the illusion that we are separate beings and to force us to admit that we cannot do it alone. (It kills off our inflated, individual stance that "I must do it all myself" and "I am in control of my life.")

• to move us from our limited, individual perspective at the trunk of the Tree, to the transpersonal vista gained only from the branches.
• to help us to develop our *Ruah*.

The spiritual paradox of this process of descent is that in order to *ascend* to our branches we must *descend* into the death experience. During spiritual awakening, the ego usually experiences regression because so many unconscious patterns are being exposed. In order to sustain the descent, we need help. The following alchemical wisdom and mythological characters help us through this most difficult passage.

1. Mortificatio

The Alchemists name the descent and death phase "Mortificatio," which paints a vivid picture of what happens to us as things in our life begin to die, decay and dismantle. Mortificatio brings a powerful confrontation with the darkness, activating our "dark night of the soul." With Mortificatio we can feel defeated, deflated, depressed and destroyed.

But Mortificatio is not about needless suffering. The purpose of Mortificatio is to cleanse and purify the *Neshamah* (personal soul) and transform it into the *Ruah* (transpersonal spirit). So the more consciously we can move into the suffering and the darkness, the more benefit we can derive from the Mortificatio experience.

Returning to our example of Dana, we see that to the outside world it appeared that she had a good marriage and family, a house, money, social status and a life many people envied. But what could not be seen from the outside was that something inside Dana was dying. The reality was that her marriage was an empty shell and there was no intimacy to sustain her. She was also being eaten alive by her secret disgust and disdain of her husband for being so "weak" and "powerless." During her Mortificatio phase, she felt as if she was rotting from the inside out. Her life began to "smell bad" as the marriage decayed more and more. The thought of totally dismantling her marriage, family, house, money and social status filled her with dread – so she stayed in a slowly rotting Mortificatio for several years, diving in and out of depression.

At some point she was forced to admit that perceiving her husband as weak and powerless was a projection of *her own inner state*, which she had been unable to see. This new insight required her to face her own weakness and powerlessness and the horror that she had unconsciously forced her husband to carry these difficult feelings for her. With this revelation she felt "mortified", but it released her to move on.

During Mortificatio, we may have dreams with violence, death, mutilation, torture, decay and darkness. We can feel grief, depression, disgust, dread and terror. These are appropriate images and feelings for this stage. With consciousness, these states do eventually transform.

2. Ereshkigal

There is a powerful story of descent from Sumerian mythology, called the myth of Innana and Ereshkigal.

Ereshkigal is the death goddess who reigns in the Underworld, and is sister to Innana. In the story, Ereshkigal's husband dies and Innana is sent to tell and comfort her sister in the Underworld. Innana must descend into the Underworld to inform her sister, mark the death, and deal with her grief.

As Innana begins her descent, she is dressed in all her finery – lots of jewelry and beautiful clothes. But as she descends into the Underworld, she must move through seven gateways to reach her destination. At each gateway Ereshkigal demands that Innana remove a piece of her clothing or jewelry, so that by the end of her journey she is completely naked and stripped of everything. As she takes off layer upon layer of clothing and jewels, all her outer protection and defenses are stripped away. There, naked and defenseless in the Underworld, she faces Ereshkigal and the intense grief of being so raw and exposed.

This is exactly what Dana experienced when she chose to take action and separate from her husband. Over the first year she was stripped of her marriage, home, many friends, her husband's income and her social standing in the community. She felt naked, exposed, mortified and defenseless. There was no more protection for her core wounded self, and so she had to sit in Ereshkigal's Underworld and grieve for the part of her that felt abandoned long ago by her mother and excluded by her father and siblings.

3. Kali

The Hindu Goddess Kali is another archetype that aids descent and surrendering of control. Kali wears a necklace of skulls around her neck and she has many arms that wield swords to decapitate people. Kali's job is to kill all the illusions and all ego attachments, to destroy all evil forces and to shatter all obstacles on our spiritual path. Kali also strips us to the bones with her fierce energy and she has the "skulls" to prove her might. Kali cuts all threads of bondage and liberates us to live from a place of Spirit. Her chopping arms accomplish the dethroning of the ego and its illusions and fantasies in order to make room for more growth and development.

Kali helps us to dismember and remember. She dismembers the false self so that we can remember our true nature, dismantling the old temple so that we can rebuild one that is more spiritually alive.

During a Kali experience, Dana felt as if she had been cut to the core. Her children were siding with her husband and seeing her as the bad mother for leaving their poor, helpless, victimized father. Any inflation or feelings of superiority she held over her husband had crumbled like a ruined house all around her. Now it was no longer the husband who embodied the weak and powerless position, but she herself who had finally stepped into those shoes. Her ego attachment to seeing him as weak was chopped into little pieces and she was left with herself – cut and bleeding. Her Kali energy had identified exactly what kept her in bondage and simply cut off the head of her projection so that she could experience her own feelings of weakness and, hopefully, return to her spiritual path unencumbered.

4. Pluto

We were introduced to the god Pluto in the Persephone story during the second initiation. Pluto's name, as we recall, means "bringer of riches" – and although Pluto is the god of the Underworld presiding over the descent and death, his job is to bring us the riches from this experience.

In the Persephone myth, Pluto is in service of the Great Mother who renews all of life. On the collective level, Pluto is pushing humanity through symbolic death, descent and dismemberment, for the purpose of spiritual transformation, so that humanity can evolve. The energy of Pluto is similar to the action of a wildfire burning our house to the ground so that all we are left with are the ashes. On the Tree of Life, Pluto is placed at Daat, the place of transformation. When his archetypal energy abducts us into the Underworld, we experience our lack of control over our environment, over our circumstances, and over our internal chaos.

What happened to Dana during her Pluto experience was that, as her children and friends retreated from her, she went into a state of paralysis and depression. She felt assaulted by compulsive thoughts of what she called "crazy, jealous possessiveness" towards her children and ex-husband and gnawing envy towards friends who seemed to be in happy relationships.

The core belief of "I am excluded" gripped her feverishly and she felt as if her world was being burnt to the ground. She sat for months in grief, envy and the fear that she was going mad. Like Persephone, her Pluto experience forced her to the depths of despair and suffering – she felt paralyzed and trapped in the darkness. Pluto forced Dana to her knees and kept her in the Underworld until she let go and fully surrendered. When she was finally humbled, all her hard crust fell off and her defenses fell away. Only then did her paralysis and numbness awaken into pain as her sleepy nerves came back to life.

When Pluto hits, it is neither an ego choice nor a soul choice. Pluto does not operate from the roots or the trunk of the Tree. Pluto's center of operation is in the branches as he serves Spirit and the spiritual development of humankind. Pluto crashes in through real experiences. He zeroes in on our deepest wounds and our most ingrained negative core beliefs, in order to shake them loose.

During her Pluto encounter, Dana hit rock bottom where her wounded self said to her, "There is no God. There are no other resources but myself. I am the only one who will ever look after me. I have to be in total control. See, everybody always betrays me. There are always more interesting people than me. No wonder I am excluded. I can trust no one."

All of these death voices were once living within Dana's being unconsciously. Lurking underground, the death voices discouraged her from engaging fully in life. Now that they were living consciously within her, she could awaken to their deadly nature and, from a place of free will, choose life. But again, choosing life means surrendering control and awakening all the corners of life that are asleep, numb and under Death's spell.

Going numb is one of our biggest defenses against moving through our death energy and facing pain, loss and grief. Pluto breaks death's spell by forcing us into the pain and embodying the feelings. *If we stay numb, we can never move fully into Spirit.*

Numbness signals our inability or unwillingness to face the fears, anxieties, abandonment and betrayals from our past. Numbness prevents a full descent and does not serve our wholeness. It is a feeble protection against the power of Pluto and his plans for us in the Underworld. Pluto is not interested in how our numbness is serving us; his job is to shake down our old, wobbly house. Pluto is totally unconcerned with personal issues of discomfort during transformation, because he stays focused on the end goal: the rebirth, the rebuilding of our house. He serves the resurrection principle – death in service of new life.

During an important Pluto descent in my own life, I had the following dream:

I am walking through a hospital parking lot, knowing that there is a frightening woman stalking me. Terrified, I grab two strong men who are nearby and hold them arm in arm on either side of me for protection and help. We're standing against a fence in the wide-open expanse of the parking lot, trying to hide from the frightening woman. Suddenly, a gunshot is fired and I realize with horror that this woman has shot me right between the eyes. The bullet penetrates into me and – instead of dying – my body begins to shake violently and a reverberation begins throughout my entire being, from the base of my feet to the top of my head. Cell by cell, I can feel my body awaken with vibrant life.

In the dream, a Pluto-like character showed up as an evil and frightening woman. She initiated me against my conscious will by shooting me in the third eye, the chakra center that helps facilitate initiation at Stage 6. When she "opened" my third eye with the gunshot, my entire being awakened from some deep and pervasive slumber. When I woke up, I felt alive as never before. It was as if bright sunlight surged into my body and tingled throughout my being. There was no way for me to see how numb I had been until my Pluto experience shook me awake.

Ereshkigal, Kali and Pluto initiate us into the descent. They help us sustain the descent when otherwise we would run rapidly in the opposite direction – avoiding, procrastinating, and remaining numb and under the spell of our own death energy. They strip us of illusions, force us to our knees, and help us surrender to the greater forces at work in life. With them, no stone is left unturned, no corner left unilluminated. They are our greatest allies during the death phase, for they move us all the way through the dark tunnel and prepare us for the ascent.

Exercise 7: Surrendering control and sustaining the descent

1. Identify and write down what part of you needs to surrender control in order to radically transform spiritually. Return to the list of the negative core beliefs you want to transform from Step 3, Exercise 5. Put this list on your altar and create a spiritual practice to help you surrender control. It could be a simple prayer, body posture, breathing exercise, mantra, movement or ritual that helps you let go and surrender control.

2. If you have experienced a descent, what has been broken down for you – your pride, hubris, narcissism, ignorance, petty self-interests, narrow vision, bigotry, intolerance, disdain, attachments to status or power, your need to control?

3. What do you need to let decay and die in order to transform? What attitudes or attachments are being stripped away? What threads of bondage need to be cut in order for you to transform? What illusions and fantasies are hindering your path? Where are you still numb? What fears, anxieties, abandonment and betrayals are you still clinging on to?

Step 1: Commit to a spiritual path
Step 2: Rejuvenate your spirit
Step 3: Risk transformation
* Step 4: Become A Visionary *

The Ascent: embracing ecstasy

After we endure the agony of descent, throw away our excess baggage, shed our skin and dismantle the old house, there is an immense relief that comes. The paralysis and numbness thaw, negative core beliefs lie in rubble and ash, and deep emotional complexes clear. When we finally get to the end of that long, dark tunnel, we have a brand new appreciation of the light, the lightness of being, and the enlightenment that comes. From the Gatekeeper meditation we had a glimpse of ourselves in this enlightened state – we caught a vision of how we might look and feel during the ascent/rebirth phase. Hopefully for most of us, it is an ecstatic vision of ourselves, radiating with an open spirit and new hope.

"Ecstasy" is the best word that I can offer for the feeling that arises during this stage of initiation. "Ecstasy" literally means "being beside oneself," and is the feeling of joy and celebration that comes when we merge into something greater than ourselves and no longer feel alone in the universe. Ecstasy is often felt during communal celebrations when we drum, sing, dance or pray together. It brings a sense of merging into the whole – into an ecstatic fusion that transports us out of isolation and into a feeling of oneness with the whole world. Ecstasy dissolves the individuated Self so that we can shift our center of life from the trunk to the branches of the Tree. Now we are no longer just an individual soul but part of a vast, cosmic sea of souls. With this vision, our individual Self is woven into the fabric of destiny and intertwined with every other human being.

The Alchemists called this ecstatic phase "Solutio" – when we feel a sense of dissolving and merging. During Solutio we can be flooded with watery emotion and tears. We lose personal definition and boundaries and swim in an ocean of collectivity. We feel blissfully in love. During Solutio we connect with others, with God, with the earth and with nature. A holistic vision of life is comprehended with a powerful visceral knowing. This can feel tremendously healing if we have been viewing the world in parts – compartmentalized and separated. Solutio gathers community and brings an experience of communion. We experience that we are not alone and that we have many spiritual companions on the journey.

There are two archetypal characters that facilitate both ecstasy and Solutio. These are the figures of Dionysus and Ariadne.

We met Ariadne in Stage 5. She is the high priestess of Crete who helps Theseus to get through the Labyrinth and slay the Minotaur. At the end of that story, Theseus and Ariadne escape from Crete and sail off together for Athens. On their way to the mainland, they stop off at a small island, where Ariadne meets Dionysus. According to the story, Ariadne stays with Dionysus and Theseus returns to Athens to reign as King. Ariadne and Dionysus remain on the island and create a fruitful partnership.

As the high priestess and queen of the snake dance, Ariadne's gift is to lead her priestesses in ecstatic dancing. This makes her a perfect match for Dionysus, who is the god of ecstasy and wild, ecstatic dancing. As Ariadne and Dionysus dance together they create a dynamic intercourse of Spirit. Ariadne's snakelike movements – winding in and out, down and around, gathering her priestesses one by one to create a long snake chain – blend with Dionysus' dance of the vine, twisting and turning in an ecstatic trance. Imagining their ecstatic movements can help to put us into an altered state where we are ready to receive life from the Spirit.

This ecstatic dancing can serve as a guide to the graceful weaving we will do as our vision opens out during the ascent phase. First we move into Spirit to glimpse our next step forward, and then we move back into ordinary time to put it into action. We step into an ecstatic state for inspiration, and then back to an ordinary state to integrate what we felt and learned. As we weave in and out, we die to whatever is not serving Spirit and awaken to that which brings deep meaning and purpose. We tear down a stone from the old temple and then pick up a new stone – destroy a room and fill it with something new, dying to be reborn.

The ecstatic dancing of Dionysus and Ariadne helps us to travel in and out of the realm of Spirit with ease. If we practice abandoning ourselves to states of ecstasy, it helps loosen any rigidity that keeps us constricted. Embracing ecstasy brings separate parts of us together. It obliterates boundaries or barriers that keep us from living life fully and joyfully. Ecstasy opens our Spirit to its full range of expression.

Transforming your vision

We have seen how the ecstatic dancing of Dionysus and Ariadne can help us to weave gracefully between the worlds, between death and rebirth as we tear down an old stone wall and build a new one with better stones. The old stones are the **negative core beliefs** that now lie in rubble. But what are the new stones? What new stones will build our inner spiritual temple?

During the ascent phase, the new stones come in the form of spontaneous affirmations of spiritual truth – truths that arrive in our heart and mind that radically transform our vision of life. The following is a list of the "new stones" – the **life-affirming core beliefs** that become the building blocks of our new inner temple.

Life-affirming core beliefs:

I am not alone, we are all connected.
I can trust.
I am included, I am at the center of my life and part of the human community.
I deserve to be loved.
I deserve abundance.
I don't need to do everything myself.
I can count on reliable people to help me.
I have surrendered my addiction/problem and have survived.
I don't have to accommodate to be loved, I can be loved without performing or adapting.
I am not trapped and I have free will.
There is room for me.
Others do not have more than me, we are all in the same boat with our own particular problems to work through.
Others are not in competition with me, I will find a place for myself.
Others do not have it easier than me, life is relative to each person.

Others see me and acknowledge me as I believe in myself and let go of the need to be seen.

Others do not stop me from being whole, I am responsible for feeling whole, fulfilling my dreams and feeling good about myself.

Others can support me when I ask the right people for what I need.

Others are not a threat to me.

Others do not have more power than me, we all have power in our own way.

Life is exactly the way it should be.

When life feels unfair I will help others in need.

Life is not out to get me, it is showing me where I need to transform.

Life provides abundant resources and I don't need to deprive others or fight for my slice of the pie.

Life doesn't need to be controlled, I can surrender control.

When these powerful spiritual truths dawn in our awareness, our entire vision of life transforms. We grow in our capacity to trust, love and serve. We grow in our capacity to transform negative situations into positive ones and evil into good. We now see others and ourselves as whole and holy, rather than fragmented. We are no longer plagued by the need to control others to get what we want, but can allow others to be exactly the way they are. This releases our hold over others because we no longer expect them to serve us – rather, we come to see how we can serve them, regardless of what they give to us. We experience tremendous freedom as our inner being no longer panics with unmet needs but feels more relaxed, relieved, soothed and supple. All of these new life-affirming and spiritually mature qualities are the stones that build our beautiful and lasting temple.

Exercise 8: New stones for the Inner Temple

Set aside some time to do an active imagination, visualizing each one of the life-affirming core beliefs as a stone placed around your temple. Prepare by having beside you the list of negative core beliefs you want to transform (from Step 3, Exercise 5) and the above list of life-affirming core beliefs you want to integrate.

Close your eyes and imagine a sacred clearing where your temple will be built. Imagine the place, the landscape, the country and the time period of the architecture in which you want your temple to be built. Now imagine a crew of helpers, builders, masons, stonecutters and whoever else you need to build this temple. Before this new temple can be built, you must first clear the ground. Scattered around the construction site are your negative core beliefs lying in rubble. Name each "stone", each negative core belief and clear it out of the way. Ask your crew of workers to help get rid of each old stone.

When the foundation area is totally cleared, read aloud each of the life-affirming core beliefs, slowly, and visualize placing each new stone around your temple. Begin with "I am not alone" and wait to place the next stone until you can clearly visualize that spiritual stone incorporated into the wall of your temple. Go through each affirmation, or pick out the most important and relevant "stones."

By the end of your visualization, you should have a powerful temple built with strong, life-affirming spiritual principles. Notice how you feel about this temple. Walk around it. Then walk inside. What is it like to be inside? Imagine going through your daily life with this temple consciously living inside you. How will your life be different?

For a creative exercise you can draw a picture of your inner Temple with the stones of life-affirming core beliefs.

Activating the Visionary

As our temple is being built and our spiritual awakening underway, the needs of our Tree of Life radically transform.

At the beginning of the journey, when we grounded our roots, we attended to the needs of the *Nefesh* – including needs for comfort, instinctive survival and communal belonging. When we strengthened the trunk of our Tree, we attended to the needs of the *Neshamah* – needs for separation and individual self-expression. Now, as we build the branches, we must attend to the needs of the *Ruah*.

The *Ruah*, our spiritual body, needs to connect with the wider vision of life and express universal spiritual values such as wisdom, understanding, love, compassion, reconciliation, peace and justice. Our *Ruah* also needs to express our true purpose and destiny.

When we awaken the *Ruah* within us, we gain access to the part of us that has the faculty and capability to **envision our higher purpose**. Our *Ruah* is encoded with our destiny, which is permanently emblazoned with our spiritual DNA code. The way to decode this message is to activate the Visionary who can access the *Ruah* and read the code, giving us insight into what we were born to do.

The Visionary within us is capable of many things. The Visionary sits on the cutting edge of life – seeing beyond ordinary reality, seeing the future and all the possibilities that could be. Our inner Visionary sees the whole of our life, including past, present and future. The Visionary is able to integrate our past and point us into the future, directing us at each step as we move towards our destination. The Visionary can see the end product that we are to produce, the person that we are to become, how we are to serve and contribute our gifts, and how this will benefit others. The Visionary inspires the creativity we need to make our destiny a reality.

The next step to becoming a Visionary is to learn to **hold the Visionary's gaze** so that inspirations bubbling up from Spirit can take form and have an impact in the real world. The Visionary within us receives inspiration by spending time around the "cauldron of inspiration," the bubbling kettle of creativity that lives deep within our being and rises miraculously from an underground source.

On the Tree of Life, our cauldron of inspiration resides at Daat and is the contact point with the world of Spirit. In Celtic mythology there is a special Visionary goddess named Cerridwen, who is keeper of this cauldron of inspiration. Her magical cauldron is always boiling and bubbling with creative juices. If we feel dry or uninspired, we can call up Cerridwen, move closer to the hot, steamy cauldron and then lean over and let our Visionary look inside.

But what is it exactly that bubbles up from our cauldron of inspiration? What rises is an upsurge of poetry, myth, story, fairy tale, music, chant, scientific innovation, new ideas, prophecy, divination, sacred images, visions, and inspirations in every field of work imaginable (see Diagram 24).

Diagram 24: Inspirations from Spirit
The Visionary within us receives inspiration by spending time around the "cauldron of inspiration. If we can learn to hold the visionary's gaze, inspirations bubbling up from Spirit can take form and have an impact in the real world.

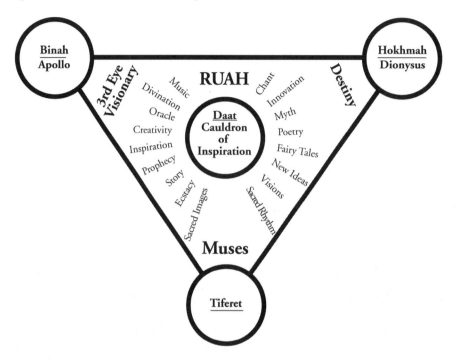

The Temple at Delphi in ancient Greece was an actual place that represented both the cauldron of inspiration and the place of Daat. In ancient times, the Visionary at the Delphi Temple who peered into the cauldron for divination and inspiration was called the "Pythia" or "Pythoness." She was the high priestess of the Temple – a snake priestess, and therefore connected to the cult of Ariadne. She was often depicted as sitting on a throne above a pit of snakes in a state of ecstasy. Symbolically, this implies that the Visionary archetype has befriended the snake and its powers, has learned to shed old skins, and can open wide to ecstatic states and new life coming from Spirit.

The Temple at Delphi was called the "omphalos" or "navel of the world" and it was thought to be a sacred axis point between heaven and earth. The Pythoness acted as a link between these two realms, and she had to be strong enough to endure the inspirations and messages from Spirit without injury. It was believed that – as she sat over the fumes steaming from a fissure in the underground cave at Delphi and breathed them in – the Spirit impregnated her. The Pythoness who sits over the steaming fissure in the cave is like our Visionary who looks into the bubbling cauldron.

The more we practice these techniques of peering into the cauldron or sitting over the steaming fissure, the longer our Visionary can maintain his or her gaze into the source of inspiration. And it is important for our Visionary to be able to sustain that gaze so that we can move beyond just getting the flash of inspiration, to the point where we can receive detailed guidance so that our inspiration can unfold. It is the Visionary who holds the larger scope for our vision and it is the Visionary who can intuit the steps that need to be taken. It is the Visionary who can also imagine and "see" the future and the people who will benefit from the manifestation of our inspiration – be it a book, a product or a teaching – and the ultimate contribution that our gift will make to the collective.

The next step in becoming a Visionary and envisioning our higher purpose is to **find our Muse**, the sacred rhythm from Spirit that most attracts us. In Western mythology, the Muses are nine sister goddesses who motivate us with song, dance and poetry and help us bring our inspirations into form. In Greek mythology, the nine Muses are the goddesses of astronomy/astrology, history, tragedy, comedy, choral song, love poetry, epic poetry, lyric poetry, and sacred hymns/sacred poetry. For our purposes, let's imagine the Muses as the creative inspirations bubbling forth from our cauldron at Daat (see Diagram 24).

The Muses are the mediators between the Dionysian and Apollonian experiences of Spirit. They transmute the raw and unrefined Dionysian material coming from Spirit and help us to envision what to do with the inspirations we receive. As we look back over the course of our life, we can often see which particular Muse has been calling to us and inspiring us over time. The Muses help us weave our particular dance from Spirit into the collective tapestry that represents humanity's highest intellectual, artistic and cultural pursuits. Doing our sacred dance therefore, builds the stones of the great temple of humanity – for as we bring our Muse to life, she weaves our golden thread into the human tapestry. The satisfaction comes when we can see clearly how our craft or sacred dance is beautifully woven into the collective weaving of humankind.

Exercise 9: Activating your Visionary

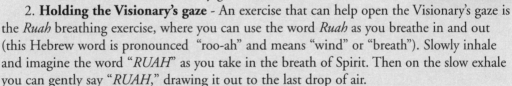

1. **Envision your higher purpose** - One of the most helpful ways to activate your Visionary is to carve out time to envision who you want to become. Sit down with a paper and pen and ask yourself these questions:

What is my highest vision for myself?

What was I born to do?

What cause would I die for?

How am I to serve? How will my gifts benefit others?

2. **Holding the Visionary's gaze** - An exercise that can help open the Visionary's gaze is the *Ruah* breathing exercise, where you can use the word *Ruah* as you breathe in and out (this Hebrew word is pronounced "roo-ah" and means "wind" or "breath"). Slowly inhale and imagine the word "*RUAH*" as you take in the breath of Spirit. Then on the slow exhale you can gently say "*RUAH*," drawing it out to the last drop of air.

3. **Attracting your Muse** - Take some time to brainstorm about your Muse. From the list of creative Muses in Diagram 24 or from your own list, which Muse calls you? What brings you ecstasy and bliss? Which creative expression captures your imagination most? Where do you experience Spirit? Are you attracted to words, voice or music? Does movement or dance capture you? Are you drawn to poetry? Are you drawn to dreams? Are you drawn to beauty? Are you excited by painting or the visual arts? For a creative exercise, make a timeline of your life and see what Muse has consistently been knocking on your door and inspiring you to creative activity.

The Visionary's powers and responsibilities

So far in Step 4 of this sixth initiation, we have embraced ecstasy, transformed our vision, envisioned our higher purpose, held the Visionary's gaze and discovered our Muse. The next step in becoming a Visionary is to *take on the spiritual responsibility that comes with the wisdom, understanding and knowledge* that we now possess.

During the sixth initiation we have developed and fine-tuned our *Ruah* to the extent that we are now able to transform our own personal life, which can shift the collective tide of consciousness in a profound way. Because of this, we must use our spiritual gifts wisely.

On the Tree of Life diagram we have now developed the "Spirit triad" of Tiferet, Binah, Hokhmah and Daat – or cosmic truth, understanding, wisdom and higher knowledge. With this level of development, consciousness and capability, we have become increasingly valuable to Spirit. Our job description now includes increased responsibility, so we must understand how to use these spiritual powers appropriately and dedicate them to the highest good. We must acknowledge that these powers come from Spirit and are not to be used for personal power or gratification. *The proper use of cosmic truth, wisdom, understanding and knowledge is for individual and collective healing and for renewal of body, heart, mind and spirit.*

Let's look now at some of the Visionary's powers and responsibilities. One of the Visionary's powers is *objectivity*, the ability to climb up into the branches of the Tree for a bird's eye view in order to see life less personally and more objectively. In the sixth initiation, this is not a defensive flight away from feelings and difficulties, for this kind of objectivity only emerges after the descent and death phase, after we have faced our pain and difficulties and integrated them into our conscious life.

The Alchemists called this stage of growing objectivity and spiritual maturity "Sublimatio." Sublimatio often follows Mortificatio and is therefore seen as the ascent stage after the death. During Sublimatio we can experience states of distilling, purifying and concentrating. This is when we try to distill our experiences and attempt to look at the meaning behind events rather than react to them. Insights begin to rise.

During Sublimatio, our level of awareness increases so that we are able to see an event multi-dimensionally - how it came to be, what it means, and how we can take appropriate action rather than passively reacting to the situation. From personal activities to cultural occurrences, we are now conscious of reading the higher value and trying to distill what is happening around us or in us. We begin to view world events from a spiritual perspective, asking ourselves why and how this war or disaster or political conflict is happening in light of the entire web of life on earth. We ask ourselves why and how we attracted this into our life at this particular time and what the bigger picture is.

Imagine the Alchemists gazing into the glass container where the Prima Materia is transmuting, and seeing the vapor rising, the water or substance distilling. As they watch and observe, they witness the substance being purified through successive evaporation and condensation, resulting in a concentration of the liquid. Like the Alchemist who extracts the essence out of a substance, it is our job during this stage of our initiation to *extract the essence out of every situation.*

It is no wonder then that during Sublimatio, images of ladders, towers, airplanes, flight and elevators arrive in our dreams. As we climb or rise into the air, we gain a higher perspective to reach an objective viewpoint. This brings a tremendous power to our waking life, as we are able to break free of emotional complexes that cloud our vision or hold us back from living our destiny.

In the Shamanic tradition, this kind of objectivity is gained through Shamanic flight or journeying. There are also accounts of Shaman initiates who are required to build and climb their own ladder, often with seven rungs, representing the World Tree or Tree of Life. In ascending the ladder, the initiates access the cosmic realm where they can talk to spirits, heal others, and perform divination for the community. The labyrinth mysteries from Crete have a similar theme. As the initiate finds the center of the Labyrinth, she then has access to the Cosmic Tree, the axis point between heaven and earth. As she climbs the Tree, she takes on the responsibility of her destiny.

What happens internally during Sublimatio is that *intuition and insight sharpen* and *consciousness increases*. We become more objective about our own life and have a brand new perspective on why were born into our particular family and how this experience helped us reach our destiny. We understand clearly why various events occurred and how they forged us into who we are. We clearly see the choices we have made to get to where we are. We gain wisdom from our mistakes instead of dwelling on the pain or the shame. We stop identifying with people and events that previously caught us in a fury of emotional entanglements.

We also gain clarity into historical and current events, which helps us to make wise choices for the future and to give wise counsel to others. There is always a feeling of upward movement in Sublimatio as we climb our Tree to get an ever broader and higher perspective. The view from the branches of our Tree can be ecstatic, joyful, relieving and peaceful – but it can also be shocking when we really see with open and conscious eyes what is happening in our life and in the world.

Changing perceptions at will

From the branches of our Tree of Life, our Visionary has access to what has been called the "perceptual field." In Kabbalah it is called "Beriah" – the world of Spirit, the plane of cosmic consciousness – and it is where our *Ruah* is centered. From this level, we have the power to change our perceptions at will because we are no longer subject to the will of the *Nefesh* or the *Neshamah*. We can perceive the past, present and future all at once. This enables us to see clearly where we have come from, why we are here, and where we are going. It enables us to see the series of free-will choices we have made to get to where we are, so that we can take full responsibility for our personal and spiritual life, no longer blaming others. It also gives us tremendous freedom to change situations – within and without – in an instant, by moving our consciousness to the highest good of any situation. We have the power to transform our thought patterns, transform our negativity and transform our destructive energy. We have the power to change evil situations into good. The following are examples of some perceptions we can now change at will:

1. My relationship is not the way I want it to be. I never find relationships that are good for me. **Changed to:** *I picked this relationship to learn a particular lesson (e.g., patience, love, tolerance, forgiveness, etc.).*
2. This is a terrible thing happening to me. It is clear that I am not loved. **Changed to:** *This terrible thing is happening and I am open to learning what this means for me.*

3. I was born into the wrong family. **Changed to:** *I can see the lessons that I have learned from this particular family.*

4. People are always dominating me. **Changed to:** *My boundaries are not strong enough and I allow people to push me around. I can change this situation.*

5. My father did not prepare me for manhood and I feel deprived. **Changed to:** *There is some passivity in me that holds me back from asking for guidance. Part of me is afraid to embrace my manhood. I now want to connect with my masculinity.*

6. My mother was unavailable to initiate me into my femininity. **Changed to:** *I have aligned with more masculine ways of being, and part of me rejects the feminine way. This has made me unreceptive to the feminine. I am ready to connect with my femininity.*

7. I am powerless to change my fate. **Changed to:** *I have free will and can choose to go in the direction of my destiny.*

8. This horrible situation is happening in a faraway country and I feel powerless to do anything. **Changed to:** *I pray for Divine light to be directed to this place, and I pray for balance to be restored in the government. I will find ways to help.*

Changing perceptions at will can now be added to our repertoire of spiritual disciplines. It is a skill that can be developed and honed with practice. The more we practice, the more rapidly *we recognize our own part in the scenario, the lesson to be learned, and the right action to be taken.* We have the power now to observe every life situation and assess: This is what is happening; this is what I need to learn; this is the energy being exchanged; this is what needs to be done. This power of observation and the ability to change our perceptions at will is one of the most sophisticated tools for good available to us as humans.

As we learn to change our perceptions at will and practice this kind of spiritual consciousness, it is possible to set off a radical shift in the entire perceptual field. As more and more of us wake up and go through this kind of spiritual initiation, we have the ability to create a global transformation. During this sixth initiation, we have a growing concern for the state of others – the state of their suffering, their pain, their frustration and, most importantly, their potential. Every human being has the potential to grow in consciousness and awaken spiritually, which in turn adds to the pool of awakened beings. In the sixth initiation we learn how we can play a part in bringing this about.

We have arrived now at the place of miracle, the place where the most horrific person or scenario can be redeemed, the most ignorant can be enlightened, and the most rigid can be softened. By the power of a word, a thought, or a shift in perception, we can transform our entire lives. We can take a radical new direction; bring healing to a person or community, or change generations of negative karma or family curses. As we are initiated here in the final step, we should not hold back or hesitate to work for the good, for the next miracle may be up to each of us.

Exercise 10: Changing perceptions at will

1. Write down the perceptions that you want to transform at will, such as, "People are always dominating me" or "I always retreat when faced with a dominant character" or "The world is in a horrible state." Then write down your new perception and how you feel about it. Note whether you are, indeed, acting from your new perception. When you first begin this practice, you will probably focus on the personal, psychological perceptions that affect your immediate life and relationships. When you master this practice, you will grow in your ability to shift collective perceptions and collective symbols that are holding back larger groups of people.

2. Climb up into the branches of your Tree and dedicate yourself to staying awake in every situation. Keep the following questions in mind:

What is really happening here?

What is the energy being exchanged?

What is my part in this scenario?

What am I to learn?

What action needs to be taken?

With practice you will become more adept at shifting perceptions at will. You will be clearer about what lessons you are learning and what action needs to be taken to achieve the desired outcome of any situation.

Signs of genuine transformation

As we come to the end of the sixth initiation, I want to talk about signs of genuine transformation.

Most spiritual traditions warn us of awakening to higher levels of consciousness too soon and burning out or going mad if our inner container is not strong enough. During the sixth initiation, true and lasting transformation only occurs if we can open to Spirit safely and successfully. To do this, we must strengthen our internal container by practicing our spiritual disciplines and developing the roots, trunk and branches of our Tree. If any part of our tree is out of sync, we may not be able to make use of the creative inspirations, visions and insight that awaken as we open to Spirit.

Over the years I have worked with many people who report a wide variety of spiritual awakenings that have activated memories and penetrating insights both of a personal and collective nature. Some people have the capacity to make use of these awakenings because they have developed the faculty to think through the experiences with objectivity and curiosity. Others have amazing flashes of insight – they are given an inspiration from Spirit or realize their wrongdoing - but then are unable to make use of the information. Their lives do not really change and their relationships do not change.

Genuine transformation is only successful when our internal container is solid enough and developed enough to hold and integrate these powerful experiences. Genuine transformation is only successful when we have walked the initiation path step by step. Genuine transformation is only successful when things in our life actually change. Our relationships improve. We love more and become more generous. We grow in intelligence. We become less judgmental and more tolerant. We are more conscious and compassionate. We have more space inside for intimacy. Our vision widens and we have more objectivity. We contemplate our spiritual experience, talk it through and begin integrating it into real life.

Conclusion – Initiation 6: Transformation

As we conclude this sixth initiation, we can look back and see that it has led us on an odyssey of transformation – through death and rebirth to a new level of being. We have solidified our commitment to a spiritual path and are open to spiritual guidance. We know how to rejuvenate our spirit by releasing old energy patterns that keep us bound and stuck, freeing us to live out our destiny and our higher purpose. We can surrender control and sustain the descent if change and transformation are necessary. We have gained the clarity and objectivity of our higher mind and are now capable of changing our perceptions at will. We have gained a spiritual perspective of life and developed the branches of our Tree.

Now we are ready to cross the threshold and enter the seventh and final initiation, where our Tree of Life will flower, bear fruit, and offer its bounty to others.

Chapter 7

Sacred Marriage
Robe 7

Initiation 7 - WHOLENESS

The seventh initiation celebrates the culmination of the journey, when our personal Tree of Life comes into alignment and we experience healing and inner peace. Through the Native American story of the Sacred Snake, we will discover the mysterious sacred spring and connect with our longing for the Divine. When the seventh initiation is successful, our Tree of Life will bloom and bear fruit and we will share our bountiful gifts and talents with the world. We will feel empowered to fulfill our life task and will be able to bless and initiate fellow seekers, becoming a healing sanctuary for others along the path.

To activate this initiation we call upon the archetype of the **Healer** who is responsible for integrating our body, mind and spirit together into a unified whole. The Healer aligns the roots, trunk and branches of our Tree into a living and thriving system that brings profound inner stability, fulfillment and satisfaction. The Healer acknowledges the Divine within us, activating feelings of deep inner peace, well-being and unconditional acceptance of self and others. The Healer sees our life as perfectly whole and holy and helps us to burn away anything that keeps us from experiencing ourselves as whole and complete.

Qualities if initiated:

Fulfilled

Content

Satisfied

Sense of wholeness and well-being

Inner peace

Empowered to fulfill our task and use our gifts

Alignment of body, psyche, spirit

Unconditional acceptance of self and others

Experiences revitalization and rejuvenation

Able to reconcile and forgive

Problems if initiation is not complete:

Unable to heal

Feeling fragmented

Never satisfied or fulfilled

General dis-ease, lack of well-being

Inner restlessness, lack of contentment

Unable to share our gifts

Feeling disconnected from the source

Stuck in self-judgements and blame

Inner dryness, unable to rejuvenate

Unwilling or unable to heal others

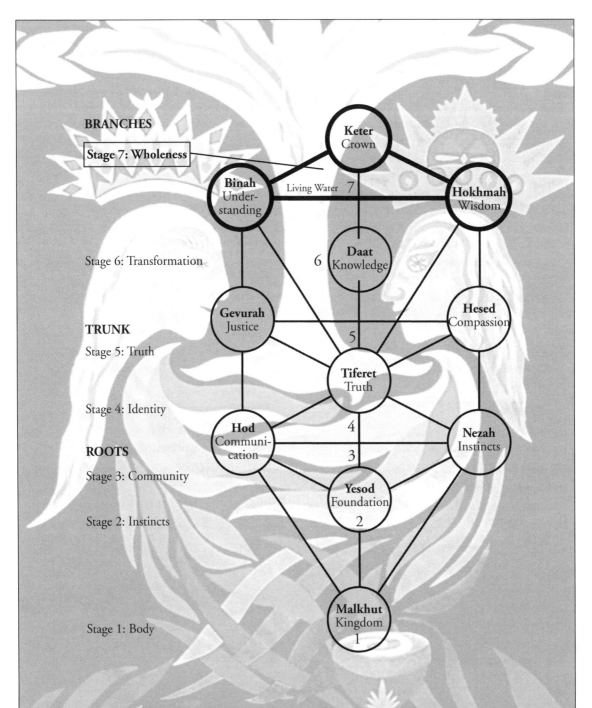

BRANCHES

Stage 7: Wholeness

Keter
Crown

Binah
Under-
standing

Living Water   7

Hokhmah
Wisdom

Stage 6: Transformation

Daat
Knowledge

6

TRUNK

Gevurah
Justice

5

Hesed
Compassion

Stage 5: Truth

Tiferet
Truth

Stage 4: Identity

Hod
Communi-
cation

4

Nezah
Instincts

ROOTS

3

Stage 3: Community

Yesod
Foundation

Stage 2: Instincts

2

Malkhut
Kingdom

1

Stage 1: Body

Diagram 25: Stage 7
The seventh initiation celebrates the culmination of the journey, where our personal Tree of Life comes into alignment and we experience healing and inner peace. Here we are reunited with the source of life, an eternal source of light and consciousness, feeding our entire being. When our Tree of Life flowers and bears fruit, we can provide physical, emotional and spiritual nourishment to ourselves and others.

Chapter 7 - Experience Wholeness

Exercise 1: Meditation - Bringing forth fruit

Imagine your great Tree of Life, rooted firmly into the rich earth. Your roots are deep and they spread wide.

Focus next on the trunk of your Tree and find its center. Stand firm in the powerful center of the trunk. Feel this place of balance. Now stretch up towards the branches and widen out your consciousness to encompass the entire branch system of your Tree. Feel the heat of the sun beaming down on your leaves. Allow the sun to energize your whole Tree.

As the sun heats the leaves, you feel it bringing to life some tiny buds on the branches. The sun coaxes these buds to begin to bloom. Pulling up the nutrients and water from the ground and soaking in light and heat from the sun fills your buds with ripening fruit.

What kind of fruit is growing on your Tree? Imagine your fruit growing and growing until it is ripe and full. Feel the fulfillment of having produced such beautiful fruit. Take some time to acknowledge your roots, your sturdy trunk, and the intricate branchwork of your Tree. Acknowledge the abundance of your fruit, and imagine the pleasure and sustenance that you can bring to others when they enjoy your gifts. See the totality of your Tree, see yourself as whole and complete.

Bring your awareness back now to the present, to ordinary time and ordinary reality; and when you feel ready, open your eyes.

The Completed Tree of Life

The seventh initiation marks the culmination of the journey and the completion of our Tree of Life. Here we are reunited with the source of all life, an eternal source of light and consciousness, feeding our entire being. Without this divine illumination, our Tree would die, just as a physical tree would die without the light and energy from the sun.

So far on our journey we have rooted our Tree, strengthened our trunk, and branched out to widen our vision of life. Now in the seventh initiation we can *blossom and bear fruit*, feeling a sense of completion and wholeness to our Tree.

In order for a tree to bear fruit, it must have the inner code to do so, it must be a flowering and fruit-bearing tree according to its DNA. It must also have the capacity to fertilize or pollinate in some way, for it takes the intercourse of the "masculine" and "feminine" components to generate flower and fruit. For our own Tree of Life to be fruitful, we too must awaken the inner code to blossom, flower and produce our fruit. We must grow in our capacity to be fertilized and pollinated by the generative life force accessed during the seventh initiation.

Mystics have many names for this life force: Holy Other, the Beloved, God, the Divine Mother or Ecstatic Love. Mystics spend much of their lives cultivating divine union and sacred dialogue with this life force. It is from this union that we can bear our fruit, which then becomes a sacred offering of our gifts to the world. During this seventh initiation we will discover ways to dialogue with the Divine so that we can conceive and bear our fruit.

The seventh Sacred Robe, called "The Sacred Marriage", depicts a completed Tree of Life that is bearing its bountiful fruit. The roots, trunk and branches of the Tree are in alignment and working together. This "Initiated" Tree is rooted in the divine soil and has found the fertile sacred ground. Its trunk consists of a divine pair whose strength is seen in their focused gaze and centered heart and will. The branches of the tree are reaching out and up towards a widened vision of life and are bearing the sacred fruit of light, a constantly generative source of unification and healing.

We have journeyed far and well to make it to Stage 7. We have passed the tests of the Gatekeeper and walked through the gateway of transformation. We have arrived here through our hard work on the road of initiation. After all this dedication, it is certain we have not arrived here by chance. We are here because we have yearned for the truth, longed to be reconnected to the source, and have desired healing. We have been like every seeker of the grail and every initiate who longs to taste the elixir of life. We have worked hard and we have gone through the fire.

So here we are at the foot of the completed Tree of Life. What can we expect to receive at this last phase of the journey? What do we now have access to?

One of the most important things we now have access to is the **unifying power of the Divine**, a binding force found everywhere in creation. It has been here all the time; we just did not have the consciousness to recognize it before now. This divine force is dwelling at the heart of everything, every part of creation and every person. It is an active force, in the process of drawing everything back into its original unity.

At Stage 7 we also have direct access to the collective storehouses of **understanding and wisdom**, Binah and Hokhmah on the Tree of Life diagram (see Diagram 25). Binah brings order, meaning and understanding to life. Binah helps us to put life in proper perspective and to accept limitations. With the experience of Binah we can understand the universal laws at work in nature and human nature, and we can learn to work with these Laws rather than against them. Hokhmah provides the expansion of ideas and consciousness to all areas of our life. With the insight of Hokhmah, we can expand our awareness far beyond the ordinary mind and glimpse the universal ideas at work in the world. These flashes of insight can bring us wisdom far beyond our years.

We also have access to Keter, the **divine will**, the spark of light permeating all existence. This is our direct contact point with the Divine Being who says "YES" to creation and declares, "It is good." The place of Keter is also our access point to the source of **inner renewal** and **rejuvenation**.

In Kabbalah, the divine will at Keter is sometimes called "Grace." Grace is imparted from Keter down the central pillar, illuminating our Sapphire Staff and bringing feelings of bliss, assurance, unconditional acceptance, acceptability, goodness, rightness, being in the right place at the right time, contentedness and well-being. All of these qualities can be embodied if initiation is successful at this final stage in the process.

* Step 1: Connect to the Divine *
Step 2: Unify all aspects of being
Step 3: Receive the blessing
Step 4: Heal yourself and others

For initiation to be successful and in order to experience healing that is lasting, we can follow the four steps of the seventh initiation and *connect to the Divine, unify all aspects of being, receive the blessing for our life purpose, and heal ourselves and others* by passing on the gifts of initiation. These four steps are portrayed as four sets of symbols on the seventh Sacred Robe.

The first step – connecting with the Divine – is portrayed at the base of the robe as a white, swirling, abundant wellspring of life that revitalizes our body, mind and spirit. The second step is portrayed as the bread and wine, a symbol of the sacred marriage and the powerful, universal binding force that unifies all aspects of being. The third step is shown on the robe as the crowned divine pair, who shows us how to gracefully receive the blessing that empowers us to live our vision and fulfill our purpose. The fourth step is portrayed as the Tree of Life, generating the divine fire that makes us feel alive with love and life, bringing healing and inner peace, which in turn helps us to heal others.

The following is a wonderful Native American story called "Sacred Snake." It addresses many aspects of the seventh initiation, especially our longing to connect with that mysterious source of inner renewal that many call the "elixir of life" or the "living water."

The Story of Sacred Snake

The Zuni Indians of the Southwest speak of the majestic village under Thunder Loud Mountain. It was called the Place of the Eagles, but today there is only skelton ruin.

At one time, there was an elder in the Place of the Eagles. He was the Priest-Chief who held the wisdom of the spirit world and sacred healing powers. He had many daughters, but one he could not understand. His oldest daughter was continually worried about being dirty or about wearing soiled clothing. She washed her hands in water buckets kept by the door of her special, solitary, clean little house. She washed her body from dawn to dusk in the spring at the base of the village. She washed her hair whenever the wind blew. She had very little time for anything else but cleanliness.

The spring at the edge of the village was a sacred spring. People stayed away from it. Nearby was an altar place of offerings and prayer, so the sacred spring was not a place to bathe. The father had told this to his daughter time and time again. She did not listen. The water in the spring was fresh, clear and cool every day.

A drought came upon the land. Water became scarce and this daughter could no longer get water from the fast flowing river to wash her clothes. So she washed them in the sacred spring. When there was no water from the ground wells for cooking her food, she gathered water from the sacred spring. She bathed, washed, cooked, and drank the water from the sacred spring.

But the spring was not without a life of its own. The dark hole that seeped Mother Earth's clear liquid held a creature, which was a coiled spirit keeping his watchful eye on the beauty who came to him. He watched her cautiously. He appreciated the curves of her body, her grace, and her love for the water. He waited.

The eldest daughter brought her tree-sap baskets to the sacred spring, submerging them in the water. The coiled spirit shrank away from the baskets and then they disappeared. The spirit knew she would return.

He floated to the surface of the sacred spring, breathed in Father Sky's strength and became a small human male infant. He knew that a human baby infant would drown in the water, so he cried out for help. The oldest daughter heard the crying. There, in the sacred spring, was a newborn infant. She lifted him out of the water and let him suckle at her breast. Holding him, she searched for the mother, but there was no one. She took him to her clean little home and lay down with him. Soon the two of them were fast asleep.

The massive body of the powerful snake was cramped in the tiny infant's body. The snake breathed and grew, filling every space of the small, clean home. The oldest daughter slept.

The father had asked his entire family to meet at his home for dinner. His oldest daughter did not arrive, and the others were eager to eat. He asked his youngest daughter to get her sister, and so she ran to the small, clean home. She tried to pull open the blanket door, but there was something massive holding it down.

She ran to the window and, standing tall, peered into the home. All she could see were massive scales. Then she saw them move. The youngest daughter ran to her father and told him what she had seen. He gathered up his medicine pouch, two prayer sticks, cornmeal, and followed his youngest daughter. There in the window, he saw the huge snake.

The father said, "I am your priest. I ask you to let my daughter leave. She is yours, but let her come to us for blessings before you take her."

The father's voice woke the oldest daughter. She saw the massive scales. She was so frightened that she could not move. The father cried out, "I am your priest. I ask you to let my daughter go. We shall have a ceremony for you."

The massive snake gathered up his coils. He could not move to speak. The father cried out, "I am your priest. Let my daughter go. We know that you have won her. She needs a blessing before she leaves."

The snake coiled his neck up to the ceiling. He swallowed part of his tail. The father cried, "Your priest asks you to let his daughter come out for a blessing." The snake lifted his tail into an arch, and the daughter crawled out on all fours and ran to her father. The father took the two prayer sticks and placed them at the door. He sprinkled cornmeal around the home. The medicine pouch remained in his hand.

The father took his daughters home, and the family listened quietly as he spoke. "You have done something which we have told you not to do, my daughter. You used the sacred spring. Since you love water and need water around you all day, it is perhaps for the best that you go with the Sacred Snake. Tomorrow, at dawn, you will begin the rest of your life with him. Tonight we shall have a blessing feast."

The oldest daughter was frightened. Her father sent the family to call the people of the village together. Meanwhile, Sacred Snake breathed in the air of Father Sky, and he lifted the massive body, placing it back in the sacred spring. There was much to do.

The next morning, the village was alive with excitement. Sacred Snake slowly slithered his massive scaled body out of the sacred spring. He ate the offerings of food. He took the prayer sticks. He slowly moved to the village. His giant head entered the village while the middle of his body was leaving the spring. It was not until midday that his tail was coiling around him in the village.

The father started a chant. The people followed. The oldest daughter was brought out of her father's home. She wore a white manta, white moccasins, a headdress of feathers and snake skins. Her face was painted with colors of corn. She walked to Sacred Snake. Sacred Snake lifted his head onto her back.

The drums began to beat as the eldest daughter started her journey back to the sacred spring, carrying Sacred Snake on her back. Sacred Snake's head was intensely heavy, and the daughter pulled strength from within her and tried to stand. She staggered and fell many times, but the strong body of Sacred Snake righted her on her path. She pulled through the day and into the early night.

Sacred Snake's long body had hardly moved and the daughter felt tired and frustrated. Darkness was now upon the land. The people had gone to their homes.

Sacred Snake breathed in the air of Father Sky. His long, scaly body shrank, and his heavy head changed form. The strong, handsome face of a brave warrior appeared. The scales gathered on the ground like a long blanket of silver; and a young man now walked beside the daughter, who continued to bend in her efforts. The brave warrior reached down and pulled up the long blanket of silver scales. He rolled it and placed it on his back, tying the blanket with a leather thong.

"Young maiden, why do you bend forward as one with a burden?" A man's voice echoed out to her in the dark night.

"Oh, I have such a load. I carry Sacred Snake, and he is so heavy I can but barely hold his head. His body is the length of four mountains and we have far to go. Could you help?" The eldest daughter did not turn.

"Beautiful maiden, I stand beside you and see that you are walking alone. There is no one on your back. There is no long body following. You are alone."

The oldest daughter lifted her hand to her shoulder, for she could feel the weight of the massive head but nothing was there. She stopped and turned to see the long body that she was sure she felt. Nothing was there. Brother Moon lifted above the mountain and lit the dark night sky.

The oldest daughter stared into the face of the warrior. "Who are you? You are not from my village. Where is Sacred Snake?"

The brave warrior smiled. "I am Sacred Snake," he said. "I have decided to walk with you rather than have you carry me."

The eldest daughter stepped back. "You are not Sacred Snake. Sacred Snake is huge and heavy. You are not he!"

The brave warrior turned his back to her. "Here is my skin. I will carry it and give you a rest."

The oldest daughter sat on the ground. "Will you let me return to my family? Will you let me go?"

The brave warrior knelt beside her. "No, I have admired you for a long time. Now that I have you, you are mine and I am yours. We shall live long. We shall have a good life. Come, let me help you."

The brave warrior carried the oldest daughter. They went to the sacred spring. Brother Moon hid behind a large, grey night cloud as Sacred Snake carried his maiden into the sacred spring water. They disappeared and were never seen again. [1]

Longing for the sacred spring

This story depicts a woman who longs for the fresh, cool, clear, sacred water. In the story she is portrayed as being overly concerned with cleanliness, which might be interpreted by therapists as an obsessive/compulsive disorder. However, when I hear this story with my sacred ear, this woman becomes the one who is refreshingly aware of her longing to be near the source. Her concern for cleanliness can be seen as her desire to remain pure and clean in the sense of being spiritually open and untouched by what others think and say. In fact, she blatantly disregards her father's warnings about her penchant for the sacred water. Despite opposition, she is willing to forge her own path and follow an inner longing to be near the spring. Her whole life eventually revolves around the sacred water as she bathes, washes, cooks, cleans and drinks the water of the spring.

This woman has some kind of inner vision and single-mindedness that is reminiscent of the saints, sages and mystics through the ages. She has dedicated her whole life to this longing. I think of this eldest daughter as doing exactly what she wants and loves to do. She remains loyal to her purpose, with purity of heart, mind and soul. This begs the questions: What do you long for? What have you dedicated your being to? What path would you follow despite all opposition? Do you have the purity of heart and mind to go after your longing?

Like the woman in the story, mystics and initiates long for the sacred spring, that hidden and mysterious underground source that has an ever-abundant flow. Human beings throughout the ages have searched for this source. Legends and myths tell of quests for the fountain of youth, the elixir of life and the Holy Grail. We all long for the vitality and rejuvenating effect that this source has on the psyche and spirit. Mystical traditions refer to this awakened level of consciousness by calling it *illumination, unconditional love or the awakened Kundalini.* The coiled serpent in the spring is a reference to the awakening Kundalini energy, which eventually rises up, signifying a fully awakened, divine consciousness.

The sacred spring, the source for which we long, is depicted on the seventh Sacred Robe at the base of the Tree as a swirling mass of white substance guarded by two white angels. I see this as the primal substance, the living water or the elixir of life. It is the ever-flowing source, the drink that every initiate longs to taste. We do not go on this sacred journey lightly or frivolously. We do it because we have had an inkling of a taste of this living water. Somewhere inside our bones we know that we have been separated from this source, and we will go through anything to return to it.

Firewater

The Sacred Spring in the story is not an ordinary spring. This is no ordinary water. It is home to a lively inner inhabitant, Sacred Snake. He provides the extraordinary element, giving this spring its magical and sacred quality.

On the seventh robe, the Sacred Spring is the central image at the base of the robe and the Sacred Snake is depicted as a swirl of light, enlivening the water and giving it movement and potential life. Spiraling out of this living water is a swirling chain of gold and silver DNA that is unfolding and replicating in a spiral dance. This bubbling soup, and Sacred Snake within it, represents the source of creation.

The Genesis Creation story offers a wonderful image to describe this watery substance that births all of life. From Genesis 1:1-2, the English translation reads:

"In the beginning when God created the heavens and the earth, the earth was a formless

void and darkness covered the face of the deep, while a wind from God swept over the face of the waters." [2]

In the Hebrew language, the usual word for water is "mayim." But in the Creation story, the water is called "Ha-Shamayim," which translates "firewater." So the mayim has been transformed into the Ha-Shamayim, meaning that the primal substance out of which all creation springs is *water infused with divine fire*. Here we find the primal soup, the potential of creation that is moving and full of power. In the story, it is Sacred Snake who infuses the spring with divine fire, creating the sacred firewater.

When the first two verses of Genesis are read in Hebrew, a very different picture emerges, for the original language brings multi-dimensionality to the text with many layers of image and meaning. The following poem is my own interpretation of Genesis 1:1-2, which flowed out of an inspirational weekend that I spent with a fellow Kabbalah teacher. I tried to incorporate the many word pictures conjured by the Hebrew language for these two verses. It speaks to the powerfully active divine life-force infusing its creation with the substance that will bring it to life and burst it into flame. As you read, try to get a sense of the firewater.

> *In the beginning, out of the Fire of all Being,*
> *Flowed the spiral dance of creation.*
> *A movement in time and space, being in the process of becoming.*
> *And this dance of the Elohim, Goddess and God, Creatress and Creator,*
> *And this dance of the Elohim is the dialogue of creation.*
> *They make love, and in their whirling dance of embracing,*
> *They lift up one voice and sing all of creation into Being.*
> *They hear the sacred sound, its echoing return,*
> *Of the sacred music of the spheres.*
> *Resounding from one end of creation to the other*
> *The octave of eternal life complete.*
> *And now all is waiting, like a silent desert,*
> *And darkness descends upon the face of the deep,*
> *And the Spirit of God, the Ruah of the Goddess*
> *Moves over the face of the waters,*
> *Hovering and stirring and shaking and trembling the surface of the water.*
> *Like a brooding eagle with fluttering wings,*
> *She holds the space, active, pregnant, gestating,*
> *Drawing out from the darkened waters*
> *All of her children.*

The Hebrew language is filled with images and symbols that help us to understand the nature of the creative life force that sits at the heart of all creation. The poem offers several images that we might use to help us gain a clearer image of the true nature of the firewater. This firewater is *enlightening, dancing, singing, dialoguing, engaging, resounding, moving, hovering, shaking, stirring, trembling and fluttering.*

This is very much like the water that lives within the sacred spring. It is no wonder that the oldest daughter wants to spend her days near it. The massive snake coiled in the spring is what gives the water its pregnant potential and infuses the ordinary water with extraordinary fire. The eldest daughter wants to relate to this energy and does what it takes to make this a reality. She actively pursues a sacred dialogue with the firewater by taking her basket and drawing out the water. In this way, she is co-creating with the Elohim (which in Hebrew refers to the creative aspect of the Godhead that is both male and female).

There is another Biblical story that uses a similar image of drawing out the firewater. This water of life, the primal water infused with divine fire, is the living water that Jesus speaks about in the Gospel of John, Chapter 4: 4-15. He is speaking to a woman from Samaria as they are both seated on the side of a well.

"Jesus had to go through Samaria and he came to a city called Sinchar, near the plot of ground Jacob had given to his son Joseph. Jacob's well was there and Jesus, tired out by his journey, was sitting by the well. It was about noon. A Samaritan woman came to draw water and Jesus said to her, "Give me a drink." The Samaritan woman said to Jesus, "How is it that you, a Jew, ask a drink of me, a woman of Samaria? Jews do not share things in common with Samaritans." Jesus answered her, "If you knew the gift of God and who it is that is saying to you 'give me a drink,' you would have asked him and he would have given you living water." The woman said to him, "Sir, you have no bucket and the well is deep. Where do you get that living water? Are you greater than our ancestor Jacob who gave us this well and with his sons and his flocks drank from it?" Jesus said to her, "Everyone who drinks of this water will be thirsty again, but those who drink of the water that I will give them will never thirst. The water that I will give will become in them a spring of water gushing up to eternal life." And the woman said to him, "Sir, give me this water so that I may never be thirsty or have to keep coming here to draw water." [3]

Jesus is speaking about the firewater, the water that has an eternal source and is an abundant resource, always accessible to us. If we are ready and willing to receive it, the living water will spring up within us as a gushing wellspring of life. It springs up from a mysterious place inside when we open ourselves to the unconditional fountain of love and vibrant life offered by the Divine. Once we are aware of its availability, we are free to partake of it.

Sometimes, as is depicted in the story, we are led to the living water in ways that we do not expect. According to the social law of the time, Jews and Samaritans did not mix, and therefore it was a surprise to the woman of Samaria that she encountered such treasure from an unexpected source. It may be that you are introduced to the firewater by someone or something outside of your comfort zone or from a source that you could not even imagine. Be open and awake. Be willing, as the Samaritan woman is, to overcome your doubts, fears and social rules of engagement.

At first, the woman must get over the *social and cultural aspect* of this sacred dialogue: "How is it that you, a Jew (for yourself, fill in the blank), ask a drink of me, a woman of Samaria (fill in the blank)?" Then she must transcend her *rational mind*, "Sir, you have no bucket and the well is deep, where do you get this living water?" Then she must transcend some *spiritual dogma from her tradition*, "Are you greater than Jacob?"

Once we can transcend hindrances from our limited expectations, rational mind or religious training and open up to the deeper reality of the Divine, we can have access to the living water. I have worked with many people who cannot open to the firewater because they get tripped up in their own doubts or intellectual stumbling blocks, such as: "Connecting with the Divine doesn't make rational sense," or "This text says you must connect with the Divine in this particular culturally defined way."

Following the lead of the woman at the well, we can take a different approach. When offered the living water, we can open ourselves enthusiastically to receive, "Give me this water that I may never be thirsty!" We do not need to go without when the well is right here, ready for us to dip in and drink.

Another powerful image in this story is that of dipping deep into Jacob's well. Here is Jesus at the well of his own ancestors, offering the living firewater at the exact same physical place that has watered and nurtured his people for generations. As we dip into the well of our spiritual ancestors and into the well of the tradition, we can be refreshed and be fed by other spiritual seekers, teachers and mystics. Likewise, as we go to our internal Jacob's well and dip into the spring that gushes forth within our own being, we can taste the firewater of our own inner life. In doing this, we are rejuvenated with the Ha-Shamayim, the firewater given to us by the Divine.

Activating the Healer Archetype

When we access the living water, the Ha-Shamayim, it opens an inner gateway to the archetype of the Healer, bringing an experience of *psychological well-being* and *spiritual fulfillment*. The Healer archetype is responsible for integrating body, mind and spirit, aligning the roots, trunk and branches of our Tree of Life. This brings profound stability to our inner life and feelings of *contentment* and *satisfaction*.

Drinking the firewater and activating the Healer archetype give us the mirroring that we need at the deepest level of our being. We spoke about mirroring in Stage 2, as one of the ways that we internalize a good mother and build the roots of our Tree. During Initiations 6 and 7, as we build the branches of our Tree, we need mirroring from another source, one appropriate to this stage of development. We need mirroring from those brave spiritual teachers who have gone before us, and we need mirroring from the Divine. When we receive deep acknowledgement for our spiritual and divine natures, we begin to hear the voice that says, "You are perfectly acceptable. You are exactly the way you are supposed to be. All is well." The wellspring of living water is full of these unconditionally loving voices, because from the Divine perspective, all is well and each circumstance, person and relationship is exactly the way it is supposed to be.

When we drink of this firewater, healing occurs because we awaken the divine fire within us that carries the unifying energy of the universe. Once awakened, it works to unify all aspects of our physical, psychological and spiritual being. There is a coming together, a drawing together, of all the lost and alienated parts of the self. When we thirst for radical healing, we activate the Healer within us to retrieve all fragmented parts and states of mind that have kept us scattered and unable to heal.

Radical healing requires surrendering to our own inner fire, which has the power to awaken our divine consciousness and burn away everything preventing us from experiencing ourselves as whole. The Healer sees our life as perfectly whole and holy.

One of the challenges of this step of the seventh initiation is getting the Healer's perspective on our life and seeing our self through the Healer's eyes. What would it be like to see our self as whole and holy, right and acceptable, perfect and integrated? What would it be like to walk around today experiencing our life from the Divine's perspective, as if all is well and as it should be?

Exercise 2: Meditation - Activating the Healer

The following is a meditation to activate the Healer in order to see your life from the Divine's perspective.

Close your eyes and listen to the rhythmic breathing of your lungs. Slow down your breathing and relax. Loosen the tightness in your muscles and make yourself receptive.

Imagine yourself in the middle of a beautiful garden. At the center of the garden is a beautiful fountain, with water pouring or spouting in a continuous flow. From this fountain comes the purest, cleanest, clearest water you have ever seen. This is the living water at the heart of your being. Look around the garden and take it in. Sit by the fountain for a time and rest.

It is time now to take a drink. Near the fountain, you see a bucket and a beautiful chalice. Dip the bucket into the water and pour it into your chalice. Now drink of this living water and feel it permeate your being. As you drink the water, it becomes a fountain within your body, gurgling, spouting and moving. Allow this living water to circulate through your body, flowing and refreshing your whole system. As the fountain rises within your being, notice how you are feeling.

As you allow the fountain to circulate within your body, you notice a secret gateway is opened in the garden. You hadn't seen it before. Through this secret gate walks a Healer. As this being walks near to you, notice what your Healer looks like. What age is your Healer? Is it a man or woman? What is the Healer wearing? The Healer acknowledges and honors you and then takes a drink from the fountain. The Healer feels refreshed and rejuvenated. Your Healer then takes you by the hands and looks lovingly into your eyes. Breathe in and receive the healing love. The Healer asks, "What healing do you need right now in your life? What is keeping you from being whole?"

You answer.

Your Healer then reaches for a full-length mirror, a magic mirror from the land beyond the garden. The Healer places the magic mirror in front of you. When you look into the magic mirror, you can see your divine essence. Light is dancing around your body and dancing inside your body. You are transformed, radiant and beautiful. See yourself as the Divine sees you – whole, perfect, healed and holy.

Then you hear your Healer say, "You are unconditionally loved. You are perfectly acceptable. You are exactly the way you are supposed to be. All is well." Breathe deeply and allow any resistances to simply flow out of your body. As you breathe deeply, say to yourself, "I am whole, healed and holy."

The Healer then puts the mirror aside and the two of you sit by the fountain, contemplating what has happened. If you wish, you can dance with your Healer or play or walk around your garden. When you are finished, you bid your Healer farewell and he or she disappears through the secret gate. You bid the garden and the fountain farewell, knowing that you can return anytime.

Breathe deeply and return to your body. Feel the flow of the living water within your body as you bring this sensation back with you into present time and present reality. Feel the weight of your body and when you feel ready, open your eyes.

When you are finished, write down in your journal all that transpired. Who was your Healer? What is significant to you about his or her age, gender or clothing? What healing do you need right now in your life? What is keeping you from being whole? Do you have any resistances to seeing yourself as lovable or acceptable?

The Inner Sanctuary

So far in Step 1, we have longed for the sacred spring and tasted the firewater that renews and rejuvenates our inner life. We have also activated the Healer archetype who begins the radical healing process. To deepen the first step of the seventh initiation and connect to the Divine, we will **build an inner sanctuary** to house the sacred spring so that we have a permanent place inside to access the living water.

For thousands of years, mystical traditions have presented the idea of the inner temple, sanctum or sanctuary. The inner temple, as opposed to an exterior temple, can never be destroyed and therefore represents the initiate's contact with the Divine that is eternal and indestructible. The inner temple is different from our inner psychological house, where we tackle family complexes and develop our emotional body. In the inner temple, we develop our *Ruah* – our spiritual body – and remember our divine body. This is the dancing light body experienced in the previous meditation that is radiant with the ever-present light of the Divine.

One of the main purposes of a mystical group is to help initiates to develop the inner sanctuary by means of various spiritual disciplines. In Kabbalah, guided meditation is frequently used to help initiates create a detailed visual image of their inner temple. Modeled after the great temple in Jerusalem and based on the Kabbalistic notion of the four worlds, the inner temple has a loose architectural structure of 1) an outer courtyard, 2) an inner courtyard, 3) a sanctuary and 4) within the sanctuary, a private "Holy of Holies." Our inner temple can be modeled after this or we can imagine our temple like a Native American round house, the garden from our last meditation, or any kind of architecture we like. Our inner sanctum could have an altar, candles, sacred water, earth, bread, wine, flowers or incense. It can be from any culture or time period. Over time, after repeated meditation, our inner temple will take solid shape and will have a certain look and feel to it.

In ancient Greece, most healing sanctuaries were built near fresh water springs because of the sacred qualities of the water. These sanctuaries were wellsprings of life for healing, cleansing, forgiveness and rest. Like the woman who lived near the sacred spring, we can build our inner sanctuary located centrally around the source of the sacred spring. This we can easily do in meditation by imagining our inner sanctum with a fountain of living water.

When I was in Crete co-leading a women's workshop, we hiked one day to Lyssos, the site of an ancient *asklepion*, a healing sanctuary. It was built on the side of a steep mountainside, out of which was flowing a fresh water spring. During our visit to the ruins, we took some time in silence to meditate at this peaceful site. When I closed my eyes, a scene came to life before me of the original temple, with beautiful mosaic floors and walls. The temple priestesses were attending visitors who came to the sanctuary for the healing waters. The pure, fresh water gushing from the spring was diverted into the interior of the temple, flowing out of the walls into small basins. The priestesses then used the water to bathe, sprinkle, give drink, cleanse, baptize or heal the seekers coming to the sacred sanctuary. This powerful image is forever etched in my mind and I can return to this place whenever I need to access the living water within myself.

When we build the foundation of our inner sanctum near this gushing spring, we can go there regularly to worship and reconnect with the Divine. We can also continually develop and encourage the flow of this living water so that our inner temple becomes the focal point within us where the Divine presence can come to dwell.

The first step in building our inner sanctum or Temple is to imagine an outer courtyard, a place where we can *ground* ourselves and gather ourselves together. The element associated with this level is **Earth**. So we can imagine this to be a place with gardens where we can walk on the earth or sit under a tree and allow nature to soothe, quiet and prepare us to enter the deeper levels of our Temple.

The next level is the inner courtyard, the place where we prepare ourselves *psychologically*. The element associated with this level is **Water**. In the inner courtyard we let go of emotional cares, worries and concerns and allow the cool waters to bring cleansing, healing and forgiveness.

Next we move into the sanctuary, the place of *spiritual* preparation. This can be either an indoor or outdoor setting, and should facilitate a calming and centering of the Spirit. The element associated with this level is **Air**, and we can imagine incense burning or a cool breeze blowing or song vibrating the air. In the sanctuary we gain clarity of mind and heart and clarity of our life purpose. Here we meet the essence of our being.

Now we are ready to *encounter the Divine* in what is referred to as the "Holy of Holies." This can be a special, curtained off section in the sanctuary where we can meet the Divine in an intimate way. The element associated with this level is **Fire**, so we can imagine candles, the eternal flame or even the Ha-Shamayim, the creative firewater in some form.

Exercise 3: Meditation - The Inner Sanctum

The following is a meditation to give us direct experience of our inner Temple and to guide us step by step through the four levels of preparation.

Imagine yourself overlooking a vast landscape. Deep within the heart of this land is your Inner Temple. Today you are on a journey to visit your Temple. Notice what landscape you are in. You travel for many miles. Perhaps you travel over land, perhaps over sea. Take some time and move at your own pace to your temple............ Many miles and many hours later, you are now approaching your temple. What does it look like? Note the architecture and the materials that it is made of. Take some time and observe the outside of your temple.

As you approach the entrance, you meet a gatekeeper who guards and protects your temple while you are away. As you approach, does the gatekeeper recognize you? Does the gatekeeper say anything to you?

The gate is opened and you enter the Outer Courtyard. This is the place where you can ground yourself and prepare yourself as you anticipate moving closer to the center of your Inner Sanctuary.

What do you do to ground yourself? If there are gardens for you to wander around, feel the earth beneath your bare feet. Perhaps you sit or walk on stone. If there are other people present, what are they doing? Take some time to ground and gather yourself.

You are ready now to move into the Inner Courtyard. As you enter the Inner Courtyard you notice there is water to help calm and cleanse you as you prepare your soul to go to the center. What kind of water is available to you here in the Inner Courtyard? The water helps center your heart and settle your emotions. You might simply dip your hands in and wash your face. You may need to cleanse your whole being by taking a bath or a shower in the healing water.

You now feel grounded, centered and emotionally cleansed. You are ready to move into the Inner Sanctuary, the place of the Spirit, the *Ruah*, the breath of the Holy One.

Move to the entrance and go in. The air is markedly different. What does your Sanctuary look like? Take some time to calm and center your spirit. Breathe in the essence of your being. Breathe with the breath of the Great Spirit. In the Sanctuary, there is an altar of your own design and making. It is where you come to access your Spirit, where you have clarity of mind and clarity of purpose for your life. What does your altar look like? Approach the altar and pay homage to Spirit in whatever way feels right to you at this time.

Now you are ready to approach the Holy of Holies. This is the central focal point of your Inner Temple. Go and stand before it. Are there candles or flames to honor the divine fire? You approach the entrance to the Holy of Holies and open it. You step into the chamber and find the Ha-Shamayim, a pool of water that appears to be filled with fire. It doesn't feel overly hot, but invitingly warm. You are drawn to it and step in. There is liveliness about it.

As you stand in this firewater, you are aware of a great light filling the room. It engulfs you and permeates your being. You feel at one with the light and lose all sense of everything but the light. You surrender to it and allow it to fill your entire being with radiance and a sense of well-being. Allow the divine light to awaken your own divine body. Let your light body come alive. Feel the light dancing around you and within you. Breathe and take it in.

After some time, the light begins to fade and disappear. You can still feel the light dancing in your body. Hold on to that sensation and try to bring this back with you when you leave your Temple.

The light has faded and it is time to leave. You bow or make some gesture of acknowledgment and make your way out of the Holy of Holies, back through the Sanctuary. Is there anything different about it? Now move through the Inner Courtyard and through the Outer Courtyard. You pass the gatekeeper on the way out. Perhaps the gatekeeper says something to you.

Make your way back through the landscape. Has it changed any? If so, how? Return to the place from which you began this journey.

As you come back from this place, pause to remember the feeling of the light permeating your being. Take the feeling back with you as you come back into this time and this reality. Be aware of the weight of your body and the rhythm of your breathing and, in your own time, open your eyes.

When you are finished, write down what happened. If you practice this meditation frequently, you will be able to quickly transport yourself back to your Inner Temple, where you can reconnect with the Divine, ask for guidance and feel refreshed and rejuvenated. You can go there when you need to center yourself, calm your anxiety, quiet your mind, make a decision, or get ideas for a creative project. You can go there to remember who you really are: a child of the Divine.

Step 1: Connect to the Divine
* Step 2: Unify all aspects of being *
Step 3: Receive the blessing
Step 4: Heal yourself and others

Mysteries of the Sacred Marriage

In Step 1, we connected to the Divine by longing for the sacred spring, drinking the firewater, activating the Healer archetype and building our inner sanctum around this rejuvenating source. Now in Step 2, we will discover how the divine force can *unify all aspects of our being*. Let's begin by looking at the Mysteries of the Sacred Marriage.

Returning to the seventh Sacred Robe, the Sacred Marriage is depicted as the couple swirling together and forming the body of the Tree of Life itself. Within the trunk of the Tree, we see the product of this fruitful union, the sacred bread and wine. For thousands of years, bread and wine have been celebrated in ceremonies from traditions spanning the globe, as a consummation of the Sacred Marriage. In most traditions, the bread represents the earth or the feminine principle and the wine represents the spirit or the masculine principle. When these elements are partaken of in sacred ceremony, ingesting them is said to *facilitate a unification of all parts of our being*.

On the Robe, the couple has ingested the bread and wine and are in the process of integrating whatever has been separate and individual into a sacred union, where all separations and divisions are accepted, respected and harmonized. The Sacred Marriage is meant to hold, contain and unify what feels estranged, opposed and divided.

According to Kabbalah, the Sacred Marriage happens internally when we are grounded at Malkhut, are able to hold a focus of consciousness of the Divine (Keter), with Wisdom, Understanding and Knowledge (Hokhmah, Binah, Daat), and are able to unite the left and right pillars within our being (see Diagram 26). This means that we can balance our psyche at will so that it is not subject to the swings of instinct or emotion that used to sway us back and forth between left and right pillars of contraction and expansion. At this point, the Sacred Marriage is attained within and we can now unite heaven to earth and earth to heaven. This means that we are able to focus the divine perspective onto earth, in the here and now. We are also then able to raise consciousness from the Earth, up to the Divine. As we participate in this two-directional flow between earth and heaven, we are participating in the mystery of the Sacred Marriage.

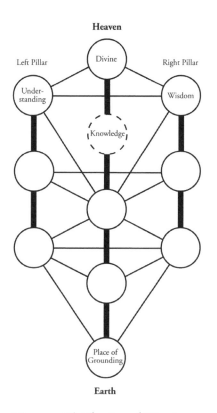

Diagram 26: The Sacred Marriage

The purpose of this mystical union is to create *unity within the individual soul, unity among creation and union with the Divine.* This unification of above and below, and from side to side, forms the sacred shape of the cross, which is the main symbol of divine union in the Christian mystical tradition.

The Jewish tradition preserves this knowledge of unification in the symbol of the Star of David. The downward-pointing triangle represents the Divine reaching towards us and the upward-pointing triangle represents the human soul reaching up towards the Source. The center of the star is where we unite in mystical union with the Creator and where our body, soul and spirit are aligned and enlightened.

Exercise 4: The Mystical Cross and the Star of David

The following are psycho-spiritual practices to help facilitate the Sacred Marriage.

1. **The Mystical Cross** (see Diagram 27) There are different ways to use the Mystical Cross to help in the unification process. Here are two suggestions. It is beneficial to do both cross exercises one after the other.

"Open Heart" Mystical Cross This cross focuses on activating the qualities of justice and compassion and is designed to *open your heart.*

Stand with your arms outstretched from side to side, shoulder height. As you stand and breathe, open your heart and chest region wide and keep stretching out your arms. At your crown chakra, at the top of your head, become conscious of Divine Will. At your feet, become aware of the earth that grounds and roots you and the Divine Will that wants to manifest through you so that you can be a divine representative on earth. With your left hand, imagine holding divine justice. With your right hand, imagine holding divine compassion.

Now balance all four points within your being, from the top of your head to your feet, and side to side with your arms – Divine Will, the Divine manifesting through you, Justice and Compassion. You have made a sacred cross with your body.

Now focus on your heart center and imagine your heart as the central point of this

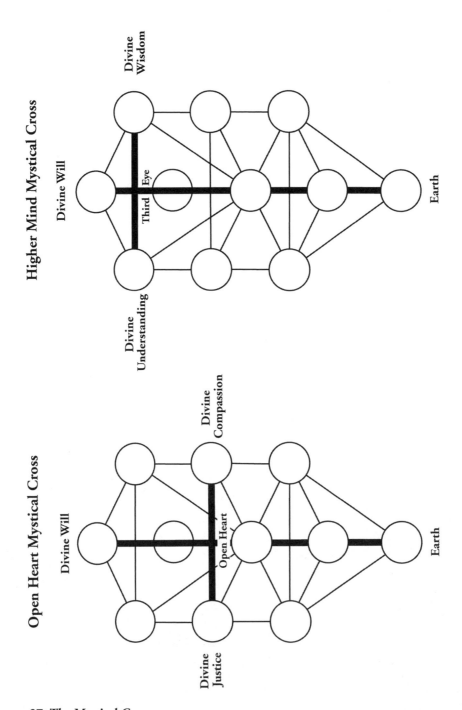

Diagram 27: The Mystical Crosses

The purpose of mystical union is to create unity within the individual soul, unity among creation and union with the Divine. This unification of above and below, and from side to side, forms the sacred shape of the cross. The "Open Heart" mystical cross focuses on justice and compassion and is designed to open the heart. The "Higher Mind" mystical cross focuses on understanding and wisdom and is designed to open the higher mind.

cross. Open your heart center wide and embody justice and compassion within your being. Notice how you feel. Perceive life from this place of heart knowledge. Embody this Mystical Cross by saying, *"May the Divine Will manifest through me as I carry justice and compassion into the world."*

"Higher Mind" Mystical Cross This cross focuses on on activating the qualities of *understanding* and *wisdom* and is designed to *open your higher mind.*

Stand with your arms down, relaxed by your side. At your crown chakra, at the top of your head, become conscious of Divine Will. At your feet, become aware of the earth that grounds and roots you and the Divine Will that wants to manifest through you so that you can be a divine representative on earth.

Shift your focus now to the left and right hemispheres of your brain. On the left side, hold a focus of divine understanding. On the right side, hold a focus of divine wisdom.

Now balance the four points of Divine Will (at the top of your head), Divine manifestation through you (at your feet), Divine Understanding and Divine Wisdom. You have created another sacred cross with your body. Now focus on your third eye (the energy center between your eyes and up about a half inch), and feel this as the central point of the cross. Open your third eye wide and embody understanding and wisdom. Notice how you feel. Perceive life from this place of knowledge with the higher mind. Embody this Mystical Cross by saying, *"May the Divine Will manifest through me as I carry understanding and wisdom into the world."*

Bring your awareness back now to your whole body. Feel the sacred shape of the cross in your body, unifying all parts of yourself. Feel how the cross unifies your whole being. Breathe deeply. Your body is a powerful instrument for justice, compassion, understanding and wisdom. Go forth and live according to these divine principles.

2. **The Star of David** (see Diagram 28) The sacred shape of the Star of David consists of two superimposed triangles, one pointing down and the other pointing up. In the Kabbalistic teachings, the triangle pointing down represents the Divine Tree of Life, rooted in the divine world and reaching its branches down towards us. This is the Great Tree of Illumination. The triangle pointing upwards represents our own individual Tree of Life, rooted in the earth and reaching its branches up towards the Divine. This is the Tree of Initiation that we climb during our life journey. The center of the Star of David is where the two Trees meet, where the Divine meets the individual in space and time, creating a sacred union.

One way to use this sacred star is to place a representation of the Star of David on the floor of your meditation room or a place where you do rituals with a small group of companions. Make the star big enough for someone to stand inside it. After dedicating the ritual to the Holy One and the highest good of the participants, explain the meaning of the star. The purpose of this ritual is to experience the Mystery of the Sacred Marriage between each person and the Divine.

Have people step inside the center, one by one. As each person experiences the center and is witnessed by the others, sacred poetry or scripture can be read that has to do with the Sacred Marriage. Another idea is to have each person stand in the center and the leader can simply repeat phrases such as "this is the meeting ground between you and the Divine" or "In the center of this circle you meet the Divine" or "As you reach up to the Divine, the

Divine is reaching down to you" or "Here in the center of the star your body, soul and spirit are aligned and enlightened." When the ritual is over, thank the Holy One and say a prayer of closing. Do a check-in around the circle and see what was experienced.

Diagram 28:
Star of David

Communion

Another expression of the Mysteries of the Sacred Marriage is the *universal ritual of ingesting bread and wine*, elements that have been blessed and set aside for sacred ceremony. Different traditions place different meaning and emphasis on the sacred bread and wine. In some Wiccan and Goddess traditions, the bread is seen as the feminine principle and the wine as the masculine principle. Ingesting them in sacred ceremony is said to unify the feminine and masculine aspects within the individual and in the world. In the Christian tradition, the bread and wine are seen as the body and blood of Christ. Partaking of the elements is said to unify the seeker with Christ himself and to unify the community as the "body of Christ."

The Friday night Shabbat service in Jewish homes also has a ceremony celebrating the bread and wine. During Shabbat, the wine and bread are blessed with ancient prayers and the Holy One is thanked for the fruit of the vine and for the sustaining bread of life. The wine and bread are then eaten together around the table, solidifying the community. At the very end of the Shabbat evening, it is a tradition for the husband and wife to retire and make love, thereby reenacting and consummating the Sacred Marriage.

The Christian tradition calls the bread and wine ceremony "communion", which literally means "with union". This brings to mind a celebration of community. This implies that we not only make space within our own body to unify all aspects of being, but we also make space in the community for reconciliation and unification. Communion invites the community together to experience wholeness.

In the Christian tradition, communion is celebrated on the *Sabbath* and in the Jewish tradition the sacred bread and wine is blessed and eaten during *Shabbat*. Both rites are celebrated on the *seventh* day, which corresponds to the seventh stage of initiation, the stage of unification. The seventh day is a holy day set apart after the six days of creation, in which God rests in order to see the whole.

According to Genesis, on the seventh day of Creation, God surveyed the six days and declared, "It is good." This declaration of goodness blesses all seven days, all seven initiations, as "good." As the Divine was reflecting on the seventh day and acknowledging everything as good, God was giving a divine seal of totality, acknowledging that all seven levels within us fit together in a whole.

This seal of divine approval and acceptance is ours to take inside, to eat and drink until every ounce of it enters the pores of our being. There is such deep satisfaction when we feel initiated into the Mysteries of the Sacred Marriage. When we connect to this unconditional acceptance of goodness and rightness, we have access to internal voices that say "You are whole and holy. All is well. You are acceptable the way you are. You are deeply loved and acknowledged." This brings satisfaction and contentment at the deepest level.

On the seventh Sacred Robe, the bread and wine are placed in the genital area of the sacred couple, to show the generative quality of the sacred elements, a sexual union of two different parts. When the bread and wine come together, there is regeneration, just as there is when a man and woman come together in sexual union to conceive a child, which initiates the genesis of something completely new.

Alchemical Coniunctio

The Alchemical tradition has preserved the knowledge of the Sacred Marriage in what is called the Coniunctio, the final stage of the transmutation process (for the Alchemical stages on the Tree of Life, see Appendix F). The Coniunctio is depicted visually as a united pair of opposites such as the sun and moon, king and queen, or masculine and feminine. They are depicted as an intertwined pair, sometimes in a bath or lying down or relating intimately to each other in some way. The goal of the Alchemical transmutation process is to realize the Coniunctio and to access this dynamic mystery of intercourse, the mystery of what happens when two opposing forces, emotions, attitudes or opinions are invited into union.

Sometimes the union of opposites is blissful, when the two opposites are complementary. Other times, when two opposing forces come together, there are sparks, explosions and chaos. The Coniunctio is achieved by holding these two dynamic energies together in one space, without either overpowering the other. Think of a skilled negotiator in diplomatic relations or a marriage counselor who must hold the energies of two opposing forces in the room. When you can do this for others and within your own being, you have activated the Alchemical Coniunctio. The purpose of the Coniunctio is to consciously realize the new creation that is birthed from the union of opposites.

The new creation that is birthed when we can integrate body and mind, heart and will, masculine activity and feminine receptivity is *an inner experience of resolution to conflicted feelings, opposing attitudes and ambivalent emotions.* We know that we have reached this stage when there is no longer a struggle between mind and heart – as when the mind attempts to block out the heart or the heart overrides the mind with senseless emotion. During Coniunctio, we have the ability to resolve internal conflicts – not by obliterating them, but by holding them together in a dynamic dialogue. From this sacred union, *new points of view emerge, solutions come, and internal balance is achieved.*

The Coniunctio is reached internally when we have done the work that the initiation journey demands, when we have tightly held the alchemical container and successfully endured the transformations and changes within our vessel through all seven stages. We know that we have experienced the Coniunctio when opposing forces within us have found synthesis, when warring internal factions can make peace, and when we can love our enemies. We grow in our capacity to experience good and bad at the same time without repressing either one in a defensive way. This means integrating shadow aspects and tolerating the things that we despise in ourselves.

The Coniunctio state of being *stops our internal swinging between two extreme positions* such as "my partner can do no wrong" vs. "my partner is all bad," or "this is the fundamentally right way to do things" vs. "this is the wrong way." When the extreme positions transform into more balanced and realistic assessments, life becomes much more stabilized. When our partner is more realistically perceived as good and bad at the same time, this can release profound acceptance and loving compassion. From the position of the Coniunctio, we can observe each experience as neutral and perfect just as it is, rather than all good or all bad.

Finally, and most importantly, the Coniunctio point of view demands that we *hold paradox and even tolerate a position of not knowing*. The Coniunctio position is two-sided, rather than one-sided, and includes and embraces the perspectives of masculine and feminine, the yin and yang, the solar and lunar consciousness. Achieving Coniunctio and establishing secure contact with the central pillar of consciousness at Stage 7, stabilizes us in a profound way and allows us to flow with the awesome mystery of life.

Cultivating the inner lover

So far in Step 2, we have looked at ways to unify aspects of our being, experience the Sacred Marriage, and begin the process of Coniunctio. Now we will focus on moving into closer union with ourselves by cultivating the inner lover.

One of the mysteries of life is that each person seems to be blessed with an inner lover, an inner figure who, at some point in our development, comes to life and brings awakening, growth, maturity, resolution and healing. In Depth Psychology, the inner lover is often referred to as the "Anima" for men and the "Animus" for women, the contra-sexual inner partner. In our Native American story, the inner lover is the Sacred Snake, who changes form as the cultivation of this relationship matures.

The task of the inner lover is to entice us into an inner union, which helps us feel completed, satisfied and loved. Think of a time when you fell in love and remember the feelings of warmth, bliss and contentment that were generated. Our inner lover draws us towards consummation and union by engaging us in ever-deepening levels of intimacy. Once we become conscious of this character within us who desires inner union, we will be drawn towards him or her and will move through various stages of this inner relationship.

When the eldest daughter in the Sacred Snake story first meets her inner lover in the form of a baby, she feels protective and nurturing. Then the baby changes into the coiled snake and she encounters this inner lover as a heavy and crushing entity. Then Sacred Snake becomes an even heavier burden and she must carry his entire body out of the village. At the point when she encounters this inner lover as the true Warrior, she is afraid and becomes resistant. Finally, she surrenders to the inner lover and allows him to carry her into the spring, where she can experience resolution, comfort and satisfaction.

One important way to cultivate our inner lover is to watch our dreams and see how this character tries to relate to us through our unconscious dream language. The more attention we give this inner lover and the more we listen to what he or she wants and needs from us, the more benevolent a dream figure he or she will become.

Let's return to the story of Sacred Snake to learn about the process of cultivating the lover inside so that we feel internally satisfied and ready to enter into true dialogue and intercourse.

Every day, the eldest daughter goes to the sacred spring and dips her basket into the fresh water, which attracts her spirit lover. Like Pluto in the Persephone story, Sacred Snake admires the woman. He desires her and longs for her. At first, the woman at the spring is unaware of her spirit lover. She is aware of her longing, but this longing is not yet grounded in the personal, it is only targeted at the impersonal spring. The eldest daughter is still unaware that her longing is for true intimacy and intercourse, but she has enough longing to awaken Sacred Snake to life.

When the eldest daughter arrives daily at the side of the pool and dips her basket in the sacred spring, she is erotically engaging with her inner lover. She simply does what she loves to do - be near the spring.

If we want to cultivate the lover within us, we need to do what brings us joy, and dip our basket into our sacred spring. We can do this by being intentional about our devotional life, by reading poetry, dancing in the living room or singing and chanting and drumming and praying. We can make offerings at our "spring," drink the sacred water, and engage our Muse. Sooner or later, our Sacred Snake will find us, and the marriage ritual will begin. The inner Coniunctio will come to life.

When Sacred Snake appears to the woman as an infant, they have an appropriate exchange as they are first getting to know each other. The eldest daughter suckles the baby. So it is inside us when we begin to cultivate the inner lover. Initially, this relationship will resemble the one between the woman and Sacred Snake, which begins in a fresh, new, infantile state. We provide this part of us with basic care and sustenance. This means that we pursue our Sacred Snake in the form of life-giving hobbies and interests, spending time exploring what brings us joy.

The next stage of cultivating our inner lover occurs when the demands of the inner lover become greater. We wake up one morning and suddenly our Sacred Snake is huge, crushing and constraining, as it was for the woman in the story when Sacred Snake transformed from a baby into the enormous snake, who fills her house so that she can barely breathe. This inner situation feels similar to the stage in any relationship after the honeymoon period of bliss, when the relationship starts to bring up our shadow aspects or demands us to be more honest and open. Any intimate encounter – whether with an outer or inner lover – forces us to stretch beyond our comfort zone. When the inner lover (our calling from Spirit) becomes demanding or our passion becomes consuming, we may feel suffocated and want to be left alone, free and unconstrained.

In the story, the only way to move on from this stage of relating to Sacred Snake is to get help from the father, who rescues his daughter by convincing the snake to let her go so that he can give her a final blessing before their sacred union. The father in the story represents the father principle inside us that steers us towards growth and differentiation. He forces the daughter to grow up, take responsibility and become conscious of her relationship with her inner lover.

Like the daughter, at some point we have to face up to what this intimate inner encounter with Spirit demands of us emotionally and spiritually. We need to decide whether we are willing to dedicate our whole being to this longing, if we are willing to face the shadow parts that come up for review and if we are willing to take conscious responsibility for our Sacred Snake, whatever that may be.

If we commit ourselves to our passion and go through with the wedding as the woman does in the story, in time, our relationship with the inner lover changes from a crushing one to a more mature one. Our passion takes on more weight, more seriousness. Perhaps we spend more and more time perfecting our art, writing, skills, voice or dance.

Like an outer marriage, the inner marriage is a life-long partnership that is forged over time with much experience and hard work. Like the eldest daughter, we too must carry the weight of Sacred Snake on our back. We must tenaciously ride through the ups and downs of our inner marriage, the trials and joys, the struggles and agonies. This is not something that suddenly happens and we arrive in blissful Coniunctio. We must cultivate this relationship over time.

However, the hard work of forging an internal intimate partnership does pay off in the end. At some point, the magic begins to happen and our Sacred Snake is no longer a burden, but transforms from a burden into the inner partner who is ready and willing to assist, love, and escort us to our real home – the sacred spring. This can become evident in our dreams, as dream characters will stop blocking our path or stop chasing us, and we may dream of union with an inner lover. *This inner lover prepares a space inside us so that we can receive and contain the gifts flowing from the sacred spring.*

Imagine the inner lover as the Divine who shows up in our psyche as a personal character, wooing us into relationship. This inner lover knows us in a way that no one else can. The inner lover knows our heart and our mind, what we need, how to engage us, how to fulfill us and satisfy us in a way that we never dreamed of. Remember the words of Sacred Snake, "Now that I have you, you are mine and I am yours. We shall live long. We shall have a good life. Come, let me help you."

Surprisingly, many people have difficulty handling the unconditional love and acceptance available during this seventh initiation, even though it is what they have longed for. We must grow big enough inside to receive, hold and contain the unconditional love that is offered by the inner lover.

The eldest daughter at first doubts the miracle and grace when the inner lover reveals his true nature. He is not heavy and burdensome, but *light and the bringer of true freedom*. Instead of immediately embracing him, she wants to run back to her family. "You are not Sacred Snake. Sacred Snake is huge and heavy. You are not he! Will you let me return to my family? Will you let me go?" Like the daughter, sometimes we are afraid of the freedom that our destiny brings when we finally realize what we could be doing with our lives.

The end of the story however, brings resolution as the woman does follow Sacred Snake/Warrior into the spring, consummating the partnership forever. When the inner Coniunctio is consummated, not only do we feel whole and complete internally, but our outer relationships transform because we no longer need others in the same hungry way.

For example, when I no longer see you as "my parent who should meet my needs," my projection falls away and I am free to relate to YOU, not you with the overlay of all my projections. Only then can I develop a true and free relationship with you, a sacred dialogue. This is a simple way of talking about the true nature of intercourse. True intercourse is when two separate and differentiated people, entities or energies come together in union and produce a third thing, a creative new life - a "baby".

When we follow our inner lover home to the sacred spring, we can expect to experience some or all of the following states of mind:
- we can tolerate the "otherness" in our partner
- love our enemies
- love others with less attachment to our own gain
- receive love
- be free of chronic depression
- release our addictions
- grow in patience and acceptance
- forgive ourselves
- forgive others
- laugh in the face of adversity
- experience deep joy
- be available for more and more intimacy
- open to other people's thoughts, feelings and ideas without feeling swamped or overwhelmed
- actively listen to partners, friends, children, parents and colleagues
- facilitate reconciliation in the world, in our relationships, families and the larger community.

Birthing the divine child - fruiting our Tree

After we successfully cultivate the inner lover, move through our resistances and overcome the blockades to our union, we will be able to consummate our union and be carried off into our sacred spring. The main purpose in cultivating the inner lover is to *blast through everything within us that has been closed off to true relating* – the parts of us that are afraid, ashamed, embarrassed or walled off. Once we have blasted through, we are open to relate, open to be penetrated, open to new ideas, open to be fertilized, open to learn, open to love and open to live. Our body and senses open, our heart opens, our mind opens and our spirit opens. We have finally cultivated the capacity for our Tree of Life to be pollinated and fertilized by the union with our inner lover.

The natural outcome of this union is the conception and birth of something new. When we become impregnated with the seed of Spirit, our inner lover or deep inner self, and birth our own creativity, our Tree of Life begins to flower and fruit. The fruit of this union is often called the "divine child." When we birth the divine child, the roots, trunk and branches of our Tree come into alignment and coordinate into a beautiful system that brings forth luscious fruit.

When we practice our craft and dance our sacred dance, we give birth to the divine child. When we fulfill our deepest nature by doing what we love, we express the unity of existence. In this way, we become the gardener and landscape architect of our Tree – watering, planting, nurturing, pruning and weaving our Tree's branches into the forest of the collective. Whatever our particular divine child or fruit, it will express our deepest nature and will also feed the kingdom, and this fruit is a vital contribution to society. In Kabbalah, we call this kind of manifestation "bringing it all the way down" - grounding our gifts in Malkhut, the Kingdom.

Exercise 5: Exercises of unification

1. **Communion** - One way to activate initiation and partake of the divine unifying force is to participate in a ritual reenactment of the Sacred Marriage. You can do this by having a bread and wine ritual, where the bread is seen as the feminine and the wine as the masculine aspects of being. Imagine bringing all the various parts of yourself to the ritual table and as you eat the bread and wine, imagine the Divine knitting your being into a unified whole.

If you are from a Christian background, which has a tradition of celebrating communion, you can go to church and remember to stay conscious of the mystical meaning of the bread and wine. During the ceremony, imagine the unifying power of Christ knitting all the various parts of you together. Imagine your body and blood unifying with the body and blood of Christ. See the web of love from Christ surround you and all beings.

2. **The union of opposites** - Make a list of the main characters in your life, the people with whom you have intimate contact: mother, father, siblings, children, spouse, business partner, lover, boss, mentor, therapist, spiritual teacher, best friend. Include anyone with whom you have an intensely negative relationship. On a piece of paper, make two columns labeled "Positive" and "Negative" and write down both the positive and negative feelings that each relationship stirs in you. Then ask yourself, what is the nature of this union – explosive, blissful, stirring, loving, challenging, calming, hateful? Do you have any idea as to why you are being asked to form a "Coniunctio" with this person or what the purpose of this union is for you?

Now place one unlit candle on your altar. Go through each relationship, or pick the most important one at the moment, and imagine holding both the good and bad aspects and good and bad feelings together. Imagine placing the opposing energies on either side of the candle. Light the candle and imagine the flame of the candle uniting you and that person in a kind of Coniunctio. Allow the opposing forces and feelings to just be. Allow the good, the bad, the uncomfortable, the joy, the pain and the disappointment to simply be. Do not try to fix or change it or make it better. Pray for divine light to surround this relationship and be present, blessing the union. Ask for guidance as to the nature and purpose of this union.

3. **Cultivating the inner lover** – One way to cultivate your inner lover is to watch how your dreams present your inner lover character to you. Whenever a significant dream character engages you in some way, write down the dream. The inner lover often appears as a person of the opposite sex, but he or she can appear in many guises or in an unexpected form, such as an animal, and can be either positive or negative. For example, your inner lover may appear in a dream in which he is angry with you (perhaps you have not been listening to him), is chasing you or is violent towards you (perhaps he cannot get through to you any other way). Try not to judge the way that your inner lover is getting your attention.

After writing down the dream, ask yourself the following: What does this character *want* from me? How am I *responding* to this character? What *blocks* us from relating positively? How do I resist my inner lover? What can I do to cultivate this relationship? Over time, as you pay attention to this character, your inner lover can *transform* into the helping partner who can escort you to your real home, the sacred spring.

4. **Manifesting the fruit of your Tree** - Spend some time imagining what kind of fruit your Tree is bringing forth. Are you sharing your fruit with others? Are you feeding the Kingdom? How is this manifesting?

Step 1: Connect to the Divine
Step 2: Unify all aspects of being
* **Step 3: Receive the blessing** *
Step 4: Heal yourself and others

So far in the seventh initiation, we have tasted the revitalizing waters of the sacred spring and have activated the Sacred Marriage so we feel psychologically integrated and spiritually unified. The next step is to *search for and receive the blessing for our life task*. In order to receive this blessing, we must know what our path is and recognize Sacred Snake, the calling towards our destiny, when it appears. Like the woman at the spring, we can invite the father's blessing – the priestly, Shamanic, elder blessing – by holding diligently to our sacred focus. The blessing is given when we find our life task and are willing to dedicate our life to it.

Crowning

Returning to the seventh Sacred Robe, we can see the two figures that are facing each other in a sacred dialogue, working together towards the goal of unification. On their heads are two luscious crowns, demonstrating that the royalty of this divine pair is crowned and legitimized. This acknowledgement comes from someone (or a body of people) invested with the power to crown and consecrate. The person who has the power to crown another is someone with a connection to the divine source, someone who has already been initiated into the seventh stage. Our own crowning happens when we receive a blessing from our elders, those who have walked the path before and have mastered the initiation journey.

When I lived in London, I often visited the Tower of London to see the Crown Jewels, an exquisite collection of royal crowns, staffs and jewels worn by kings and queens throughout the ages. The crowns themselves are made of the most precious materials: diamonds, sapphires, rubies, emeralds and the finest gold. Each crown is constructed either as an open laurel design or as a rounded cap with a pointed apex.

A crown is placed over the crown chakra and is designed to focus the divine will that comes from "above" - from a higher state of consciousness - consecrating the crowning ceremony and acknowledging the completion of the initiation journey. The hollow crown design creates an open channel for light and higher consciousness to pour into the seventh chakra and the pointed crown design acts as a lightning rod. Both types focus our connection with the Divine.

Anyone who has ever watched a coronation ceremony can see this principle in action. While one waits in line at the Tower of London to see the Crown Jewels, a video plays, showing the coronation ceremony of Queen Elizabeth II. When the Archbishop of Canterbury crowns Elizabeth, one can sense the moment when this divine connection is made, just as the crown is placed upon her head and she is consecrated as the Queen. This is a profound moment, when the timelessness of the Divine breaks in upon ordinary, historical time.

This miracle can happen for us as well, when we are symbolically crowned and consecrated for our life task. When the sacred comes into ordinary time and we become the focus of divine will, we will experience a profound shift. We will become an awakened spark of divine light bursting into flame.

Finding an elder to bless you

Many of us feel invisible when our genius is not seen and acknowledged. This can plunge us into depression, apathy or despair. Sometimes we waste our gifts or we give up because of the fatigue that comes when we are not seen. When we *are* seen however, our Tree of Life can happily bear its natural fruit. A blessing relieves our weariness and fatigue and gives us renewed strength to carry on.

Who will be your Archbishop of Canterbury? Who will crown you? Who will notice your genius? Who will know how to bless you? How can you attract or call up this blessing?

In the story of Sacred Snake, the eldest daughter has a father who understands the need for blessing, and he fights for her to have one. He must wrestle with Sacred Snake and use his powers of persuasion and knowledge of Spirit. The father says, "I am your priest. I ask you to let my daughter leave. She is yours but let her come to us for blessings before you take her."

The woman's father is a priest and medicine man. Like the eldest daughter, we have to access the medicine man/priest or medicine woman/priestess within us who values the sacred and knows when a blessing is needed. The father does not understand the woman's calling and he even advises against it. Nevertheless, he graciously acknowledges her need for a blessing and initiates action to get it accomplished. He says to her, "Since you love water and need water around you all day, it is perhaps best that you go with Sacred Snake." The father in the story represents the part of us that can fight for and attract a blessing to us.

The best elder to offer a blessing is the one who does know and understand the significance of our particular genius. Perhaps he or she has a similar Sacred Snake, a similar Muse. We need to find that Archbishop of Canterbury in our life who will say, "I bless your life task."

I need to add here that sometimes our elder is no longer alive, but we can still gain strength from her or him. Many people are tremendously uplifted by the artists or writers, or others in their particular line of genius, who are no longer alive but whose life story and pursuit of their craft brings inspiration to those of us struggling to produce our fruit.

It is still crucial, however, to find a live elder who can see you now. What this does is set you apart from other people – not in an inflated, narcissistic way, but in a way that allows you to do your particular, unique task and fulfill your life purpose. *The purpose of a blessing and crowning is to give you the confidence and the support from the community of elders that enables you to do your work of service.* A blessing creates the ultimate feeling of belonging in the human community.

There is a wonderful blessing story in the book of Genesis (chapter 32) about Jacob who wrestled with the angel. During a crucial point in his development, Jacob found just the right elder to bless him – an elder in the form of an angel. Together they wrestled "all night long" and Jacob would not let the angel go until he got a blessing. In this story, Jacob is a man at the crossroads, at the threshold of his initiation, who has enough courage to ask for what he needs and demand his blessing. He knows that he needs to be blessed and seen by this particular angel.

If we look at the blessing psychologically, human beings naturally tend to project the divine archetype onto someone outside themselves. We project our own unrealized elder, sage or saint onto an external elder because we have not yet developed it ourselves. So we need our angel/elder to give our blessing back to us. Jacob recognized that this was the right angel to bless him because he found something in this angel that he wanted. And so it is with us that the right person is usually the person that we admire or respect, the person who has a quality we want to cultivate in ourselves.

In order to receive a powerful blessing, it is helpful to find an elder who has knowledge and experience of your particular path. If oil painting is your path, find a painter that you deeply respect to give you a blessing. If nursing is your path, find an experienced nurse to bless your work. If your path is teaching, find a learned teacher to bless you. If raising a family is your path, find an awakened parent to bless and crown your task. These elders are the ones who can truly see you. Ask your elder for some of her time, ask for advice, ask for her experience, her knowledge, her vision and guidance.

In the story of Jacob, the result of his blessing was a permanent wound in his hip. He awoke in the morning after wrestling the angel and found that he had a limp that affected him for the rest of his life. It was a sign of his initiation. These sacrificial scars – either wounds on the body or in the psyche – frequently accompany initiations. They are a kind of testimony to remind us of our journey. They symbolize crossing the threshold and remind us that we have received the blessing.

Think about times in your life when you have been wounded psychologically or physically, and consider whether you were attempting to get a blessing. Contemplate also whom you are drawn to get blessings from – a grandfather figure, a boss or favorite guru or teacher? Do you want blessing from a man or a woman?

When we are young we often instinctively look for someone to crown or bless us, but in fact blessing is something we can ask for at any point in our life. It is important to ask for blessing anytime you need it, at any age, no matter what our stage of physical, emotional or spiritual development. This is an archetypal stage, not an age-specific stage.

Exercise 6: Finding an elder to bless you

1. Who would you like to be your Archbishop of Canterbury? Who would you like to bless you? Who might notice your genius? Who might know how to bless you? Are you drawn to a man or a woman?

2. Why is this person the perfect choice for you?

3. What specifically do you want from them - acknowledgement, advice, time, help, resources, guidance, counseling, mentoring, apprenticeship, friendship, a blessing ceremony?

4. What are you willing to ask for? When will you do it?

Feeling empowered to serve

In order to live our vision and fulfill the purpose for which we were born, we need to feel empowered to do so. We need confidence and inner strength. We need to be seen and witnessed. When our genius is crowned and acknowledged, we feel internally equipped to step into our power and serve.

Some years ago, I had an interesting dream about crowning, blessing and empowering. It addressed my own struggle to be acknowledged by my elders and to feel empowered by their strength and wisdom. The dream also offered a resolution to old feelings of disempowerment and disappointment, bitter feelings that were hindering me from fulfilling my purpose and offering my fruit. It is a dream of hope and of feeling empowered to move ahead with my mission and purpose. I call this dream "Baptism by Wine."

> *I am at a church youth conference as a guest leader with my husband. There are hundreds of youths and many leaders present. At some point during the conference, a magic show begins on the main stage. The magician is a woman who specializes in spinning small, snakelike coils of clay on top of people's heads. One by one, teenagers and leaders are coming up onto the stage to have the magic snake spinning demonstrated on their heads. As each person steps up onto the stage, the woman magician attaches the clay snake shapes to the head and then spins them. The crowd is amazed; what a fantastic sight it is to see 50 clay snakes spinning on people's heads, like a wig of writhing hair.*
>
> *Soon it is my turn to approach the woman magician. I walk up on stage and, to my surprise, she puts the clay snakes aside and instead hands me a large glass of full-bodied red wine. She indicates that I should spin it on my head. One by one she hands me glass after glass, and I place them on my head, spinning each one myself. Defying gravity, the red wine remains within the wine glasses as I place more and more upon my head – until finally my entire head is covered with glorious, spinning wine glasses. I feel triumphant.*
>
> *Suddenly, as if synchronized together, the glasses stop their spinning and the red wine pours out over my body, like a red baptism of rich and fragrant perfume, soaking everything from my head to my toes. No glass breaks in the process. I am stunned. Silence fills the auditorium. Welling up inside of me is a feeling of ecstasy, excitement and a kind of freedom that I have never known. I look up at the crowd of church people through drops of wine. I throw my head back and from the depths of my being shout, "I am a Jewess and a Christian!"*

Crowning and baptism are blessings that do not come easily – they come through the hard work of the initiation journey and seeking out the right people to bless us. The dream offers an interesting and creative crowning ceremony that has transformed what was a crown of snakes into a crown of baptismal wine.

The dream also evokes some questions like: Who is the magician woman spinning her snakes? Why does the magic trick involve the head region of the body? What is significant about the setting and the community of witnesses?

My first association with the magician woman is Medusa, the mythological Gorgon with hair of snakes who has the power to turn anyone she looks upon to stone. On the one hand, the magician woman has the power to recreate a "Medusa" effect on each person she works on, which is potentially destructive and deadly. On the other hand, she transforms into a benevolent, initiating mother who baptizes me with wine.

For many years I wrestled internally with destructive aspects of Medusa, an inner mother who did not see me with loving eyes but stony eyes, resulting in feelings of disempowerment and loss. At times it felt as if the Medusa mother/magician was actually "spinning snakes on my head," because for years I suffered with debilitating migraine headaches, sometimes three or four times a week. The Medusa mother represents my felt experience of the elder who could not see me, acknowledge me or offer me a blessing. With this kind of internalized mother figure, it felt both excruciating to be seen - for then I turned to stone - and excruciating not to be seen – for then I felt abandoned. I believe that the migraines were in part a response to this inner dilemma that kept me from seeking and obtaining a blessing from a real elder and kept me from serving as the rabbi/minister/teacher that I was destined to be.

The snakes could also represent bits of untransformed snake energy, primitive bits of the psyche that are unprocessed and therefore potentially poisonous or venomous. The way that these poisonous snakes manifested for me was to feel split between my head and my body, which literally made my head ache. It was difficult to access the soothing internal mother who could help relieve the mind/body split. One of the internal challenges for me – and for many people raised in Western culture – is to get the mind and body back together again into a sacred dialogue. In order to do this, I spent years descending into the depths to face my inner Medusa mother, to try to transform her. After a long, confrontational battle and learning to internalize a good mother, I made some progress. By the time I had this dream, my Medusa mother had moved through a transformation. She was no longer a magician handing me poisonous and spinning snakes that kept me in a distracted, manic or defensive state. She transformed into a feminine figure capable of baptizing me with the living water and able to help me get my mind and body back together again.

The dream marks the archetypal passageway out of the descent, when we are freed from the grip of the negative complex. After the hard work of initiation, our inner figures transform. Even our stoniest Medusa can transform into an initiating elder who can baptize us with a full-bodied red wine. The Medusa changed into the helpful magician because I had, in my waking life, been demanding another kind of blessing, one that would honor my whole being, both mind and body. In the dream, as wine spills over my entire body, this baptism acts as an integrating force, knitting my mind and body together, facilitating an experience of body wholeness.

In addition to my physical suffering and the feeling of being split between body and mind, other things were also contributing to my feelings of disempowerment and failure to move ahead with my life purpose and serve in my full capacity. During my twenties, as I was training to be a therapist and also a minister, I lived in constant tension regarding my identifications with both Judaism and Christianity. I struggled with the Christian view of Judaism and the Jewish view of Christianity. I felt deeply connected to the teachings of Jesus and yet disconnected from the Christian expression of these teachings. Having both Jewish and Christian ancestry, I struggled with many questions: Who am I - Jewish or Christian, a

Christian Jew or Jewish Christian, neither one or somehow both? These deep questions of identity were painful and yet fruitful, for they led me to broaden my worldview tremendously in the end – but that came later.

When I was in the midst of this struggle, I was counting on the "Church" to see me, hear me, acknowledge me and bless me. What I did not yet understand, was that I really needed help transforming my negative mother complex. This expectation was impossible for anyone to fulfill, especially the church as it was struggling to acknowledge women and Jewish perspectives of faith, as well as the kinds of ideas and questions that I was raising. When the church and its elders were unable to help me with my struggles, I was deeply disappointed and disillusioned. I could not yet recognize my projections onto the church, and as a result I felt unseen, unheard and betrayed. I was also deeply divided and split off from an important aspect of my identity, my Jewish heritage. In the dream, I was released from the grips of both the Medusa mother and my expectations and projections onto the church. I was then able to declare and embrace my Jewish inheritance, retrieving a lost part of myself, which I had long denied.

With this beautiful dream of baptismal blessing, I felt reconciled between my body and mind, between my Christian and Jewish inheritance and between the exoteric community of spirit (the church) and my internal, ecstatic experience of the Divine. The snakes had finally turned to wine and the negative energy of my complex had transformed into a life-giving, empowering force. In my moment of ecstasy at the end of the dream, I felt blessed, crowned, and seen. This helped me catch a glimpse of my future, my destiny – which is to help reconcile that which is split, bringing opposites of body and mind, psyche and spirit, masculine and feminine together into sacred dialogue. The only way that I can achieve this with integrity is to achieve this unified state within myself, by coexisting peacefully with my opposing natures. Only then can I effectively teach these principles externally in the world, offering my students the possibilities of ecstatic union both psychologically and spiritually. The blessing elder empowers me to serve and fulfill my life purpose.

Exercise 7: Feeling empowered to serve

1. Is there anything in your life that is disempowering you and keeping you from feeling excited, able and energized to move forward with your life task?

2. Have you been looking for a blessing in the wrong place or from the wrong person – from someone who cannot or will not bless you? Are you willing to move your focus towards someone better suited to bless you, one who will not disappoint you?

3. If your genius has not been acknowledged or your gifts not supported, do you carry old feelings of bitterness or disappointment? Are you ready to let them go?

4. What do you need in order to feel empowered to carry out your task? What do you need in order to feel confidence, inner strength, seen and acknowledged, supported and legitimized? When will you meet that need?

Step 1: Connect to the Divine
Step 2: Unify all aspects of being
Step 3: Receive the blessing
* Step 4: Heal yourself and others *

Reconciliation

So far in Stage 7, we have connected to the Divine, worked to unify all aspects of our being, and received the blessing for our life task. The final step in the seventh initiation is to *receive healing and inner peace* so that we can become a healing sanctuary for others, exuding an atmosphere of love, vitality and peace. In the final step of this initiation we will experience profound healing through *practicing reconciliation, receiving the baptism of fire, and working with healing symbols.*

Let's return to the "Baptism by Wine" dream in the previous section to begin our discussion on reconciliation.

At the end of the dream, a resolution occurs as two opposing and unreconciled parts of myself are brought together in an interesting ritual of reconciliation. These two parts are named "Jewish and Christian" in the dream, but for our purposes they could represent any two seemingly oppositional forces within us that have somehow been separated and distanced. Other opposites can be seen in the dream such as body and mind, good mother and negative mother, magician and initiator, pain and pleasure.

It is important to learn how to creatively embrace the many oppositions and tensions that we hold in our life on a daily basis. Rather than holding the tension, we often split our world into separate categories of good and bad or body and mind because we cannot handle the pressure that these opposing forces create. It is, however, possible to heal and reconcile these splits and live with a container inside that is big enough to gracefully hold all the various parts of our life.

From the perspective of the Divine, nothing is separated and distanced. All facets of the self are various expressions of the One. Thus, *true reconciliation can only occur when we are able to live with this inner attitude, that all is One and all diversity is simply another interesting and lively expression of the One.* This inner attitude matures as we develop more compassion and tolerance, until we get to the point where all points of view and all differences can be contained within one internal space.

It is not that all our various identities merge or that we lose self-definition during this stage of reconciliation. On the contrary, we can hold all of our diversity without merging and without splitting. We can be "both/and" rather than "either/or". At the end of the dream, I no longer need to split myself into two opposing parts (Jewish or Christian) but can live with both these identities occupying the same house, "I am a Jewess *and* a Christian."

All around us we see evidence that people are not moving towards reconciliation and healing. They refuse to reconcile with their perceived enemy and steadfastly maintain the projection that the evil is "out there" and "in others." This leads people to try to eradicate what is "bad" and to kill off their enemy. In this scenario, there is no possibility for the reconciliation container to expand.

One of the reasons that it is so hard to expand our inner container of reconciliation is because it is much easier to believe that the enemy is "out there" rather than embracing the idea that the enemy is also "in here".   If we have the courage to see our own potential destructiveness, badness, evil, unconsciousness and ignorance, it becomes much easier to move towards embracing all parts of ourselves and embracing all parts of others. Expanding our container often involves seeing our own brokenness, weeping over the splits within our own being, and surrendering to the Divine – whose container is infinite and filled with enough conscious love to melt and heal the splits in ourselves and our world. We must be able to see that the badness in the world is not only located in "you," it is also located in "me."

Exercise 8: *The circle of reconciliation*

In this exercise, we will use the powerful image of the sacred circle of reconciliation, the infinite circle originating from the Divine that is big enough to surround all oppositional forces. This exercise is designed to expand our sacred circle in an ever-widening circumference, so that we can grow to the point where we become healing sanctuaries for other individuals and groups struggling with the difficulties of reconciliation.

1. **Reconciling core parts of yourself** - Make a list of any two parts of you that feel in opposition or in tension, parts that you want to reconcile. For example, you might feel tension between your roles of father/husband or mother/wife. Or you may feel tension between your sexual self/spiritual self. Write down any "pairs" in your life that you want to reconcile. After each pair, write what the tension is that you feel and what kind of reconciliation you need.

After writing about each pair, create a circle in your meditation room with a rope or string or scarves – anything you choose that is big enough to sit in with room to spare. Invite all the various aspects of yourself that need reconciliation into the circle. Invite the Divine to be present and then you can say this prayer of reconciliation:

"From the perspective of the Divine, nothing is separated and distanced. All facets of the self are various expressions of the One. May Divine compassion and unconditional love enter this circle and work to heal all within me that needs reconciliation."

2. **Reconciling personal relationships** - Now imagine inviting someone into this sacred circle with whom you want reconciliation. This could be a father, mother, child or political figure. This person can be alive or dead, it does not matter. When you can imagine this person within your circle, verbalize what kind of reconciliation you want and also allow space for that person to "speak" to you through active imagination. Invite the Divine into this circle and then say the prayer of reconciliation:

"From the perspective of the Divine, nothing is separated and distanced. All people are various expressions of the One. May Divine compassion and unconditional love enter this circle and work to heal all hate, all prejudice, and all divisions that need reconciliation."

3. **Reconciling the world** - Now imagine extending the circle of reconciliation to all beings, not just those with whom you are personally involved. Imagine tribal and national enemies coming into the sacred circle. Imagine all beings brought into the great circle of reconciliation. Repeat the prayer:

"From the perspective of the Divine, nothing is separated and distanced. All beings are various expressions of the One. May Divine compassion and unconditional love enter this circle and work to heal all hate, all prejudice, and all divisions that need reconciliation."

Baptism by fire

The last image at the top of the seventh Sacred Robe is the great illuminated Tree of Life, with flames shooting out of the branches. These flames extend into fruits of divine light, which are continually illuminating all beings and enlivening all things with divine consciousness. This fire is the divine presence that we invite into the sacred circle of reconciliation and the same fiery presence that we invite into our life and heart on a daily basis to receive healing and inner peace.

In the sixth initiation we spoke of the baptism of air or Spirit, and its rejuvenating effects on individuals and the wider collective. In the seventh initiation we encounter the baptism of fire, an initiation that awakens our divine nature and activates our fruit to burst forth from the branches of our Tree. When we are able to consciously realize the divine fire within ourselves, we know where we come from, who we are and where we are going – we recognize that we are one spark of the universal Tree of Light.

In previous initiations we have encountered the kind of fire that burns away the destructive aspects of the *Nefesh*, the fire that tames the power drives, the fire that eradicates the dross and forges the pure gold of the soul. Now that we are further along the initiation journey and our internal container is more developed, *the fire that once burned us in uncomfortable or painful ways now enlivens us, bringing enlightenment and insight from the divine perspective.*

The baptism of fire can be activated during deep prayer or meditation or during a moment of awakening in an ordinary circumstance. It happened to me one afternoon when I was hiking near a river in Spain. I stopped to rest and was admiring a small, beautiful tree standing by the banks of the river. Suddenly, without warning, a kind of veil peeled back and I "saw" the tree as a tree of light; I saw the divine aspect of the tree. The trunk, branches and leaves seemed to be made of dancing fire. Then everything around me seemed to be connected in a kind of web. The divine insight I received seemed so simple – all things are interconnected. The result of this subtle baptism by fire left me feeling joyful, more trusting in life, less anxious and more grounded in my being.

Sometimes the baptism of fire can be more dramatic and can happen during a crisis. For example, during an acrimonious divorce, a father has a moment of *profound enlightenment* and realizes the terrific pain and suffering he is causing his children. He recognizes the bigger picture and the long-term effects this suffering will have on his children and on subsequent generations of children if parents cannot find more compassionate solutions to their own problems. The father is convicted to stop fighting for his own selfish needs and desires some kind of reconciliation. He finds a new attitude of forgiveness, his heart begins to melt and he can now consider the needs of his children and ex-wife. With the insight from his baptism of fire, he exercises a powerful act of divine love in the world.

Another dramatic story of baptism by fire is the Christian account of Pentecost recorded in the book of Acts, chapter 2:1-11. After the death of Jesus, his disciples had gathered in Jerusalem for the Feast of Weeks (or "Pentecost" meaning 50 days after the Passover), which is the Jewish celebration of the grain harvest, the celebration of the first fruits. During this festival, the disciples and the many people gathered for the celebration, received a baptism of fire.

"When Pentecost day came around, the disciples had all met in one place, when suddenly they heard what sounded like a powerful wind from heaven, which filled the entire place in which they were sitting. Something appeared to them that seemed like tongues of fire, they separated and came to rest on the head of each of them. They were all filled with the Holy Spirit, and began to speak in foreign languages as the Spirit gave them the gift of speech. Now there were devout people from every nation under heaven living in Jerusalem, and at this sound they all assembled, each one bewildered to hear these men speaking his own language. They were amazed and astonished. "Surely," they said, "All these men speaking are Galileans? How does it happen that each of us hears in his own native language? Parthians, Medes, and Elamites, people from Mesopotamia, Judaea and Cappadocia, Pontus and Asia, Phrygia and Pamphylia, Egypt and parts of Libya around Cyrene, Rome - Jews and Proselytes alike - Cretans and Arabs, we hear them preaching in our own language about the power of God." [4]

When the disciples experienced the baptism of fire, "tongues of fire" alighted on their heads and they began communicating the power of God in different languages. This had the amazing effect of unifying the diverse crowd under a common umbrella of understanding. People from all walks of life were able to hear the same message but in languages they could comprehend. From this story we see that the baptism of fire creates the possibility of some *unity*, some *common understanding*, between diverse groups of people. It creates the possibility of some *reconciliation*, where differences are considered, honored and held within the divine container. When we create this kind of atmosphere for others we are, in Kabbalistic terms, aiding in "the great work of unification."

It is significant that the baptism of fire occurs on the Festival of Weeks because that is the time to celebrate the first fruits of the harvest. So as we receive the baptism of fire, we are to celebrate the fruits from our bountiful Tree of Life, the fruits that will feed others with sweetness and sustenance. What might these fruits be? Our fruits can be potent "fireballs" of truth and enlightenment enacted wherever we go. Our fruits can be words of wisdom, understanding, and knowledge. Our fruits can be salves of healing and reconciliation, soothing those in need. Our fruits can be potent acts of courage and compassion, touching the lives of those around us. When the divine fire is activated within us, we are called to *speak, honor diversity, take action and heal those in need.*

Exercise 9: Baptism of fire - manifesting your fruits

1. Write a list of the fruit you are currently producing or what fruit you would like to produce in your daily life. If you can, draw a picture of your Tree manifesting these fruits of fire.

What "fireballs" of truth and enlightenment are you willing to offer in your daily life?

What words of wisdom, understanding and knowledge can you share?

What acts of healing and reconciliation are you offering?

What potent acts of courage and compassion are you offering now in your life?

2. For a creative exercise, draw or paint an image of your own baptism of fire, either a symbol that captures the essence of your fire initiation or a picture of your own fire body/divine body. Be creative.

The "I Am"

The Jewish tradition offers us another account of the baptism of fire in the story of Moses and the burning bush. The story of Moses, which was discussed in Stage 6, shows us a powerful aspect of the divine fire, revealed in the "I Am," the fiery name of God.

Moses has fled Egypt and is living in the wilderness with Jethro's family. He has undergone a death and rebirth and has survived the sixth initiation. He has taken on a new life and stands poised at the threshold of his initiation into discovering his destiny. One day when Moses is off by himself, shepherding his sheep, he is confronted with "an angel of God in the shape of a flame of fire coming from the middle of a bush". [5] This burning bush is an image of the Tree of Life that is ablaze but never consumed.

Out of the fire Moses hears the divine voice, the divine will, asking him to come nearer and to take off his shoes because it is holy ground. God then reveals the situation – Moses is to lead the Hebrew people out of slavery in Egypt and into the Promised Land. With this pronouncement, God hands Moses his destiny papers, mapping out his job to lead Israel out of slavery and into freedom. Moses then asks, "But if they ask me what <your> name is, what am I to tell them?" God responds to Moses saying, "I Am that I Am. Tell them I Am has sent me to you." [6]

In this story, the name of God is revealed in a personal way to Moses through the burning bush. Here, before Moses' eyes, is a manifestation of the fire that lives in the heart of everything, the fire that burns but never consumes. This is the fire that gives *life, animation, movement* and the *ability to be*. It is not the hungry fire that destroys or reduces life to ashes, but the fire that sustains life with *warmth, light* and *consciousness*.

In Kabbalah, the I Am is found at the very top of the Tree at Keter and is also the force of life and consciousness running all the way down the central pillar of the Tree. When Moses encountered the burning bush, it is said that he ascended to the I Am at Keter and encountered the fiery aspect of the Divine; he experienced the unification of all existence. When this happened to Moses and when the baptism of fire happens to us, we encounter both the I Am nature of God and the I Am that dwells within the heart of our own being. Unlocking this door reveals the divine being, presence, able-ness and willingness of the I Am. Realizing the I Am within us produces an internal state of mind where there is *stillness, calm,* and *love* – with no separation and no striving. Encountering the I Am brings deep inner peace.

When we can sustain an experience of the I Am, we discover how it is the central, stabilizing force in life. Nothing rocks the stability of the I Am because it knows both the good and evil in our hearts. Nothing is outside its container. It accepts all and sees all. The I Am is the biggest container that we can imagine.

From the perspective of the I Am, all of life is exactly the way it should be. As we embrace this perspective, *we can bring a powerful sense of acceptance to any situation,* which others find tremendously comforting and healing. We can accept our life circumstances and experience everything being exactly as it should be. I do not mean putting up with abuse or horrible injustices. We should continually fight against the hatred and ignorance in our hearts and in our world. The deep acceptance of the I Am is the most life-affirming stance we can take. With the inner stability of trust and acceptance of life, we can find the resolve necessary to move in a positive and life-giving direction. We can move towards what feels whole. Feeling a sense of well-being and deep trust in life means trusting that life will bring us exactly what we need in exactly the right time, in exactly the right place with exactly the right people.

The other capability developed after our encounter with the I Am is the capacity to *remain in the present* for longer and longer periods of time. Every time we find ourselves slipping back into the past or looking forward to the future, we can try focusing on the I Am that permeates the present. Most mystical traditions advise us to take one day at a time, one step at a time, one moment at a time. At each moment we must decide to surrender to life, decide to move towards our wholeness. If we do not have to worry about what happens in the next moment, maybe we will have more courage to be bold and take the necessary risks to radically change our life or to make intimate contact. If we are overly concerned, fearful or anxious about what happens in the next moment, this may paralyze us to move forward and make courageous decisions.

The ultimate healing that comes from the seventh initiation is our feeling of connection to the I Am as an ever-present reality and revitalizing source. It is such a relief to realize that we do not have to generate everything ourselves. There is a universal energy source in the I Am that is constantly generating the energy and consciousness we need. It is not up to us to generate everything. In fact, one of the tasks here at Stage 7 is to get out of the way enough to let this eternal spring flow and watch with wonder how it heals us.

Working with healing symbols and images

So far in this last step of Initiation 7, we have extended our circle of reconciliation, received the baptism of fire and embraced the I Am. Another way to heal ourselves and others is to pay attention to healing symbols and images. Healing symbols are visual archetypes that bring us a sense of wholeness and completion. Healing images, such as mandalas, circles, gold rings, hearts, diamonds etc., bring hope, courage, strength, healing, new insight and release.

Healing symbols are handed down to us from our living traditions to help us through our initiations. Some symbols we have already discussed, such as the Cross, the Star of David and the chalice or Holy Grail. In addition to collective symbols, each of us has *personal healing symbols* that emerge from our unconscious when they are needed, coming to us in dreams, visions or meditations. Both collective and personal symbols are designed to bring a sense of restoration, repair, redemption, reconciliation and wholeness when our Tree of Life system is out of balance.

So often, when our Tree is out of alignment, we do not know the exact origin of the wound, nor are we clear about the remedy that will soothe our pain and bring lasting change. Sometimes the only thing that feels healing is a symbol or image that brings meaning and hope and touches us at some deep, primal level.

A few years ago I worked with a woman who was struggling with a physical disability as well as undergoing a career change. She felt generally anxious and uneasy with this transition, until she dreamed that she was handed a beautiful red crystal heart. This symbol emerged at just the right time and gave her a feeling of hope and support.

Other students and clients have reported receiving healing symbols such as a golden disc or sphere, a diamond, a golden ring, eyeglasses, the moon, a wooden box, a jeweled chalice, a lotus flower, a golden book, a sacred Tree, a purple cloak, a rainbow, a holy mountain, a snake, a bear, a wolf, a butterfly, a waterfall, a crystalline rock, a wand and a staff, to name a few.

The following is a list of healing symbols that are associated with each of the seven initiations. When we want to activate initiation, complete initiation or heal a wound at any stage, we can use the healing symbols associated with each stage, using them in ritual or any creative way we choose. It is also vitally important to watch our dreams, for our unconscious surprises us with powerful, unusual and meaningful symbols. When you receive a healing symbol, you can manifest it by drawing, painting, sculpting or writing about it. The following are various symbols associated with each stage.

Symbols for Initiation 1: BODY

The Midwife, *Anima Mundi*, Adamah (Original Human), the Earth, dirt, underground, cauldron, sacred vessel, roots, *Prima Materia*, cave, the naked body, a garden of rich soil, womb, hermetically sealed vessel, the Tabernacle in the wilderness.

Symbols for Initiation 2: INSTINCTS

The Great Mother, the triple goddess of Maiden, Mother and Crone (spinner, measurer and cutter of the string of fate), labyrinth, waves, ocean, spirals, circles, the moon, swirls, spider's web, changing seasons, silver, night, sand box, child, playing children.

Symbols for Initiation 3: COMMUNITY

The Storyteller, family crests, campfire, totem pole, communal scenes of crafting, drumming, weaving or cooking in a circle of people, tribal council, ancestors, the family home, ancestral land.

Symbols for Initiation 4: IDENTITY

The Adventurer, The Wildman or Wildwoman, animal allies, sword, shield, heart, wild masks, desert, wilderness, blacksmith's furnace, Jordan River.

Symbols for Initiation 5: TRUTH

The Hero/Heroine, Warrior/Warrioress, King/Queen, chalice, Holy Grail, sun, throne, chariot, lion/lioness, the Philosopher's Stone, gold, day, captain of the ship, caduceus (intertwined snakes up a central staff, used as a medical healing symbol).

Symbols for Initiation 6: TRANSFORMATION

The Visionary, Seer, Prophet, Sage, Mystic, Shaman, Shapeshifter, white dove of the Spirit, third eye, gateways, portals, the Abyss, birds, ladders, towers, wind, a sailboat with full sail, feathers, smoke, sky, bubbling cauldron, Kali.

Symbols for Initiation 7: WHOLENESS

The Healer, the Lovers, Mystical Cross, Star of David, Uroborus (the snake eating its tail), the circle, the sphere, bread and wine, living water, Tree of Life, fire, temple, sanctuary, crown, fountain, river of light, the well of wisdom, a diamond, the Sapphire Staff.

Exercise 10: Finding your core healing symbols

1. Write down the **core symbols** that have held meaning for you over the years – symbols of healing that have come to you in dreams, meditations, visions or through any means. Include symbols that were meaningful in the past that may not hold meaning any longer. Hopefully you have been keeping a journal throughout this journey and have sketched or written down the healing symbols that have emerged for you during each initiation. These healing symbols can be animals, colors, objects or religious symbols. For example, your favorite symbols may be as diverse as the color blue, the sky, a wolf, a chalice, the cross, a crystal heart and many more.

2. Next to each symbol or image on your list, write down what was/is **meaningful** about it and how it has helped you. For example, did it bring hope, courage, strength, healing, new insight, release or a sense of repair, restoration, redemption, reconciliation or wholeness? In what way?

3. Now pick out your **top three healing symbols** with their various healing associations and see if you can come up with a creative name for yourself using one, two or all three symbols. Pretend that you are an elder initiating "you" into this final phase. What name would you give to yourself based on these three significant symbols? For example, if your top three symbols are blue, sky and wolf and the healing these symbols bring is peace, you might name yourself "Peaceful Blue Skywolf" or "Peaceful Wolf." You do not need to be that literal. Play around and add or change if you want.

4. Now represent your "Name" creatively by making a **sacred object** that reflects the essence of your core symbols. It is a powerful exercise to actually make a three-dimensional sacred object. Be creative. You can make a staff or small altarpiece. You can use wood, stones, a tree branch, leather, ribbons, feathers or whatever you choose. Go all out on this project. This last creative exercise in the initiation process is designed to capture the essence of your healing journey so far in your life. This name and sacred object may change as you develop your Tree, but for now, honor yourself and all that you have accomplished so far.

Becoming a healing sanctuary for others

As initiation into Stage 7 completes, we find that we now have access to the revitalizing waters, we celebrate the inner marriage, we are blessed and empowered to fulfill our vision, and we feel healed and enlivened with our core healing symbols. With this kind of emotional and spiritual stability, we can become a *healing sanctuary for others*. Our Tree of Life is now producing abundant fruit. In this awakened and initiated state, our presence draws others to come and rest beneath our branches and eat of our fruits. We create an atmosphere around us of love, vitality and peace, where people can come to have sacred dialogue and where people can come to be healed.

In Stage 1, we spoke about the sanctuary set up in the wilderness, called the Tabernacle. This "tent of meeting" was the healing sanctuary where the people would meet with the Shekhinah, the divine presence. As a result of wandering in our own wilderness and successfully walking the initiation journey, we too have created a tent of meeting that can be a refuge and light to others. By simply accessing our sacred spring, we can feel like a cup full to the brim and spilling over. We can give out of our abundant resources and not feel drained or depleted. We feel a sense of having a full storehouse because we have access to the universal treasury of understanding and wisdom. We have also developed an open channel to receive knowledge of the Divine and of universal light and healing. Once we open that door, we have continual access.

Now our Tree of Life is a sanctuary for others. Under the branches of our Tree, other companions can be seen for their own particular genius and can be blessed and crowned and receive acknowledgment. We can now help others walk the way of a true Adamah, a true human being, offering hope and encouragement. We can heal others by escorting them to the sacred spring, where they too can feel quenched and satisfied.

Now the journey of the seven stages has come full circle. We began by finding our sacred ground and worked diligently through the seven stages to build a solid inner sanctuary. This has connected us to abundant resources that can now be shared with others. Our enlightened, awakened Tree of Life now radiates out and becomes a living Tabernacle, a living Temple.

Blessing and initiating others on the path

As a healing sanctuary, you can do more than just point the way to the sacred spring. You can now become an important elder for other initiates who needs to wrestle with their angels. You can be the elder who *wrestles, blesses, crowns, sees* and *initiates*. This is an honored, respected and privileged position to be in. It is a very active role, one you can delight in, for you have so much to give. You have your experience, your wounds, your failures, your successes, your loves and your wondrous adventures with Spirit.

Watch carefully for those who are on your particular path of transformation. Sooner or later they will begin to wrestle with you. Wrestle with them all night long, until they demand from you and call out of you your power to bless them. See what happens. Watch for the kind of wound they will or have already acquired. Listen carefully to what they demand of you. Devise interesting initiation scenarios for them as part of the wrestling. Say the unexpected. Empower them to be strong. See the Divine within them. Play the fool. Laugh a lot. Confront their weaknesses. Baptize them with wine. Set alight the fire under their soul. Teach them well. Hold nothing back.

Conclusion – Initiation 7: Wholeness

As we conclude the seventh initiation, we can now experience the fullness and fulfillment of our Tree of Life. We have connected to the Divine by longing for our sacred spring, drinking the firewater, activating the Healer and building our inner sanctum around this rejuvenating source. We have activated the Sacred Marriage and called forth our inner partner who helps us feel psychologically integrated and spiritually unified. We have searched for and received the blessing for our life task, and we feel fulfilled, content, peaceful and whole. We feel an inner alignment of body, soul and spirit. The branches of our Tree are now flowering and bearing fruit and we are able to offer our bounty to others along the initiation path.

The Initiation Journey

The initiation journey is a lifelong process. As you spiral your way through life, there will be times to strengthen your trunk and times to replant some of your roots. At times you will climb your branches and connect for long periods of time with Spirit. Sometimes your fruit will be abundant and falling off the Tree. Then you will reach an appropriate season of pruning those branches. The art of following the growth and development of your Tree is to flow with the inevitable changing seasons of your life and pull out the tools from the toolbox that you have acquired through the stages of initiation. For a review of successful initiation mapped out on the Tree of Life, see Diagrams 3 and 4.

From **Initiation 1** you have found the sacred ground, the creative and generative soil that will hold and anchor your life task in a profound way. You are grounded, rooted and contained and bring a solid presence to any situation.

From **Initiation 2** you have built a firm emotional foundation, trusting your instincts and natural rhythms. You have internalized the Good Mother and can experience healthy attachments with others.

From **Initiation 3** you can connect with community and have found a sense of belonging. You have the support that you need around you. Your self-esteem springs from an internal source and you are using your inherited gifts in a positive way.

From **Initiation 4** you can manage healthy separations, especially from your village, and can venture off into unknown territory to focus your energies and discover your true identity. You can survive the wilderness times when your creative path brings confrontation with the establishment or the established ways of doing things.

From **Initiation 5** you know how to individuate and live your truth. You can commit yourself to your own path. You can lead your kingdom (or queendom) with a balance of power between your heart and will.

From **Initiation 6** you can surrender to the guidance of Spirit, risk inner transformation and let go of addictions, habits and fears that keep you from your creative life expression and from your magnificence. You can envision your higher purpose and dance your sacred dance.

From **Initiation 7** you can connect in a permanent way to the divine source that gives you the juice to carry on with your life task, no matter what life brings your way. You offer a unique gift of fruit to the whole human community and are a healing sanctuary for others along the path. You can now bless and initiate other seekers, showing them how to walk the path of a true Adamah.

Healing your Tree of Life requires dedication, stamina and commitment. The journey itself frequently invites pain, confusion, confrontation, chaos and fear. Birthing yourself has its reward, however, as you are flooded with feelings of joy, well-being, satisfaction, and childlike wonder.

As you heal your Tree of Life, the vistas of your inner landscape open. You begin to see a picture of yourself from the divine perspective, as the beautiful creation that you are. As your individual Tree is fulfilled, you realize that you are a part of a vast forest of Trees, gathered around the foot of the great illuminated Tree of Life, its roots rising upward and its branches reaching down toward all of us, protecting us, illuminating us, nourishing us and guiding us on our journey through life.

May you travel well.

Chapter Notes:

Introduction

1. This intriguing quote from the Alchemical text *Teatrum Chemicum,* is quoted in a compendium of Alchemical works called *Alchemy and Mysticism,* by Alexander Roob. It was published by Taschen in 1997 and is filled with hundreds of color and black and white alchemical images.

2. This quote is found on the first page of the Introduction from the book, *The Work of the Kabbalist,* by Z'ev ben Shimon Halevi. Gateway Books, Bath, England, 1984 (the current publisher is Red Wheel/Weiser, Boston, MA and York Beach, ME. To order call: 1-800-423-7087. Also see website www.redwheelweiser.com). I highly recommend Halevi's many excellent books on Kabbalah. They give a thorough background of the tradition of Kabbalah and a working method through the Tree of Life.

Chapter 1:

1. This quote is found in Genesis, chapter 2, verses 5-7 and 9-10 from *The Jerusalem Bible,* Doubleday & Company, Inc., Garden City, New York, 1966. The second sentence informing us of the nature of the Tree of Life with its four rivers, comes from the Seder Gan Eden, a midrash (a Biblical commentary) describing the Garden of Eden.

2. The Gospel of Mark 4:3-9. From *The Holy Bible - New Revised Standard Version,* Oxford University Press, New York and Oxford, 1989.

3. The story of Bezalel is found in The Book of Exodus 35:30-35 and Exodus 40:34-38. From *The Jerusalem Bible,* Doubleday & Company, Inc., Garden City, New York, 1966.

Chapter 3:

1. The story, "The Woman Who Honored the Bones", comes from a marvelous book called *The Woman Who Was Wild and Other Tales.* The story begins on page 148. The collection of stories is written by Karla Andersdatter and has additional commentary by C.E. Brooks. Chiron Publications, 1995.

2. The story, "The Demon in the Tree", comes from a book called *Lilith's Cave: Jewish Tales of the Supernatural.* The story begins on page 104. The book is a compilation of stories selected and retold by Howard Schwartz. Harper and Row, San Francisco, 1988.

Chapter 4:

1. The Story of John the Baptist is found in the Gospels of Matthew 3:1-17, Mark 1:1-11, Luke 1:1-80 and 3:1-32, and John 1:15-34. I used two versions, from *The Holy Bible - New Revised Standard Version,* Oxford University Press, New York and Oxford, 1989 and *The Holy Bible - New Revised Standard Version,* Oxford University Press, New York and Oxford, 1989.

2. The Gospel of Matthew 3:7-9. From *The Holy Bible - New Revised Standard Version,* Oxford University Press, New York and Oxford, 1989.

Chapter 5:

1. For an extended version of the ancient Greek myth of Theseus and Ariadne, King Minos and the Minotaur, I recommend *The King Must Die* and *The Bull from the Sea*. These marvelous books of historical fiction have captured the essence of the myth and are written by a novelist named Mary Renault, Penguin Books, 1962.

2. Some of the dialogue from the David and Goliath story comes from I Samuel, chapters 16 and 17, from *The Jerusalem Bible*, Doubleday & Company, Inc., Garden City, New York, 1966.

Chapter 6:

1. The story of Moses' birth, early childhood, young adulthood and "calling" is described in Exodus, chapters 2 and 3. The quotes are taken from *The Jerusalem Bible*, Doubleday & Company, Inc., Garden City, New York, 1966.

2. For a wonderful rendition of the Dionysus story, I recommend Robert Johnson's book, *Ecstasy: Understanding the Psychology of Joy*. This was published by Harper San Francisco in 1987.

Chapter 7:

1. The story of "Sacred Snake" comes from a book called *White Wolf Woman and Other Native American Transformation Myths*. This story begins on page 44. These stories were collected and retold by Teresa Pijoan. August House Publishers, Inc., 1992.

2. This quote from the beginning of the Book of Genesis is from *The Holy Bible - New Revised Standard Version*, Oxford University Press, New York and Oxford, 1989.

3. The full story of Jesus and the Woman at the Well can be found in chapter 4 in the Gospel of John. The portion quoted here is from *The Holy Bible - New Revised Standard Version*, Oxford University Press, New York and Oxford, 1989.

4. This version of the story of the Pentecost is taken from *The Jerusalem Bible*, Doubleday & Company, Inc., Garden City, New York, 1966.

5. This partial quote is taken from the broader story of Moses and the Burning Bush and is found in the book of Exodus 3:2. The version is from *The Jerusalem Bible*, Doubleday & Company, Inc., Garden City, New York, 1966.

6. The "I AM" statement from God is found in Exodus 3:14. This quote is taken from *The Jerusalem Bible*, Doubleday & Company, Inc., Garden City, New York, 1966.

Appendix A

The Tree of Life and the Sephirot

The Tree of Life diagram consists of divine qualities called "Sephirot" - the sapphires on the staff of knowledge. These archetypal qualities are said to originate from the Divine Being and are echoed in human nature (see Diagram 2).

Starting from the base of the Tree, **Malkhut** represents the body and our anchor point to the earth. Here we consciously connect with nature and feel grounded and embodied in the present. **Yesod** represents the ego, the foundation of the psyche concerned with safety, comfort and survival needs. Yesod knows exactly what we want and need to feel secure in life. **Hod** is our communication system, our ability to receive information, process and analyze and make the appropriate connections. It facilitates our intuition. **Nezah** represents our instinctive, "gut" responses to life, attractions and repulsions that naturally draw us to or away from people and situations.

Tiferet is the captain of the psyche's ship, our true Self that can harmonize and integrate the personality into a working whole. Tiferet is our radiant, shining core Self concerned with our individual truth and self expression. **Gevurah** means discipline and is that warrior-like energy that sets boundaries and protects our truth and what we stand for. Gevurah focuses our energies and harnesses our will. **Hesed** is our ability to love and show mercy and compassion. Hesed is an active, powerful force leading us to our passion and heart's true desire. **Daat** means knowledge, direct experience that brings a profound sense of knowing without a doubt. Daat enables us to transform our heart and renew our mind.

Binah is Divine understanding, the ability to see the universal laws at work in the world and in our own life. Binah understands the workings of fate and how all events are woven together in a vast cosmic plan. **Hokhmah** is Divine wisdom, the flash of revelation, inspiration and Divine insight that can radically change our world in an instant. Hokhmah is our expansive, creative energy, always thinking of new possibilities and new horizons. **Keter** means crown and is our connection to the Divine, the source of all life. Keter dissolves all boundaries keeping us from the Divine and enables us to experience profound healing and inner peace.

The Tree is structured with three vertical pillars that are in a constant, interactive dance: the **left pillar of form**, the **right pillar of force** and the **central pillar of consciousness.** Alternatively, they are called the pillars of structure, dynamic and equilibrium. As we develop, we dance back and forth between the left and right pillars, experiencing contraction and expansion, reflection and action, rest and play.

The goal of initiation is to continually touch base with the central pillar of consciousness, thus stabilizing the psyche and integrating our diverse experiences, emotions, revelations and dreams into a meaningful whole. With this powerful harmonizing and equalizing tool, we can develop, flourish and find purpose in life.

Appendix B

Roots, Trunk and Branches

The initiation process requires us to attend equally to all three systems of the Tree of Life through grounding our roots, strengthening our trunk and reaching out our branches for healing and wholeness.

Roots: The roots represent the body with its physical and instinctual needs that must be honored and nurtured. They also represent the family matrix that undergirds and feeds the Tree from an underground source. Healthy roots stabilize the entire tree, building a platform for a healthy trunk and branches.

Trunk: The trunk represents the individual that arises out of the complex root system. It symbolizes the individual heart and our need to express our individual truth and passion. With a strong individual focus, this sturdy trunk can become an effective vessel for Spirit, holding the weight of the branches as they fan out to a wider vision of life.

Branches: The branches of the Tree represent our yearning to branch out and connect with the Divine source and with all of life. They can only flourish if they are supported by healthy roots and trunk.

Nefesh, Neshamah and *Ruah*

From the teachings of Kabbalah, the three stages of consciousness connected to roots, trunk and branches are referred to as the *Nefesh*, the *Neshamah*, and the *Ruah*.

The **Nefesh** is the vital soul connected primarily to the body, the **Neshamah** is the living soul connected primarily to the psyche, and the **Ruah** is our spiritual body, connected to the transpersonal aspect of our being but also interfacing with the Divine. As we climb the Tree of Life and work through each of the seven initiations, the *Nefesh*, *Neshamah* and *Ruah* develop and begin to function in their awakened and optimum state.

When we awaken and harness the *Nefesh*, we will know how to bring our instinctive power into the world. When we awaken and harness the *Neshamah*, we will know how to express our heart and truth to the world. When we awaken and harness the *Ruah*, we will know how to bring our spiritual wisdom and knowledge into the world.

In order to awaken and harness the *Nefesh*, *Neshamah* and *Ruah*, we must climb the seven stages of the Tree and as we do, shift our center of consciousness up the central pillar from Yesod to Tiferet and, finally, to living with Daat as the center of our conscious life.

Yesod lies at the center of the root system and when healthy, provides the Tree with a strong foundation. The *Nefesh* or vital soul is located here, nourishing the roots of the Tree with physical and instinctual vitality.

The central Sephirah, Tiferet, translates as "truth, beauty and goodness", and lies at the heart of the trunk section, providing the integrity of the Tree and the upward thrusting direction of the Tree. The *Neshamah* or living soul is found here, nourishing the trunk.

The upper circle is focused around Daat, which translates as "knowledge", and lies at the center of the branches, helping us to branch out to a spiritual perspective and increase in wisdom and knowledge. The *Ruah* is located here, nourishing the branches and the fruit that will eventually flower and ripen.

The purpose of the initiation journey is to climb the Tree in order to awaken, develop and coordinate the three systems of the Tree: roots, trunk and branches. This means strengthening our emotional foundation, creating our individual focus and offering our collective contribution to the spiritual development of all living things. The roots, trunk and branches of our Tree of Life must align and work together so that we can experience the healing of body, mind and spirit which is our birthright. As we heal ourselves and come into true alignment with our passion and purpose, we become a human being capable of healing others. In this way, we fulfill our human destiny to help creation evolve in a life-giving direction.

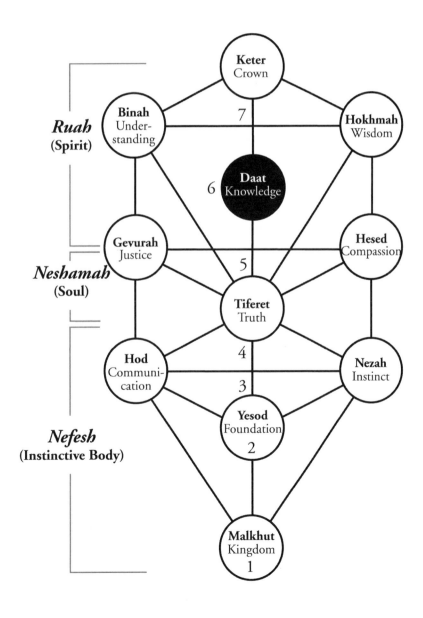

Appendix C

Initiating Archetypes

Let's look at the unique archetypal helpers in Stages 1, 2 and 3 who help to build the roots of the Tree. In Stage 1 (BODY), we meet the archetypal **Midwife** who births us into life, helping us to become embodied, grounded and present. In Stage 2 (INSTINCTS), we can call upon the **Great Mother** who steers us toward our natural instinctive rhythms, bringing emotional stability as we learn to love and nurture ourselves. In Stage 3 (COMMUNITY), we meet the **Storyteller** who can make sense of our life within the context of our family stories, giving us communal support and tribal belonging.

The initiating archetypes for Stages 4 and 5 help to build the trunk of our Tree of Life. In Stage 4 (IDENTITY), we meet the **Adventurer** who arouses us from the comfort of community, calling us to leave home and establish a separate identity away from the tribe and the pull of the family. In Stage 5 (TRUTH), we call upon the **Hero, Warrior** and **King** or the feminine Heroine, Warrioress and Queen. These particular archetypes help us to develop a truly individual focus, speaking our truth and living authentically with passion. Now we have a solid trunk that will support our unique individual efforts in the world.

The initiating archetypes for Stages 6 and 7 are the **Visionary** and the **Healer**. These archetypes help us to build the branches of the Tree, branching out of an individual focus towards the Spirit and collective life. In Stage 6 (TRANSFORMATION), we call upon the Visionary to help us dream and envision our contribution to the collective. The Visionary inspires and encourages us to transform what is dead and no longer serving us. The Visionary also aids the collective vision by breathing new life and Spirit into the culture. In Stage 7 (WHOLENESS), we encounter the Healer archetype who connects us to the Divine, bringing a deep sense of satisfaction and healing. We can now see ourselves as one part of a vast whole, bearing a unique gift which fits perfectly into the grand design. When we exercise this gift, we heal ourselves and create a sacred space that allows others to awaken and heal.

Appendix D

The Solar Mysteries

My research on the Solar Mysteries brought me time and again to the British Museum, where black granite statues of the solar goddess Sekhmet are scattered about the Egyptian collection. One day as I was meditating in front of Sekhmet, my imagination opened, and with my inner eye, I experienced Sekhmet's sun disk filling with light and expanding into a solar flare that radiated outward from her head. The vision that I had that day became the inspiration for the fifth Sacred Robe. This experience deepened my understanding of Sekhmet as the solar goddess who is both warrioress and healer. She is proud, regal and dignified, strong and fierce in battle, yet compassionate and openhearted. It is as if the sun disc began as a seed in her heart, growing larger and finally rising triumphantly above her head into a halo.

In one of her many forms, Sekhmet holds a papyrus scepter, the vegetable staff, which is rooted in the earth, connecting her to the origins of the earth and the creative energies of the Feminine principle. In her other hand she holds the ankh, which is the symbol of life, connecting her to the masculine principle of the spirit. Part of her function is to integrate both masculine and feminine energies, thereby balancing the soul.

The Sekhmet energy helps us in many ways, and for that reason she has many names. Sekhmet the Powerful – holds the true Self position and represents the sun goddess with both warlike and beneficent aspects. She is a powerful lioness with solar strengths of courage, focus and inner radiance. Sekhmet the Lady of Life – whose powers, according to legend, were not only called upon for winning battles but also in the service of healing. Sekhmet's priests were physicians who held a detailed knowledge of the workings of the heart and who used knives – not as weapons – but for healing.

Appendix E

Collective Myths and the Mystery Traditions

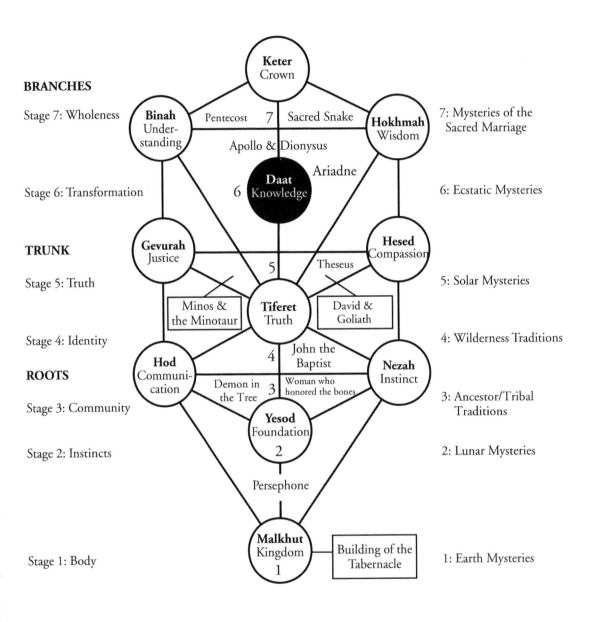

BRANCHES

Stage 7: Wholeness

Stage 6: Transformation

TRUNK

Stage 5: Truth

Stage 4: Identity

ROOTS

Stage 3: Community

Stage 2: Instincts

Stage 1: Body

7: Mysteries of the Sacred Marriage

6: Ecstatic Mysteries

5: Solar Mysteries

4: Wilderness Traditions

3: Ancestor/Tribal Traditions

2: Lunar Mysteries

1: Earth Mysteries

Keter
Crown

Binah
Under-
standing

Hokhmah
Wisdom

Pentecost   7   Sacred Snake

Apollo & Dionysus

Ariadne

Daat
Knowledge   6

Gevurah
Justice

Hesed
Compassion

5   Theseus

Minos &
the Minotaur

Tiferet
Truth

David &
Goliath

John the
Baptist   4

Hod
Communi-
cation

Nezah
Instinct

Demon in
the Tree   3   Woman who
honored the bones

Yesod
Foundation   2

Persephone

Malkhut
Kingdom   1

Building of the
Tabernacle

Appendix F

Alchemy and the Tree of Life

The alchemical metals are placed within the Sephirot/spheres and stages of the alchemical process are placed within the triads, paralleling the seven stages. There are often several alchemical operations in one stage.

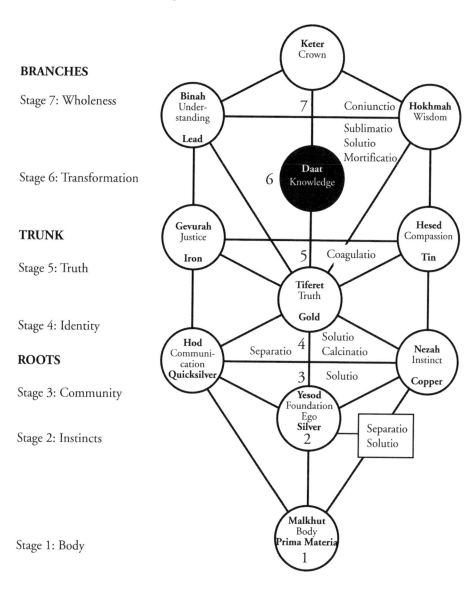

Exercises and Meditations

Myths and Stories

Acknowledgements

I am deeply grateful to my spiritual teacher, Warren Kenton (Z'ev ben Shimon Halevi), who inadvertently inspired me to write this book years ago when I asked him innocently in a Kabbalah class, "Why isn't there more psychology on the Tree?" and he answered, "That's your job!"

To my Kabbalah companions in England, I am grateful for all you have taught me about the Tree of Life - Mark Jeoffroy (incalculable thanks for your unconventional wisdom), Steve Pope, Marie-Elsa Bragg, John Powderly, Joanna Lapage-Browne, Sue Smethurst, Jon Taylor, Maggy Whitehouse, Peter Dickenson, Celia Bain and David Cohen.

I want to thank and honor my mentors in Depth Psychology, who guided me through the storms and adventures of the inner path. Thanks to Dr. Richard Auger for introducing me to the journey of the soul and to Elizabeth Urban for her brilliant clinical skills and insights. From the depth of my heart, I offer special thanks to Vernon Yorke for his love and dynamic presence in my life. Much of this book is the result of our many years of dialogue and travel into the emotional landscape.

This book could not have been possible without Liz Kalloch, my book designer extraordinaire. Thank you for your artistic eye, expert layout advice, interior and exterior design and occasional "book therapy".

Thanks to all the "angels" who helped with the manuscript - to my sister-in-law, Carol Crocker, for the hours of transcription, to "Book Midwife" Caroline Pincus for her encouragement and expert eye, to Tamara Chin for her excellent feedback and to Linda Matthew for her precise copy editing.

I want to thank my parents Roger Wagner and Roz Wagner who encouraged my education and taught me to follow my bliss. A special thanks to my mother, who has not only supported me in many ways but has also offered helpful advice and feedback and entertained my son, Jacob, with creative projects and games while I wrote this book. My other family "angels" have spent time taking wonderful care of Jacob so that I could write – my husband, Jim Larkin and my parents-in-law, Jim and Lois Larkin. Thank you for your love and support.

I am deeply indebted to Alzak Amlani, my weekly writing partner, who has heard every word of this book and has given me valuable feedback and helpful counsel. Thank you for discussing, dialoguing, commiserating and sharing your heart with me.

I also extend gratitude to Gina Rose Halpern, for her enthusiastic support and for giving me the opportunity to teach much of the material of my book at her creative Institute.

Finally, I want to thank my wonderful students, clients and friends whose bravery and truth-seeking has been an inspiration to me over many years. I honor your struggles, triumphs and healings, and hope that we continue this awesome journey together as companions on The Way.

About the Author

Megan Wagner, MA

(BA Stanford University, MA Marriage and Family Therapy, MA Theology, Fuller Theological Seminary)

Megan is a Therapist, Artist, Kabbalah Teacher and Ordained Interfaith Minister. She trained in Family Systems, Depth Psychology and Christian and Jewish Mysticism. She has 20 years of counseling experience and 12 years of experience in personal analysis and supervision in psychodynamic counseling and analytic depth psychology.

In London, England, Megan trained extensively with Kabbalah Master Z'ev ben Shimon Halevi and has lectured on Kabbalah in England, Spain and in the USA, where she runs a Kabbalistic School of the Soul with her husband, Jim Larkin. Both Megan and Jim are on the Board of Directors of the International Kabbalah Society.

Megan is founding director of the *Tree of Life Training*, a holistic model of healing that attends to emotional, individual and spiritual development. The training combines modern Western therapy techniques with the ancient healing arts of drumming, chanting, storytelling and ritual. Megan developed this method of healing after years of traveling and experiencing the sacred arts of other cultures, working with ritual experts and studying Kabbalah, Depth Psychology, Astrology, Alchemy, Mythology and the Western Mystery Traditions.

Megan is also an accomplished artist and creates ceremonial robes for meditation and ritual. She performs live with her Sacred Robes using dancing, drumming, story and song to celebrate the soul's journey through life. She also trains interfaith ministers and teaches Spiritual Psychology at The Chaplaincy Institute for Arts and Interfaith Ministry. Megan has a special interest in women's rites of passage and for ten years has been leading women's groups to the island of Crete.

Megan lives in the San Francisco Bay Area with her husband and son.

Further Resources

Tree of Life Training

The Tree of Life Training is an intensive, year-long training facilitated by Megan Wagner and her husband, Jim Larkin. It is designed to give you a full experience of the Tree of Life path of healing through indiviual and group work, personal consultations with Megan and powerful group rituals. During the **Tree of Life Training**, you will set goals for what needs to be transformed in your life and find tools to reach your goals and manifest your dreams.

For further details see **www.TreeofLifeTeachings.com**

CDs

The Sapphire Staff: Companion CDs to the Book (Volumes 1-4)

Join author Megan Wagner as she presents the Tree of Life path of healing, a powerful tool to align the roots, trunk and branches of our Tree for optimum health. Through live drumming and storytelling and guided meditations, she will help you to complete the seven initiations needed for psychological and spiritual transformation.

Introduction to the Tree of Life – Volume 1

Discover Ms. Wagner's practical and dynamic teachings of Kabbalah and Depth Psychology in this comprehensive overview of the Tree of Life. Included are meditations to visualize and heal our personal Tree and guidance through Initiation 1: BODY, so that we feel profoundly connected to our body and nature. Volume 1 - Intro / 75 minutes $17.00

Heal and Nurture the Roots – Volume 2

With live drumming and storytelling, Megan Wagner leads us on an unforgetable journey with Persephone into the instinctive ground of being. We learn to call back our instinctive power and connect with our ancestors during Initiations 2 & 3: INSTINCTS and COMMUNITY. Volume 2 - Roots / 75 minutes $17.00

Strengthen and Balance the Trunk – Volume 3

Through the story of John the Baptist and the Myth of Theseus and the Minotaur, we learn to forge a strong individual identity, open our heart and stand in our truth. Initiations 4 & 5: IDENTITY and TRUTH strengthen and balance the trunk of our Tree. Volume 3 - Trunk / 75 minutes $17.00

Extend the Branches and Harvest your Fruit – Volume 4

The myth of Dionysus opens us to the inspiration and ecstasy of Spirit. As we extend the branches of our Tree during Initiations 6 & 7: TRANSFORMATION and WHOLENESS, we discover our higher purpose, connect with the Divine and experience wholeness. Volume 4 - Branches / 75 minutes $17.00

Full set of CDs Volumes 1-4 / 5 hours $60.00

Further Resources (cont.)

<u>CDs</u>

Kabbalah Meditations

Join author Megan Wagner and husband, Jim Larkin, as they unlock the secrets of Kabbalah meditation, revealing techniques that have been used for thousands of years to develop psychological integrity and spiritual maturity. No prior Kabbalah training is needed to make use of these powerful meditations.

1. **"Visiting your Soul Kingdom"** and **"Journey for Guidance"** by Megan Wagner

Megan guides us to visit the inner kingdom of our soul, where we learn to rule our inner kingdom with integrity. In the second meditation we travel into the future to envision who we want to be and learn how to make our visions and dreams a reality. 40 minutes $17.00

2. **"Whole Life Meditation"** and **"Annual Life Review"** by Jim Larkin

Jim guides us on a journey to view the whole of our life, from birth through childhood, adulthood, old age and even our passage through death and union with the Divine. In the second meditation we see a movie of our life as we have lived it in the last year so that we can make wise decisions for the coming year. 30 minutes $17.00

<u>Meditation Cards</u>

The seven Sacred Robes - created by artist Megan Wagner and displayed in the book in black and white - are now available in full-colored packaged sets. These powerful sacred art images can be used for meditation and spiritual guidance. Each Meditation Card depicts one of the seven robes on the Tree of Life path of healing and activates one of the seven chakras, inviting this particular archetypal energy to flow into your life. On the back of each card you will find the qualities evoked by each robe.

1. **Meditation Cards - set of seven (4x6)** $20.00/set
2. **Individual Images (8x10)** $25.00 each

<u>Sacred Robes</u>

Sacred Robes: Art of Initiation

Artist Megan Wagner brings the seven Sacred Robes to life! You can have your own beautiful silk robe that can be used for meditation, ceremony and ritual or displayed as a sacred art piece. The Sacred Robes are reminiscent of ancient initiation garments and make wonderful gifts for important rites of passage such as weddings, birthdays, anniversaries and significant initiations. Each Sacred Robe is 100% silk and is one-of-a-kind, hand-painted by the artist. Inquire for a quote.

**All products are available through the Tree of Life website
(see Training and Gallery/Store) www.TreeofLifeTeachings.com**

**For written inquiries,
Tree of Life Teachings, P.O. Box 81, Redwood City, California, 94064**